Palgrave Studies in Prisons and Penology

This is a unique and innovative series, the first of its kind dedicated entirely to prison scholarship. At a historical point in which the prison population has reached an all-time high, the series seeks to analyse the form, nature and consequences of incarceration and related forms of punishment. *Palgrave Studies in Prisons and Penology* provides an important forum for burgeoning prison research across the world.

Series editors:

Dr. Ben Crewe
Institute of Criminology, University of Cambridge, UK

Professor Yvonne Jewkes
Department of Criminology, Leicester University, UK

Dr. Thomas Ugelvik
Associate Professor in the Department of Sociology, Political Science and Community Planning, UiT The Arctic University of Norway, Norway

Series advisory board:

Anna Eriksson, Monash University, Australia
Andrew M. Jefferson, DIGNITY – Danish Institute Against Torture
Shadd Maruna, Queen's University Belfast, UK
Jonathon Simon, University of California, Berkeley, USA
Michael Welch, Rutgers University, USA

Titles include:

Jamie Bennett
THE WORKING LIVES OF PRISON MANAGERS
Global Change, Local Culture and Individual Agency in the Late Modern Prison

David Brown, Chris Cunneen, Melanie Schwartz, Julie Stubbs and
Courtney Young
JUSTICE REINVESTMENT
Winding Back Imprisonment

Deborah H. Drake, Rod Earle and Jennifer Sloan (eds)
PALGRAVE HANDBOOK OF PRISON ETHNOGRAPHY

Mark Halsey and Simon Deegan
YOUNG OFFENDERS
Crime, Prison and Struggles for Desistance

Andrew M. Jefferson and Liv S. Gaborit
HUMAN RIGHTS IN PRISONS
Comparing Institutional Encounters in Kosovo, Sierra Leone and the Philippines

Keramet Reiter and Alexa Koenig (eds)
EXTREME PUNISHMENT
Comparative Studies in Detention, Incarceration and Solitary Confinement

Vincenzo Ruggiero and Mick Ryan (eds)
PUNISHMENT IN EUROPE
A Critical Anatomy of Penal Systems

Peter Scharff Smith
WHEN THE INNOCENT ARE PUNISHED
The Children of Imprisoned Parents

Marguerite Schinkel
BEING IMPRISONED
Punishment, Adaptation and Desistance

Phil Scraton and Linda Moore
THE INCARCERATION OF WOMEN
Punishing Bodies, Breaking Spirits

Thomas Ugelvik
POWER AND RESISTANCE IN PRISON
Doing Time, Doing Freedom

Palgrave Studies in Prisons and Penology
Series Standing Order ISBN 978–1–13727090–0 hardback
(*outside North America only*)

You can receive future titles in this series as they are published by placing a standing order. Please contact your bookseller or, in case of difficulty, write to us at the address below with your name and address, the title of the series and the ISBNs quoted above.

Customer Services Department, Macmillan Distribution Ltd, Houndmills, Basingstoke, Hampshire RG21 6XS, England

Justice Reinvestment
Winding Back Imprisonment

David Brown, Chris Cunneen, Melanie Schwartz,
Julie Stubbs and Courtney Young
University of New South Wales, Australia

© David Brown, Chris Cunneen, Melanie Schwartz, Julie Stubbs and Courtney Young 2016

All rights reserved. No reproduction, copy or transmission of this publication may be made without written permission.

No portion of this publication may be reproduced, copied or transmitted save with written permission or in accordance with the provisions of the Copyright, Designs and Patents Act 1988, or under the terms of any licence permitting limited copying issued by the Copyright Licensing Agency, Saffron House, 6–10 Kirby Street, London EC1N 8TS.

Any person who does any unauthorized act in relation to this publication may be liable to criminal prosecution and civil claims for damages.

The authors have asserted their rights to be identified as the authors of this work in accordance with the Copyright, Designs and Patents Act 1988.

First published 2016 by
PALGRAVE MACMILLAN

Palgrave Macmillan in the UK is an imprint of Macmillan Publishers Limited, registered in England, company number 785998, of Houndmills, Basingstoke, Hampshire RG21 6XS.

Palgrave Macmillan in the US is a division of St Martin's Press LLC, 175 Fifth Avenue, New York, NY 10010.

Palgrave Macmillan is the global academic imprint of the above companies and has companies and representatives throughout the world.

Palgrave® and Macmillan® are registered trademarks in the United States, the United Kingdom, Europe and other countries.

ISBN: 978–1–137–44910–8

This book is printed on paper suitable for recycling and made from fully managed and sustained forest sources. Logging, pulping and manufacturing processes are expected to conform to the environmental regulations of the country of origin.

A catalogue record for this book is available from the British Library.

A catalog record for this book is available from the Library of Congress.

Contents

List of Illustrations — vi

Acknowledgements — viii

List of Abbreviations — ix

Books by the Authors — xi

Introduction — 1

1. Justice Reinvestment: A Response to Mass Incarceration and Racial Disparity — 17
2. How Has Justice Reinvestment Worked in the USA? — 54
3. The Politics of Locality and Community — 94
4. Justice Reinvestment, Evidence-based Policy and Practice: In Search of Social Justice — 141
5. How Does Justice Reinvestment Travel? Criminal Justice Policy Transfer and the Importance of Context: Policy, Politics and Populism — 189
6. Conclusion — 239

Appendix: Record of Interviews in the USA and Australia — 251

Notes — 256

List of Cases — 257

List of Legislation — 258

References — 259

Index — 283

List of Illustrations

Figures

1.1	US Incarceration – Rates of supervision comparing total correctional population, with offenders subject to community supervision (probation and parole), and federal, state and jail populations in 2013	19
1.2	US Incarceration – Rates of custody comparing federal, state and local jail populations in 2013	21
1.3	US Incarceration – Persons subject to correctional supervision in 2013 comparing groups across demographic lines, using a 1 in X analysis	25
1.4	US Imprisonment – Rates of custody (state and federal prison) for US males, by age and race/ethnicity in 2013	26
1.5	US Imprisonment – Rates of custody (state and federal prison) for US females, by age and race/ethnicity in 2013	26
1.6	UK Imprisonment – Rates of imprisonment for England and Wales in increments from 1980 to 2014	40
1.7	UK Incarceration – Number of persons comparing types of supervision (remand, sentenced prisoners and persons on probation or parole)	41
1.8	Australian Incarceration – Crude imprisonment rates, per state and territory, in increments from 1980 to 2014	45
1.9	Australian Imprisonment – Rates of imprisonment vs violent crime from 1995 to 2013–14	46
1.10	Australian Imprisonment – Age standardised imprisonment rates, by state and territory and Indigenous status in 2014	46
1.11	Australian Imprisonment – Male rates of imprisonment by age and Indigenous status in 2014	48
1.12	Australian Imprisonment – Female rates of imprisonment by age and Indigenous status in 2014	49
2.1	JRI Step 1	76
2.2	JRI Step 2	76
2.3	JRI Step 3	77
2.4	JRI Step 4	77
2.5	Five Steps to Local JRI	78

Table

1.1 UK Imprisonment – Prison population by self-identified ethnicity in 2004 and 2013   42

Acknowledgements

We would like to gratefully acknowledge the contribution of the many individuals who have worked on various aspects of the research which form the basis of this book. They include Samara Hand, Laura Heaney, Eleanor Holden, Louise Lau, Shannon Longhurst and Scarlet Wilcock.

We would also like to acknowledge the assistance of the various government and non-government organisations in both the USA and Australia. A full list of the interviews we conducted and the relevant organisations can be found in the Appendix. The material published in this book cannot be considered as either endorsed by these organisations or as an expression of their policies or views.

The Australian Justice Reinvestment Project was generously funded by the Australian Research Council (DP130101121).

List of Abbreviations

ACLU	American Civil Liberties Union
ACT	Australian Capital Territory
AJR Project	Australian Justice Reinvestment Project
ALP	Australian Labor Party
ATSISJC	Aboriginal and Torres Strait Islander Social Justice Commissioner
BJA	Bureau of Justice Assistance
CBA	cost–benefit analysis
CBT	cognitive behavioural therapy
CEPP	Center for Effective Public Policy
CJI	Crime and Justice Institute
COAG	Council of Australian Governments
CRJ	Community Resources for Justice
CSG	Council of State Governments
Cth	Commonwealth
EBP	evidence-based policy (and/or practice)
FUSE	Frequent User Service Enhancement program
FY	financial year
GFC	Global Financial Crisis
HCJC	House of Commons Justice Committee (UK)
IPP	Imprisonment for Public Protection (UK)
JR	Justice Reinvestment
JRI	Justice Reinvestment Initiative
LCARC	Legal and Constitutional Affairs Reference Committee
LNC	Liberal-National Coalition (Australia)
MOJ	Ministry of Justice (UK)
NAAJA	North Australian Aboriginal Justice Agency
NATSILS	National Aboriginal and Torres Strait Islander Legal Services
NeON	Neighborhood Opportunity Network (NYC)
NGOs	non-governmental organisations
NSW	New South Wales
NT	Northern Territory
NYC	New York City
PbR	Payment by Results

QLD	Queensland
SA	South Australia
SIBs	Social Impact Bonds
SIDL	Spatial Information Design Lab
SROI	Social Return on Investment
TCJC	Texas Criminal Justice Coalition
WA	Western Australia
WACOSS	Western Australian Council of Social Services
WIPAN	Women in Prison Advocacy Network
WSIPP	Washington State Institute for Public Policy

Books by the Authors

Brown

Brown, D., Farrier, D., McNamara, L., Steel, A., Grewcock, M., Quilter, J. and Schwartz, M. (2015) *Criminal Laws: Materials and Commentary on Criminal Law and Process in NSW,* (6th edition) The Federation Press: Sydney.

Cunneen, C., Baldry, E., Brown, D., Brown, M., Steel, A. and Schwartz, M. (2013) *Penal Culture and Hyperincarceration: The Revival of the Prison,* Ashgate: London, UK.

Brown, D., Farrier, D., Egger, S., McNamara, L., Steel, A., Grewcock, M. and Spears, D. (2011) *Criminal Laws: Materials and Commentary on Criminal Law and Process of New South Wales,* (5th edition) The Federation Press: Sydney.

Brown, D., Farrier, D., Egger, S., McNamara, L. and Steel, A. (2006) *Criminal Laws: Materials and Commentary on Criminal Law and Process in NSW,* (4th edition) The Federation Press: Sydney.

Pratt, J., Brown, D., Brown, M., Hallsworth, S. and Morrison, W. (eds) (2005) *The New Punitiveness: Trends, Theories, Perspectives,* Willan Press: Devon.

Brown, D. and Wilkie, M. (eds) (2002) *Prisoners as Citizens,* The Federation Press: Sydney.

Brown, D., Farrier, D., Egger, S. and McNamara, L. (2001) *Criminal Laws: Materials and Commentary on Criminal Law and Process in NSW,* (3rd edition) The Federation Press: Sydney.

Hogg, R. and Brown, D. (1998) *Rethinking Law and Order,* Pluto Press: Sydney.

Brown, D., Farrier, D., Weisbrot, D. (1996) *Criminal Laws: Material and Commentary on Criminal Law and Process in NSW,* (2nd edition) The Federation Press: Sydney.

Brown, D., Farrier, D. and Neal, D. and Weisbrot, D. (1990) *Criminal Laws in NSW: Cases and Materials,* The Federation Press: Sydney.

Hogan, M., Brown, D. and Hogg, R. (eds) (1988) *Death in the Hands of the State,* Redfern Legal Centre Publishing: Sydney.

Blackshield, A., Brown, D. Coper, M. and Krever, R. (1986) *The Judgments of Lionel Murphy,* Primavera Press: Sydney.

Zdenkowski, G. and Brown, D. (1982) *The Prison Struggle,* Penguin: Melbourne.

Cunneen

Cunneen, C., Baldry, E., Brown, D., Brown, M., Schwartz, M. and Steel, A. (2013) *Penal Culture and Hyperincarceration,* Ashgate: Farnham.

Cunneen, C. and White, R. (2011) *Juvenile Justice: Youth and Crime in Australia,* (4th edition), Oxford University Press: Melbourne.

Cunneen, C. and Hoyle, C. (2010) *Debating Restorative Justice,* Hart Publishing: Oxford.

Behrendt, L., Cunneen, C. and Libesman, T. (2009) *Indigenous Legal Relations in Australia*, Oxford University Press: Melbourne.

Cunneen, C. and Anthony, T. (eds) (2008) *The Critical Criminology Companion*, The Hawkins Press (an Imprint of Federation Press): Annandale.

Cunneen, C. (2001) *Conflict, Politics and Crime: Aboriginal Communities and the Police*, Allen and Unwin: Sydney.

Cunneen, C. and Stubbs, J. (1997) *Gender, 'Race' and International Relations*, Institute of Criminology Monograph Series: Sydney.

Cunneen, C., Fraser, D. and Tomsen, S. (eds) (1997) *Faces of Hate, Essays on the Incidence and Nature of Hate Crime in Australia*, Federation Press: Annandale.

Cunneen, C. and Libesman, T. (1995) *Indigenous People and the Law in Australia*, Butterworths: North Ryde.

Cunneen, C. (ed.) (1992) *Aboriginal Perspectives on Criminal Justice*, Institute of Criminology Monograph Series: Sydney.

Cunneen, C., Findlay, M., Lynch, R. and V. Tupper (1989) *The Dynamics of Collective Conflict*, Law Book Company: North Ryde.

Stubbs

Stubbs, J. and Tomsen, S. (eds) (forthcoming 2015) *Australian Violence*, Leichhardt, NSW: Federation Press.

Cunneen, C. and Stubbs, J. (1997) *Gender, Race and International Relations: Violence against Filipino Women in Australia*, Institute of Criminology: Sydney.

Stubbs, J. (ed.) (1994) *Women, Male, Violence and the Law*, Institute of Criminology: Sydney.

Schwartz

Brown, D., Farrier, D., McNamara, L., Steel, A., Grewcock, M., Quilter, J. and Schwartz, M. (2015) *Criminal Laws: Materials and Commentary on Criminal Law and Process in NSW,* (6th edition) The Federation Press: Sydney.

Cunneen, C., Baldry, E., Brown, D., Brown, M., Schwartz, M. and Steel, A. (2013) *Penal Culture and Hyperincarceration*, Ashgate: Farnham.

Young

Zahra, P. and Young, C. (2014) *Zahra and Arden's Drug Laws in NSW* (3rd edition), Federation Press: Annandale.

Introduction

Point of departure

This book has its point of departure in a previous work, *Penal Culture and Hyperincarceration: The Revival of the Prison* (Cunneen et al., 2013), which involves some of the same authors. That book sought to identify 'changes in penal culture over the last 40 years, which have led to the re-valorisation of imprisonment as a frontline criminal justice strategy'. The notion of penal culture was used: 'to refer to the broad complex of law, policy and practice which frames the use of imprisonment, and to the broad system of meanings, beliefs, ideas and symbols through which people understand and make sense of the prison' (ibid.:1–2). The chapters explored what we called the 'penal/colonial complex'; local variations in imprisonment rates within the Australian federal system; the emergence of risk in correctional paradigms; the positioning of three particular social groups within penal regimes: those with mental and cognitive impairment, women, and Indigenous and racialised peoples, and the reconstitution of the prison as a 'therapeutic institution'; the reinvigoration of the prison through the emergence of new penal subjects, such as terrorists and sex offenders; and the way that the prison is reproduced and spread through the growth in transcarceral regulation and forms of popular culture.

Having thus identified some of the ways in which the prison had been reinvigorated, normalised and reproduced, we questioned whether 'after nearly 30 years of increasing imprisonment rates we were at something of a conjuncture or turning point, presaging a period of falling imprisonment rates, a movement away from the era of mass imprisonment' (ibid.: 194). What were the prospects for 'winding back imprisonment?' It was at this point, among the various forces that might herald a 'turning point', that the emergence of 'justice reinvestment' strategies was discussed. While noting that in the longer term it may turn out to have been a 'passing fad' we raised the possibility (and hope) that:

> it is a notion that captures the deep disillusion with more than three decades of popular punitive approaches to law and order across the political spectrum and gives expression to the desire for more social and cost effective strategies to rebuild local communities blighted by crime and other forms of social dysfunction. (ibid.: 175)

We emphasised throughout *Penal Culture and Hyperincarceration* the highly selective nature of imprisonment rates, with particular reference to race and to mental and cognitive impairment, and to the way racial disparities (Aboriginality in the Australian context) were obscured by reliance on national or state prison census figures. Accordingly, our conclusion was that:

> while the moment looks promising in terms of rolling back nearly three decades of increasing imprisonment rates and their drivers, unless reform movements confront the highly selective nature of penality and the way it bears so disproportionately on marginalised groups, then any gains to be made through political and popular attitudinal shifts through widespread adoption of policies such as justice reinvestment or penal reductionism, are likely to be limited in practice. (ibid.:195)

This conclusion was thus the departure point for the current project. We had already been struck by the spectacular rise of justice reinvestment on the political and policy agenda internationally (Allen and Stern, 2007) and the way that in Australia, the idea was gaining traction among politicians and community advocates (Brown, 2010, 2011a, 2013a; Brown, Schwartz and Boseley, 2012) with particular emphasis on its potential in the Indigenous context (Schwartz, 2010). A research project was born; we were successful in an application to the Australian Research Council for a grant beginning in 2013.

The justice reinvestment groundswell in Australia

In Australia the interest in justice reinvestment is being expressed in both government and community sectors. The call has been led by the Aboriginal and Torres Strait Islander Social Justice Commissioners

(ATSISJC) (2009), beginning with the 2009 *Social Justice Report*. Also in 2009, the Legal and Constitutional Affairs Reference Committee (2009) recommended a pilot program of justice reinvestment strategies and exploration of the potential for justice reinvestment in regional and remote Indigenous communities. Building on this momentum Schwartz argued that 'justice reinvestment could be part of a justice renewal strategy for Indigenous people' (2010:12) which points to the links between important national Indigenous policy documents and the foundational principles of justice reinvestment, including the Australian Federal Government *Social Inclusion Agenda* (2009) and the *National Indigenous Law and Justice Framework 2009–2015* (Standing Committee of Attorneys General, 2010). The Framework sought to build a government and community partnership approach to law and justice issues to reduce the evident levels of disadvantage that are directly related to adverse contact with the justice systems (ibid.: 6). Schwartz (2010: 7–8) argued:

> The Framework sets out five core goals, three of which are equally central tenets of justice reinvestment. The goal to '[r]educe over-representation of Aboriginal and Torres Strait Islander offenders, defendants and victims in the criminal justice system', commits to an expansion of diversionary programs and other interventions for Indigenous people. Like justice reinvestment, the Framework recognises the centrality of community ownership and responsibility to the development of successful initiatives, calling for communities to be partners in the 'identification, development and implementation of solutions'. Goal 3.2, to '[r]ecognise and strengthen Indigenous community responses to justice issues to support community ownership of safety and crime prevention', is likewise consistent with the collaborative, community centred approach in justice reinvestment. Goal 5 ... is to '[s]trengthen Indigenous communities through working in partnership with governments and other stakeholders to achieve sustained improvements in justice and community safety'. This goal focuses on building community resilience and emphasizes the fact that maintaining 'not simply functional but thriving communities, healthy families and individual wellbeing is crucial to improving justice outcomes.' The strategies nominated for achieving these goals are, as in the justice reinvestment approach, not necessarily focused on criminal justice, but are geared to allowing communities to develop their own capacity and their own solutions. These include to '[c]ontribute to the provision of measures needed to sustain the

social and cultural resilience of strong communities' by providing the support necessary to develop leadership, and to engage in community affairs, policy development and service delivery. Community justice groups are singled out as vehicles to establish links between health, education, housing, employment and welfare services so that an integrated approach to crime prevention can be developed (references omitted).

In 2010, the Australian Greens adopted justice reinvestment as part of their justice policy platform, and a review of the New South Wales (NSW) Juvenile Justice system proposed the implementation of justice reinvestment strategies in the juvenile context (Noetic Solutions, 2010). In 2011 the House of Representatives Standing Committee on Aboriginal and Torres Strait Islander Affairs lent its support to justice reinvestment in its report on the over-incarceration of Indigenous young people, *Doing Time – Time for Doing* (HRSC, 2011). Three months later, a Northern Territory government review (2011) of its youth justice system supported the use of justice reinvestment to address youth incarceration. *Doing Time*'s recommendation that further research be conducted to investigate the potential for justice reinvestment in Australia (Rec. 40) was accepted by the federal government, and the National Justice CEOs established a working group to develop options for working towards justice reinvestment in Australia.

In 2012 the ALP federal government, with the support of the Greens, initiated a Senate inquiry into the value of justice reinvestment in Australia. The Inquiry was chaired by South Australian Greens Senator, Penny Wright. The terms of reference for the inquiry included:

   c) the over-representation of disadvantaged groups within Australian prisons, including Aboriginal and Torres Strait Islander peoples and people experiencing mental ill-health, cognitive disability and hearing loss;
   d) the cost, availability and effectiveness of alternatives to imprisonment, including prevention, early intervention, diversionary and rehabilitation measures;
   e) the methodology and objectives of justice reinvestment;
   f) the benefits of, and challenges to, implementing a justice reinvestment approach in Australia;
   g) the collection, availability and sharing of data necessary to implement a justice reinvestment approach;

h) the implementation and effectiveness of justice reinvestment in other countries, including the United States of America;
i) the scope for federal government action which would encourage the adoption of justice reinvestment policies by state and territory governments... (LCARC, 2013: iii)

The outcomes of the inquiry are discussed in Chapter 1.

Indigenous democracy

In an early contribution to the Australian debate it was noted that the processes which characterise justice reinvestment aligned well with what was acknowledged to be the most desirable approach to program implementation in Indigenous communities.

> These processes include the necessity for bipartisanship and consensus-driven solutions, the devolution of decision-making to the local level, the localization of solutions, and the high-level of input from the high-stakes communities about what might address criminogenic factors in that particular place. The democratic nature of decision-making in the JR methodology is a significant departure from the way that government has traditionally approached policy making for Indigenous communities, but it coheres with what Indigenous advocates have always said about how to give programs implemented in Indigenous communities the best chance of success: by letting communities lead the direction of those strategies. (Brown, Schwartz and Boseley, 2012: 100)

In a report, *Addressing Aboriginal Disadvantage: The Need to Do Things Differently*, the NSW Ombudsman (2011) highlighted aspects of existing Indigenous affairs programming and policy production which were obstructing positive outcomes. The Ombudsman identified the failure to achieve a whole-of government approach to program management in Indigenous communities; poor communication and co-ordination between relevant agencies; weak accountability mechanisms; and a lack of formal mechanisms to engage Aboriginal people (ibid.: 2.1, 2.2, 3.1). The report concluded that 'government needs to adopt a very different way of doing business with Aboriginal communities. While for many years there has been rhetoric about "partnering" with communities, too often this is not translated into communities having genuine involvement in decision-making about the solutions to their problems.' (ibid.: 2.2) The report went on to recommend that formal mechanisms be established to engage with Aboriginal people, including providing community leaders with the authority to facilitate outcomes. These recommendations met with high levels of support from Indigenous groups.

In an interview for the project, Sarah Hopkins from the Just Reinvest NSW campaign, encapsulated the importance of Indigenous democracy, given the history of a lack of trust in Aboriginal government relations.

> It's an interesting time when it comes to looking at justice reinvestment and Aboriginal communities in New South Wales, because it is the time of this theoretically new idea of local decision-making and different grades of devolving control to Aboriginal communities. But I think that the reality is, if you look at the Aboriginal experience in terms of government, their relationship with government, support from government funding... it's so fraught that this is the only way to do it because there's no trust there... I think for community leaders to actually begin to trust a process I think that's when you see that real community capacity building.

What was striking here then was that in the developing interest in justice reinvestment in the Australian context, parallels were emerging between some of the key principles in the original justice reinvestment process and methodology and the ongoing criticisms by Indigenous leaders and others of the way Indigenous policies and programs were formulated and administered with little or no Indigenous involvement. The potential of justice reinvestment policies in Australia is thus bound up with issues of Indigenous governance, empowerment, self determination and nation-building: what we have called in short hand, 'Indigenous democracy'.

'Tipping point' and 'criminogenic' arguments gather force

The uptake of justice reinvestment in the USA and UK, and the high-level of interest in it in Australia and elsewhere, is in large part a response to the fact that ever increasing imprisonment rates are hugely expensive at a time of fiscal stringency and global financial crisis, and provide very little return in terms of high recidivism rates. There is another argument that is gathering force within criminology, that the effects of mass imprisonment in high-stakes communities, predominantly defined in terms of race, may be counter-productive and criminogenic, contributing to social breakdown and crime (Rose and Clear, 1998; Stemen,

2007; Durlaf and Nagin, 2011; Pritikin, 2008; Daoust, 2008; Vieraitis, Kovandzic and Marvell, 2007; Brown, 2010, 2011a).

Rose and Clear (1998) argued that there was a 'tipping point' in certain communities, where crime increased once incarceration reached a certain level. This was because:

> high rates of imprisonment break down the social and family bonds that guide individuals away from crime, remove adults who would otherwise nurture children, deprive communities of income, reduce future income potential, and engender a deep resentment toward the legal system. As a result, as communities become less capable of managing social order through family or social groups, crime rates go up (ibid.: 457).

The tipping point effect, in particular marginalised and racialised communities, developed in subsequent work (Clear, 2002; 2007a; 2007b; Clear and Frost, 2014; Clear, Rose and Ryder, 2001; Clear et al., 2003; Western, 2002; 2006; Western, Kling and Weiman, 2001; Western, Lopoo and McLanahan, 2004; Mauer and Chesney-Lind, 2002) became a significant component in the development of the 'mass imprisonment' analysis. It revealed the inadequacies of explanations of imprisonment rates and their effects in terms of an accumulation of individual instances of offending. Rather, the issue was about effects on whole communities. As Garland (2001a: 2) put it in the seminal collection on mass imprisonment, it:

> becomes part of the socialisation process. Every family, every householder, every individual in these neighbourhoods has direct personal knowledge of the prison...through the spouse, a child, a neighbor, a friend. Imprisonment ceases to be a fate of a few criminal individuals and becomes a shaping institution for whole sectors of the population.

One of our interviewees, Eddie Cubillo, National Aboriginal and Torres Strait Islander Legal Services (NATSILS) put it succinctly: 'being Indigenous, you know you're never far from the issues, and coming from the Territory you're either affected by the justice system or having family in it. So, it's a constant I suppose for Aboriginal people'.

The 'tipping point' research spelt out the 'collateral consequences' of mass imprisonment, which include worsening inequality, 'deepened by reducing the pay and employment of ex-prisoners' (Western,

2006: 190). In a book length analysis subtitled 'How Mass Incarceration Makes Disadvantaged Neighborhoods Worse', Clear (2007a: 105) summarised the effects of incarceration on families:

> Children experience developmental and emotional strains, have less parental supervision, are at greater risk of parental abuse, and face an increased risk of having their own problems with the criminal justice system. Mothers find it harder to sustain stable intimate relationships with men who have gone to prison, and they have an increased risk of contracting sexually transmitted diseases. Families are more likely to break up, and they encounter economic strains. Girls raised in these high imprisonment places are more likely to become pregnant in their teen years; boys are more likely to become involved in delinquency.

Epidemiologists like Ernest Drucker (2011:9) liken the effects of mass incarceration to a 'large scale disaster', an 'epidemic' (ibid.: 78) or a 'toxic exposure' (ibid.: 113). Drucker argued that mass incarceration 'imposes the same burden for our society as many chronic diseases associated with occupational hazards (for example, coal, asbestos, or nuclear radiation), the physical and emotional trauma of war, or the deprivations of severe poverty and family disintegration' (ibid.: 113–4). He detailed the range of disabilities imposed by time spent within prisons, especially deteriorating health issues, including drug and alcohol problems; exposure to HIV/AIDS transmission; increasing mental health problems; and the prevalence of homicide and suicide in prisons (ibid.: 114–129). In terms of life on the outside, he noted 'chronic incapacitation after prison'; difficulties in obtaining housing and consequent homelessness; bars to employment; bars to receiving public assistance; civil death consequences such as the loss of the right to vote in some states (ibid.: 129–140). Collateral damage to children and the families of prisoners, which Drucker saw as a form of 'contagion', included marriage breakdown, family violence, child removal, shortened life expectancy for children of prisoners and increased likelihood of gang membership, drug use, and criminal offending (ibid.: 141–162).

While all of this research took place in the USA, it seems likely 'that such effects apply in the Australian context, particularly amongst vulnerable populations and communities, such as Aboriginal communities and certain geographical or "postcode" areas, where we may already have reached that "tipping point" where excessive imprisonment rates are actually causing crime' (Brown, 2010:141). One of the obstacles to broader acceptance of the tipping point and criminogenic arguments and evidence is the belief that the law applies equally to all individuals and groups, reflected in a popular metaphor we heard a number of times in our interviews, that 'a rising tide floats all boats'. This was usually posed to suggest that criminal justice reforms would apply equally and thus remedy racial disparity. However the flaws in the notion can be illustrated by looking at the 'rising tide' of imprisonment. Clearly this does not 'float all boats', as the evidence of worsening racial disparity in Australian imprisonment rates, spelled out in Chapters 1 and 3, demonstrates. To continue the metaphor, not all boats are equally seaworthy; some are holed and need repair; some are adrift, or hauled up on the shore, out of reach of the tides; some are ocean liners moored across from the Sydney Opera House; and others tinnies, long abandoned in suburban backyards. As Weatherburn (in NSW Law Reform Commission, 2012: 62) put it succinctly, 'Whenever the justice system gets tougher, as it has in New South Wales and other states, it always has a bigger impact on Aboriginal people than it does on non-Aboriginal people'. Similarly, it is not automatic that justice reinvestment reforms will necessarily address racial disparity, unless either they are fashioned to achieve this, or they affect policing, or substantive criminal or sentencing laws, which have disparate effects on Indigenous people and other racialised groups. There are preliminary indications that some criminal justice reforms in three US states may have produced drops in both prison admissions and prison populations that are greater for blacks and Hispanics than for whites (CSG Justice Center, 2015a).

The tipping point and criminogenic arguments were supplemented by studies which demonstrated the limited role of imprisonment in reducing crime. Western estimates that the growth in US 'incarceration rates explains only one-tenth of the decline in serious crime at the end of the 1990s' (Western, 2006: 7, 168–188). Spelman (2006: 484) concluded that a 10 per cent increase in imprisonment rates will produce at most a 2–4 per cent decrease in crime rates and that only 25 per cent of the US drop in crime rates could be attributed to increased incarceration rates (see also Spelman; 2000a; Levitt, 2004; Useem, Piehl and Liedka, 2001; Pritikin 2008; Mauer and Chesney-Lind, 2002; Daoust, 2008; Weatherburn, Hua, and Moffatt, 2006). Research indicated that:

> incarceration has, at best, a modest effect in reducing crime; that this crime-reduction effect diminishes over time the higher incarceration rates climb; and that in relation to particular communities and groups, such as African Americans in the US and Aborigines in

Australia, it is likely to have a negative or crime-producing effect in the long term. (Brown, 2010: 142)

These arguments are discussed in more detail in later chapters.

The research project

Our conception of the project at this point was as a ground clearing exercise in a social democratic, social justice mode. This is similar to Loader and Sparks' (2010: 124–133) notion of a 'democratic under-labourer', reflecting that the task is not just one within criminology or criminal justice but is also about developing a democratic politics around criminal justice issues. This politics is fashioned, they suggest, by the generation of knowledge, the attempt to understand how criminological knowledge is deployed within criminal justice and political institutions, and the adoption of a normative dimension which seeks to theorise and set forth 'alternative ways of thinking about and responding to crime, and in forging connections with groups in civil society which are seeking to advance an alternative justice politics' (ibid.: 131). Loader and Sparks see the normative task as 'to supply a constant reminder that there is always more at stake in crime-reduction than reducing crime, and hence more to evaluation than finding out 'what works' (ibid.: 127).

While acknowledging the evident promise of justice reinvestment, we were concerned to address the fact that the groundswell of commitment to justice reinvestment in Australia was arising without a clear understanding of (1) the defining features of justice reinvestment; (2) its conceptual and theoretical components; (3) how it related to other concepts in current criminal justice policy; and (4) the possibility and likely effects of its introduction in the Australian context. The danger we saw was that without a robust and critical consideration of the conceptual foundations of justice reinvestment, Australian states risked committing to a policy trajectory without a clear understanding of whether it fitted the particular conditions that attend the high rates of imprisonment among Indigenous people, the disabled and intellectually impaired, and marginalised women in Australia, or its potential effects in practice (Weatherburn, Snowball and Hunter, 2006; Fitzgerald, 2009; Dowse, Baldry and Snoyman, 2009). Given the growing calls for adoption of justice reinvestment in the Australian context, it looked as though policy decisions were likely to be made in the near future. We feared that to make these decisions without addressing some research questions, might distort or undermine the promise of justice reinvestment in the Australian context. Accordingly we identified four core research questions.

Research questions

1 Towards a clear definition: what assumptions underpin justice reinvestment?

One of the main criticisms of justice reinvestment is that it was conceptually vague, meaning different things to different people, so that apparent bi-partisan support was built on unstable ground (Tonry, 2011a). Partly this was because there had been little academic or critical treatment of justice reinvestment. Clear (2011: 587) noted that the success of justice reinvestment strategies in the USA had been achieved despite the fact that it is 'an idea in progress rather than a full-fledged strategy'. Maruna (2011: 661) argued that the concept has been only 'sort of' defined, is not based on a 'strong empirical foundation', and does not really qualify as being a proper 'theory'. While application of justice reinvestment strategies had led to significant savings in corrections costs in numerous US states, Clear (2011: 590) observed that 'the implementation of these strategies has sometimes been problematic' and, at this stage, largely unexamined. In the light of these sorts of criticisms we thought it would be useful to identify firstly, the common threads to various approaches associated with the justice reinvestment banner (primarily in the USA); secondly, the theoretical, legal, criminological and public policy assumptions which underpin these approaches; and thirdly, the broader sociohistorical factors that have given rise to current interest in or adoption of a justice reinvestment approach.

2 What are the social-moral aspects of justice reinvestment policy and limitations of the rational approach?

Justice reinvestment is allied with both 'evidence-led' approaches to criminal justice policy and the increasing concern with fiscal imperatives, or 'value for public money', in criminal justice policy and incarceration in particular. We hoped to investigate the extent to which justice reinvestment approaches might overcome a reliance on economic rationalities and be theoretically articulated with various moral and social approaches to penality. We were also concerned to examine what is accepted as 'evidence' and the need to develop measures relevant to Indigenous and other communities. Among ourselves we were grappling with desires to achieve practical reform effects while also expounding social justice-oriented normative positions. Even where agreement could be reached on a particular normative position, how is it possible to formulate and deploy such normative positions while acknowledging the complexity and autonomy of politics, being wary as Loader and Sparks (2010: 128) argue, 'of attempts to place theories, topics and methodologies in some kind of hierarchy, or to champion any one of them as the only true path'? Does it, as they argue, involve abandoning 'the hope that criminological knowledge can engineer outcomes, end political discussion, trump the ill informed concerns of others' (ibid.: 131); are our achievements likely to be more modest, perhaps informing public debate, highlighting pitfalls, and advocating for informed change?

3 Can place-based approaches respond effectively to entrenched disadvantage?

Justice reinvestment is often described as a 'place-based' approach in that it uses a geographical bounding of high crime communities as a basis for the delivery of programs. We wished to examine and identify place-based responses to crime in Australia in order to identify key divergences, both theoretical and empirical, from justice reinvestment approaches in the USA. Given that high crime communities in Australia have historically also been spaces of social, economic and political marginality and Indigeneity, we were concerned to ask how justice reinvestment approaches might affect marginalised and socially excluded groups (e.g., Indigenous people, women, people with mental health or cognitive disorders). To pose such questions was only to generate others – how do place-based approaches render social disadvantage? Do they tend to impede or promote recognition of various historical, structural, cultural and interpersonal roots of disadvantage? How do they interact with human rights-based, or 'needs-based,' approaches to working with vulnerable groups? Is a focus on community as a 'whole' likely to mask gendered needs, or fail to take into account underlying community power dynamics (along gendered or other lines) that may be present?

4 How might justice reinvestment translate into the Australian context?

Given that most of the existing literature and programs based on justice reinvestment are from the USA and to a much lesser extent the UK, a key question is how well it might translate into the Australian context. One feature of globalisation is an often rapid and sometimes inappropriate transmission of new concepts and programs to widely different local, regional and national contexts without sufficient consideration of the different conditions of reception. Accordingly we proposed to reflect on the nature of policy transfer in the criminal justice sphere more generally and to attempt to map out some of the significant differences in political, social, economic and cultural contexts between the USA and Australia that might present barriers to adoption or transmission of US-derived justice reinvestment policies, as well as the 'conditions of penal hope' (Brown, 2013a).

This then was the task we set ourselves. As the research progressed the ground, as always, shifted, as did our take on some of the key issues. One important development was the Senate Inquiry, discussed in Chapter 1. A second important development was a re-evaluation by a significant number of justice reinvestment's early proponents (Austin *et al.*, 2013) which suggested that its original progressive edge, stemming from its origins in a response to the racial selectivity of imprisonment rates under conditions of mass imprisonment, had been transmuted into a program of implementation known as the Justice Reinvestment Initiative (JRI). The program had lost its local neighbourhood reinvestment focus in favour of predominantly back-end efficiency reforms to parole and community corrections aimed at reducing recidivism and revocation rates, outlined in Chapter 2.

Program of interviews

The authors conducted two series of interviews in the USA, one in late 2013 and a second in mid 2014. The first set of interviews concentrated on some of the leading proponents of justice reinvestment, the key think tanks and other leading and long-standing players, located mainly in New York and Washington. The second round of interviews focussed on six states where justice reinvestment schemes had been initiated on the ground so that we could get a more detailed, empirically informed view of justice reinvestment programs in operation in a selection of locations. The states were Hawaii, South Dakota, New York, Rhode Island, North Carolina and Texas. Chapter 2, where we summarise justice reinvestment developments, describes how these states were chosen.

The first round of US interviews in particular tended to confirm the split argued by Austin *et al.* (2013) between the original conception of justice reinvestment and the form it had taken in the process of implementation (JRI). Two key features of this split were the general lack of neighbourhood reinvestment and the almost total absence of any discussion of the racial disparity of imprisonment rates. Such reinvestment that is taking place in the USA typically involves boosting parole and probation officer numbers, programs and training, in an attempt to stem the flow of revocations into prison, especially revocations on 'technical' grounds. Racial disparity seemed an absent discourse, largely unspoken and apparently unspeakable, too sensitive to confront directly, something 'everybody knows', but cannot address. The second round of interviews basically confirmed but also mitigated these impressions somewhat, and brought home to us the varied nature of developments in different states and locations, and thus the importance of context. We were struck by the political appetite for change amongst all our interviewees, whatever their affiliations and perspectives; an appetite for change reflected in both debates around justice reinvestment, and debates around criminal justice reform not conducted in the terms of justice reinvestment, such as the need for juvenile justice reform. The two rounds of US interviews were followed with a program of Australian fieldwork. These interviews focused on a range of advocacy organisations which reflected the interests of criminalised women, Indigenous peoples and people with mental illness and cognitive impairment. The discussion centred on the possibilities and challenges that justice reinvestment presented for their constituents.

We are indebted to all those people who agreed to be interviewed, all very busy and many in very senior positions, who so willingly gave of their time, extended us considerable hospitality, and were so open in their responses to our questions, in some cases also answering follow-up questions. A list of those interviewed and their organisational affiliation is attached as an appendix.

We have attempted to use the interview material liberally throughout our discussion. We hope this provides a more grounded and earthy feel, as often results from oral as against written responses. We were struck by the enthusiasm, commitment and frankness with which interviewees from widely different perspectives offered responses to our questions and tolerated our outsider ignorance of US conditions, politics, cultures and sensibilities. Part of the requirement for success of any social movement is its ability to inspire, and we were inspired in various ways by the passion and pride with which those we interviewed explained developments they had been involved in and worked for.

Structure of the argument

Chapter 1 locates the emergence of justice reinvestment in the USA, and also the UK and Australia, in the historical context of responses to the phenomenon of mass imprisonment, which has neighbourhood, vulnerable communities and racial disparity at its core. Tracing the concept from its origins as conceptualised by Tucker and Cadora

(2003), through its early development in the USA as a product of many masters, and its progression towards the JRI, the chapter concludes with an overview of the momentum building around justice reinvestment in the Australian context. Having highlighted key moments during the history of justice reinvestment, this chapter serves as a means of grounding the discussion to come and contextualising the portability analysis.

Chapter 2 outlines some of the key features of the justice reinvestment approach before providing a critical assessment of the conceptual shifts that occurred in the process of implementation in the US context, the shift from justice reinvestment to JRI. This is illustrated through information obtained from interviews with leading participants in JRI implementation. While providing key empirical information, neither of these chapters is simply descriptive; they offer a critical overview of the history of the emergence, political uptake and implementation in the US context, elaborating on the critique offered by Austin *et al.* (2013).

Chapter 3 examines the claims of justice reinvestment to be a place-based strategy. It unpacks the meaning of place-based and draws distinctions between 'top-down' and 'bottom-up' approaches to public policy development and implementation and considers how place-based approaches might coalesce with a social-justice vision of justice reinvestment. We seek to unpack the various meanings of 'community' and consider their impact on our understanding of 'place' and justice reinvestment more generally. There is specific consideration of whether a place-based approach is likely to provide adequate recognition of the needs of three social groups who have been particularly affected by the growth in imprisonment: people with mental illness and/or cognitive impairment, women and Indigenous peoples. We draw attention to a case study of the Just Reinvest NSW initiative in Bourke, Australia, which we see as an especially instructive example of a bottom-up approach to justice reinvestment that has been developed and sustained through community initiatives.

Chapter 4 critically examines the methodologies promoted under the 'evidence-based' and 'what works' frameworks used in justice reinvestment. It traces the kinds of economic analysis commonly used and how evidence is conceived and applied, and how a focus on cost cutting and evidence-based programs can work against the possibility of social justice and rights-based approaches. It considers the extent to which different groups, such as those with mental illness and/or cognitive disability, women or racialised people, are recognised, or remain invisible, within these frameworks. The chapter demonstrates that the methodological choices made are not just technical matters but also have significant implications for who benefits from justice reinvestment.

Chapter 5 addresses the issue of portability – how well does justice reinvestment travel? Wacquant's (2009a; 2009b) arguments about the globalisation of a US-derived punitive common sense, and Jones and Newburn's (2007) testing of such claims in the UK context, are examined. This is followed by a brief overview of policy transfer in Australia. The issue of context is essential to any consideration of policy transfer and the chapter examines a number of potential barriers to the reception of US notions of justice reinvestment in Australia. Among the issues considered are: differences in legal and political structures; differences in the extent to which there is widespread acknowledgement that mass incarceration has resulted in a 'broken' system; differences in the levels of bipartisanship and in the role played by faith-based constituencies; and differences in the capacity for co-ordination among various criminal justice agencies. The chapter goes on to scrutinise the notion of policy formulation and transfer more carefully in an attempt to highlight problematic conceptions of policy transfer. These include simplistic notions that policy is the direct manifestation of the intentions of policy-makers, which can be simply 'rolled out'. This is followed by a discussion of the inadequacies of rationalist conceptions of policy-driven processes, reflected in the common 'roll out' metaphor, and in the ever-present possibility of populist backlash.

Chapter 6, the conclusion, offers summaries of the arguments in each chapter, followed by a distillation of our own position on the way justice reinvestment might be most fruitfully promoted in Australia.

The book draws on a broad range of critical criminological, penological and criminal justice scholarship in support of the positions being argued and will hopefully be read not just as a work of critical scholarship for teaching and research purposes but also as a useful resource for a wide range of policy-makers, and others interested in debates about incarceration, including those within government, non-government and not-for-profit organisations, politics and the media.

1
Justice Reinvestment: A Response to Mass Incarceration and Racial Disparity

In little over a decade, the concept of justice reinvestment has captured the imagination of communities, the actors in the criminal justice system and legislatures alike in a range of Western countries. With its promise of reduced spending, decarceration and improved public safety, justice reinvestment emerged at a unique point in time as a reaction to mass incarceration. In the USA, and increasingly elsewhere, a combination of fiscal, political and societal conditions are favourable to the emergence of strategies of penal reduction, including justice reinvestment, to an extent not seen since the 1970s.

The evolution of the practical implementation of justice reinvestment has differed significantly in the UK and Australia in comparison to the USA. Whereas the approach in the USA has concentrated on legislative reform and technical assistance measures, the UK model has adopted a 'payment by results' (PbR) approach. By comparison, the embrace of justice reinvestment in Australia to date has been distinctive, focused on a non-government and community-driven approach. However, what is common across all three countries is the recognition that traditional criminal justice policies are failing and are disproportionately failing vulnerable groups.

This chapter examines the emergence of justice reinvestment in the USA, the UK and Australia. Tracing the concept from its origins, this chapter locates the birth of justice reinvestment initially as a reaction to mass incarceration and racial disparity, through its early development in the USA and its progression towards the JRI. Further, it briefly considers the adaptation of the principles of justice reinvestment to suit the UK context before canvassing the momentum building towards justice reinvestment in Australia to date.

18 *Justice Reinvestment*

Justice reinvestment has come to mean many things to many people. As the story of justice reinvestment is a mere 12 years old, it is still a work in progress. This chapter begins by looking back at key moments during the history of justice reinvestment as a means of grounding the discussion to come and contextualising the analysis of the portability of the concept.

A term is coined

Justice reinvestment is a term that owes its origins to Susan Tucker and Eric Cadora. In an article first published in *Open Society*, Tucker and Cadora (2003: 3) lament the 'cumulative failure of three decades of "prison fundamentalism"' and argue for a place-based approach 'driven by the realities of crime and punishment'. In an oft quoted passage, Tucker and Cadora (ibid.: 2) assert:

> The goal of justice reinvestment is to redirect some portion of the $54 billion America now spends on prisons to rebuilding the human resources and physical infrastructure – the schools, healthcare facilities, parks, and public spaces – of neighborhoods devastated by high levels of incarceration.

This sentiment has resonated widely. As Austin *et al.* (2013: 1) explain, 'the intent was to reduce corrections populations and budgets, thereby generating savings for the purpose of reinvesting in high incarceration communities to make them safer, stronger, more prosperous and equitable'. However, it is important to acknowledge that Tucker and Cadora intended justice reinvestment to generate change well beyond the cost saving to taxpayers. As the authors state, '[i]t is also about devolving accountability and responsibility to the local level. Justice reinvestment seeks community level solutions to community level problems' (Tucker and Cadora, 2003: 2).

An important inspiration for the concept of justice reinvestment was the research conducted by Cadora, Clear, Gonnerman, Kurgan and others identifying 'million dollar blocks': literally city blocks in locations such as Brooklyn where the state was spending a million dollars incarcerating the residents (Cadora, 2008; Clear, 2012; Gonnerman, 2004; SIDL, 2009). The focus on geography evident in this analysis of blocks in Brooklyn and elsewhere, is demonstrated in Tucker and Cadora's (2003: 3) assertion that '[a] critical component of reinvestment thinking is stopping the debilitating pattern of cyclical imprisonment', not least because '[t]he "coercive mobility" of cyclical imprisonment disrupts the fragile economic, social and political bonds that are the basis for informal social control in the community'. Ultimately, as Susan Tucker explained in an interview, 'we were really looking for some kind of mechanism that would in a sense depoliticise the issue of mass incarceration'.

The context of mass incarceration in the USA

Despite what appears to be recent stabilisation, a more than fourfold increase in the prison population nationally since 1975 has left imprisonment and incarceration levels, both in raw numbers and rates in the USA, at historic highs (Green and Mauer, 2010: 2; Tonry, 2014: 525). This exponential growth in incarceration led to the crossing of the dubious milestone of one in 100 Americans being imprisoned by the end of the first decade of the millennium (Pew, 2008: James, Eisen and Subramanian, 2012: 821).

On 31 December 2013, 6,899,000 adult residents in the USA were under some form of supervision through the criminal justice system. This number includes probation, parole, prison and jail (Glaze and Kaeble, 2014; 1). Of those, approximately 1,574,700 were detained in state and federal prisons and a further 731,208 in local jails (Carson, 2014: 1–2; Minton and Golinelli, 2014). These numbers, converted into rates of incarceration per 100,000 of the US adult population, are represented in Figure 1.1.

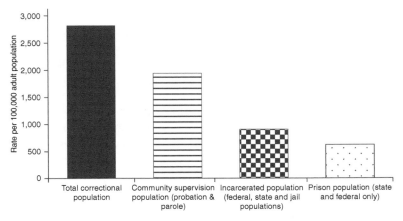

Figure 1.1 US Incarceration – Rates of supervision comparing total correctional population, with offenders subject to community supervision (probation and parole), and federal, state and jail populations in 2013

Source: Authors' graph (Carson, 2014: Table 5; Glaze and Kaeble, 2014 Table 2)

For a cross-jurisdictional analysis it is important to understand what the terms jail, prison, parole and probation mean in the USA. A small number of US jurisdictions are unified, which is similar to the position in Australia, where there is no distinction drawn between prisons and jails. However, generally:

- Prison refers to state- or federal-based custody
- Jail denotes local- or county-level custody
- Probation is court-ordered supervision, as an alternative to full-time custody
- Parole means supervision in the community, usually after a term of full-time custody.

The distinction between the term prison and jail is an important one in the US context. Prison populations refer to offenders sentenced under state or federal regimes. State prisons almost exclusively house people serving state sentences. The terms 'sentenced prisoners' or 'imprisonment' usually refer to offenders sentenced to prison (state, federal or both) for a term of more than one year (Carson, 2014: 1).

Local jails operate at the local or county level. They house primarily pretrial detainees and locally sentenced inmates convicted of minor offences. However, the jail population can also include state-sentenced inmates awaiting transfer to a state prison, people on probation and/or parole who have allegedly violated their supervision orders, accused or sentenced persons from other jurisdictions due to the unavailability of beds, and immigration and customs enforcement detainees (Subramanian *et al.*, 2015: 6–7).

Offenders subject to probation or parole are supervised in the community. Offenders on probation serve their sentence in the community as an alternative to full-time custody. Offenders on parole have generally already served a period of full-time custody and have been conditionally released into the community. However, the latter group can also include persons sentenced to a term of supervised release. Some offenders can be at the same time serving separate probation and parole sentences (Herberman and Bonczar, 2014: 2).

Thus, as Simon (2012: 28) rightly suggests, mass incarceration is a more appropriate phrase as it incorporates populations held in US jails and thus can better 'facilitate cross-national comparison' with unified jurisdictions.

In 1973 the imprisonment rate, which counts state and federal prisoners only, was 150 per 100,000 (Tonry, 2014: 525). In 2013, the imprisonment rate was 478 per 100,000 of the whole US population. This comprises a rate of 61 per 100,000 for federal prisoners and 417 per 100,000 for state prisoners, as demonstrated in Figure 1.2 (Carsen, 2014: 6).

The rate of imprisonment for the US adult population is 623 per 100,000 (Carson, 2014: 6). However, the rate of incarceration, which includes jail populations as well as state and federal prisoners, for the adult population in 2013 was 910 per 100,000, which represents a slight decrease from a peak rate of 1,000 per 100,000 in the years 2006–08 (Glaze and Kaeble, 2014: 4). (See Figure 1.1)

Nevertheless, these statistics do not present a true portrait of incarceration in the USA as they are merely a snapshot of the levels of incarceration on a particular day. In fact, such statistics can dramatically under-represent the true numbers of people entering some type of custody each year. This is best demonstrated by reviewing the jail population. Since 1983, the number of people entering jail has doubled to 11.7 million admissions in 2013. Therefore, while there were 731,208 people in jail on a single day in 2013, nearly 12 million people cycled through jails throughout the USA in that same year (Subramanian *et al.*, 2015: 7; Minton and Golinelli, 2014: 6).

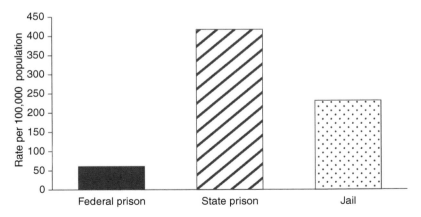

Figure 1.2 US Incarceration – Rates of custody comparing federal, state and local jail populations in 2013

Source: Authors' graph (Carson, 2014; Table 5; Minton and Golinelli, 2014; Table 1; Glaze and Kaeble, 2014: Table 2).

Difficulties also surround the collection of data for mentally ill or cognitively impaired persons in contact with the criminal justice system. An estimated 25 per cent of the US correctional population has a 'severe' mental illness; and it has also been estimated that 56 per cent of state prisoners, 45 per cent of federal prisoners, and 64 per cent of jail inmates have a mental health problem (Kim, Becker-Cohen and Serakos, 2015: 1, v).

The story of mass incarceration

The story of the dramatic rise in incarceration in the USA from the 1970s is one that has been told in detail elsewhere (Garland, 2001a; Drucker, 2011; Tonry, 2014; Alexander, 2012; Cunneen *et al.*, 2013).

David Garland (2001a: 1) first used the phrase 'mass imprisonment' in 2001 to characterise what he saw as a unique development in imprisonment in the USA from the mid-1970s onwards: a 'phenomenon...that has no parallel in the Western world'. Mass imprisonment, according to Garland (ibid.: 1–2), has two defining features:

> One is sheer numbers. Mass imprisonment implies a rate of imprisonment and a size of prison population that is markedly above the historical and comparative norm for societies of this type. The US prison system clearly meets these criteria. The other feature is the social concentration of imprisonment's effects. Imprisonment becomes mass imprisonment when it ceases to be the incarceration of individual offenders and becomes the systematic imprisonment of whole groups of the population. In the case of the USA, the group concerned is, of course, young black males in large urban centres. For these sections of the population, imprisonment has become normalized.

Mass imprisonment, he explains:

> was not a policy that was proposed, researched, costed, debated and democratically agreed. America did not collectively decide to get into the business of mass imprisonment...Instead, mass imprisonment emerged as the overdetermined outcome of a converging series of policies and decisions. (ibid.: 2)

Thus, a key feature of Garland's (2001a: 2) description of mass imprisonment as a 'systemic imprisonment' is, as Cunneen *et al.*, (2013: 141) explain that, 'penal culture extends well beyond the prison gates to form part of the defining social conditions of being young, black and male in the USA, the UK, Canada, New Zealand and Australia'.

While the original conception of mass imprisonment as defined by Garland (2001a: 1) clearly entails 'the social concentration of imprisonment's effects' on selected, usually racialised groups, some commentators suggest that the term might (wrongly) imply that the risk of incarceration is uniform (Simon, 2012: 28; Cunneen *et al.*, 2013: 3–4). Wacquant coined the term 'hyperincarceration' in order to place class and race at the forefront of the mass incarceration debate. Thus:

> the stupendous expansion and intensification of the activities of the American police, criminal courts, and prison over the past thirty years have been finely targeted, first by class, second by race, and third by place, leading not to mass incarceration but to the hyperincarceration of (sub)proletarian African American men from the imploding ghetto. This triple selectivity reveals that the building of the hyperactive and hypertrophic penal state that has made the United States world champion in incarceration is at once a delayed reaction to the civil rights movement and the ghetto riots of the mid-1960s and a disciplinary instrument unfurled to foster the neoliberal revolution by helping to impose insecure labor as the normal horizon of work for the unskilled fractions of the postindustrial laboring class. (Wacquant, 2010: 74, footnotes omitted)

Wacquant (2010, 74) continues:

> [t]he concomitant downsizing of the welfare wing and upsizing of the criminal justice wing of the American state have not been driven by raw trends in poverty and crime, but fuelled by a politics of resentment toward categories deemed undeserving and unruly.

In *The New Jim Crow Mass Incarceration in the Age of Colour Blindness* (2012), Michelle Alexander has rejuvenated the analysis of how mass incarceration occurred in the USA. Her analogy is derived from Jim Crow – so-called after a black character in minstrel shows – a term used collectively to describe the laws, policies, regulations and practices operational across the USA between the 1880s and 1960s that drove racial exclusion, discrimination and segregation (Alexander, 2012: 35). Describing the transition from the Reconstruction period to Jim Crow, Alexander (ibid.: 30) suggests, '[e]ven amongst those most hostile to Reconstruction, few would have predicted that racial segregation would soon evolve into a new racial caste system as stunningly comprehensive and repressive as the one that came to be known simply as Jim Crow.'

Drawing parallels between mass incarceration and Jim Crow laws, Alexander (ibid.: 13) explains, '[l]ike Jim Crow (and slavery), mass incarceration operates as a tightly networked system of laws, policies, customs, and institutions that operate collectively to ensure the subordinate status of a group defined largely by race.'

She continues:

> Arguably the most important parallel between mass incarceration and Jim Crow is that both have served to define the meaning and significance of race in America. Indeed, a primary function of any racial caste system is to define the meaning of race in its time. Slavery defined what it meant to be black (a slave), and Jim Crow defined what it meant to be black (a second-class citizen). Today mass incarceration defines the meaning of blackness in America: black people, especially black men, are criminals. That is what it means to be black. (ibid.: 197)

As Tonry (2014: 504) concludes, '[t]he criminal law and sentencing became means to other ends such as winning elections, fighting cultural wars, and refusing to accept that the United States had become a multi-ethnic and multiracial country'.

The racial character of incarceration rates

The numbers and rates of incarceration in prisons, jails and community corrections across the USA were set out above. However, as Cunneen *et al.* (2013: 141) note the 'racial dynamic that generally underpins the concentration of prisoners in certain areas' can often be obscured in general corrections statistics.

In December 2013, 37 per cent of the imprisoned males were black, 32 per cent white and 22 per cent Hispanic. This translates to almost 3 per cent of the black males in the USA being imprisoned or, put another way, an imprisonment rate of 2,805 per 100,000. The imprisonment rate for Hispanic males is 1,134 per 100,000 compared to 466 per 100,000 for white males (Carson, 2014: 8).

Since 1980, 'the rate of growth of women in prison has exceeded the rate of increase for men, rising 646% from 1980 to 2010, compared to a 419% increase for men' (Mauer, 2013: 9). In December 2013, 22 per cent of the women in prison were black and 17 per cent were Hispanic. This translates to an imprisonment rate for black women that is double that of white women (Carson, 2014: 8). There have been recent declines in the rate for black women but increases for white women and Hispanic women. Mauer (2013: 18) explains, 'the nearly 30-year trend of women's incarceration increases outpacing that of men has not abated; rather, the racial dynamics of those changes have shifted'. Thus, while no one factor is adequate to explain this shift, as Mauer (ibid.) suggests, 'it is likely that reduced numbers of drug incarcerations explain a significant portion of the trend'.

Figure 1.3 presents the ratio of adults subject to some form of correctional supervision in the USA in 2013, highlighting significant variations for different demographic categories. Thus, the racial character of mass incarceration is undeniable.

These trends are repeated at the jail level, with blacks and Hispanics representing 51 per cent of the jail population compared with 30 per cent of the general population (Subramanian *et al.*, 2015: 15). Black Americans are jailed at four times the rate of white Americans (ibid.: 11).

Once age is factored in, the racial character of imprisonment rates becomes even starker. As demonstrated in Figures 1.4 and 1.5, black Americans, both male and female, have higher rates of imprisonment in every age bracket.

For black males aged between 30–39 years, the rates of imprisonment exceed 6,000 per 100,000 (Carson, 2014: Table 8). Black males aged 18–19 have an imprisonment rate six times higher than white 18–19 year olds (ibid.: 8). Or put another way, excluding the population of county jails, '1 in 13 young Black men' were detained in federal or state prison on a single night in 2014 (Tonry, 2014: 504).

1 in X Analysis : Persons subject to correctional supervision in 2013 in the USA					
TOTAL 1 in 35	WOMEN 1 in 98	MEN 1 in 21	WHITE 1 in 46	HISPANIC 1 in 37	BLACK 1 in 14

Figure 1.3 US Incarceration – Persons subject to correctional supervision in 2013 comparing groups across demographic lines, using a 1 in X analysis

Source: Authors' calculations (United States Census Bureau, 2014; Glaze and Kaeble, 2014: Table 5; Herberman and Bonczar, 2015, appendix Tables 3, 6; Minton and Golinelli, 2014: Table 2; Carson, 2014: Table 7; Pew 2009, 7).

26 *Justice Reinvestment*

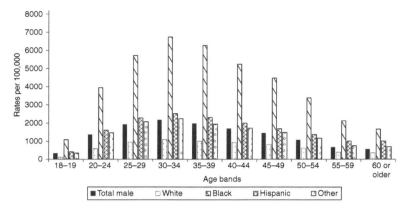

Figure 1.4 US Imprisonment – Rates of custody (state and federal prison) for US males, by age and race/ethnicity in 2013

Notes: '"Other" includes American Indians, Alaska Natives, Asians, Native Hawaiians, Pacific Islanders, persons of two or more races, or additional racial categories in the reporting information systems. White excludes persons of Hispanic or Latino origin'. Rate is calculated 'per 100,000 US residents of corresponding sex, age, and race for Hispanic origin'. (Carson, 2014: Table 8).

Source: Authors' graph (Carson, 2014: Table 8).

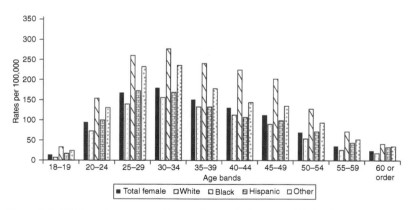

Figure 1.5 US Imprisonment – Rates of custody (state and federal prison) for US females, by age and race/ethnicity in 2013

Notes: '"Other" includes American Indians, Alaska Natives, Asians, Native Hawaiians, Pacific Islanders, persons of two or more races, or additional racial categories in the reporting information systems. White excludes persons of Hispanic or Latino origin'. Rate is calculated 'per 100,000 US residents of corresponding sex, age, and race for Hispanic origin'. (Carson, 2014: Table 8).

Source: Authors' graph (Carson, 2014: Table 8).

For black females aged between 25–34 years, rates of imprisonment exceed 250 per 100,000 (Carson, 2014: Table 8).Though relatively small in raw numbers, with a total of 111,287 women incarcerated in US prisons (state and federal) on 31 December 2014, the percentage increase of the female population is significant. The adult female imprisonment rate increased 2 per cent in 2013 (Carson, 2014: 6); and in jails, women represent the fastest growing category, with an average increase of 3.4 per cent annually since 2010 (Glaze and Kaeble, 2014: 1).

As originally conceived, this was the very thing justice reinvestment was designed to combat. In Susan Tucker's own words during an interview in 2013:

> The whole purpose of justice reinvestment was about addressing disproportionate incarceration and punishment of people of colour. That was the whole thing. If you're talking about mass incarceration, that's what you're talking about.

Drivers of mass incarceration

The drivers of mass incarceration are complex and heavily intertwined but not invisible. In summary, they have been identified as: harsh sentencing laws, especially mandatory sentences and mandatory minimums; drug laws which over-criminalise nonviolent offenders; and probation and parole policies which focus on incarceration as the primary response to technical violations (see Clear and Austin, 2009; Cole, 2011). Simon (2012: 24) argues the 'intent of mass incarceration as a policy is wonderfully transparent'. With reference to the experience in California where 22 new prisons housing an extra 52,000 offenders were built between 1983 and 2000, he suggests that the state:

> has 'removed' people from 'neighbourhoods' and sent them to 'state prison' – end of story. There is no pretense that this will effectuate change among those imprisoned; it will only provide security through removal and custody in prison. (ibid.: 24)

Tonry (2014: 504–5) recounts how the story of incarceration has been told through a range of lenses; firstly, there is the penal populism account which emphasises the role of rising crime rates and with them, public fear and political agendas; secondly, there is the argument that late modernity has produced a 'culture of control', highlighting the significance of sentencing policy; and thirdly, there is the argument which suggests that the rise of neoliberalism supported 'tough on crime' rhetoric and individualism, which in turn drove harsh judgements of criminalised behaviour. Tonry (ibid.: 505–6) proposes that '[n]one of those stories provides an adequate explanation for American developments', preferring instead to highlight the unique 'political culture and history' of the USA, concluding '[c]ountries and, within the United States, states, have the policies and prison populations they choose'.

Ferguson (2014) blames the combination of social, economic, historical, political, religious, philosophical and legal elements for the creation of 'a perfect storm of punishment'. Arguably, this 'perfect storm' has so permeated the community in the USA that incarceration has gone mainstream, from being featured on Sesame Street where characters sing about what it is like to have a parent incarcerated to John Legend's 2015 Oscar acceptance speech deploring the overrepresentation of black Americans in the criminal justice system (Sesame Street Workshop, 2013; Smith, 2015). Clear and Austin (2009: 316) emphasised in describing the 'iron law of prison populations' that:

> [t]here is no getting around it. If the problem is mass imprisonment, then the solution is to change the laws that send people to prison and sometimes keep them there for lengthy terms. That means reducing the number going in, their length of stay, or both.

The core difficulty with reversing the trend of mass incarceration lies in the fact that mass incarceration has been likened to a disease that is itself 'criminogenic' (Morrison, 2012: 954). As Drucker (2011: 67) asserts, '[v]ery high rates of imprisonment concentrated in specific communities cause social disorganisation, undermining the normal social controls of family and community that are the best (and most natural) guarantors of good behaviour'.

Shifting ground – opening up a reform dialogue.

In 2013 then US Attorney General Eric Holder (in Roberts and McVeigh: 2013) declared: 'Our system is in many ways broken…Too many Americans go to too many prisons for far too long and for no truly good law enforcement reason…We cannot simply prosecute or incarcerate our way to becoming a safer country'. Two years later, during a congressional hearing, when asked about the capacity of the US prison system, US Supreme Court Justice Anthony Kennedy (in Flatow: 2015) similarly declared that '[i]n many respects, I think it's broken…This idea of total incarceration just isn't working, and it's not humane'. This sentiment that the 'system was broken' was shared by many of the interviewees. Chapter 5 explores this theme further.

There are a number of overlapping theories attempting to explain the emergence of a developing consensus that the system is broken in the USA. This is particularly relevant in terms of considering what may have changed in criminal justice policy, politics and importantly in the public's view, to enable the 'justice reinvestment conversation' to occur.

Fiscal constraints

The most obvious answer is fiscal constraints. As the number of individuals subject to criminal justice systems grew dramatically, so too did the cost of supervising or housing them. Mitchell and Leachman (2014: 8) calculate that between 1986 and 2013, state corrections spending more than doubled from US$20 billion to $47 billon, adjusted for inflation. In the federal sphere, between 1980 and 2013, annual spending increased from US$970 million to more than $6.7 billion, adjusted for inflation (Pew, 2015a).

State budgets were stretched beyond capacity. Traditionally 'tough on crime' states like Texas were facing the very real prospect of not being able to fund their corrections costs; and thus in the early promotional materials surrounding justice reinvestment in Texas, finances feature significantly (CSG Justice Center, 2009). Nonetheless, even in Texas, the adoption of justice reinvestment was not driven by a purely financial argument. In an interview, Marc Levin of the Center for Effective Justice in Texas explains:

> When Texas embarked on this course in 2007 the state had a budget surplus of six billion dollars. So Texas could have just kept building prisons which is certainly what we had been doing... I think of course it was their impression because of course once 2008 hit as it turned out we ended up with a significant budget shortfall due to the economic downturn but in any case frankly in 2007 the biggest problem was we couldn't staff all the prisons that we had.

The Bureau of Justice Administration (BJA) (2015) also denies the JRI was a direct response to the global financial downturn:

> While JRI is not directly responsive to our current economic climate, the core principles of collaboration, identifying cost drivers, analyzing

relevant criminal justice data, and using evidence-based practices to increase public safety with dwindling budgets are more important than ever.

Moreover, when budgets are strained, criminal justice reform is not the only option available. As Morrison (2012: 956) notes, some states adopted 'downright miserly and short-sighted' adjustments including billing inmates for the period of their incarceration or costs incurred during their stay, including their underwear.

Therefore, the fiscal aspect should be seen as a necessary element but not sufficient in and of itself to shift momentum towards a reform movement. Rather, an appetite for change had developed which, heightened by the stressors associated with the global downturn and the rising costs of incarceration, gave focus to the shift away from 'tough on crime' policies. La Vigne *et al.* (2014: 6) conclude that 'states, already facing increasingly strained budgets, were frustrated with stubbornly high recidivism rates, the attendant public safety concerns, and the costs associated with both', thereby linking the economic argument with a crime one (see also Fox and Albertson 2010).

Beyond the dollars

Cadora (2014: 278) attributes the shift to 15 years of 'socioeconomic megatrends' as helping the diminution of the rising imprisonment rate. In particular, he highlights the effect of the 1990s economic boom and the decline in crime as a public concern in conjunction with the absence of a corresponding decrease in prison populations and state budgets. In 2013, the US violent crime rate was an estimated 367.9 per 100, 000 of the population. This rate represents a 14.5 per cent decrease in comparison to 2004. In fact the US crime rate has been decreasing since the 1990s (FBI, 2014: Table 1).

Greene and Mauer (2010: 1) suggest a 'new political environment' was emerging even prior to the fiscal crisis, wherein states were beginning to shift focus from traditional 'tough on crime' attitudes to approaches focused on evidence-based practices. In part this shift was enabled by conservatives adopting the rhetoric of being 'smart on crime' in preference to 'tough on crime', as discussed below.

Legal challenges have also played a significant role driving states, perhaps reluctantly, towards reform. Across the USA there is a long history of activists appealing to the authority of the courts to drive change. In the high profile case of *Brown v Plata*, the level of population reduction in California's prison system ordered by the Supreme Court was the most substantial in history (Simon, 2014: 133). Legal challenges have also played a role in other jurisdictions, including North Carolina and Rhode Island, as will be noted in Chapter 2.

Additionally, in the early 2000s a strong focus on prisoner re-entry emerged, as demonstrated by the *Second Chance Act* 2008, the *Fair Sentencing Act* 2010 and most recently, the *Criminal Justice Reinvestment Act* 2010. Money was made available which generated some momentum towards reform. Consequently, Cadora (2014: 278) contends:

> The eruption of reform was not simply an organic development of the socio economic megatrends of that time. It is in good part the fruit of the indefatigable labor of research and advocacy organizations around the country, including The Sentencing Project, Families against Mandatory Minimums, the Drug Policy Alliance, the American Civil Liberties Union, the Justice Policy Institute, the Center for Effective Public Policy, the Crime and Justice Institute, Justice Strategies, the Safer Foundation, and the Brennan Center for Justice, to name just a few. It is due as well to the adoption of the same goals by a range of independent institutes and national associations, including The JFA Institute, The Urban Institute, the Vera Institute of Justice, the Council of State Governments, and the Pew Center on the States. Apart from the many innovators and policy leaders working from within these organizations, one must also count the plethora of academic researchers whose reams of new inquiries have begun to shift the center of research away from a near-exclusive focus on crime analysis and recidivism evaluation, towards the multidimensional impact of incarceration and re-entry.

Justice reinvestment as the product of think tanks

The advancement of justice reinvestment is a product of a multitude of think tanks and agencies. With support from the Open Society Foundations, and the championing by criminologists and other experts, justice reinvestment found traction in the early states (Connecticut, Texas, Kansas, Rhode Island and Arizona). With that success came interest, support and further funding from a number of sources including Open Society, CSG, BJA and Pew. As the concept gained more support, other organisations including the Vera Institute and the Urban Institute contributed in a variety of ways, including the provision of technical assistance. Subsequently, other individuals and organisations including the American Civil Liberties Union (ACLU) and The Sentencing Project have played roles as supporters and critics.

Consequently, the complex arrangements of support and interaction between the various organisations and groups can be seen as key contributors to the unique development of the concept of justice reinvestment and its transition to the JRI. The Justice Reinvestment Initiative refers to a version of justice reinvestment for which the implementation has been spearheaded by the CSG, and funded by Pew Charitable Trusts and the BJA (Austin *et al.*, 2013: 1). (See Chapter 2) For this reason, it is useful to briefly identify the origins, nature and activities of these think tanks and other organisations.

Open Society Foundations

Founded in 1979 by George Soros, the Open Society Foundations has a strong history of promoting reform around the world. Its mission focuses on 'protecting and improving the lives of people in marginalized communities' both within America and internationally (Open Society Foundations, 2015). In 2013, the Open Society Foundations had expenditures of US$873 million, with US$242 million directed specifically towards rights and justice (ibid.). The Open Society, through The After Prison Initiative, provided the initial footing, both in terms of publication avenues and financial support, from which justice reinvestment was launched.

Bureau of Justice Assistance

The BJA is part of the US Department of Justice and is involved in both policy development and the delivery of grants at national, state, local and tribal levels. As a publicly funded entity, BJA's primary strategic goal is to '[r]educe crime, recidivism, and unnecessary confinement, and promote a safe and fair criminal justice system' (BJA, 2012: 2). The BJA coordinates nearly 40 separate funding schemes including the JRI (BJA, n.d). The BJA has taken a lead role in defining and implementing the major JRI state site selection process. In conjunction with Pew, BJA supports both state and local level JRI by funding technical assistance through organisations like the Urban Institute, the Center for Effective Public Policy (CEPP) and the Crime and Justice Institute (CJI) (BJA, 2015).

Pew

In 2004 the Pew Charitable Trusts established the Pew Research Center, a non-profit, non-partisan and non-advocacy think tank focused on 'data driven social science research' (Pew, 2015b). Its mission focuses on generating 'a foundation of facts that enriches the public dialogue and supports sound decision-making' (ibid.). The Public Safety Performance Project of the Pew Center on the States is involved in the JRI at the state level, partnering with BJA in support of the CSG and, for a period, Vera (Pew, 2015c).

Council of State Governments

The CSG is a national non-government organisation which represents all 50 states. It primarily provides advice to government policy-makers. The CSG's mission is to 'champion excellence in state governments to advance the common good' (CSG, 2015b). The CSG works on a myriad of projects including education, health, the environment, transportation and public safety. The CSG Justice Center is funded by a diverse combination of federal, private and local funds including the BJA. The CSG's Justice Center is the primary implementation arm of the JRI. The JRI is only one of eight areas of focus for the Justice Center, the others being corrections, courts, law enforcement, youth, substance abuse, re-entry and mental health (CSG Justice Center, 2015a).

Vera Institute of Justice

The Vera Institute is a non-partisan, non-profit entity focused on 'justice policy and practice' (Vera Institute, 2015). The aim of Vera is to bring together research and 'program innovation to plan, implement, and evaluate improvements in systems that deliver justice, such as courts, law enforcement, immigration, and social services' (Vera Institute, 2012a). Funded by grants from a variety of sources including government of all levels, foundations and private donors, Vera's involvement with the JRI is as a technical assistance provider to states. (Vera Institute, 2015)

The Urban Institute

The Urban Institute is a non-profit, non-partisan research-based think tank which aims to 'offer solutions through economic and social policy research' (Urban Institute 2015). The Urban Institute is primarily funded by external sources including grants from all levels of government, foundations and private donors. Its work covers a broad range of areas from health and tax to well-being of neighbourhoods and trends in work and wealth. In the context of the JRI, the Urban Institute is funded by BJA. Originally playing a role providing technical assistance to local level JRI schemes, the Urban Institute most recently completed a large-scale assessment of the development of the JRI in 17 states (La Vigne et al., 2014). It has also produced a number of tool kits and manuals for implementing justice reinvestment at the local level (e.g., La Vigne *et al.*, 2010; La Vigne *et al.*, 2013). The Urban Institute continues to review and report on the progress of state and local level JRI sites (Cramer *et al.*, 2014).

Center for Effective Public Policy

The CEPP is a non-profit organisation providing research and practical expertise to federal, state and local governmental agencies and private foundations on a variety of criminal justice related issues. In the context of the JRI, the CEPP is engaged at the local level only. Funded by the BJA, CEPP has been providing technical assistance to county sites since 2011 (CEPP, 2015).

Crime and Justice Institute

The CJI is the research and consultancy limb of Community Resources for Justice that is a charitable business which focuses on community strategies and social justice services to support those involved with the adult and juvenile justice systems (CRJ, 2014: 5, 11). Since 2010, the CJI has received funding from the BJA to provide technical assistance to counties as part of the JRI (CRJ, 2015).

Justice Mapping Center

The Justice Mapping Center (JMC) is the brainchild of Eric Cadora and Charles Swartz. Formed in 1998, the Justice Center has produced 'justice mapping analyses in numerous states around the country in partnership with many organizations, including the Open Society Institute, the JFA Institute, the Council of State Governments, and the Urban Institute' (JMC, 2015). Cadora, in addition to coining the term justice reinvestment with Tucker as project officer for The After Prison Initiative at Open Society, provided guidance on asset and justice mapping for the early efforts to implement justice reinvestment, in locations such as Wichita, Kansas (Susan Tucker; JMC, 2010).

The Sentencing Project

The Sentencing Project has been working to promote just reforms to sentencing policy since 1986 (The Sentencing Project, 2015). The Sentencing Project has connections with Open Society Foundations and while broadly supportive of justice reinvestment, 'never played a substantial role in the development of the concept' (Mark Mauer, The Sentencing Project). Therefore, The Sentencing Project's role in the JRI has been 'from a little bit of distance', with Mauer being one of the authors of the Austin *et al.* (2013) review.

American Civil Liberties Union

Founded in 1920, the ACLU is a non-partisan, non-profit organisation self-described as 'our nation's guardian of liberty' (ACLU, 2015). The ACLU's interest in justice reinvestment aligns with its national campaign to end mass incarceration. In an interview with Vanita Gupta, she describes how the ACLU's interest in the JRI grew out of concern regarding 'some of the dynamics around the current implementation of the Justice Reinvestment Initiative', which led to the ACLU contributing to the Austin *et al.* (2013) critical review.

JFA Institute

The JFA Institute is a non-profit agency focused on generating 'research-based policy solutions' for criminal justice (JFA, 2012). Led by James Austin, the JFA Institute was involved in justice reinvestment between 2004 and 2007, taking a prominent role which included producing a series of reports and publications in conjunction with a number of other organisations including the BJA and CSG (ibid.).

Other players

There are a range of organisations and actors beyond those noted above who have shaped justice reinvestment. These include community activists, philanthropic foundations, academics and organisations like the National District Attorneys Association, National Association for Public Defence, Right on Crime, lobbyists, and a range of victims' advocates.

The many masters of justice reinvestment

Tucker and Cadora's initial articulation of justice reinvestment was published by Open Society Foundations (formally Open Society Institute). As a stepping stone to turning theory into practice, Tucker and Cadora, supported by the Soros Foundation, funded Mike Thompson from the CSG Justice Center, to begin the process of developing a method for implementing justice reinvestment. With less than US$100,000 to begin with, Tucker describes Thompson as 'a one person operation at the time' (Susan Tucker).

In 2005, Marshall Clement joined the CSG Justice Center to further the development of justice reinvestment. Clement explains that in those early days 'no one really knew about justice reinvestment or really cared' (Marshall Clement, CSG Justice Center). The process in Kansas took two years, during which time Clement worked with Dr Tony Fabelo who provided substantial data analysis and liaised with policy-makers, and also Eric Cadora, who consulted with the CSG around asset mapping (Marshall Clement, CSG Justice Center). The focus was on collecting and analysing data, isolating the drivers of incarceration and fine-tuning the implementation plans in terms of 'applying what works in evidence-based practices to what they were doing' (Marshall Clement, CSG Justice Center). In Clement's own words it has been 'just kind of going on gangbusters ever since, state after state' (Marshall Clement, CSG Justice Center).

Through the early 2000s, a number of criminologists contributed to the process of revising the concept of justice reinvestment as originally envisaged by Tucker and Cadora into a specific set of initiatives. In early attempts to develop a method for implementing justice reinvestment, CSG had significant success 'bringing State legislators to the table' (Susan Tucker). This enabled the key players to build on the small amount of funding initially provided by the Soros Foundation. The BJA provided seed funding out of discretionary funds to CSG Justice Center. By 2010, federal funding for justice reinvestment peaked, with the BJA receiving US$10 million for the JRI as part of the *Consolidated Appropriations Act, 2010*. Based on this figure, the BJA made the decision to expand its work with the Urban Institute and others to fund JRI technical assistance at the local or county level (Gary Dennis, BJA). To this end, the BJA funded CEPP and CJI to provide 'technical assistance and then ultimately providing some money' (Gary Dennis, BJA).

The federal government continued to support the JRI, though in subsequent years the funding amount dropped to US$6.5million for financial years (FY) 2011–12 (Gary Dennis, BJA). In the FY 2014 budget President Obama asked for $85 million for justice reinvestment initiatives (*Consolidated Appropriations Act 2014*). However, in part a consequence of the budget crisis, in FY 2014 and FY 2015 respectively, justice reinvestment received US$27.5 million. Out of a proposed budget of US$4 trillion dollars, of which $1.14 billion relates to state and local law enforcement assistance, the FY 2016 budget request for justice reinvestment is US$45 million (CSG, 2015c). In addition to funds derived for the BJA from congressional appropriations, in some instances Pew provides funds, and JRI sites themselves are encouraged to look for sources of funding internally from government or private sources (BJA, 2015).

The joint financial and procedural arrangements between primarily the BJA, Pew and CSG, but also the Urban Institute, Vera, CJI and CEPP has led to a complex coalition arrangement between private, public, for-profit and non-profit organisations (La Vigne, Urban). This has shaped the continued development of justice reinvestment into the JRI, cementing the difference between the two. Most recently, the ties between the entities was demonstrated with the Pew Charitable Trusts, BJA and CSG co-hosting the Justice Reinvestment National Summit in late 2014 (Pew, 2014).

Implementation of JRI

With the transition from justice reinvestment to the JRI, the process of converting states was increasingly streamlined. As La Vigne et al (2014: 6) have stated, 'JRI was launched as a public-private partnership' between BJA and Pew, with CSG Justice Center, Pew or Vera providing technical assistance. This formalised efforts to 'fund, coordinate, assess, and disseminate state and local justice reinvestment efforts across the United States' (ibid.).

The elements of the JRI are discussed in Chapter 2. However, three key aspects to the adoption of justice reinvestment that are worth acknowledging are the value placed on bipartisanship, the support from an early stage from conservative political organisations and the role played by faith-based organisations.

Valuing bipartisanship

The extent of bipartisanship demonstrated in the context of the JRI is, at face value, striking. To some extent the bipartisan nature of justice reinvestment has been imposed on states and local sites because of the value placed on it by the CSG. In order to receive funding and technical assistance, states or counties must first demonstrate they have the support of key stakeholders including from both sides of politics and others including the judiciary, corrections, prosecutors, and defence lawyers (BJA, 2015). The approach taken in South Dakota is an example of such bipartisanship and also the capacity for coordination (see Chapter 6). However, the emphasis on bipartisanship also represents a shift in politics in the USA, and a new approach to the language used in criminal justice which focuses on being 'smart on crime' instead of 'tough on crime'. Consequently, though perhaps not surprisingly, some of the bipartisan agreements have proved to be more stable and resilient than others.

Sources of support and promotion

Justice reinvestment and the JRI have enjoyed significant popularity in traditionally hard-on-crime conservative states like Texas, South

Dakota, Kansas, Nevada and Arizona. In part this could be seen as a product of the bipartisanship demanded by the CSG and BJA. However, beyond the mandate for bipartisanship, another unique aspect of the uptake of justice reinvestment and the JRI has been the varied sources of support and advocacy, in particular from Right on Crime (Right on Crime, 2015).

In 2011, Newt Gingrich and Pat Nolan (2011), promoting Right on Crime in *The Washington Post,* wrote:

> We can no longer afford business as usual with prisons. The criminal justice system is broken, and conservatives must lead the way in fixing it...If our prison policies are failing half of the time, and we know that there are more humane, effective alternatives, it is time to fundamentally rethink how we treat and rehabilitate our prisoners.

Right on Crime (2015) characterises its role as a 'national campaign to promote successful, conservative solutions on American criminal justice policy- reforming the system to ensure public safety, shrink government, and save taxpayers money'. It also describes itself as 'transforming the debate on criminal justice in America' (ibid.). Though more often drawing on the language of 'performance incentive funding' or 'public safety' and 'cost-effectiveness', as opposed to using the labels of justice reinvestment or the JRI, Right on Crime continues to play a high profile role in criminal justice reform associated with JRI states (see ibid.; Reddy and Levin, 2014). Most recently, Right on Crime signatory and former Speaker of the US House of Representatives, Republican Newt Gingrich opened the 2015 Bipartisan Summit on Criminal Justice Reform in Washington, DC (Muldrow, 2015).

To this end, the flexibility of the concept of justice reinvestment, and the fact that it appeals to both sides of politics, has enabled the reframing of the reform conversation. As Clear (2012:1) asserts, '[j]ustice reinvestment treats all correctional costs as public safety investments'. This is a sentiment which equally suits conservative Christians talking of redemption and libertarians who have come to see the prison system as the embodiment of a heavy-handed state. As Morrison (2012, 958) concludes, '[t]hough the motivations of the conservative and the liberal may diverge, their goals may be aligned'.

Reflecting on the increasingly high profile role of conservatives in reforming criminal justice away from imprisonment-only solutions, Tonry (2014: 508) argues:

The same kind of emotive language about lost human potential, ruined lives, heavy-handed and arbitrary laws, simplistic and ineffectual policies, and immorality has appeared regularly over the past 20 years in statements by representatives of the American Civil Liberties Union and other liberal reform groups.

Moreover, as Vitiello (in Morrison 2012: 956) asserts, criminal justice reform is no longer simply the province of well-meaning liberals and rehabilitation advocates.

Role of faith-based organisations

The importance of faith-based organisations in the context of criminal justice policy in the USA is facilitated by uniquely American structures. The election and partisan selection of judges and prosecutors gives these positions a particularly influential role in criminal justice policy, including justice reinvestment and re-entry schemes (Tonry, 2014: 513) (see Chapter 5). Organisations such as Justice Fellowship (2015), which is the criminal justice reform arm of Prison Fellowship, seek to 'change our criminal justice system at every level so that it reflects the principles of restorative justice found in the Bible'. The Prison Fellowship expressly promotes the JRI:

> Justice Fellowship, the policy arm of Prison Fellowship, promotes the understanding that being "smart on crime" – and not just being "hard on crime" – is the key to reducing incarceration and recidivism rates. By implementing common sense reforms like those proposed by the Justice Reinvestment Initiative, the criminal justice system can become more effective in breaking the cycle of crime that all too often enslaves individuals, families, and communities – all while saving taxpayer money. (Rempe, 2014)

Demonstrating the prominence of faith in justice reform, and the power of such organisations to communicate with the general public, Prison Fellowship actively campaigns for reforms in states adopting the JRI, one example of which is in Michigan:

> Justice in Crisis: Justice Fellowship's Call to Action
>
> Justice Fellowship is committed to reforming the justice system according to the principles of restorative justice – encouraging safer communities, respect for victims, and transformation for men

and women who have been convicted of crimes. We are working with the Council of State Governments to bring justice reform to Michigan, and look forward to partnering with you. (Justice Fellowship, 2015)

Justice reinvestment in the UK

In 2014, England and Wales had an imprisonment rate of 149 per 100,000 of the population. Scotland had a rate of 146 per 100,000 and Northern Ireland had a rate of 100 per 100,000 of the population (Prison Reform Trust, 2014: 2). From the early 1990s the UK prison population increased significantly, at an average of 4 per cent per annum (MOJ, 2015a: 4). Following the *Criminal Justice and Immigration Act* 2008, the population has continued to rise, albeit at a slower rate of 1–2 per cent per annum (MOJ, 2014a: 6–7; 2015a: 5). Figure 1.6 demonstrates this increase in rates per 100,000. However, the crime rate between 2003 and 2012 decreased from 1,018 to 833 violent crimes per 100,000 of the population (Institute for Economics and Peace, 2013: 8).

As at March 2015, persons on remand made up 11.8 per cent of the prison population (MOJ, 2015b: Tables 1.1, 1.2a). Growth in the adult remand population was 5 per cent for 2014 and is thus a key contributor to the growth in the prison population (MOJ, 2015a: 5). As at April 2015 the prison population was 85,432 (MOJ, 2015c). But on any day more than an additional 180,000 persons are subject to either community

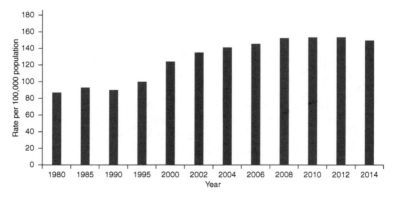

Figure 1.6 UK Imprisonment – Rates of imprisonment for England and Wales in increments from 1980 to 2014

Source: Authors' graph (ICPS, 2015).

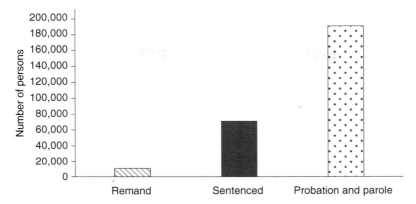

Figure 1.7 UK Incarceration – Number of persons comparing types of supervision (remand, sentenced prisoners and persons on probation or parole)
Source: Authors' graph (MOJ, 2014a: Table A1.1, A4.1).

sentences, suspended sentences, pre-release supervision or post-release supervision. Thus, as represented in Figure 1.7, the majority of offenders in the UK criminal justice system are subject to supervision by the Probation Service (MOJ, 2014a).

The women's prison population in England and Wales more than doubled between 1995 and 2010, from 1,979 to 4,236. More recently the numbers have declined a little – with 3,929 women in prison in June 2014 (Prison Reform Trust, 2014: 35). As at April 2015 women represented 4.5 per cent of the prison population (MOJ, 2015c). However, this tends to understate female involvement in the criminal justice system as the most common sentence type for women is a community sentence, and women are less likely to receive a prison sentence of greater than 12 months (MOJ, 2014b: 47, 49).

Table 1.1 shows the prison population in the UK classified by self-identified ethnicity. The disparity between the ethnicity of prisoners varies the greatest when the British national population is compared to the foreign national population as 'the proportion of Black and Asian offenders in the foreign national prison population was nearly three times as high as those in the British national prison population' (MOJ, 2013a: 16). From 2008–12, the proportion of offenders sentenced to immediate custody increased for all ethnicities, despite a decrease in the total number of persons sentenced for indictable offences during the same period (ibid.: 76).

Table 1.1 UK Imprisonment – Prison population by self-identified ethnicity in 2004 and 2013

Offenders	2004 (No)	2004 (%)	2013 (No)	2013 (%)
All nationalities	74,488		83,842	
White	51,281	68.8	60,706	72.4
Mixed	1,859	2.5	3,208	3.8
Asian or Asian British	3,837	5.2	6,474	7.7
Black or Black British	10,044	13.5	10,847	12.9
Chinese or Other ethnic	694	0.9	1,014	1.2
Not stated or Unrecorded	301	0.4	1593	1.9

Note: Identity is self-identified. The 2004 percentage does not total 100 as prior to 2004 the 1991 census ethnic codes were used. Thus 6,742 offenders are not accounted for within the six specified categories.

Source: Authors' calculations (MOJ, 2014a: Table, A1.8).

The costs of imprisonment in the UK are significant. In 2009–10 the Ministry of Justice (MOJ) budget was £10 billion, of which approximately £4 billion were allocated to the cost of prisons (Fox, Albertson and Wong, 2013a: 19). However, since 2009 expenditure has fallen. In 2013–14, 'overall resource expenditure', which represents the 'net expenditure met at a regional or national level' for prisons as managed by the National Offender Management Service, had dropped to £2.8 billion, translating to an average cost per prisoner of £33,785 per year (MOJ, 2014c: Table 1).

Embracing justice reinvestment

In its report *Do Better Do Less* (2009: 55), the Commission on English Prisons Today profiled justice reinvestment as a new model 'for reducing conflict and crime' and recommended 'fundamental reform':

> With local authorities as lead partners, we suggest local strategic partnerships should be formed that bring together representatives from the criminal justice, health and education sectors, with local prison and probation budgets fully devolved and made available for justice reinvestment initiatives.

The following year the UK House of Commons Justice Committee (HCJC) Report, *Cutting Crime: The Case for Justice Reinvestment*, argued that the criminal justice system 'is facing a crisis of sustainability' and noted that '[t]he overall system seems to treat prison as a "free commodity"' (HCJC, 2010: 5–6). The Justice Committee drew heavily on the four-stage JRI model from the CSG in support of a holistic approach to criminal justice reform (Fox, Albertson and Wong, 2013a: 38). In addition, the Justice Committee specifically recommended capping the prison population at current levels, followed by phased reductions to two-thirds of the current population and a devolution of custodial budgets so that there is 'a direct financial incentive for local agencies to spend money in ways which will reduce prison numbers' (HCJC, 2010: 143).

After the May 2010 election, the Justice Secretary in the new Conservative/Liberal Democrat coalition government deplored the 'bang 'em up culture' and pledged to cut the prison population in England and Wales within four years via sentencing reforms and a 'rehabilitation revolution' (Travis and Herch, 2010). Allen (2011: 620) argues the coalition government's support of justice reinvestment represented at the time a 'somewhat surprising change of direction in penal policy', given that the party, in adopting a justice reinvestment approach was not only resiling from a commitment to create 5,000 prison beds but actually promising to reduce the population by 3,000 in 2014–15.

A new trajectory

Justice reinvestment, as adopted, or, as some commentators have argued, 'partially implemented' or 'misappropriated', has its own trajectory in the UK (Allen in Wong, Fox and Albertson, 2014a: 80; Fox, Albertson and Wong, 2013a: 41). It has followed a PbR-orientated approach (Fox and Albertson, 2012).

In 2010 the MOJ launched two justice reinvestment related pilots: the *Local Justice Reinvestment Pilots* and the *Youth Justice Reinvestment Pathfinder Initiative*. Pilots also operated under the banner of payment by results: *HMP Peterborough Social Impact Bond* and *HMP Doncaster PbR Pilot*. These pilots do not follow the Tucker and Cadora concept of justice reinvestment and differ also from the approach taken in the implementation of the JRI in the USA. Rather, Fox, Albertson and Wong (2013a: 27) describe the approach as one in which 'the government has appropriated the term to motivate innovations in criminal justice delivery'.

Fox, Albertson and Wong (2013a, 4) foreshadowed this by arguing, 'the version of JR dominant in the UK policy dialogue is fairly narrow and focused primarily [on] re-offending by individual offenders'. In part this can be attributed to the complexity of UK criminal justice structures (ibid.: 13), but it also represents a choice by politicians and key figures in criminal justice as to the use of language and approach. This is demonstrated clearly in a contemporaneous statement made by Nick Herbert (2010: 9), Minister of State for Policing and Criminal Justice (2010–12):

> We call this payment by results, but you might call it "justice reinvestment." Whatever the name, it represents a radical new focus on rehabilitating offenders, recognising that it no longer makes sense to incur such costs on the public purse through high rates of reoffending. It allows us to make the "reinvestment" a reality by capturing savings to the criminal justice system.

The *Youth Justice Reinvestment Pathfinder Initiative* was designed to incentivise local criminal justice actors to reduce the use of custody for juveniles. Described as a 'form of justice reinvestment', the pilot ended in September 2013 (Wong, Ellingworth and Meadows, 2015: 5). Only two of the four original sites completed the pilot, underscoring 'the importance of having the capacity and capability in data analysis and interpretation, problem-solving approaches, and project implementation' (ibid.: 31).

The *Local Justice Reinvestment Pilot*, which operated in six sites (Greater Manchester and five London Boroughs) ended in mid-2013. The pilot aimed to reduce the criminal justice system's costs by reducing demand, and if successful the local area was to be 'rewarded' on the basis of their results. Those payments were to be reinvested into services aimed at reducing reoffending. The Ministry of Justice reported that of the five sites that completed the pilot all five received payments ranging from £659,000 to £4,986,000 (MOJ, 2013b). However, significant concerns about the structure and data measurement systems of the pilots have been raised. (See Wong *et al.*, 2013a; Wong, 2013a; Wong, 2013b; see also Chapter 4). Having been involved in the interim evaluation of the sites, Wong, Fox and Albertson (2014a, 86) conclude:

> Assessed against the four-step approach to JR proposed by the Justice Committee ... only one of the six sites in the pilot (Greater Manchester) appeared to take up the opportunity to attempt a JR approach to the delivery of local criminal justice services.

Justice reinvestment in Australia

Mass incarceration in Australia has a different character to that in the USA and the UK. While the Australian overall rate of imprisonment in

2014 of 185.6 per 100,000 of the adult population is significantly lower than the general US imprisonment rate of 623 per 100,000 of the adult population, it still represents a substantial increase from a low of 90 per 100,000 in 1982 (ABS, 2014a; Carson, 2014: 6) (See Figure 1.8). However, the overall Australian imprisonment rates include sentenced and un-sentenced prisoners, and is irrespective of sentence length. Thus the more appropriate comparison is with the US rate inclusive of jails and state and federal prisons, which was 910 per 100,000 of the adult population in 2013 (Glaze and Kaeble, 2014: 4). While the imprisonment rate has been increasing, the violent crime rate has been decreasing consistently since 2001 as per Figure 1.9.

The imprisonment rate for Indigenous Australians often exceeds the incarceration rates for black Americans, making mass incarceration a very real issue in Australia. In 2014, the crude Indigenous imprisonment rate was 2,174 per 100,000 (ABS, 2014a: Table 19). The state-based rates of imprisonment demonstrate even starker disparities, as portrayed in Figure 1.10. In 2014, Western Australia (WA) had the highest age-standardised imprisonment rate for Aboriginal and Torres Strait Islanders of 3,013 per 100,000 (ABS, 2014a: Table 17) (see also Chapter 3).

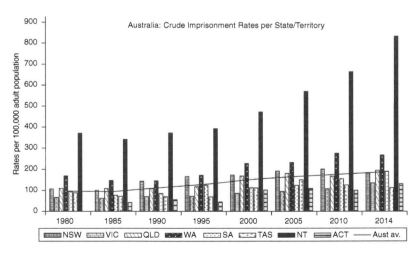

Figure 1.8 Australian Incarceration – Crude imprisonment rates, per state and territory, in increments from 1980 to 2014

Source: Authors' graph (Stephens *et al.*, n.d: 3; ABS, 2014a: Table 18).

46 *Justice Reinvestment*

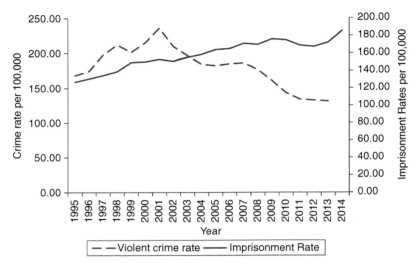

Figure 1.9 Australian Imprisonment – Rates of imprisonment vs violent crime from 1995 to 2013–14

Note: The crime rate graphed is for serious violent offences (murder, manslaughter, attempted murder, sexual assault, kidnapping, robbery and blackmail/extortion).

Source: Authors' graph (ABS, 2014a: Table 18; ABS, 2014b: Table 6; Stephens *et al.*, n.d: 3).

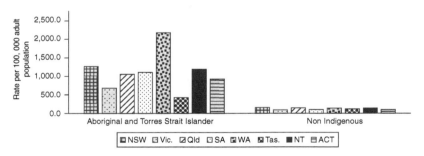

Figure 1.10 Australian Imprisonment – Age-standardised imprisonment rates, by state and territory and Indigenous status in 2014

Note: Age-standardised rates better accommodate the age based population differences between Indigenous and non-Indigenous Australians.

Source: Authors' graph (ABS, 2014a: Table 17).

Age and gender in combination with Indigenous status affect the imprisonment rate dramatically, as demonstrated in Figures 1.11 and 1.12. For Indigenous males aged between 25–39 years, rates exceed 6,000 per 100,000. For Indigenous women in the same age band, rates exceed 600 per 100,000 (ABS, 2014a: Table 20). When gender, race and age are examined simultaneously, the vulnerabilities of Indigenous women emerge.

Justice reinvestment finds traction

The groundswell of support for justice reinvestment in Australia in both community and government sectors, leading up to the Australian Senate inquiry, was outlined in the introduction. The terms of reference of that inquiry canvassed both the state of imprisonment and the potential of justice reinvestment in Australia. Attracting 131 submissions from all over Australia that were overwhelmingly supportive of justice reinvestment, the committee (LCARC, 2013: xii–xiii) produced a report that made nine recommendations. Of particular note, the committee recommended that the Commonwealth adopt a leadership role in supporting the implementation of justice reinvestment including the collection and sharing of data, (Recs 1, 2, 4, 5) establishing and funding a trial, including in at least one remote Indigenous community, to be robustly evaluated (Recs 6 and 7), and promoting through the Standing Committee on Law and Justice the establishment of an independent central coordinating body (Rec 8).

The majority of the committee acknowledged concerns raised by contributors in submissions around the data collection, the suitability and availability of programs, and the challenges associated with quantifying savings to ensure genuine reinvestment. Nonetheless, the majority remained optimistic:

> Addressing disadvantage, particularly where disadvantage is deep and persistent, is complex. There will be significant challenges in identifying the right policies, services and criminal justice responses; implementing those policies, and conducting evaluations. Also the benefits of justice reinvestment may take some time to eventuate. However, the committee considers that justice reinvestment has sufficiently attractive attributes to warrant genuine consideration in Australia. (ibid.: 112)

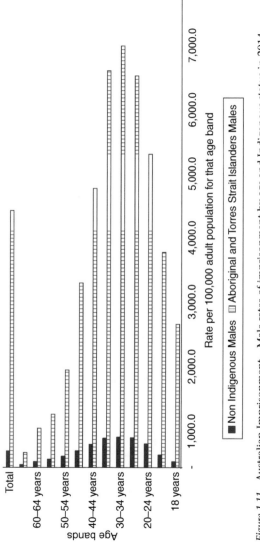

Figure 1.11 Australian Imprisonment – Male rates of imprisonment by age and Indigenous status in 2014
Source: Authors' graph (ABS, 2014a: Table 20).

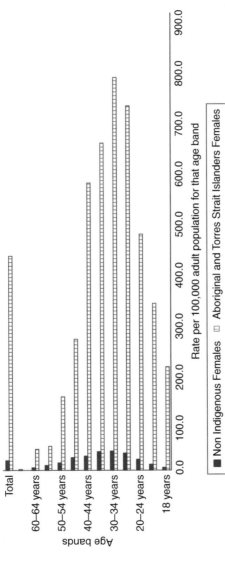

Figure 1.12 Australian Imprisonment – Female rates of imprisonment by age and Indigenous status in 2014
Source: Authors' graph (ABS, 2014a: Table 20).

Conservative Liberal-National Coalition (L-NC) senators produced a minority report endorsing the 'principle' of justice reinvestment but rejecting any leadership role for the Commonwealth:

> Coalition senators are broadly supportive of further investment in exploring the potential of JR, but we see the approach emerging from the majority report as one of the Commonwealth assuming policy and funding leadership over JR across the nation, an approach which is potentially very costly and which intrudes into the fundamental responsibilities of the second-tier of Australian government. (ibid.: 127)

Following this split result and a change of government in 2013, there has been no further action adopting a justice reinvestment policy or assisting states to implement their own policies. Rather, the momentum in Australia is being driven at the community level.

The evolving nature of justice reinvestment

The profile of justice reinvestment continues to develop in Australia, as do the disparate contexts within which it is referenced as a possible solution to criminal justice and social justice issues. These contexts include: being proposed as a means of drastically cutting juvenile corrections in Queensland (QLD) (Bratanova and Robinson, 2014); being considered as an option for furthering drug diversion as part of Victoria's methamphetamine inquiry (Parliament of Victoria, 2014); and as a model to follow in the development of a 'care reinvestment' strategy by the Secretariat of National Aboriginal and Islander Child Care (Secretariat of National Aboriginal and Islander Child Care, 2013).

Given the constantly evolving nature of justice reinvestment endeavours in Australia, it is not possible to be comprehensive about every group, organisation or government investigating the potential of justice reinvestment. Therefore, what follows below is a snapshot of the more prominent developments as at March 2015.

Summary of key Australian developments

- Pilots

The most advanced pilot in Australia currently is running in Bourke, NSW, launched by Just Reinvest NSW in 2013. Just Reinvest NSW has as its priority redressing the overrepresentation of Aboriginal young people in custody (Just Reinvest, 2015a). The Bourke pilot is a community led project which benefits from a number of philanthropic and corporate relationships and has progressed from community consultation to the collection of data (see Chapter 3). In South Australia (SA), development of a justice reinvestment pilot has reached the stage of nominating locations, with two sites having been identified. In Queensland (QLD), there are discussions occurring with Griffith University and James Cook University with respect to a justice reinvestment project on Palm Island. In the Northern Territory (NT), the development of a pilot project for justice reinvestment to be implemented in Katherine is being supported by the NT Council of Social Services and the North Australian Aboriginal Justice Association (NAAJA) (Allison, 2015).

- Working groups and other organisations

In NSW, Just Reinvest NSW (2015b) has a public profile advocating for justice reinvestment, most recently launching *Justice Reinvestment Policy: Thinking Differently for a safer Community*. In Victoria, Smart Justice for Young People (2015) launched a new campaign calling for the adoption of a 'youth justice reinvestment approach to criminal justice in Victoria'. Smart Justice (2015) explains that the 'campaign will look at data, learnings from the experience of JR in other jurisdictions and various related projects happening around Australia in order to help facilitate the discussion and exploration of justice reinvestment's potential within a Victorian context'. In Tasmania, a justice reinvestment framework was recommended in the context of a review of youth detention (Daly, 2013). In SA, the South Australian Justice Reinvestment Working Group is active. In WA, a coalition, Justice Reinvestment WA, developed early on; however it has since disbanded with the focus in WA shifting to Social Reinvestment (Solonec, 2014: 14; Chris Twomey, WACOSS). The Australian Red Cross (2012) has embraced justice reinvestment and is supporting the development of pilots.

- Government Support

At the federal level, the Australian Greens have adopted justice reinvestment as a policy (Australian Greens, 2013). In NSW former Attorney General Brad Hazzard and Shadow Attorney General Paul Lynch both spoke at the launch of Just Reinvest NSW's election policy in a rare show of bipartisanship alongside the ATSISJC Mick Gooda and Sarah Hopkins from Just Reinvest NSW (2015a). In early 2015, NSW Labor announced their election commitment to a justice reinvestment approach: 'In an Australian first, Labor will invest $4 million into three pilot projects run by non-government organisations based on the strategy of Justice Reinvestment' (NSW Labor 2015). In the Australian Capital Territory (ACT), the Government announced in 2015 a 'Justice Reinvestment Strategy' as a 'whole of government justice reinvestment approach aimed at reducing recidivism and diverting offenders, and those at risk of becoming offenders, from the justice system' (ACT Government 2015). In WA, while there has not been any sustained support for justice reinvestment, key public figures including Chief Justice Wayne Martin, Police Commissioner Karl O'Callaghan and Shadow Corrective Services Minister Paul Papalia have all emphasised the potential of justice reinvestment for the specific needs of that state (Egan, 2013; O'Callaghan, 2015; Papalia, 2010).

- Academic projects and literature

A number of academic projects with a justice reinvestment focus have been developed in Australia. Apart from our project, the Australian Justice Reinvestment Project (AJR Project), Dr Jill Guthrie from the National Centre for Indigenous Studies at the Australian National University leads a research project, *Reducing Incarceration using Justice Reinvestment: An Exploratory Case Study*, exploring potential reinvestment options for young people in the regional town of Cowra, NSW. Also, the Human Rights Law Centre has philanthropic funding to investigate justice reinvestment in Australia, to reduce Aboriginal imprisonment and better promote community safety. Additionally, a growing body of Australian literature, led by the AJR Project, has resulted in a number of conferences, presentations, forums and discussions about the relevance of justice reinvestment at the community, state and national level.

Conclusion

Across all three jurisdictions, there is increasing recognition that imprisonment is criminogenic. As Clear (2012: 2) quips, 'think of this as a sort of very expensive dysfunctional timeout for where you are spending a lot of money to put people away so that they can come back to you worse'. As discussed earlier, the only way to change corrections population numbers is to change how many people are incarcerated and for how long. Thus Clear (ibid.: 20) suggests, 'we don't have to get the perfect set of reforms, we just have to beat the current system, we have to improve on the current problem'.

In surveying the history of justice reinvestment to date, this chapter has sought to locate the emergence of justice reinvestment in the historical context of responses to the phenomenon of mass incarceration, a phenomenon which has neighbourhood, vulnerable communities and racial disparity at its core. As demonstrated through the data presented in this chapter, across all three jurisdictions, rates of incarceration and imprisonment stand at historic highs, particularly for vulnerable groups. This laid the foundation for a discussion of the development of justice reinvestment.

Having briefly covered the changes in the conceptualisation of mass incarceration from Garland to Wacquant to Alexander, this chapter traced the shifts in the concept of justice reinvestment from its US origins, grounded in community and social innovation, through to the uptake of the JRI by think tanks, political and state actors. Reflecting on the unique features of the US context which facilitated a predominately bipartisan reform dialogue, this chapter identified it was more than merely fiscal concerns, rather a combination of factors that coalesced to create a unique opportunity in response to 'the perfect storm of punishment'.

The adoption of justice reinvestment in the UK was then briefly surveyed, highlighting the transformation of the principles of justice reinvestment to suit the UK context. The emphasis on PbR schemes in the UK was explored in the context of the 2010 local justice reinvestment pilots. Finally, turning to the Australian context, the growing enthusiasm for justice reinvestment was canvassed. The outcome of the Senate inquiry was briefly summarised along with an overview of the key justice reinvestment initiatives being championed by community groups and other organisations, and to a lesser extent, state governments. This highlights the evolving nature of justice reinvestment in Australia currently, and reinforces the importance of the research questions set out in the introduction of this text.

Through this chapter, what unfolds is a story that highlights the potential of justice reinvestment to open up a new dialogue.

2
How Has Justice Reinvestment Worked in the USA?

As more US states have taken up justice reinvestment to deal with ballooning corrections populations and the budgetary realities that go with them, justice reinvestment has taken a range of shapes. Cumulatively, these strategies have contributed to a change in the political climate whereby lowering imprisonment rates can be seriously entertained by public officials (Austin *et al.*, 2013: 1). Moreover, according to Gary Dennis of the BJA, JRI initiatives have led to improvements in levels of professionalism within the not-for-profit sector and faith-based organisations as their work gets drawn into a framework involving stronger oversight and evaluation.

In the decade or so in which JRI has been implemented in various US jurisdictions, gaps have emerged, perhaps inevitably, between the way that it was originally conceived and the way that it has been applied in practice. This chapter sets out some of the original principles of justice reinvestment and discusses a number of the strategies that were identified as its defining features. We then compare those originating principles to the on-the-ground realities of the JRI in the USA. The analysis here is not exhaustive, but rather is based around the literature from organisations involved with the JRI and interviews with key stakeholders involved in the implementation of various strategies.

The instrumental approach taken by the CSG has been remarkably successful at securing the expeditious passage of legislation aimed at reducing incarceration rates. It has also been at odds in some respects with the normative principles that shaped the original formulation of justice reinvestment. One of the architects of the concept, Susan Tucker, says that the success of the CSG in shaping the criminal justice reform narrative around justice reinvestment means that 'to be in a position to get money, I think people feel like they have to come under the banner of justice reinvestment. And so then justice reinvestment itself gets watered down'. She is referring here to the aspects of the strategy, as originally conceived, that go beyond budgetary imperatives – such as (re)investment in disadvantaged communities – which reflect deeper values like social and racial justice; indeed, justice reinvestment was devised as an elegant structure through which funds could be found to achieve such reinvestment. While it also has the advantage of being marketable as a strategy which recognises that there is 'no logic to spending a million dollars a year to incarcerate people from one block in Brooklyn' (Tucker and Cadora, 2003: 2), the idea, as originally conceived, was ultimately a vehicle for achieving 'community-level solutions to community-level problems' (ibid.: 2, 3).

The variance of the JRI in practice from justice reinvestment in theory in some respects reflects the necessary adaptation of an idea to political and practical realities. Its various iterations also raise the question of whether or not the term 'justice reinvestment' has a conceptual core in the absence of which an enterprise can no longer be considered justice reinvestment. This is a significant question for new jurisdictions, such as Australia, which are exploring the possibilities of justice reinvestment. Has the term become a 'floating signifier' with no essential defining features? This chapter begins to explore this question. The discussion is taken up further in Chapter 5.

Back to the beginning: principles of justice reinvestment

Justice reinvestment is a public policy response to over-incarceration which takes a holistic approach to both the systemic drivers of the prison population and to underlying issues that lead to offending. Because of this breadth of approach, it was conceived as a strategy that would work both inside and beyond the criminal justice system to achieve reduced levels of incarceration; as suggested by the Commission on English Prisons Today (2009: 49), justice reinvestment 'is not about alternatives within the criminal justice process, it is about alternatives outside of it'.

Its key strategy is to quantify savings from the corrections budget and to then reinvest those savings to address the causes of reoffending in places where large numbers of people spend time in prison, and to make communities safer. To appeal to progressives and conservatives alike, justice reinvestment rhetoric can speak both in the language of saving taxpayer dollars/increasing community safety, and of neighbourhood renewal/racial justice.

Justice reinvestment is grounded in the fact that the geographies of imprisonment intersect with the geographies of poverty and race. As such, the first element of the strategy is the collection and analysis of available data about, among other things, where prisoners come from and where they go home to. Other relevant criminal justice-related data may include (by locality): prison admission numbers, interaction with police including arrests and cautions, court appearances; types of offences charged; grants of bail, length of sentences, alternative dispositions handed down and grants and revocation figures for probation and parole. Each of these criminal justice costs is then calculated and mapped back to the locations that are identified as yielding large numbers of prisoners. An analysis of the costs attached to criminal justice interventions go beyond the direct costs of housing an inmate to associated and indirect costs which may include (by location): costs of policing, court costs, the costs associated with transporting defendants to court (if they live in more remote communities), hospital costs for victims of violent crime and for other victim services.

The analysis of data around criminal offending provides the basis for justice reinvestment's place-based approach. Not only does the data yield information about the characteristics and drivers of incarceration in general, but it also identifies those places where the degree of criminal justice intervention and control is most concentrated, and the spending is the highest. In the USA, it is governments (generally aided by technical assistance providers) who collect and analyse these data. In the Australian context, the Just Reinvest NSW campaign has assisted the community in Bourke, NSW (via Maranguka, a grassroots representative body) to request and analyse the data themselves.

Based on the evidence that the data provides about the drivers of incarceration, a package of policy options is devised. Where there are stand-out issues, such as very high rates of parole or probation revocations, the systems that govern those arenas can be examined to see what changes might decrease revocations without impacting on public safety. If there are particular demographics (like young people) disproportionately contributing to the prison population from a particular area, innovative options can be explored focusing on that group.

There are different models that can be used to generate, first, either budgetary savings or reductions in rates of imprisonment (there can be a chicken and egg dynamic here). Either 'quick-hitting' policy changes can be put in place to realise swift reductions in prison numbers which can translate into seed funding for other justice reinvestment initiatives (which would then, it is hoped, lead to further reductions in admissions, revocations or reoffending down the track). Alternatively, initial funding can be made available by government to kick-start a justice reinvestment program (usually in the form of grants), and funds recovered once the programs put in place translate into reduced corrections spending.

While a PbR approach has been strongly taken up in the UK (see Chapter 1), use of this model is more contested in the USA and has not been the primary vehicle for justice reinvestment schemes. Some advocate for the inclusion of the private sector in the justice reinvestment process to provide start-up funds or, indeed, to spearhead innovative programs to reduce offending (Clear: 2011; Rudd *et al.*, 2013; see also the social impact bond proposal in NSW). Incentives are also sometimes used to provide momentum for change in agency practices. This can be particularly important where there are structural incentives to *increase* rates of imprisonment. Examples include the existence of formal or informal 'breaching' quotas for parole officers or where performance measures reward arrests and prosecutions. Prison privatisation as a category creates business-model incentives for increased inmate numbers. Tonry (2011a: 642) has noted that except for a few states, corrections is not a unified system: states pay for prisons; county governments pay for jails, sheriffs and district attorneys; and municipal governments pay for local police. In many states, probation and community corrections are county responsibilities. The absence of a unified system means that savings and reinvestment costs do not necessarily belong to the same entities. For example, a state realises savings from closing a prison, but it is the counties that have to implement community corrections programs. Conversely, there is no incentive for counties to attempt to reduce the number of people going into prisons when it is the state, and not the county, paying for them. A further disincentive is the difficult politics of closing prisons: both unions and particularly rural communities where prisons are located will resist closure (ibid.: 641). Austin *et al.* (2013:10) note that these disincentives were addressed in the early years in Connecticut and Kansas but have not been followed through more recently.

Whichever justice reinvestment model is employed, the intended outcome is to reduce the number of people in prison, to strengthen the communities that are most vulnerable to imprisonment, and to facilitate the permanent closure of prison facilities, which is where the opportunities for the most significant cost savings lie. As stated by the head of The Sentencing Project, an advocacy body working for 'a fair and effective U.S. criminal justice system' (The Sentencing Project, 2015a):

> at the very least is it possible to reduce the prison population, have no adverse effect on public safety, save a little bit of money by closing

some prisons and targeting some of those funds for some kind of reinvestment. (Mark Mauer, The Sentencing Project)

Finally, evaluation of justice reinvestment programs as an integral part of the methodology helps to measure the efficacy of the strategy and to shape future directions for reinvestment.

The shapes of justice reinvestment: state and local initiatives

As discussed in Chapter 1, justice reinvestment in the USA has developed in two parallel strands. The more prevalent model works at the state level as a political and legislative process to address over-incarceration in state controlled (and funded) prisons and is largely driven by the work of the CSG. The reforms adopted differ from state to state depending on the specific drivers of incarceration in each jurisdiction. The passage of legislation helps to make reform more durable, and opportunistic punitive policy relapses less likely. In this model, there is typically no intra-state place-based component, and as such, the 'reinvestment' into high-incarceration communities proposed by Tucker and Cadora is not a feature of this strand of the JRI.

The other incarcerated population in the USA is the inmates who are imprisoned in jails run by counties. These facilities house people awaiting trial and those convicted of lower level offences. As noted in Chapter 1, almost 11 million people move through this system each year. Peggy Burke, a principal at CEPP, explains that the combination of the 'churn' through the jail system and housing less serious offenders presents a strong opportunity for the JRI at the local level:

> Individuals who are a low risk, basically the less you do with them the better, in terms of affecting their future... at the local level there are many, many people who are low level offenders, fairly low risk, and so it seemed as though from a logical point of view there would be opportunities at the local level.

The justice reinvestment vision at the local level is different; because the issues that arise with the jail population differ from those emerging at the state level, and reform paths other than legislative action must be used. The processes involved in the JRI at the local level have tended to involve more interaction with stakeholders working on the ground. The local JRI sites often have histories of progressive criminal justice reform, as explained by a CEPP senior manager:

> They tend to pick sites where there were some good things already afloat, some good kind of pre-planning activities or other previous work that had kind of prepared them to be successful at this. If you were starting with a jurisdiction that didn't have any kind of planning going on, that didn't have any kind of collaboration going on, that had people with very kind of silo-oriented approaches to criminal justice, you'd have to overcome all of that first, and you'd have to create an environment in which people saw that it was safe to work together and they wanted to work together towards some commonly identified objectives before you could really do this. (Richard Stroker)

Reflecting the difference in process between state and local JRI, local level initiatives are managed not by the CSG but by agencies with more experience working with local players. These are the CEPP (Maryland) and the CJI (Boston). The local JRI is not as far progressed as the state-level model, with only a small handful of jurisdictions having moved from the first phase (collaborative identification of policy options through data analysis) to phase two (implementation).

In phase one of the local JRI, a consortium of agencies and groups involved in the criminal justice system (often already existing within a locality) provide a written expression of interest in participating. The signatories generally include members of the judiciary, jail administrators, local community supervision, probation and parole, prosecution and defense attorneys, and allied service providers such as mental health. Once accepted to the JRI program, stakeholders meet and, with help from a technical assistance provider, they analyse the available data to identify the drivers of imprisonment and to develop strategies to address these. While bodies like the CEPP have been doing systems analysis with policy-makers for decades, the JRI umbrella brings with it a great deal more sophistication in analytic capability and an increase in resources.

The local JRI would seem to be better situated to align with the place-based model articulated in the original conception of justice reinvestment, including holistic attention to the needs of specific communities from which large numbers of prisoners are drawn (see Chapter 3 for a discussion of the parameters of place-based initiatives). However this is not, in general, the path that the local JRI has followed. Rather than zeroing in on specific communities or 'million dollar blocks', local initiatives tend to target a small number of drivers of incarceration *countywide*.

The local JRI in Travis County, Texas provides one example. It focuses on the (local stakeholder identified) need to provide permanent supported housing for people exiting jails, particularly those with complex needs such as homelessness, mental illness and drug use. The candidates for the scheme are those whom the data shows to be cycling through county jails ten or more times each year. Those involved with the program state:

> A lot of the JRI clients that are in housing were frequent, very high radar, very high [re]cycling. They were very known to police and so got picked up weekly. (Quiana Fisher, Foundation Communities)
>
> They're homeless and they're visible and they have substance abuse or a mental health problem. (Timothy Miles, Foundation Communities)

The JRI has made use of existing initiatives at the county level which were geared towards dealing with a number of the same issues:

> They do quite a lot of use of good data and analysis in Travis and they have been rebuilding their justice system for a number of years, but the thing that they're using JRI for, they did a really careful analysis of a population that comes into their jail, some of them 10 and 12 times a year, or more... Housing officials in Travis County, as in many counties in this country, they have developed their 10-year plan to end homelessness. So there are prominent citizens who are on the board of the Housing Authority who also are on the board of the JRI initiative. (Peggy Burke, CEPP)

At the implementation level, Foundation Communities provide a holistic service for those accessing supported accommodation through the scheme, reflecting the complex needs of the cohort:

> When people come in, a lot of times they don't have the documentation that they need. Navigating those systems can be really intimidating and confusing, especially for someone that's just coming off chronic homelessness. So we help them with that, help them with securing any treatment that they need for physical health problems,

mental health problems... We have individual supportive services that are focused on what the individual resident needs and then we do property activities. We have socialisation activities like coffee hour once a week, movie nights, ice cream socials. Then we'll have things that are geared more towards education purposes. We're starting a Healthy Eating on a Budget, through a local agency here. It's a four-week class. We do things like we've just started a community garden. So that's helping with nutrition and mental health and socialisation. They're all rolled into one. (Heather Courson, Foundation Communities)

Participants in the program are drawn from the county as a whole, which is a large area with a population of more than 1.21 million people. Thus local JRI initiatives are more geographically contained compared with state-based programs, and they address salient issues affecting the jail population. However at the same time, they do not bear out the kind of intensive community-specific focus envisaged by the original proponents of justice reinvestment.

Some of the implementation challenges in Travis County are articulated by the County-level senior planner:

The pilot has gone, I would say, a lot slower than we anticipated. One of the reasons has been the criminal histories as a barrier, the other one is these are really difficult clients to locate in the first place. Just finding them, you have to have resources and even though the social workers know what bridge these people live under, what area of town they camp in, it's really hard to find some of them. We've had people on the list who nobody can locate; we've had people on the list who have died; we've had people on the list who aren't interested; we have some people on the list who are so severely mentally incapacitated that they are not capable of living on their own. That's one of the requirements of this pilot, is they have to be able to live sufficiently, independently, and some of them can't – they need a guardian and they need to be in a place where they have more supervision. Not a lot of mental health services in Texas. (Cathy McClaugherty, Travis County Criminal Justice Planning)

Nancy La Vigne, from the Urban Institute, more generally expressed some doubt about the efficacy of the local-JRI approach of focusing on just one or two drivers, commenting that, 'if you only focus on one piece of it at the expense of everything else you're not going to have an impact'.

The Justice Reinvestment Initiative in practice

Many JRI states are in relatively early stages of implementation. However, there are a number of early adopter states that have a longer track record with justice reinvestment and about which more can be said. Between 2004 and 2008, legislation was adopted by Connecticut (2004), Kansas (2007), Texas (2007), Rhode Island (2008) and Arizona (2008). Initial successes are said to have resulted from targeting correctional administrative policies and practices that were 'low-hanging fruit', such as 'reducing revocations for technical violations of parole and probation, holding parole hearings at the point of parole eligibility, or re-establishing earned "good-time" credits' (Austin *et al.*, 2013: 6). These measures helped to win bipartisan support, achieve some level of reduction in correctional populations and served as a wedge for more ambitious reforms.

Austin *et al.* (2013: 6) report that the longer term results in these states have been mixed:

- In Connecticut, the prison population fell by 2,400 prisoners in 2011 (but was already on the decline when JRI legislation was enacted) from 20,720 in 2002 to 18,324.
- In Kansas the prison population rose by nearly 800 inmates from 8,539 in 2008 to 9,327 by 2011.
- In Texas, the prison population remained stable (171,790 in 2007 to 172,224 in 2011).
- In Rhode Island the prison population fell slightly from 3,654 in 2006 to 3,337 in 2011.
- In Arizona the prison population rose slightly from 39,589 in 2008 to 40,020 in 2011.

At present there are 17 local JRIs and 24 operating at the state level in varying degrees of progress. This section describes a selection of those initiatives, based on the fieldwork conducted in the USA by the AJR Project. Fieldwork sites were chosen to reflect a range of characteristics which encompass both state and local JRI sites, with some running concurrently in the same jurisdiction. Some states were chosen because they are unified jurisdictions, meaning that there is no system of local jails but only a state-based corrections system (making it more akin to the Australian situation). Other states, like South Dakota and Hawaii, were selected because they were JRI states with substantial Indigenous populations.

State-wide justice reinvestment was examined through visits to Hawaii, South Dakota, Rhode Island, North Carolina, Texas and New York. Local level initiatives were the focus of visits to Mecklenburg County, North Carolina and, Travis County. In New York the research team examined a distinctive model of justice reinvestment used within the Department of Probation.

Texas

Texas was one of the early adopter JRI states and is often cited as a justice reinvestment success story. The JRI began in Texas in 2006, when data analysis found that people revoked to prison from probation had increased 18 per cent in the previous decade, despite a 3 per cent decline in the probation population and that more than 2,000 individuals were awaiting placement for substance abuse and mental health programs due to a reduction in funding and the subsequent closure of various community-based programs and facilities. Parole grant rates fell far short of the parole board's own guidelines – among low-risk individuals, the board fell short of its minimum approval rate by 2,252 releases (CSG Justice Center, 2015b).

Policies were adopted in the 2008–09 budget to address the issues identified, such as an increase in the treatment capacity in the prison system by 5,200 program slots for substance abuse treatment (outpatient, in-prison, and post-release) and mental health treatment; and the expansion of the diversion options in the probation and parole system by 4,500 beds for technical violations of supervision, transitional treatment and substance abuse treatment. Texas' 2007 legislative reform package, developed through the JRI, was said to be 'the most expansive redirection in state correctional policy since the early 1990s' (Austin *et al.*, 2013: 24). The JRI strategies were said to have averted projected growth in the state prison population of about 9,000 people, producing savings of US$443 million from 2008–09. The state reinvested US$241 million to expand in-prison and community-based treatment and diversion programs.

However, as Austin *et al.* (2013) point out, touting the Texan experience as a success story presupposes firstly that the projections of future prison growth were valid, and secondly that it was the JRI rather than other factors which led to the outcomes reached. Austin *et al.* (ibid.: 14–15) argue that the attribution of the stabilisation of the Texas prison population to the JRI was the result of faulty assumptions by the state Legislative Budget Board on prison admissions (the predictions were too high) and parole grant rates (too low): 'Once those two faulty assumptions were corrected by the [Legislative Budget Board], its pre-JRI projection was no growth, suggesting that the JRI is far less responsible for averted growth in Texas than it has claimed'.

This view is supported somewhat by comments from CSG staff which locate the JRI in a broader trajectory of criminal justice reform in Texas:

> The model has been here for a while, at least in Texas... The assumption [around JRI is] that we're so genius that we came up with a new model... [But] Texas has been doing that for years, believe it or not it started in 1993 when we had a major reform... [of] reducing penalties for drug offenders... In 07 [JRI] came back to basically enhance what has been done before. (Tony Fabelo, CSG Austin)

Travis County

As discussed above, the local level JRI pilot in Travis County, Texas, centres around the identification of inadequate housing as a key driver for those who cycle with the most frequency in and out of jail. With the Urban Institute providing technical assistance to analyse corrections data, county officials discovered that:

> 1/3 of all bookings to the county jail during a three-year period were non-unique (revealing a sub-population of frequent residents). This population, which had two or more bookings per offender, accounted for just 32.7% of the jail population, but consumed 69.3% of jail bed days. (CEPP, 2012a: 1)

In association with the CEPP and the Urban Institute, the Travis County Community Justice Council convened a community consortium, composed of key justice stakeholders (the sheriff, courts, prosecution, defence, pre-trial services, probation, criminal justice planning), other county and city agencies (city and county health, human services and veterans affairs, county and city management and county purchasing office), as well as community stakeholders (business alliance, health care providers, housing advocates, and the Corporation for Supportive Housing). The consortium developed the strategy of increasing supportive housing resources in partnership with the Foundation Communities, a social service and housing provider in Austin. Targeting the most frequent users of the jail system, the JRI pilot involved housing former prisoners in Foundation Communities housing, including provision of social services. Speaking of its confidence in this approach to impact on recidivism rates, the CEPP (ibid.: 3) states that:

> research has shown that residents in permanent supportive housing have incarceration rates reduced by 50%; have 50% fewer hospital emergency room visits; are 85% less likely to need emergency detoxification services; and have a 50% increase in earned income.

Foundation Communities works not only to provide individual case management to residents, but also to 'build a sense of community here':

> since a survival skill for a lot of our population has been to keep to themselves – to kind of unravel a bit of that and build a sense of community. This provides a sense of stability for a lot of the residents as they get comfortable here and start to make relationships. (Edward Crawford, Foundation Communities)

There are certainly reasons to believe that the program is making a difference. This case study is given by a director at the Downtown Austin Alliance:

> The 20th person housed, which was at the very end of the first year we were trying to get them housed, was the number one Community Court offender. This person had more than 300 cases with Community Court. Everyone knew this person by name... [he] was sleeping, urinating, defecating in doorways, he would curse, he was just as nasty as any individual could possibly be and terribly disruptive to our membership, to property owners, business owners, to the residents, anyone downtown.
>
> Arthur was the 20th person housed, has not had a recurrence with the criminal justice system. He's been in housing for a year and a half now, I understand he's in love, he's planning to get married, he's no longer abusing whatever substances of choice he used to. That's a great success story. (Bill Brice, Downtown Austin Alliance)

Rhode Island

Rhode Island is the smallest state in the USA and a unified jurisdiction. It was an early adopter of the JRI after an independent prison population projection estimated that its prison population would increase

21 per cent between 2007 and 2017, with a cost to taxpayers of an additional US$300 million. Lawsuits about prison overcrowding were also a driver in the decision to adopt the JRI. Policy-makers accepted three from a basket of a dozen or so potential areas of reform, with a focus on 'reducing the need for beds and saving money' (Mr A.T. Wall, Department of Corrections), and enacted a legislative package in 2008. The new laws standardised the calculation of earned time credits (to remedy an existing disincentivisation of people serving short sentences), established risk reduction program credits and required the use of risk assessments to inform parole release decisions (CSG Justice Center, 2015b; see also CSG, 2007). Interviewees reported that one in 11 men in Rhode Island were on parole on any given day.

The positive outcomes attributed to the JRI include the closure of a medium security prison. The state showed significant reduction in the prison population from a high of about 4,000 in 2006 to 3,200 in 2011. Austin *et al.* (2013: 4) write that this reduction was largely brought about via the 2008 legislation:

> which increased the amount of good-time credits all individuals could receive by participating in meaningful programs. There were also adjustments to parole board decision-making and a general decline in prison admissions (non-JRI factors).

Some reinvestment occurred within corrections:

> We put in $1 million to expand the capacity of the treatment system so that these individuals would not have to wait in prison for any substance abuse bed, and that created some movement. (Mr Costantino, Health and Human Services)

> Yes. It created movement out and it also reduced the likelihood of recidivism for those drug dependant people...the legislature projected some savings as a result of these initiatives, and true to the model, reserved some of those savings and reinvested them into the programs that we were offering in prison, the idea being that for those risk reduction credits to have meaning, there needed to be programs, substantive programs that inmates could access – in a robust way, and money was reinvested to expand those programs so that it would give meaningful opportunities to the inmates, and also because that was one of the engines that kept the population down (Mr A.T. Wall, Department of Corrections).

A pilot program, 9 Yards, which works with prisoners in custody prior to their release and provides intensive post-release support, including accommodation, is currently being trialled (OpenDoors, 2015). Despite the benefits of such programs, concerns have been expressed about sustaining the JRI into the future. The funding of 9 Yards is particularly precarious.

North Carolina

In 2010, an analysis of the prison population in North Carolina predicted a growth of 10 per cent over the next decade. The data showed that probation revocations accounted for more than half of prison admissions and that only about 15 per cent of the people released from prison received supervision. The *Justice Reinvestment Act,* which was signed into law in 2011, introduced policy options developed to address the current state of imprisonment. These included:

- The mandatory supervision of people leaving prison who were incarcerated for a serious offence
- New powers for probation officers to use 'swift and certain' jail sanctions for violations of conditions of supervision
- Increased sentences for repeat offenders of breaking and entering
- Diversion of nonviolent, first-time felony drug offenders from prison using second chance incentives (CSG Justice Center, 2015b)

Parole officers employ a strategy called 'quick dips', where minor violations of probation are met with a swift response of two to three days in jail, as opposed to immediately revoking probation and issuing a lengthier, more expensive and less effective prison stay. The range of reforms around parole are said to have led to a 50 per cent drop in probation revocations since 2011 (CSG, 2014a: 1).

The policy package was projected to save the state up to US$560 million over six years in reduced spending and averted costs. The CSG reports that since 2011, the incarcerated population has fallen by nearly 3,400 people, resulting in the closure of ten prisons. The state is using some of the savings generated to focus on improving supervision practices by adding 175 probation and parole officers and investing in cognitive interventions and substance abuse treatment for individuals with the greatest need and who are at the highest risk of reoffending (CSG, 2014b: 1). In the FY2012 budget, US$8 million was allocated to existing community-based treatment facilities.

However, some qualifications to these outcomes must be noted. A portion of the reduction in prison population is attributable to the movement of 1,200 people convicted of misdemeanours to local jails, which does not have an impact on the state's overall incarceration rate. Further, Austin *et al.* (2013: 15) point out that the projections on which the impact of the JRI are based were inaccurate and that later projections showed that 'the pre-JRI prison population estimates and the post-JRI estimates are virtually the same, which suggests the JRI has had little impact'. According to Austin *et al.* (ibid.), the JRI legislation is expected to add nearly 2,000 people to the projected incarcerated population by increasing the lengths of sentences for breaking and entering and lengthening the terms of parole supervision.

Mecklenberg County

At the local level in Mecklenberg County, changes had already been made to redress acknowledged problems in the criminal justice system before the JRI was introduced. With the JRI, county officials were able to interrogate the evidence base to explain and sustain the improvements that had been made:

> Things were starting to turn around as a result of investments that we made in our criminal justice system and they were starting to get better. We really couldn't explain why things were getting better... We weren't necessarily convinced that they would stay better without really getting involved in some data analysis and really exploring what would make our system truly work better... We wanted to sustain what we already had. (Tom Eberly, Mecklenberg County)

Existing programs include a supported accommodation project for chronically homeless people who were frequently jailed (CEPP, 2012b: 1). Through the JRI process, the focus has been on developing an evidence base to support proposals for change:

> One of the things that we developed was for our chronic homeless frequent fliers that were coming in, what we call FUSE, our 'Frequent User Service Enhancement Program'... You take the individuals on that top 200, the ones that come in four or more times a year, who also tend to show up in the shelters for many days or the emergency department at the hospital over and over again, ... give them sustainable housing for free and it really works. We've done that. We have 36 individuals off that top 200 list in sustainable housing. We also have

an apartment building that we built specifically for the homeless that houses these individuals. They are allowed to bring in guests; they're allowed to drink...other restrictions that you see a lot of times at shelters were removed. We just want them to be somewhere safe...

It cost us $14,000, almost $15,000 to give them permanent housing or sustainable housing and it cost us, to let them do what they were doing before, about $38,000. So some faction of our society will say these people are just living off the welfare of other taxpayers, but they're not really capable of sustaining a job because of their mental health condition or substance abuse problems. So you might as well do something that's more humane and it ultimately is cheaper and more effective. (Tom Eberly)

After undertaking data analysis, areas for further work have centred on frequent system users, low level offenders, and the mentally ill (CEPP, 2012b: 2).

Challenges for local level JRI have arisen from the multiple levels of government involved in criminal justice, which requires a level of collaboration not always forthcoming at the state level:

We really wanted to do this in partnership with the state, and I thought it would have been a fantastic opportunity to dovetail our initiative and really be in sync with our ideas and bounce up in significance because we're the largest county and the largest contributor to the prison population, the largest place of people on community supervision...Unfortunately, the state never really engaged, even though we tried multiple times to do so. I think that was a real downfall in terms of not reaching our potential. (Tom Eberly)

The significance of a neutral party (e.g., the CEPP or CSG) to provide data analysis and policy advice was stressed.

Hawaii

Hawaii's incarcerated population grew by 18 per cent in the decade leading up to 2010. Due to a lack of space in its correctional facilities, Hawaii contracted with mainland facilities, particularly in Arizona, to house approximately one-third of its prisoners (CSG, 2015b). A large proportion of the out-of-state prison population is Native Hawaiian (Prison Policy Initiative, 2015), which gives rise to a loss of cultural identity in addition to the problems of severed family ties and debilitating health problems, given that Arizona has one the lowest rates of spending per prisoner (Meronek, 2013). From 2006 to 2011, the state's pretrial population increased partly due to delays in the pretrial decision-making process.

In 2011–12, the CSG worked with Hawaiian state leaders. There was strong community advocate involvement in this process, including representation from criminalised people. Policy-makers enacted justice reinvestment legislation in 2012. Among other things, the law:

- Requires timely risk assessments of pretrial defendants to reduce delays in the pretrial process
- Focuses probation and parole resources on individuals most likely to reoffend
- Increases the amount individuals pay toward victim restitution and ensures institutions have the mechanisms in place to collect, track, and disperse these funds effectively (CSG Justice Center, 2015b)

These policies are estimated to reduce bed demand in correctional facilities by more than 1,000 beds, saving the state US$130 million over six years. In FY2013, the state reinvested US$3.4 million to expand the availability of community-based treatment programs, hire additional corrections staff to complete risk and needs assessments and support re-entry efforts, and re-establish the Department of Public Safety's research and planning office (ibid.).

The JRI in Hawaii has some novel features. It emphasises victim restitution and is therefore strongly supported by victims' advocate groups. It also works in conjunction with an innovative court program, Hawaii's Opportunity Probation with Enforcement (HOPE), which was established prior to the JRI. The HOPE program focuses on providing positive and negative consequences for probationers and has the discretion to impose short prison sentences for breaches or to terminate probation early for those performing well.

Concerns have been voiced about how the JRI has been given effect in Hawaii, particularly in respect to the lack of community engagement in the process and inadequate attention to Native Hawaiian issues. Native Hawaiian prisoner issues were raised early in the process. Indeed, Kat Brady, a prisoner advocate who was responsible for drafting the initial JRI grant application, noted that the Native Hawaiian community was not included in decision making about the reforms. Initiatives focusing on Native Hawaiians were largely absent. Also, whilst prison advocates were involved early in the process, they were not given a formal role in shaping the reforms. As Kat Brady states:

> You're talking to the same people who have been talking for 25 years and how are we going to get out of the rut if we keep going to the people who got us into the rut? It's like we need new thinking...
>
> I remain hopeful because I am a pain in the arse, frankly, and I'm really tenacious and I think that's really – if I had to say what is the one quality that can make change, it's tenacity. (Kat Brady, Community Alliance on Prisons)

There was also disquiet about the degree of reinvestment into communities that was occurring. Kat Brady put it this way:

> It's so slow and it's so indiscernible for the community that it's hard for me to keep saying this is a good thing when there's really nothing to show except, you guys got more positions, your budget's back up.

The role of the Governor and political leadership was emphasised as crucial to sustaining change. Some positive developments underway in the juvenile justice sector in Hawaii are consistent with, but developed without reference to, justice reinvestment.

South Dakota

South Dakota is a relative newcomer to justice reinvestment, having begun implementing legislative reforms in 2013. Pew and the CJI (rather than the CSG) provided technical assistance for the scheme.

From 1977 to 2013, South Dakota's prison population increased by more than 500 per cent. If this trend continued, corrections spending was predicted to cost the state US$224 million over the next decade. The main drivers of this surge in population were the incarceration of nonviolent drug offenders and parole violators (South Dakota Government, 2014: 117). The 2013 reform package included:

> improving its behavioral health service and community supervision infrastructure, developing drug and DUI courts, and adopting evidence-based supervision practices. Justice reinvestment legislation also changed the criminal code to reserve prison space for the most serious offenders. (ibid.)

Over the next ten years, the intention is to reinvest US$53 million of the US$207 million projected savings: $8 million from the FY 2013 and 2014 budgets, and $4.9 million per year in the following years. The reinvestment plan includes allocations for training and implementation of evidence-based programs; pilot programs for alternative sentencing options and community-based support programs; state-wide systems to ensure victim notification and restitution accountability; expanded drink-driving and drug courts; expanded substance abuse, mental health, and cognitive behavioural therapy (CBT); increased probation and parole staff; and a pool of funds to support additional costs to counties (South Dakota Government, 2014: 119).

The over-representation of American Indians in South Dakota prisons is a significant issue. It was recognised that to reduce the state's incarceration rate this issue required attention in any JRI initiative. To this end, a pilot program on parole supervision for American Indians commenced. Three of the nine tribal governments in the state joined the trial (See Chapter 3).

Strong leadership from the Governor and interagency coordination (see Chapter 6) and data analysis were identified as critical features of the JRI in South Dakota. Interviewees were united in their emphasis on bipartisanship and engaging with key stakeholders across the criminal justice system who were prepared to work together.

New York

New York is not a JRI state. However, there are a number of schemes that have been achieving reductions in prison numbers – some drawing on justice reinvestment principles, but not under the JRI banner, and others without any connection to justice reinvestment at all. As such, New York demonstrates that there is much being done to reduce incarceration rates outside of the JRI framework, which may consciously draw on justice reinvestment principles or sit outside them altogether.

The contrast between the JRI and non-JRI states is picked up by Austin *et al.* (2013) who compare eight JRI states with other US states. They find that for 'both groups and almost all of the states, there have been negligible, if any, reductions in prison populations' over a 12-year period from 2000 (ibid.: 11). Only four non-JRI states (New York, New Jersey, Michigan and California) and one JRI state (Rhode Island) significantly reduced their prison population during this period.

In New York, reductions in the number of felony arrests coupled with increases in non-prison sentences (New York City only) have reduced the state's prison population by nearly 25 per cent. Prison admissions and lengths of stay for drug sale offenses have declined markedly since 1999. In 2009, the Rockefeller Drug Law reform eliminated mandatory prison sentences for second and third felony drug sales, as well as for nonviolent felonies if the defendant is drug dependent and willing to seek treatment

(Austin *et al.*, 2013: 12, 16fn). Between 2002 and 2011, New York City reduced institutional placements of young people by 62 per cent, and had a 31 per cent decline in major felony arrests of juveniles (ibid.: 28).

One example of a scheme considered both inside and outside the justice reinvestment framework is an initiative at New York City Probation – one which was, significantly, spearheaded by Susan Tucker over the time that she worked there. The Neighborhood Opportunity Network (NeON) program connects probation clients who live in the target neighbourhood to resources, services and opportunities to help them reintegrate, post-incarceration (New York City Department of Probation, 2015). For a detailed discussion of NeON and particularly its different construction of a place-based approach, see Chapter 3.

'Don't call it justice reinvestment': JR v JRI

While the importance of the JRI in creating the conditions for less punitive criminal justice policy is widely acknowledged, the directions that the JRI has taken has been the subject of criticism from a range of academics and advocates who have been closely involved with justice reinvestment at various stages of conceptualisation and implementation. The central critique of Austin *et al.* (2013) is that the JRI has abandoned several of its basic tenets, particularly its commitment to place-based strategies and the reinvestment of correctional savings in high-incarceration communities. Instead, the JRI has focused on working with the political leadership of a state to secure the passage of legislation containing criminal justice reform. Reflecting on this critique, a co-author of the Austin *et al.* (2013) paper, Mark Mauer of The Sentencing Project, comments that the article could have been retitled, 'What you are doing is good...but don't call it Justice Reinvestment'.

The narrowing of justice reinvestment to the JRI can be tracked through the changed framing of the explanation of what the JRI is on the CSG website. Until 2010, the website set out a four-step program for justice reinvestment, as follows:

Step 1 Analyze the prison population and spending in the communities to which people in prison often return
Step 2 Provide policymakers with options to generate savings and increase public safety
Step 3 Quantify savings and reinvest in select high-stakes communities
Step 4 Measure the impact and enhance accountability (CSG Justice Center, 2010a)

By August 2011, the four steps had been reduced to three:

1. Analyze data and develop policy options
2. Adopt new policies and put reinvestment strategies into place
3. Measure performance (CSG Justice Center, 2011a)

The step that has fallen out is step three, the place-based strategy whereby savings that have been generated through the previous step are invested back into the community (see also Austin *et al.*, 2013: 7). That same language has also become absent from step one. During the time that step three was still in place as an essential component of the JRI, the CSG website explained it in this way:

> Policymakers and the team's experts develop plans for reinvesting a portion of these savings in new or enhanced initiatives in areas where the majority of people released from prisons and jails return. For example, officials can reinvest the savings and deploy existing resources in a high-stakes neighborhood to redevelop abandoned housing and better coordinate such services as substance abuse and mental health treatment, job training, and education. (CSG Justice Center, 2008)

It is significant that the CSG's justice reinvestment strategy dispensed with the community investment component. This indicates that the intention to address the underlying causes of criminal offending in high-incarceration communities is no longer central to the process. What remains is a reform program centred on consensus-driven passage of legislation aimed at a reduction in corrections expenditure without jeopardising public safety. The Director of State Initiatives at the CSG Justice Center explains the shift in terms of the expertise base of the CSG:

> We've learned a lot. I came in with this ideal – we spent a lot of time in conceptual-idea-land thinking about how to integrate and leverage community-based resources and put together service packages.
>
> ...
>
> I wish we could do it. Again, we tried for four years [in Wichita, Kansas]. We got really, really close but we realised there's just so much to do on the structural, on the corrections side, criminal justice side, and we're not community redevelopment experts. (Marshall Clement, CSG Justice Center)

By 2013, the CSG's statement of what justice reinvestment is and how it works had been reduced to two phases. Its website stated:

> To begin this work, policymakers establish a small, high-level, inter-branch, and bipartisan team of elected and appointed officials to work with the Justice Center's nationally recognized criminal justice policy experts. These experts then consult with a broad range of stakeholders in the jurisdiction, which may include prosecutors, public defenders, judges, corrections and law enforcement officials, service providers and community leaders, victims and their advocates, and people who have been incarcerated, as well as health, housing, human service, education, and workforce professionals.
>
> Together, these policymakers, experts, and stakeholders analyse a variety of state-specific data to develop practical, consensus-based policies that reduce spending on corrections and generate savings that can be reinvested in strategies to improve public safety. In the second phase of work, jurisdictions translate the new policies into practice and monitor data to ensure that related programs and system investments achieve their projected outcomes. (CSG Justice Center, 2013a)

The current iteration on the CSG website employs an infographic which returns the JRI to four explanatory steps, while entrenching the absence of a place-based component and the lack of prioritisation of community-based reinvestment (CSG Justice Center, 2015a). Step one, it explains, is to 'Look at the big picture', specified as an investigation of spending and reoffending rates, but without the necessity for community-specific inquiries (See Figure 2.1).

The creation of policy responses to the issues raised by the data, it then follows, does not have a place-based dimension. Rather, as step 2 explains (see Figure 2.2), savings should be invested in 'what works' (see Chapter 4 for a critical discussion of the 'what works' approach).

Step three (see Figure 2.3) gives further clues to the meaning of 'what works'. There is an emphasis on the reform of supervision regimes (chiefly parole), and serial recidivists are the primary focus for these efforts. Without being anchored to a particular place, the strategies to address recidivism can only really be system-based, which explains the prominence of parole reform and in-prison program initiatives. There is no mention of reinvestment in incarceration-blighted communities.

Step four continues the emphasis on an evidence-led approach, explaining that 'the proof is in the numbers' (see Figure 2.4).

76 *Justice Reinvestment*

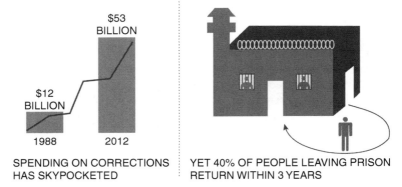

SPENDING ON CORRECTIONS HAS SKYPOCKETED

YET 40% OF PEOPLE LEAVING PRISON RETURN WITHIN 3 YEARS

Answers are in the data. Justice reinvestment synthesizes mountains of criminal justice data to help policymakers understand what is driving crime, recidivism, and prison populations.

Figure 2.1   JRI Step 1
Source: CSG Justice Center: http://csgjusticecenter.org/jr/about, used with permission.

2. CRAFT POLICY SOLUTIONS

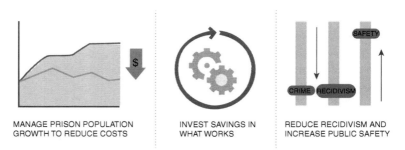

MANAGE PRISON POPULATION GROWTH TO REDUCE COSTS

INVEST SAVINGS IN WHAT WORKS

REDUCE RECIDIVISM AND INCREASE PUBLIC SAFETY

Figure 2.2   JRI Step 2
Source: CSG Justice Center: http://csgjusticecenter.org/jr/about, used with permission.

What is clear from the explanatory progression of the JRI set out here is that there has been, at best, a wavering of commitment to some of the central tenets of justice reinvestment as originally conceived. It also shows that there is some conceptual fluidity in justice reinvestment, and this is not necessarily a weakness; the capacity of the strategy to adapt

3. TURN POLICY INTO PRACTICE

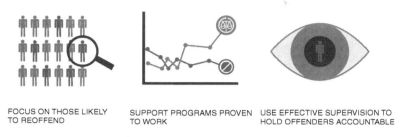

FOCUS ON THOSE LIKELY TO REOFFEND

SUPPORT PROGRAMS PROVEN TO WORK

USE EFFECTIVE SUPERVISION TO HOLD OFFENDERS ACCOUNTABLE

Figure 2.3 JRI Step 3
Source: CSG Justice Center: http://csgjusticecenter.org/jr/about, used with permission.

4. MEASURE THE IMPACT

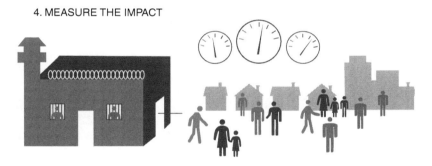

Figure 2.4 JRI Step 4
Source: CSG Justice Center: http://csgjusticecenter.org/jr/about, used with permission.

to varying implementation contexts and political realities can equally be seen as contributing to its robustness. As Figure 2.5 demonstrates, justice reinvestment at the local level (at least as set out by the Urban Institute) describes the model in five steps, despite that officially there are two 'phases' of the JRI.

It may be that this multiplicity of interpretation lends itself to adaptability, which is a key factor in the success of the JRI.

However, as evidenced by Austin *et al.* (2013), this conceptual fluidity has not been universally well received. The authors note that increasingly, a generic language is used which has less emphasis on reducing prison populations and reinvesting in communities and which reflects

Figure 2.5 Five Steps to Local JRI

Source: Urban Institute, *Justice Reinvestment at the Local Level*, http://www.urban.org/center/jpc/justice-reinvestment/upload/jrllbrief-2.pdf, used with permission.

a shifted focus onto cost savings, crime control and law enforcement (Austin *et al.*, 2013). Further, JRI goals have shifted from aiming to reduce the number of prisoners in the corrections system to averting prison *growth*. As a result, prison populations are not being reduced below historically high levels. As ACLU advocates Vanita Gupta and Kara Dansky comment, 'if you set the bar low then it's not hard to succeed...and you get to declare a victory'.

This dynamic can be observed in Texas where projected prison growth was arrested and prison numbers were stabilised. Savings were calculated on the basis of the gap between the projected and actual population. The point made by Austin *et al.* (2013) is that it is perhaps a modest overall victory to maintain imprisonment rates at an all-time high. A more ambitious and meaningful goal, they argue, would be decarceration, which would involve a *reduction* in inmate numbers.

Other key criticisms made by Austin *et al.* (2013: 4) are that savings that have been generated through the JRI have not gone to high-incarceration communities as originally envisaged, but have rather been channelled into general revenue or to community corrections or law enforcement. Additionally, local advocates and reformers have frequently been marginalized from the JRI process, whereas local organised support for community initiatives was a core part of justice reinvestment as originally conceived.

Justice reinvestment principle and practice – development and divergence

The original conception of justice reinvestment was one which allowed for complete flexibility in the *content* of the justice reinvestment strategies (given that they were to be responsive to the circumstances of the localities in question) but which was fairly specific in its articulation of the structures and processes through which these strategies would be developed and implemented.

Below, we take in turn the central tenets of justice reinvestment as set out by Tucker and Cadora (2003) and other early proponents and examine the extent to which they have been adhered to in JRI practice, incorporating in the discussion the critiques made by Austin *et al.* (2013). The principles explored in this section loosely follow the original four-step justice reinvestment program: data analysis, collaborative and bipartisan development of reform options, reinvestment of savings in high-incarceration communities, and evaluation of the strategies pursued.

An evidence-led, data driven strategy

Central to justice reinvestment is its reliance on data which acts as a type of evidence-based anchor in a policy area often driven by political imperatives, while aligning with the 'what works' approach to criminal justice reform. The data-centric nature of justice reinvestment is one characteristic that has flowed strongly through the JRI. In *Lessons from the States: Reducing Recidivism and Curbing Corrections Costs Through Justice Reinvestment* (2013a), the CSG reflects on the major lessons learned through its involvement in the JRI in 17 states over the preceding five years, such as the following:

> The level of data generally collected by states lead to gaps and inadequacies in knowledge of what factors drive crime, reoffending, and the growth of the correctional population more generally. Governments might also lack the expertise necessary to evaluate data about existing programs, so that decisions made about programming and policy are to some degree stabs in the dark.

Because some JRI states are engaging in upfront investment based on projected savings predicted by data analysis, the quality of that data is crucial. Yet, as Nancy La Vigne from the Urban Institute noted, the quality of available data can be 'a real sticking point':

> Being able to get the type of data needed to be able to identify the drivers of the population, the ability to project out, this is a critical part... that's what you want to use as your baseline to then project out the impact of various policy changes because that difference is where you get your savings. (Nancy La Vigne, Urban Institute)

This is especially true for the JRI at the local level, where data collection is generally less sophisticated and where the systems being analysed are more complex and fragmented. Thus the quality of the available data presents challenges to the fulfilment of what is a stated pillar of justice reinvestment.

However, the *availability* of data per se is not the only relevant issue. Even where adequate data is available, it is alleged that the JRI often does not tackle the issues that the evidence points to as the drivers of high-incarceration rates. Austin *et al.* (2013) argue that JRI legislative reform is generally not geared to significantly reducing the numbers of prison admissions and the lengths of stay, which are the two major drivers of incarceration levels. The authors argue that:

> Too many of the current reform efforts try to achieve population reductions by programmatic initiatives, such as increasing the availability of drug treatment slots, strengthening re-entry-related services and supervision, and funding police reform. These tactics have limited capacity to reduce admissions or lengths of stay. (Austin *et al.*, 2013: 8)

When promising strategies for affecting these two key drivers of the prison population have been proposed, 'they are too often the first to be compromised'. This is in part because according to Austin *et al.* (ibid.: 4), the 'JRI puts a premium on the passage of legislation, even when the legislation will not lead to meaningful reductions'. This is connected to the emphasis placed in justice reinvestment on bipartisanship in formulating policy options, which means that more politically controversial proposals are jettisoned early, even if they offer the most potential for penal reduction.

Clearly it is important to prevent decarceration from being a partisan issue, lest law and order politicking eclipse the reform agenda. But, as Todd Clear argues, the approach has significant limitations:

> The CSG agenda is a consensus agenda, which sounds very nice, but it means changing sentencing for people committing drug crimes, off the table; changing recidivism statutes, off the table...
>
> The consensus has been at the wrong starting point in my opinion... The problem is the consensus was that certain kinds of things can be *done*, rather than, 'we have way too many people behind bars and we ought to reduce the number of people behind bars'.
>
> There are a lot of people who came to the table on the consensus thing who started with that premise, but there are a lot of people who started with no premise: 'we can do the criminal justice system better than we're doing it now' or whatever... [Rather, the starting-point should be:] 'there are too many Black people in prison, there are too many families being disrupted by prison. Too many people who leave prison and can't do anything with their lives, it's a cycle, it's a dysfunction, nobody wants it'. That's the consensus. (Todd Clear, Rutgers University)

ACLU advocates add that beyond failing to deliver the kind of penal reduction that was originally envisaged, the JRI as it currently stands risks entrenching the status quo:

> If the JRI continues on its current trajectory, which is to say no more decarceration and no real reinvestment in high incarceration communities, but rather slowing of growth... if that continues then we run a very real risk of institutionalising mass incarceration in this country for the foreseeable future, including the racial disparities. (Kara Dansky, ACLU)

Where the JRI is pitched at the local level, the ramifications of poor data availability are particularly highlighted. A representative from The Urban Institute spoke of the technical assistance providers for the local JRI becoming frustrated at delays in acquiring and analysing data such that they convened stakeholders to move the initiative forward – including discussing policy options – in the absence of data to guide deliberations. The result was that 'it was based on anecdote and perception but not reality'. Here, the evidence-based nature of the JRI was abandoned from the outset.

It is worth noting that quantitative data is not the only material on which justice reinvestment was intended to be based. Alongside incarceration mapping – of prisoner numbers and locations, statistical drivers of incarceration, and costs associated with imprisonment – there is also the evidence base around the needs of high-incarceration communities and existing strengths within those communities. Known as 'asset mapping', this was only captured in the earliest iterations of justice reinvestment. The state level focus has largely obviated the need not only for community-level incarceration mapping but also for community asset mapping. Laura Kurgan, who was involved in asset mapping in the earliest iterations of the JRI, expressed the view that 'it's too much hard work for them. They really go top down'. She continues:

> I think it's hugely important. I think the spatial language of this project should be about the city. This is a huge country. Australia is a huge country too and I don't know how it gets spread out. You also need to come up with so many solutions in such a creative way. So often when you go into these neighbourhoods you do find a lot of not-for-profits and a lot of community organisation. So as soon as you focus those people together – so I think there is a way that something could come out of it that could become an approach. (Laura Kurgan, SIDL)

The power of asset mapping, particularly when combined with more conventional data collection, has been recognised by the Just Reinvest NSW campaign. Sarah Hopkins (Just Reinvest NSW) reflects on the use that the Bourke community are looking to make of asset mapping:

> So the community says this women's service is working and we are funding it, not cap in hand, but they need to have the ability to say this is what is being funded in this community, and that's why you need the data and the evidence and all that. That evidence base might not just be how many clients ... it might be that this has created a strong community within a community.

As alluded to here, asset mapping is a valuable component of a place-based justice reinvestment approach which draws out existing community resources and provides information about valuable sites for reinvestment that will build on current strengths.

Working at the local level: inclusion in setting the reform agenda

Working at the local level was a key element of the original justice reinvestment concept. Tucker and Cadora (2003: 5) envisaged the devolution of both decision-making and budgetary control to the local level:

> Under this proposal, local government could reclaim responsibility for dealing with residents who break the law and redeploy the funds that the state would have spent for their incarceration. The localities would have the freedom to spend justice dollars to decrease the risks of crime in the community. They could choose to spend these dollars for job training, drug treatment programs, and preschool programs... The key is making the locality accountable for solving its public safety problems.

In *Lessons from the States,* the CSG (2013a) nominates as one of its major lessons that politicians and their staff are not best placed to make decisions about what might impact on offending rates or recidivism. What is required, the report states, is the input of a wide range of stakeholders including criminal justice actors and community-based organisations and individuals. Bringing this diverse group to the table 'is essential to accurately diagnosing systemic issues and effectively responding to them' (CSG, 2013a: 3).

Austin *et al.* (2013: 8) similarly emphasise that organizing and maintaining demand for an ambitious vision of criminal justice reform requires the inclusion of reform coalitions rooted in the long-term interests of the communities they are part of, especially minority leaders and elected representatives, high-incarceration communities. However, they argue that the JRI in fact limits the voices included in decision-making around reform options, focusing on policy-makers rather than community-based stakeholders.

The make-up of the stakeholder group may shape outcomes in a number of ways. For example, according to Marshall Clement, one of the lessons learned from the early JRI was that for a target audience of policy-makers, there is a need to provide a 'diversified basket of policy strategies' to impact several parts of the criminal justice system simultaneously while catering to the political need to appear to be engaging in reform immediately:

> Some policies should have a short term immediate impact... other policies should be delayed fireworks that don't really kick in for two

to three years or five years, so that if one policy gets taken back or isn't implemented correctly, we've got other policies. (Marshall Clement, CSG Justice Center)

One outcome of a limited stakeholder pool is obviously that the voices of those best placed and most invested in the outcomes of the JRI may not be adequately represented. But structuring JRI as an initiative largely involving the legislature and criminal justice actors also delimits the scope of the enterprise. As Vanita Gupta (ACLU) states:

> It's really become a much more conservative effort ... to really appeal to the most conservative stakeholders in the country, and not trying to push or educate ... they're meeting lawmakers where they are ... [and] in this country, mass incarceration really is the new normal.

The danger, Gupta explains, is that this approach generally leads to a limited reform agenda that may ultimately be counterproductive in that it entrenches mass incarceration. This is compounded by the fact that the CSG spends, on average, only 6 to 12 months working with a state before moving on to a new jurisdiction:

> They aren't working with advocates who may have been doing this work on the ground for quite some time, know about the local dynamics, the state dynamic. They're coming in ... and getting through whatever they can get through in that short window, which of course is not going to be the higher hanging fruit – the tougher stuff, like sentencing reform – and then they leave. If you do that, then you leave law makers with the impression that they fixed their criminal justice problem, or that they've at least stabilised the levels, they're leaving all the advocates who have been pushing on much bigger, important reforms in the dust. (Vanita Gupta, ACLU)

In West Virginia, for example, several parties supportive of progressive criminal justice reform proposed legislation in 2011 to address over-crowding in jails and prisons in that state. The legislation was narrowly defeated. In 2012, the JRI presented a more modest legislative proposal which passed. While the orientation towards progressive criminal justice reform is welcome, Kara Dansky (ACLU) expresses concern that:

> They were basically torpedoing all of this energy that would have been placed towards a more comprehensive Bill. [The 2012 Bill]

has stabilised the population for three years, but the state is already talking about privatising prisons to figure out their overcrowding crisis, because the Bill did not do what it needed to do to actually address the overcrowding crisis, and now law makers feel like they've done the law reform piece.

In addition, it is argued that focusing on intensive, short-term analysis and technical assistance and aiming for legislative packages in a large number of states, 'does not build state and local capacity to assume responsibility for monitoring and evaluating implementation and outcomes for genuine justice reform over the long-term' (Austin *et al.*, 2013: 4).

Kat Brady from Hawaii voices similar concerns about the JRI in that state. As discussed above, having done a great deal of work to bring justice reinvestment to Hawaii, she found that there was no place at the table for her as a community advocate.

On the other hand, others express the view that working in partnership with advocacy groups would make it impossible for a workable consensus to be achieved. Nancy La Vigne from the Urban Institute, which plays a coordination and assessment role in the JRI, suggests that having organisations like the ACLU at the table would make collaboration challenging because 'these advocates serve a very important purpose but... their whole method of effectiveness is not to be collaborative, it's to hammer away at their points'.

The JRI at the local level would seem to provide more opportunity for ownership by local stakeholders. This is bolstered by the skill set of the supporting organisations. Peggy Burke from the CEPP says on this point:

> The real trick in my estimation is working with the community so that you are a resource for them, but that they own it. This is a way that the Center for Effective Public Policy has been doing its work for many years. We do not assume the role of [an] expert outside consultant that comes in and tells them what to do about solving their problems. We refer to ourselves as facilitators, but I would say that in many ways that we're process experts – and we try to help them set up a process that allows them to work effectively together.

One challenge to building a strong basis for local JRI is ensuring that the initiative has ongoing collective support. When working at the state level, that support is assured in the process of securing bipartisanship and by having legislative underpinning for agreed upon outcomes. On the local level, the supporting body may require letters of support from various key players, but there is a danger that this is 'just a signature':

> When you get working in the field you come to find that it's really just one person who's spearheading this effort, and they could get another job and leave and...everything falls apart. (Nancy La Vigne, Urban Institute)

Barbara Pierce Parker, managing associate at the CJI which spearheads some local JRI initiatives, adds that many people who are called upon to be involved in local JRI do not have the capacity to add another project to their workload. Gary Dennis similarly confirms that the different political and structural realities make the JRI more difficult to pull together at the local level:

> There's been so much difficulty in getting the stakeholders together, we're right now, honestly, at the point where we are seriously discussing whether we can continue to fund work at the local level. I think that what's going to happen is that we're going to probably look at a different model. (Gary Dennis, BJA)

A revised model would support the local JRI only when there was a concurrent commitment at the state level into which a local component could be blended. Given the current disappointment on the part of some local JRI sites that state actors have been unwilling to dovetail state and county JRI efforts (see discussion of Mecklenburg County above), this approach is likely to encounter obstacles of its own.

What is interesting is that the major sticking point at the local level – a difficulty in getting true buy-in and support from the focus community – is potentially the greatest strength of a localised initiative. A lack of commitment from local stakeholders is likely to signal a defect in process resulting in a lack of ownership of the project by the community. This stands in stark contrast to the process that has unfolded in Bourke NSW, where the Just Reinvest NSW campaign has spent more than 18 months being guided by the community in developing a plan of what justice reinvestment might look like. The local JRI experience in the USA reiterates the need for widespread buy-in from a range of community stakeholders, such that the initiative is deeply rooted and sustainable.

A place-based approach

As originally conceived, justice reinvestment is not just about achieving cost efficiencies in the prison system. It is concerned with affecting sustained reductions in prisoner numbers, to ultimately rebuild the human resources and physical infrastructure in communities that lose high numbers of people to prison (Tucker and Cadora, 2003: 3). In order to achieve this, justice reinvestment was conceived as a 'place-based' approach, where savings gained through de-incarceration would be redirected into local communities with high imprisonment rates (sometimes called 'million dollar blocks' or 'diamond districts'). In the original paper setting out the idea, Tucker and Cadora (ibid.: 4) make the place-based nature of the enterprise very clear: 'We advocate taking a geographic approach to public safety that targets money for programs in education, health, job creation, and job training in low-income communities'.

However, in practice, the commitment to 'improving the prospects not just of individual cases but of particular places' has fallen out of the JRI (Allen, 2007: 5). Rather, state-level initiatives have had almost exclusive focus on system-wide reform, including criminal justice system-based reinvestment. This is exemplified in the emphasis on the passage of legislation as the central JRI outcome, the rationale for which is stated by Marshall Clement of the CSG Justice Center: 'If you pass legislation it can be repealed, it can be changed...but legislation typically feels – and is – more durable than what one administration tries to put in place'. Clement explains that the analysis of state corrections systems often reveals both inefficiencies and failures to meet principles of best practice. As such, there is much to be achieved on the systemic level without needing to address the complexities of a place-based model.

Speaking about the Texan experience at the state level and the absence of a place-based component, Tony Fabelo of the CSG states:

> My justice reinvestment is the *realpolitik* justice reinvestment...I know politics, I know what is doable, I know what I can get done. Taking the amount of resources necessary to invest in one of these broader communities to have a large impact, the politics are not there. It's not going to happen...the will is not there for it to happen.

The CSG cites as one of the key lessons learned from its experiences that the focus of JRI approaches should be on the cohort most likely to reoffend, which indicates a shift away from a placed-based approach (CSG, 2013a). Instead of working with communities that produce the highest numbers of offenders, the focus has been on probation and parole supervision regimes, and the reliance on risk assessment tools, that is, on reform of the system rather than a place-based reform agenda. The relationship between justice reinvestment and other place-based initiatives is taken up in Chapter 3.

Reinvestment in high-incarceration communities

The movement away from a place-based focus gives rise to perhaps the most obvious, and fundamental, departure from the original vision of justice reinvestment: that 'increasingly, JRI has abandoned reinvestment in high-incarceration communities as a key element and goal of the initiative' (Austin *et al.*, 2013: 4).

The modification of justice reinvestment from a community to a systems level reflects the skill set of the CSG. The earliest CSG attempts did take up the original vision of addressing the underlying causes of crime within high-incarceration communities. In Wichita, Kansas, for example, an ambitious community redevelopment strategy, involving four years of work with the mayor, community groups, facilitators Urban Strategies and property developers McCormack Baron Salazar, was ultimately thwarted by the advent of the global financial crisis. Marshall Clement (CSG Justice Center), who worked on the initiative, comments:

> We were close but we didn't even get the chance to prove whether you could actually execute a community redevelopment plan as part of a justice reinvestment effort given the collapse of credit markets. In addition, funders were understandably wary of investing in helping get the effort off the ground, given the history of so many well-intentioned community redevelopment efforts not achieving significant impact.

Picking up on the frustration with the difficulties in successfully implementing community development programs, Gary Dennis from the BJA, the primary JRI funding body, emphasises a preference for investing in programs that have been positively evaluated rather than what he perceives as money being 'somehow pumped in to making the world a better place':

> Money has been ploughed back into evidence-based programs, in community corrections programs to support non-governmental [organisations] to provide drug treatment and whatever. It hasn't generally gone back into, for the good of the world...it's the first

time as a country that I can remember ... that we have taken a rational approach to incarceration. (Gary Dennis, BJA)

There were some community projects funded especially during the earliest years of the JRI. The Nurse–Family Partnership program was extended to 2,000 families in 'high-stakes' communities in Texas, through the appropriation of US$4.3 million from the 2008–09 corrections budget, is an example of a reinvestment program which aims to increase self-sufficiency, improve the health and well-being of low-income families, and prevent violence' (Clement, Schwarzfeld and Thompson, 2011: 59).

In Connecticut, US$13 million in savings were reinvested in community-based strategies for reducing recidivism and increasing public safety (CSG Justice Center, 2015b). More than US$7 million was provided for contracts for new residential beds, including drug treatment beds and halfway houses. This included 'New Day', a residential housing facility in Hartford, an identified 'high risk' community, where secure housing, programming and other services were offered to recently released prisoners. It was administered by the Connecticut Puerto Rican Forum. Participants were all male, more than half were Hispanic, and about 35 per cent were African American (Institute for the Study of Crime and Justice, 2009). The one million dollars went to community-led planning processes in New Haven and Hartford to develop neighbourhood-focused initiatives to further integrate funding streams and achieve better outcomes for residents. This was called the 'Building Bridges' program. Both the Building Bridges and New Day programs have since lost funding.

For the most part, savings are directed not into communities but towards other parts of the criminal justice system such as community corrections, or to programs for drug treatment and mental health. For instance, in North Carolina, the *Justice Reinvestment Act* (House Bill 642) was passed in June 2011; it was estimated that by 2017 there would be 5,000 fewer inmates with savings of US$214 million from averted prison construction and US$346 million in operating costs. Reinvestment has included community treatment programs targeted according to risk and need (US$8 million in 2011 and 2012, and US$4 million over 2013–14), and 175 extra probation officers (US$18 million in 2013–14) (La Vigne et al., 2014: 95).

Some US states have legislation that includes a requirement for reinvestment and in some cases this also directs where savings are to be reinvested. However, it has been noted that it is difficult to tie the hands of future legislators in terms of budget allocations or to get commitment to reinvestment over a longer term. A bill passed in Pennsylvania was cited as notable on two grounds, first because it includes a commitment for reinvestment over a five-year period and secondly because the reinvestment is stipulated by reference to a formula that calculates savings (Marshall Clement, CSG). However, criticisms have been raised that the reinvestments do not go back to communities (Austin *et al,.* 2013). Even legislated reinvestment schemes may be precarious. James, Elsem and Subramanian (2012: 844) note that despite the success of the JRI in Texas, a bill to cut reinvestment was proposed in response to the economic downturn. It was ultimately unsuccessful.

The capacity to shape the form of any reinvestment also has been limited in some schemes. For instance it was noted that:

> the Texas Department of Criminal Justice budget does not go to health and human services, does not go to education, does not go to any of that. So the only thing we could work on was on the budget that pertained to criminal justice... So we had to settle for the least harmful which is probation, parole, re-entry, substance abuse, mental health. (Ana Yanez-Correa, Texas Criminal Justice Coalition (TCJC))

Austin *et al.* (2013) note that the failure to reinvest in high-incarceration communities is probably the most glaring weakness of the JRI. They contend that in side-lining this aspect of justice reinvestment, an important ethical dimension of mass-incarceration has been ignored:

> Individually and collectively, residents of [high incarceration] communities—already suffering from social exclusion due to race, poverty, disenfranchisement, etc.– have been disproportionately subjected to the further destabilizing and downwardly mobile consequences of high incarceration rates; therefore, it is incumbent upon policy leadership to make investments that promote greater economic and social equality and stability. (Austin *et al.*, 2013: 9–10)

However, not all stakeholders believe that abandoning a place-based approach is problematic. Nancy La Vigne from the Urban Institute comments that a departure from the original vision of justice reinvestment does not necessarily compromise the integrity of the initiative. While the bulk of reinvestment in the JRI may go back into programs allied with the criminal justice system, in cases where that system needs reorientation or reform, this might be a productive use of funds. This was reiterated by Marshall Clement of the CSG: the 'system is really weak...we couldn't ask the system to further adopt evidence-based practices without making significant reinvestments to allow for those changes to take place'.

Part of the more general difficulty around reinvestment as part of the JRI is that substantial savings are only realised with the closure of a prison wing or entire prison. Without the closure of facilities, savings are only of marginal costs and the core costs of running the facilities remain. In New York, for example, where incarceration numbers dropped steadily over some time (outside of the JRI), it took several years for actual savings to arise in the state budget, following the eventual closure of facilities. Where savings are calculated according to the non-expenditure of *projected costs*, these savings are notional; there are no immediate savings to reinvest. Speaking of the Texan experience, the CSG's Tony Fabelo explains that when the JRI came to that state in 2007:

> we had a surplus of money. Billions of dollars surplus...the so-called reinvestment really was money that we had in surplus that we decided to spend this way. Because the concept of reinvestment when you have avoided deficit is very unreal.

Arguably the movement away from reinvestment in vulnerable communities bears out the danger of framing justice reinvestment largely in the language of 'smart on crime' and saving the taxpayer dollar. While this may have been politically necessary, it has also served to pull the focus away from social justice principles. In 2009, the ATSISJC (ATSISJC, 2009: 10) suggested that 'framing the problem of Indigenous imprisonment as an economic issue might be more strategic than our previous attempts to address it as a human rights or social justice issue'. The way that the JRI has unfolded in the USA has arguably veered too far from any consideration of social justice issues, especially in the absence of any attention to the racial characteristics of mass-incarceration.

Evaluation of results

For those arguing that the JRI has failed to fulfil the promise of the justice reinvestment vision, the requirement for evaluation of outcomes is a toothless one; the goals against which evaluation takes place set too low a bar. One of the central criticisms of the JRI from Austin *et al.* (2013: 9) is that the short-term investment of the CSG in states with the passage of legislation as the primary outcome against which success is measured, does not lay the groundwork for sustained change.

Under the current model, a state applies for JRI assistance to analyze and assess the drivers of its correctional population. Based on that analysis, the state receives a set of recommendations that includes estimated impacts of proposed reforms on populations and budgets... One side effect of this strategy is... that no one is onboard to ensure that reforms are implemented as intended. Absent local analytical capacity or participatory authority to track and oversee JRI implementation and reform outcomes, short-lived technical assistance eventually gives way to increasingly watered – down, risk-averse policy mechanisms and inadequate quality assurance of implementation.

ACLU advocates stress that when the goals of the JRI do not go far enough at the outset, evaluation of success is necessarily compromised:

That's what I think is really distressing. They don't open up with deep enough goals and so they're already coming in with being able to accept very low hanging reforms, and saying, 'well that's a victory because we got legislation passed', then really not leaving any long-term notion that there is a lot more work to do and it's not going to happen in 18 months... success is not the passage of legislation. (Vanita Gupta, ACLU)

Reflections on the US experience

As originally conceived in 2003, and as reimagined by Austin *et al.* in 2013, justice reinvestment has at its centre not just de-carceration, but community-driven local capacity building in the places most in need of positive change. In practice, however, we have seen that many of the cornerstone ideas of justice reinvestment have been altered, reconceived or abandoned. The most significant of these shifts has been the move away from localised, place-based justice reinvestment, and the failure to reinvest savings in communities that produce large numbers of prisoners.

While the US experience discussed above may seem to bear out justice reinvestment becoming a 'floating signifier' divorced from the principles from which it grew, the situation may equally be described as one in which justice reinvestment continues to evolve and be shaped by those engaged in its implementation. Marshall Clement from the CSG Justice Center describes the early attempts at the JRI in Kansas and Texas as exercises in proof of concept in conservative bellwether states: '[i]t's like version 1.0. If you go to North Carolina and Ohio you get version 2.0. If you see some of the things we are doing in Idaho and Michigan you get version 3.0'. He adds that the nature of the data being analysed has also changed from a narrow focus on revocations to include sentencing policy, behavioural health analyses, crime and arrest trends, victim restitution and probation data. The JRI is itself, it seems, a work in progress.

Even this being the case, the model of justice reinvestment that is emerging out of Bourke, NSW, is distinctive in current international practice. Arising through the initiative of the Bourke Indigenous community, it springs from a desire to allow a community to own and solve their own problems, rather than because of fiscal imperatives. It has developed with some government support but without, so far, government intervention or leadership. Rather it is community-driven. The Bourke model goes well beyond anything attempted in the USA. As a place-based program, it seeks to address the underlying causes of juvenile contact with the criminal justice system as they are expressed by the community and through data focusing on that location.

Mark Mauer, reflecting on the course that the JRI has taken in the USA, summarises the need to allow the concept to develop and change as follows:

> The bottom line is that each individual State and each individual jurisdiction is different. The players are different, the attitudes are different... in the final analysis it morphs into its own thing... you've got to maintain flexibility. You have to understand that it may, in two different states, in two different areas, look different. (Mark Mauer, The Sentencing Project)

The chapters that follow work to raise questions about, and to some degree destabilise, the premises upon which both the original conception of justice reinvestment and the JRI are built. As we will see, the principles of each of these models are contingent, sometimes problematic, and not easily transferrable from one political, social and geographic context to another.

3
The Politics of Locality and Community

As we have identified in earlier chapters, the origins of justice reinvestment situated it within a place-based approach to public policy. In the words of Tucker and Cadora (2003: 2, 4), 'justice reinvestment seeks community level solutions to community level problems... solutions are required that are locally tailored and locally determined'. Place-based approaches are usually conceived as initiatives specific to a particular geographic location, rather than those that operate at a state-wide or federal level. In this chapter we explore the meaning and implications of place-based approaches to justice reinvestment. We do this through a critical analysis of locality, place and community and consider whether place-based approaches can respond to social groups who have been particularly impacted through rising incarceration rates.

The importance of place-based approaches has grown over the last several decades with the social and economic research showing the high level and long-term concentration of poverty and disadvantage in particular localities including neighbourhoods and communities. In this context, place-based responses became tied to public policy initiatives attacking social exclusion and can at least at a general level, be connected with a social justice orientation. Vinson (2009: 7) discusses the 'web of disadvantage' as the appropriate metaphor to show how people become entrapped in highly disadvantaged communities:

> Progress in overcoming one limitation, say, unemployment, can be inhibited by related factors like limited funds, poor health, inadequate training or having a criminal record. This web-like structure of disadvantage restricts attempts to break free of it. And because disadvantageous conditions are often 'bundled' in this way, efforts must be

directed to loosening systemic constraints on people's life opportunities if progress is to be achieved.

According to Gilbert (2012), place-based initiatives require governments to change the way they do things in at least two ways. First there is a requirement for greater coordinated service delivery by agencies that have traditionally delivered such services at the broader state or federal level. Second, government departments need to move towards less centralised and more locally informed service delivery models. This should involve greater flexibility, collaboration and community engagement. According to Vinson (2009: 9), the characteristics of a successful place-based approach involve the 'maximum practicable *engagement of disadvantaged communities* in decisions...a local coordinating or "steering" group needs to operate on a basis of authentic community participation' (italics in original). Successful approaches also involve, inter alia, the cultivation of community capacity and adequate time for development and implementation (ibid.: 9).

Having said that, we argue that place-based approaches can be conceptualised, and operationalised, as either 'top-down' or 'bottom-up'. In a top-down approach, governments still set the policy priorities and parameters, although they may be aimed at particular communities. While there may be greater coordination in service delivery and consultation with communities, the place-based initiative is still firmly set by government agencies and their agendas. In contrast a bottom-up approach, starts with the local community. The policy priorities, linkages and service delivery models are determined through community decision-making and negotiated with different levels of government. This latter approach involves a more participatory democratic approach to determining, prioritising and delivering public policy and services.

Although justice reinvestment is defined as a place-based approach, this can have competing definitions, differing political imperatives, and contrasting priorities for policy and practice. A strong emphasis on a place-based approach was core to the original conceptualisation of justice reinvestment. However, as we noted previously, there has been a tension between the original cornerstones of justice reinvestment and the way that it has played out. As originally conceived, the strategy was not limited to achieving cost efficiencies in the prison system. Its core premises were not only effecting sustained reductions in prisoner numbers, but also 'rebuilding the human resources and physical infrastructure' (Tucker and Cadora, 2003: 3) of communities that lose high numbers of people to prison. In order to achieve this, justice reinvestment was conceived as a place-based approach, whereby resources spent on incarcerating offenders were to be redirected into local communities with high imprisonment rates. As such, justice reinvestment was described as a form of 'preventative financing, through which policymakers shift funds away from dealing with problems "downstream" (policing, prisons) and towards tackling them "upstream" (family breakdown, poverty, mental illness, drug and alcohol dependency)' (Lanning, Loader and Muir, 2011: 4).

It is worth noting that the idea of justice reinvestment as a place-based approach has also taken a different twist in the UK. Wong, Fox and Albertson (2014), referring to the work of the Commission on English Prisons Today (2009), note the way in which justice reinvestment became tied to ideas and policies of *localism*. Localising service providers and services was seen to achieve a number of beneficial outcomes including better cooperation between agencies, more efficient delivery of justice services, and greater trust in criminal justice processes (Wong *et al.*, 2014: 80). A place-based approach, as defined through localism, focuses attention on various local multi-agency approaches and localised administrative reform and innovation, perhaps at the expense of an engagement with communities in decision-making. Localism runs the risk of being limited to administrative convenience.

The social justice argument for a place-based approach to justice reinvestment was most explicitly developed by Clear (2007a). Based on a form of social disorganisation theory, Clear argued that high-incarceration rates (and concentrated cycling between prison and community) contributed to the destabilisation of poor neighbourhoods and led to increased crime. Imprisonment constituted a type of 'coercive mobility' where men and women (but particularly men) cycle back into a community from prison to be replaced by another cohort. Many who leave prison are back in a couple of months. This cycling and recycling through community and prison becomes a dynamic of the poor neighbourhood, 'so that a family is hardly ever without a son, uncle, or father who has done prison time' (Clear, 2007a: 9). The effects on the prisoner/ex-prisoner are ecologically important because the prison touches almost everyone in the neighbourhood (ibid.: 9). In this way, 'prison [becomes] woven into the fabric of these communities' (ibid.: 10).

Low formal education levels, histories of drug and alcohol abuse, of substantial physical or mental illness, and of unemployment impact negatively on human and social capital. The ability to use social networks for access to resources (such as housing, employment, medical or other assistance) is diminished. People involved in the re-entry cycle between prison and community become increasingly isolated from social (non-criminal) networks, and are sometimes forced to rely upon their families – who are often themselves poor. Families are disrupted by cycling in and out of prison in many ways: 'parenting is interrupted, role models are removed, families move and change school districts, mothers go on welfare, children receive less supervision, the number of single-parent families increases, incarceration experiences are models for children' (ibid.: 88). In addition, imprisonment disrupts marital relationships, increases the chances of foster care or other substitute care (which is itself associated with poorer long-term life outcomes) and increases the risk of juvenile offending by the children of imprisoned parents (ibid.: 96).

At the microeconomic level, high-incarceration neighbourhoods are 'created of mostly men that have depleted labour market prospects where labour markets are weak to begin with' (ibid.: 88). The concentration of formerly incarcerated people in poor neighbourhoods not only affects them, but can also damage the labour-market prospects of others in the same community. The erosion of local labour markets and employment opportunities is itself connected to higher rates of crime: 'economic hardship is one of the strongest geographic predictors of crime rates' (ibid.: 109). In addition, high crime rates lead to decreased private investment and falling property values. At the macroeconomic level, government funding is shifted away from improving impoverished communities toward penal institutions instead. 'Once they are arrested and incarcerated, these people's economic value is transformed and transferred into penal capital – the demand for salaried correctional employees to provide security. It is also transferred to the locality of the prison' (ibid.: 89). This echoes the description of the Spatial Information Design Lab (2009: 7) of prisons as 'urban exostructures, displacing investments to prison towns outside of the communities to which prisoners will return'.

The development of a community-based justice approach is central to understanding how a placed-based approach to justice reinvestment might operate. The goal of promoting community life is a central value: 'To deal with the problem we will have to make community well-being a central objective of our penal system' (Clear 2007a: 13. See also Tucker and Cadora, 2003). For Austin *et al.* (2013: 4) a key element of justice reinvestment is the requirement of 'an organised coalition of demand for prison reductions and reinvestment in community institutions from local coalitions of city and county officials, grassroots leaders, residents, and service providers'.

As we discussed in the previous chapters, justice reinvestment relies on the ability to identify which communities produce large numbers of people sent to prison (justice or incarceration mapping) and to strategically use that information to guide investment in community programs to most effectively reduce imprisonment numbers. This is one part of the technical underpinning to a place-based approach for justice reinvestment. The second part is to map the potential justice reinvestment 'assets' in the same area (e.g., homelessness support services, health clinics, community centres, local businesses, etc.). Asset mapping is then able to identify which entities already exist in particular locations that may be strengthened through justice reinvestment strategies, as well as significant gaps where services need to be developed.

At its best, justice reinvestment is a flexible strategy *because* it is place-based. Location-specific programs can be as diverse as investments in education, job training, health, parole support, housing or rehabilitation. They can include schemes like micro-loans to support job creation and 'family development loans' for education, debt consolidation or home ownership. Local coalitions, including local government, rather than central government, can decide through devolved budgets how money should be spent to produce safer local communities (Schwartz, 2010: 5). Justice reinvestment, through reinvesting money at the local level, provides greater incentive for local communities to reduce imprisonment levels among their residents. Thus, through a place-based approach 'justice reinvestment is...more than simply rethinking and redirecting public funds. It is also about devolving accountability and responsibility to the local level' (Tucker and Cadora, 2003: 2).

However, at its most limited and restricted, the place-based approach of justice reinvestment can lose its social justice focus and become simply a technical exercise of 'mapping' localities with high prisoner/ex-prisoner numbers. Even more limited is where the process is reduced to crime mapping. Various people we interviewed noted that the problem of the 'top down' approach to justice reinvestment meant that the core aspects of *reinvestment* could be lost. For example, 'I really think you have to watch out with starting from a policy level down that you have to always keep...in mind, the place-based side' (Laura Kurgan, Spatial Information Design Lab [SIDL]). Commenting on her work in New Orleans, she went on to say, 'that project really didn't start from the top down, like the Council of State Governments. It really started at the city council level. Actually, first it started at the community level'. However, losing sight of the importance of local communities in identifying and developing local programs can mean that even the asset mapping of community infrastructure falls away: 'Once they had a different concept of the reinvestment piece, they just stopped all of that local assets mapping' (Vanita Gupta, ACLU).

Certainly much of the JRI approach is focused at the state-level and with achieving bipartisan support and legislative reform. It is not surprising in this context that the focus on place-based initiatives essentially falls off the radar with the consequence that community reinvestment becomes a 'forgotten' part of justice reinvestment. As one of our interviewees in Hawaii expressed it:

> Yeah I don't think that's happening [community reinvestment] and that's a [problem]. Again we've got certain communities where the vast majority of people who go out on parole go back to these total low income communities and...there's no money gushing from the prison system back into Waiohai (Meda Chesney-Lind, University of Hawaii).

However, we note that recent government funding programs for technical assistance at the local level can lead to more localised developments. We noted in Chapter 2, specific developments in Mecklenburg County, North Carolina, and Travis County, Texas, as examples of this. As Tom Eberly (Mecklenburg County) stated in an interview:

> We had the information from people leaving the state prisons, coming back to Mecklenburg and...put a map to where they were coming back to, and we were able to see that there were certain areas that are highly concentrated with ex-prisoners. We used that as a stepping-stone for a creative reentry program. We went after federal dollars to get grant money to target that neighbourhood in particular.

We would argue then that as justice reinvestment has evolved, a number of significant limitations on the place-based approach have become evident. In the first instance, the focus on place can be dropped completely, and the emphasis is solely on reducing prison numbers. This is evident, for example, in changes to the CSG identification of the 'four steps' of justice reinvestment, which we outlined in the previous chapter. Secondly, even though the rhetoric may include reference to a place-based approach, the reality may be that the emphasis on developing local solutions by communities themselves and through existing community-based organisations, disappears and community asset mapping may be seen as no longer relevant (Austin *et al.*, 2013). As one interviewee, who preferred not to be named, told us, it is important to take 'the reinvestment part of this seriously... because justice reinvestment as it is practiced here is different from that original concept... that piece of it [reinvestment] for the most part has kind of dropped out'. A similar sentiment was echoed by a senior official with the New York City Department of Probation, who spoke of the 'frustration with the nature of justice reinvestment... that it has not reached the million dollar blocks. That it's gone to the Police Departments, it's gone to the systems. Systems need things, need resources of course, but... justice reinvestment, if it is a movement, it needs to expand or grow'.

A third issue to emerge is that, even where community reinvestment is acknowledged as desirable, the funds available may not be significant enough to tackle the depth of issues that need to be addressed. As Tom Eberly explained in relation to the Frequent User Service Enhancement (FUSE) program in North Carolina:

> That leads me to my second biggest disappointment and that is I feel like there was seed money offered from the federal Government to participate in [JRI]. This was justice reinvestment funds. We really didn't know how much it was and we had big dollars in our head, millions of dollars to do something spectacular, and it came back as $300,000 and you could just use this as seed money...
>
> Stubbs: So does that mean that the capacity to do the kind of neighbourhood development work that's part of at least some vision of justice reinvestment isn't there for you?
>
> Mr Eberly: There's just too many disconnects. It's a wonderful idea that gets unfortunately off track because there's just not that complete package of a solution.

It is instructive to consider here previous experiences with the de-institutionalisation of the mentally ill in the 1970s and 1980s where the emphasis was on closing large institutions and reinvesting the money into community-based treatment, support and accommodation. As Eileen Baldry told us in an interview, 'the lessons learned from de-institutionalisation projects around the world are that the amount of money needed never gets invested in the community, other stuff happens to it'.

It is clear that a place-based approach may be watered down to a particular type of 'localism' that has little connection to the concept of justice reinvestment as it was originally conceived. For example, pilot projects of justice reinvestment by their very nature are likely to be localised affairs, but this does not mean that they are place-based in the broader public policy sense of the term. It would appear that many of the UK experiences with justice reinvestment reflect a type of localism that is administratively convenient, but does not connect to either a social justice strategy or engagement with community (Fox, Albertson and Wong, 2013a). There are some exceptions to this such as the Greater Manchester justice reinvestment project, which we return to below.

The 'community' in a place-based approach

The concept of 'community' underpins much of the discussion on a place-based approach to justice reinvestment. It is important therefore to consider some of the problems or limitations with the concept, as well as its advantages. We note that understanding the complexity of the term and its deployment has been debated in a range of disciplines including development studies, social work and sociology through to public health and the human services literature more generally (Taylor, Wilkinson and Cheers, 2008; Ife, 2013). Defining and understanding what 'community' is has plagued other reformative approaches to criminal justice, including restorative justice (see, Cunneen and Hoyle, 2010). Despite its conceptual and pragmatic appeal, 'community' is not a natural set of relations between individuals, nor a natural social process lying at the foundation of civil society. Communities are always constructed on the broad terrain of history and politics. Communities can be defined in a range of ways based on a geographic, physical location (e.g., neighbourhoods, towns, regional centres and rural areas). Community can also be defined by a common interest (e.g., political, social, cultural, religious, etc.). The common thread to these various conceptualisations of community is the social interactions that arise and give shape to the group.

Because communities are socially constructed they are also reflective and constitutive of power, difference, inequality and potentially exploitative social and economic relations. Many communities are characterised by social exclusion, coercion and inequalities of power. We might ask where is the community for the homeless and mentally ill who cycle in and out of prison through a revolving door? Social solidarity does not come into being simply through the application of a community-based approach, although we acknowledge that it may lay the foundations for developing the social networks for such solidarity to occur.

How we understand and define community has fundamental implications for how we progress particular practices, and in particular how we envisage the development and implementation of a place-based approach in justice reinvestment. Ife's (2013: 8–9) general comments on community development work are pertinent.

> The main reason for much of the confusion, and the seeming inadequacy of what passes for community work 'theory', is that community work has often not been adequately located in its social, political and ecological context, or linked to a clearly articulated social vision, in such a way that the analysis relates to action and 'real-life' practice. Many of the stated principles of practice are fragmentary and context-free, and often the goals of community work remain vague, uncharted and contradictory. Similarly, the literature on community-based services is often rhetorical rather than substantive, and often does not relate specifically to relevant social and political theory.

A top-down understanding of place-based approaches, where the agenda is determined externally by governments and then targeted at communities, can also be seen to coalesce with ideas about 'governing at a distance'. Communities are called into existence to provide for a process of responsibilisation. In Rose's (1999) conceptualisation, this is 'government through the community'. A 'sector is brought into existence whose vectors and forces can be mobilised, enrolled, deployed in novel programs and techniques which encourage and harness active practices of self-management and identity construction, of personal ethics and collective allegiances' (ibid.: 176). Common civic duties and responsibilities are mobilised and developed by the state for particular purposes. Community activities are constituted by the state, which may design, establish, fund and staff those activities and provide authority and legitimacy. In this sense, community is not a social formation that is independent of the state. In this context, justice reinvestment may simply serve as a guise to further extend the scope of criminalisation by greater targeting of 'problem' communities and further surveillance through increased policing and substantially expanded community corrections supervision.

It is also important to note that aspects of community-based and place-based approaches *may* coalesce with particular imperatives of neo-liberalism, including a reduction in commitment to social welfare through funding less costly community alternatives, covert privatisation of services, placing greater responsibility on families (and particularly women) to provide support under the guise of the community, and the entrenchment of class and racial hierarchies (see, e.g., Ife, 2013: 18–20). There is a danger here of reframing basic government obligations to meet human needs around housing, health, education and employment. Rather than being seen as fundamental human rights, they become tied to a discourse about crime prevention. We argue throughout this book that to avoid these pitfalls a social justice-oriented approach to justice reinvestment is fundamental. Such an approach includes a commitment to a process of democratisation and empowerment, the satisfaction of human physical, social and economic needs, and respect for human rights (including principles of fairness, equity and non-discrimination).

Community and the disavowal of race in justice reinvestment

How does the concept of community sit then with broader social divisions? From a postcolonial perspective, colonial policies were directly responsible for the destruction and reconstruction of 'community' in the interests of the coloniser. The very fabric of rural and urban life in Australia has been spatially patterned through the processes of colonising strategies, policies and practices. Many contemporary Indigenous communities were created directly as a result of colonial government policies of forcibly removing and concentrating different tribal and language groups on various types of reservations, which are often now referred to as communities. The construction of 'community' took people away from their traditional areas and prevented the use of some traditional means of diffusing conflict (such as temporary exile). The provision of various types of infrastructure and services (such as housing, health and education) reinforced a particular form of sociality: service provision both presupposed and regulated a sedentary, family-based living arrangement (Cunneen 2001). 'Community' is a concept that does not translate easily into Australian Indigenous languages, where kinship and relationship to land is paramount. Thus, anthropologists and ethnographers have been critical of the application of the term 'community' to describe Aboriginal social organisation (Rowse, 1992: 53). In the above context, the application of the term 'community' to the complex interrelationships and heterogeneous groups of Indigenous people, while administratively convenient, can be misleading.

Further, contemporary racial and ethnic minority communities within first-world nations were created under conditions determined by former systems of racialised slavery and contemporary neo/postcolonial relations that influence immigration and post-immigration experiences. History and contemporary politics have shaped the social, economic and political relationships of colonised, formerly enslaved and immigrant peoples (Go, 2013). What, then, does 'community' and a 'place-based approach' mean for minority people in these situations? In this context, it has been noted that in the USA, discussions about place-based approaches have been used to disguise the importance of race. As Todd Clear notes in an interview:

> In this country it's very difficult to talk about race but it's easy to talk about place. You can talk about place, you can talk about neighbourhoods, you can talk about families, you can talk a little bit about inequality but you really have trouble – it's not because we're post racial – it's because the minute you start talking about race, the ears close.

To a significant degree, the racialisation of imprisonment has been the missing piece in the discussion, policy development and implementation of justice reinvestment.

> The reality is there is a way in which speaking about the problems of our criminal justice system in purely racial analysis, a lot of people have shut their eyes and ears to that. In this country mass incarceration is really the new normal. There's a certain degree of fatigue around hearing about race disparities. So cost has become much more relevant, especially to conservative stakeholders... I think they've just lost the whole notion that high incarceration communities is code for communities of colour in this country. (Vanita Gupta, ACLU)

In this sense, ideas about community and place can be discursively powerful concepts that may potentially silence other ways of describing and understanding social and political relationships. The disavowal of race and ethnicity can occur through various processes. Perhaps, as Tom Eberly stated in an interview in North Carolina, 'I think people are scared to talk about it'.

Even if there is a basic collection of information on the racial and ethnic profile of a community as part of the technical exercises underpinning justice reinvestment, this can be easily ignored: 'Most of the data analyses we've seen at the local level do include the basic statistics broken down by race, but a lot of the time they don't end up focusing in on one key race or ethnicity' (Lindsey Cramer, Urban Institute). It appears that the placed-based 'presence' of minority peoples can be too easily ignored. An interviewee stated the following: 'The whole purpose of justice reinvestment was about addressing disproportionate incarceration and punishment of people of colour. That was the whole thing. If you're talking about mass incarceration, that's what you're talking about' (Susan Tucker). She went on to describe a seminar where:

> Only one table out of six or seven, with policy people, community people, researchers, even mentioned race. We all took it for granted, like somehow it was there but it wasn't mentioned. It's still very unpopular to mention it here in some circles. It's like, 'do we have to talk about that now?' or if you talk about it, it's going to turn off people who don't want to talk about it and don't want to be confronted with that. (Susan Tucker)

Marshall Clement put the absence of a race conversation down to the lack of clarity in the data about how racial disparity in imprisonment rates is produced and the resultant difficulty in knowing what to do about it.

> Everyone acknowledges when you talk to people about our system, these disparities exist. While that is true, it is also true that no one in the criminal justice system understands or can tell you what to do about it. Where the problem lies, why there's racial disparity, there's a number of things that people all agree will probably contribute to it, but that list varies from person to person you could talk to. Judges would say it's never them, its maybe who was being arrested, maybe it's parenting, maybe it's poverty. So the lack of clarity about what to do about it, I think, has historically made it a very difficult and contentious conversation at least in the US context. (Marshall Clement, CSG Justice Centre)

However, as we argue further in this chapter, a place-based approach may also provide certain *opportunities* to challenge the way criminal justice agencies, politicians and bureaucrats understand and respond to the problem of crime control and mass incarceration. In the Australian context this has been particularly apparent with the support of justice reinvestment by Indigenous organisations – a point we discuss at length below. However, in the USA several people we interviewed argued that justice reinvestment provided a potentially important way of responding to the problem of racialised justice and mass incarceration through the 'back door'.

> I mean justice reinvestment, to its credit I guess, gives people a way of talking about reducing incarceration without having to deal with race, which is so hard for us to deal with. I think there is now a much stronger competing narrative or impetus around the tremendous racial disparity and [who] we incarcerate. But I think through this book, *The New Jim Crow* [Alexander, 2012], there is a sort of counter-voice that is helpful. But it's still very hard for the States, or anyone, to take this head on. And justice reinvestment, because it's talking about how you're spending resources and things like that, allows people to deal with it. (Nancy Fishman, VERA)
>
> Some folks at Pew and CSG will tell you, of course we care about racial impact, but we're not going to talk about it. We are going to use the language that is most conducive to getting us in the room and keeping us in the room, and all the reforms that we're going to be advancing are going to be ones that are going to impact racial minorities. (Vanita Gupta, ACLU)

Although Gupta went on to make the important point that the absence of a clear identification of race 'really changes the benchmarks for how they measure their success in any given jurisdiction'.

Community service providers and community-based activists also discussed the difficulties of raising the issue of race in connection with criminalisation and justice reinvestment. The following interchange between the authors and Ana Yanez-Correa from the Texas Criminal Justice Coalition captures the substantial political difficulties and contradictions facing advocates and activists:

> Cunneen: One of the things that has struck us here [in the USA] is the absence of race in all of the discussions around justice reinvestment. Do you think by and large that is a strategic decision?
>
> Ms Yanez-Correa: You bet. You bet.
>
> Schwartz: That silence around race is quite a peculiar thing for us.
>
> Ms Yanez-Correa: Yeah. We don't do it.
>
> Schwartz: Why not?
>
> Ms Yanez-Correa: Because we want our bills to pass. They will stop our bills.
>
> Schwartz: But why?
>
> Ms Yanez-Correa: My job is to pass bills and no matter whether I believe it or not, I have to meet people where they're at and my obligation is

to the people I advocate for and if I pass a bill that's going to benefit all facets of society and including the African American or the Latino population because they are the ones that have the most desperate impact, I'm going to do it. People have told me, it's like, "You've got to start leading with race", and I'm like, "I need to pass my bills. Show me that I can pass my bills leading with race and I'll do that". We passed the anti-racial profiling bill but at the time it was mainly Democrat. Right now it's going to be all Tea Party members. I'm not going to talk about race. (Ana Yanez-Correa, Texas Criminal Justice Coalition)

Timothy Miles from Foundation Communities, a social housing provider in Austin which is partially funded under the JRI, noted that with race:

I bring it up in the meetings that I go to. I've never heard anybody else bring it up. One of my big issues and concerns [is] the impact of race on homelessness. There's a big correlation between race and homelessness largely because of race and involvement with the criminal justice system. So for me it's always been an issue and it's something that I've been pushing. I get told "no" probably as many times as I get told "yes", so I have about a 50/50 success rate, so I'll take that. So for me it's been something, a big driver for my interests as much because of the issue of race as criminal justice. (Timothy Miles, Foundation Communities)

In this context, a place-based approach may provide the space to argue for more radical, localised and democratic approaches to policy development, decision-making and program implementation. This more open-ended, 'bottom-up' approach to place-based initiatives may provide opportunities for groups who fare particularly badly in the incarceration stakes, particularly but not exclusively racialised minorities, to create the political space necessary for a dialogue about justice reinvestment that is focused on reinvestment, social justice and localised democractic control.

Contrasting localised place-based approaches

The open nature of the concept of community also provides flexible interpretations of what constitutes a place-based approach. We provide two contrasting examples of place-based approaches (or localism as it is referred to in the UK). The first is in Greater Manchester in the UK, and the second, the NeON initiative in New York City.

The Greater Manchester initiative was developed as part of the Local Justice Reinvestment Pilot operating between July 2011 and June 2013. It was one of six sites (Wong *et al.*, 2013: 1). The project provided local financial incentives in the case of successful reductions in demand on criminal justice services, thus reflecting more generally the PbR approach to justice reinvestment in the UK (see Chapter 4). The pilot was focused on efficiency measures to divert individuals from more expensive interventions – what Wong *et al.* (ibid.) refer to as the criminal justice system's redesign. Its aim was to build on existing multi-agency relationships. In Greater Manchester the focus was on arrest, sentencing, and release from prison (ibid.: 1). An evaluation of the pilot found that the financial incentives were insufficient to bring about substantial changes in practice. Other disincentives were noted (ibid.: 2). However, during the period of the pilot, Greater Manchester also became involved in a separate project, the Whole Place Community Budget. The Community Budget pilot aimed to allow greater flexibility in allocating funds to preventative (pre-habilitation) work and integrating criminal justice and non-criminal justice services, including accommodation and employment (Wong, Fox and Albertson,2014:91). 'The pilot focussed on developing joint investment proposals in four thematic areas: early years; transforming criminal justice; troubled families; and health and social care' (Wong *et al.*, 2013: fn 14). The involvement in the Whole Place Community Budget pilot allowed the justice reinvestment project in Greater Manchester to develop a broader social justice focus (Wong, Fox and Albertson, 2014: 92).

In Chapter 2 we briefly described the NeON project developed by the New York City (NYC) Department of Probation. The NeON projects were established at a number of locations in NYC including Brownsville, South Bronx, Jamaica and Harlem. The NeON provides various services including probation, employment preparation, academic support, technical education, literacy and numeracy courses, healthcare, mentoring, after school activities and other community projects (e.g., NeON art and poetry projects). In the context of this chapter several points are important. Firstly, the NeON was set-up completely outside of the JRI process by a justice agency. It was a justice reinvestment-*inspired* initiative established under the leadership of Susan Tucker. As a senior official with the New York City Department of Probation, explained:

> [NeON] is our effort to...invest into local communities...The NeON concept emerged out of the justice reinvestment and system reform and community engagement...it was talking about our clients as

members of families, members of communities that were in need of an investment and need of empowerment with skills and resources and opportunities. We had a role in helping to make that happen.

The second point of interest is that engaging in the community required operational changes, including a reduction in technical violations and violations arising from minor new arrests, and a cultural change from one that was based simply on monitoring compliance with court orders. It was clear that there was substantial effort required to change the organisational culture.

> The NeON, the justice reinvestment... [both] necessitate an organisation with a culture of change, reemphasis, policy change, even reorganisation within the Department... The fact is, and that is always difficult, a veteran staff here with average 10 to 20 years, people have been here and seen different leaders come and go but certainly what we have done represented a significant shift. The thing about that, change is difficult, new concepts, different concepts, but then even the process of how you manage that, how you message that, how you work with that. I think we definitely experienced some growing pains and certainly some missed opportunities or mishandled opportunities in doing that. That is a difficult process to move something. (senior official, New York City Department of Probation)

Community engagement was a fundamental part of establishing the NeON and this took time and commitment. Catrina Prioleau, the Director of the NeON project told us:

> Our first NeON we opened in Brownsville, across the street from the [police] precinct, around the corner from the juvenile jail, down the block from the shelter. So it's, 'Here comes another government entity into our community'. There was a lot of sensitivity around that and there were a lot of conversations that we had to have. Also we had no track record with NeON... So we had to build relationships and that was just a matter of allowing time to do what time does, and let us prove who we are.

> We kept our doors open and we went to all of the community board meetings, we presented, we talked, we met. We changed our hours so that we were open later so that the community could come in. Just the physical set up was different than what probation would be. We had to also engage the precinct around how we would interact

with them. As we moved into the other communities, we now had something that we could say, okay this is how Brownsville is working and it gave them a little more, I don't know if confidence is the word, but definitely eased them somewhat as we started to go into other communities and NeON became more known in terms of how we are now doing business. We had been in the community before as an agency and it was a very law enforcement, police driven operation. We had some work to do just in terms of changing the character.

There are thus problems that need to be confronted with any place-based approach: how do we ensure a collaborative approach between government, non-government services and local community organisations in identifying specific problems and their solutions? How do we ensure that the government can overcome its own internal culture, demarcations and divisions and provide whole of government solutions to the problems identified by communities? As Chris Twomey from Western Australian Council of Social Services (WACOSS) notes:

I think that the most critical issue is around consultation, participation and ownership, actually making sure that these are not things that are being imposed but are things where we're actually getting those communities, those service providers actually involved and engaged in identifying and delivering the solutions. So for us that stuff is really critical.

The challenge is to ensure a bottom-up approach that maintains the social justice and democratising impulse of justice reinvestment. A further factor that requires consideration is how criminalised people might participate in the development of local policy, practice and implementation that is at the heart of place-based approaches. By definition, the places where ex-prisoners reside are likely to be highly disadvantaged communities. As Kat Armstrong, an ex-prisoner who is now the Director of the Women in Prison Advocacy Service (WIPAN), explains:

You will find that a lot of people from disadvantage or poverty won't want to be at the table because they won't feel confident, they can't articulate, and so that's where community organisations have a huge responsibility to ensure that they are there at the table and they're empowered in the process... empowering the people that don't know, that aren't educated, that haven't got the tools and know-how to actually do what's best for their brothers, their sisters, their children, but empower them to be the leaders of their community and to make it the best that they can be. Give them the tools and whatever they need to do that.

These are basic questions of how to provide the conditions and opportunities for meaningful participation and empowerment of otherwise silenced people. They are questions that have confronted most radical community development advocates for decades.

Over-represented and vulnerable groups

For the purposes of this book, we identify three groups of people that have been particularly affected by the politics and policies of mass incarceration: people with mental illness and/or cognitive disability, women and Indigenous and other racialised peoples. We explore whether and in what way a place-based approach might work for these groups within the context of justice reinvestment. But first, we make some comments on how, over recent decades, all of these groups have seen substantial increases in imprisonment in the Western common law countries where justice reinvestment is now being introduced or is under consideration. We outline briefly below the nature of that increasing incarceration.

People with mental and/or cognitive impairment

The prevalence of people with mental illness and/or cognitive impairment in prison systems is well established. Baldry (2014: 371) estimates that at least half of the Australian prisoner population has some form of mental, cognitive or physical impairment and the number of prisoners with a disability entering or leaving Australian prisons throughout a year, is in the tens of thousands. As we have argued elsewhere (Cunneen *et al.*, 2013: 92–94), the rise in the co-occurrence of substance abuse and mental disorder, along with a political environment of criminalisation, increased prison sentences and low tolerance of illicit drugs (the War on Drugs) has meant an increase in the imprisonment of people with mental or cognitive disability. In addition, the way the War on Drugs has translated into criminal law, policy and practice has had significant racialised effects, as has been the case in the USA.

The penal warehousing of large numbers of people with mental and/or cognitive disability is now a normalised response, with rates three to six times higher than their presence in the general population (Butler, Andrews and Allnutt, 2006). Women with mental health disorders are more highly over-represented in the prison population than men (ibid.).

And people with complex needs – those living with multiple diagnoses and disadvantages – are even more likely than those with a single diagnosis to be caught in the imprisonment cycle (Dowse, Baldry and Snoyman, 2009). There is significant over-representation of Indigenous people with mental and cognitive impairment in Australian prison populations (Butler and Allnut, 2003; Indig *et al.*, 2010; Heffernan *et al.*, 2012).

In most countries, poor historical data on the rates of mental disorders amongst prisoners makes it difficult to identify precise changes over the last 30 to 40 years. However, we do have evidence of the increasing imprisonment of people with mental and/or cognitive impairments over the last decade or so, and this supports the perception amongst judges, correctional authorities, and service providers that the proportion of prisoners with cognitive and/or mental disorders has increased (Cunneen *et al.*, 2013: 97, White and Whiteford, 2006). As one of our interviewees in New York stated:

> You will see cover story after cover story on the situation at Rikers[1] now. Its symptomatic of what's going on...the jails have become our mental health institutions and police have become our de facto mental health workers because they're faced with someone having what is clearly a mental health issue, and they have to treat it like a criminal justice issue. (Nancy Fishman, Vera)

We also note that young people with mental and cognitive impairments are over-represented in juvenile justice systems. The international assessments of juvenile offenders on community orders and in detention suggest even higher rates of mental health problems than amongst adults in prison (Teplin *et al.*, 2002; Fazel *et al.*, 2008; Indig *et al.*, 2011).

Indigenous peoples and racialised minorities

In Chapter 1 we identified the racialised nature of imprisonment in the USA, and in this chapter we have indicated the problematic silencing of race in justice reinvestment. We have argued elsewhere that imprisonment rates may be strongly linked to racial composition, colonial and postcolonial histories, immigration, refugee, and citizenship policies (Cunneen *et al.*, 2013: 180), and this is certainly the case in those countries considering justice reinvestment approaches. The highly racialised nature of imprisonment is apparent in the UK, the USA, New Zealand (NZ), Australia and Canada. For example, in September 2014, Maori comprised 51 per cent and Pasifika peoples a further 11 per cent of the

NZ prison population (Department of Corrections, 2015). In Canada, Aboriginal people are six times over-represented in provincial prisons and three times over-represented in federal prisons (Mosher and Mahon-Haft, 2010: 245).

In Australia, the imprisonment of Indigenous people has been increasing since the 1980s and growing more rapidly than non-Indigenous imprisonment rates in recent decades. At 30 June 2014, there were 9,264 prisoners in Australian prisons who were identified as Aboriginals and Torres Strait Islanders, which was a 10 per cent increase from the previous year. Indigenous people were imprisoned at a rate 13 times greater than their non-Indigenous counterparts (ABS, 2014a: Tables 2, 16). In the decade between 2004 and 2014, Indigenous imprisonment rates had risen by 37 per cent, while at the same time the non-Indigenous imprisonment rate rose by 11 per cent (ibid.: Table 19). Thus while the use of imprisonment had increased for all people, the increase was far more pronounced for Indigenous people. Similar to Canada (Mosher and Mahon-Haft, 2010), there are also significant variations in the imprisonment of Indigenous people between states and territories. For example, the Indigenous age standardised imprisonment rate in WA is 3,013 per 100,000 compared to Victoria where is it less than half that rate at 1,435 per 100,000 (ABS, 2014a: Table 17).

It is also worth noting that minority and Indigenous over-representation is even more apparent when focused on juvenile detention. For example, 51 per cent of the young people incarcerated in Australia are Indigenous. This is truly an extraordinary situation given that Indigenous young people are only 5 per cent of the nation's youth. On the basis of specific youth populations, Indigenous young people are 31 times more likely to find themselves in detention than non-Indigenous youth (AIHW, 2013: vii). The situation for Aboriginal youth in Canada is similar (Mosher and Mahon-Haft, 2010: 245). In the USA, African American youth make up 14 per cent of the youth population but 40 per cent of incarcerated young people (The Sentencing Project, 2014: 7).

As we have argued elsewhere (Cunneen et al., 2013), there has not been a uniform 'penal surge' over recent decades. Once Indigeneity, race and ethnicity are separated out from national or state-based figures, it can be seen that both high rates and rapid increases are largely the province of selected racialised groups, including African Americans and Hispanics in the USA, and Indigenous peoples in Australia and Canada, Maori and Pasifika peoples in NZ. Imprisonment rates of the remaining, predominantly white European inhabitants are much less dramatic, as are any rates of increase (ibid.: 168). The immediate drivers of increased imprisonment rates may be relatively easy to identify through various forms of technical assistance provided, for example, by the JRI process. However, recognition of the differential impact of these drivers on minority groups needs far more careful unpacking.

Women

Over recent decades the imprisonment rates for women have risen to a greater extent than male rates in several jurisdictions worldwide, including the USA, the UK and Australia (Kruttschnitt *et al.*, 2013; Kautt and Gelsthorpe, 2009, Baldry and Cunneen, 2014). In the USA between 1980 and 2010, the number of women in prison increased at nearly 1.5 times the rate of men (646 per cent compared to 419 per cent) (The Sentencing Project 2012: 1). In Australia, in 1983, women formed 3.9 per cent of the prisoner population, in 1993 the proportion was 4.8 per cent, and in 2003 it was 6.8 per cent (Baldry and Cunneen, 2014: 279). By 2014 women comprised 7.7 per cent of the Australian prisoner population (ABS, 2014a: Table 13).

Thus, while the actual number of women prisoners remains relatively small compared to men, their proportion of the total prison population has increased significantly over the longer term. In Australia there are now 55 per cent more women in prison than there were a decade ago, compared to 39 per cent more men (ibid.: Table 2). Stubbs (2013) has argued in the Australian context, that harsher bail determinations have resulted in more women remanded into custody, and that more intensive compliance surveillance of bail conditions and other conditional forms of release have contributed to the increases in women's incarceration. In particular, women may be at heightened risk of breach where the conditions or programs are inappropriate to their needs and circumstances (ibid.).

While the feminisation of imprisonment as a component of the punitive turn over recent decades has been acknowledged, perhaps less acknowledged is that the proportionate increases in women's imprisonment have been uneven, with the greatest effects falling on marginalised racialised women. For example, the numbers of Aboriginal women being sentenced to Canadian federal prison saw a 90 per cent increase over the last decade (Sapers, 2010). In the USA the lifetime likelihood of imprisonment for African American women was one in 19, compared to one in 118 for white women (The Sentencing Project, 2012: 2).

In the Australian context, much of the increase in women's imprisonment noted above can be accounted for by the increasing rate of Indigenous women's imprisonment (Stubbs, 2013; Baldry and Cunneen,

2014). The proportion of Indigenous women prisoners increased from 21 per cent of all women prisoners in 1996, to 30 per cent in 2006, and to 35 per cent in 2014 (Baldry and Cunneen, 2014: 279–80; ABS, 2014a: Table 20). Indigenous women are 22 times more likely to be imprisoned than non-Indigenous women. The complexity of the intersection between race and gender is shown by the fact that Indigenous women's rate of imprisonment (419 per 100,000) is now more than 60 per cent higher than the non-Indigenous *male* rate (260 per 100,000) (ABS, 2014a: Table 20). The often taken-for-granted criminological 'truth' that men are more likely to be imprisoned than women is simply false when race and gender are considered simultaneously: Indigenous women are far more likely to be imprisoned than non-Indigenous men (Baldry and Cunneen, 2014: 279–80).

Place-based approaches for people with mental and/or cognitive disabilities

The evidence strongly suggests that those with a mental illness and/or cognitive impairment who are most likely to be incarcerated are racialised persons from poor, highly disadvantaged families and neighbourhoods. They are people who have more than one impairment, often have been or are homeless, and have a substance abuse problem. In other words, they have multiple and complex needs, and continually cycle in and out of the courts and prisons (Baldry, 2014: 370, 373). This interconnectedness was acknowledged by many of the people we spoke to across both the United States and Australia. For example;

> I've had the chance to work with other local sites in Denver and in Seattle and in a county in Ohio, and for larger sites. [We] come to these same issues over and over again. It is this frequent jail utiliser population that has chronic homelessness, that has mental health issues, that has substance abuse issues, and we do see that folks are just kind of cycling through...they're constant participants in the local criminal justice system. So seeing them in the emergency rooms, seeing them in the mental health centres, seeing them on the street, law enforcement dealing with them continuously is very much...a common local problem, particularly in larger metropolitan areas. (Richard Stroker, CEPP)

> They get called different things, we call them frequent flyers. It's men and women, typically homeless, typically mentally ill, a lot of them have co-occurring substance abuse and alcohol disorder who cycle

in and out of our jail repeatedly and it's typically on really low level offences, it's loitering in public and things like that. They get picked up, come to jail, sometimes are out very quickly, sometimes they come in and because of the mental health problems are kept on a mental health hold. They're in and out...they probably spend more time in jail than they do out on the streets. (Cathy McClaugherty, Travis County, Texas)

However, it was also acknowledged by those we interviewed in the USA that a justice reinvestment focus on people with mental illness and cognitive impairment has been limited. There may be an expectation that they will be picked up under more general interventions. Some interviewees noted that while mental illness emerges frequently as a concern, there may not be specific interventions that target mental illness within JRI reforms.

Others noted there had only been a few initiatives:

Not much to date. Travis County is doing a supportive housing effort which they had identified [through] their frequent jail population clients, the ones that just cycle in and out repeatedly for folks that are chronically homeless and tend to also have mental health problems and drug addiction and so forth. They identified providing supportive housing for this population which is not just housing but wraparound services for all of their needs and risks...Their intent was "We're going to do this and it's going to save money...Even though supportive housing is expensive it's less expensive than jail time and then with those savings we can help or reinvest them back into the supportive housing program and help sustain it over time". So that's the theory. It will be interesting to see if they accomplish that because they only have enough money for a couple of dozen beds. (Nancy La Vigne, Urban Institute)

A place-based approach to addressing the needs of criminalised and imprisoned people with a mental illness and cognitive impairment appears to offer substantial advantages. First, we know that it is not *all* those with impairments who are vulnerable to being drawn into the criminal justice system. It is those deemed riskier and more dangerous – those from seriously disadvantaged and racialised communities and those excluded from mainstream support and advocacy who are likely to be imprisoned (Baldry *et al.*, 2011). Homelessness is a key factor. NACRO (1992) and James, Farnham and Cripps (1999) in the UK, and

Lamb *et al.*(2002, 2004) and Lamb and Weinberger (1998) in the USA, all confirm that homeless mentally ill persons were much more likely to be incarcerated than non-homeless mentally ill persons. People with dual diagnosis (both mental and cognitive impairment) or co-morbidity (mental or cognitive impairment with a substance abuse disorder) or, as is more common, with multiple diagnoses (Hayes *et al.*, 2007; Kavanagh *et al.*, 2010) are now recognised as a large and neglected group in the criminal justice system and in prisons in particular (Herrington, 2009; Baldry, 2010). This group has a much greater likelihood of having come from and returning to highly disadvantaged places. Because social and health services are more stretched in a disadvantaged community, with the lowest levels of services and programs, it is more likely that a person with a mental illness, disability and complex needs will be subjected to criminal justice control rather than mental health, disability and other support (Baldry *et al.*, 2006; Dowse, Baldry and Snoyman 2009; Cunneen *et al.*, 2013: 99). In short, place matters both for the ability to access services and for the likelihood of criminalisation and imprisonment.

Second, we argue that a place-based approach developed through the analysis of community needs and provided at the community level provides a more ethically sound and effective way of responding to the complex needs of people with mental illness and cognitive impairment, than criminalisation and imprisonment. It is sometimes argued that offenders with impairments, problematic drug use and health needs, will at least receive the health and other care in prison that they do not receive in the community. In an interview, Peta MacGillivray of the University of New South Wales (UNSW) gave the not unusual example where in one regional Australian town, 'the magistrate had the impression that there were not appropriate services in the community and therefore sending someone to prison to get some type of assessment was the best thing for them'.

We have argued against this proposition elsewhere, seeing it as a dangerous approach, but one easily made when the prison has been reconstituted as a 'therapeutic institution' providing a solution to behaviour seen as too difficult to manage in the community (Cunneen *et al.*, 2013: 95). As one of our interviewees in Hawaii noted specifically in relation to young people:

> You know the way government funding is it's so screwed up... because there were a lot of kids who needed mental health stuff but the only way they could get it was if we send them to prison. They couldn't get treatment anywhere else and I'm thinking this is so sick. You're

increasing somebody's problem to help them. (Kat Brady, Community Alliance on Prisons)

And another in North Carolina stated:

> Homeless. Drug dependent. Mentally-ill. I almost wish there were a better way or another system as opposed to criminal justice. It really is a public health issue as opposed to a criminal problem. (Tom Eberly, Mecklenburg County)

Prisoners have a right to receive good health and social care, but imprisoning a person is the most serious sanction that can be imposed in all Western states (except the USA). Being imprisoned and having a criminal record disadvantages the already disadvantaged, and creates many negative consequences particularly for those with a mental illness and/or cognitive impairment. It makes a person a target for re-arrest and re-imprisonment, and a target for assault and mistreatment within the prison; it disrupts social connections and locks people into serial incarceration. Imprisonment does not guarantee good or appropriate treatment, and often any treatment started is not continued in the community upon release; it makes homelessness more likely; and creates more connections with criminal culture, ensuring the learning of the prison culture to survive. It often leads to self-harm and depression (Cunneen *et al.*, 2013: 96; Stern 2006; Tonry and Petersilia, 1999). There are readjustment problems post-release as people with cognitive disability inherently have impaired adaptive skills (NSW Sentencing Council, 2004; Glaser and Deane, 1999). These are all outcomes that further exclude and punish the most vulnerable. Many services in the community do not want to deal with people with mental disorders or cognitive disabilities who have difficult behaviour and have a history in the criminal justice system, which contributes to the increasing acceptability of managing this group of people through imprisonment (Cunneen *et al.*, 2013: 96).

Justice Reinvestment as an opportunity for change

> What it [justice reinvestment] offers is an option outside of custody, and looking at diversionary programs – social inclusion, accommodation, support – that may be in the community as a whole. (Gowan Vyse, Office of the Public Guardian NSW Department of Justice)

The problem with existing criminal justice interventions, such as therapeutic or problem solving courts (such as drug courts, mental health courts, etc.) is that, 'despite trying to bring a range of social and health supports to each case, these courts are still managing the person [mental illness and/or cognitive impairment and complex needs] using the criminal justice system' (Baldry, 2014: 382). Justice reinvestment provides the opportunity to develop integrated and more holistic support to people in the community and potentially prior to their becoming enmeshed in the criminal justice system.

A large-scale cohort study of people with mental illness and/or cognitive impairment in prison in NSW between 2000 and 2008 showed that there was a significant geographical concentration of people in particular suburbs, and these were people with multiple impairments and complex support needs (Baldry, 2014). This geographical concentration provides opportunity for the focus on community development which lies at the heart of a social justice-oriented approach to justice reinvestment. Yet at the moment there are few community-based support services available. Examples of these in Australia are the Multiple and Complex Needs Initiative (MACNI) in Victoria and the Integrates Services Program (ISP) in NSW. Both these programs work with people who have been in the criminal justice system, but are not criminal justice responses. As Eileen Baldry (UNSW) explained in an interview, 'they do work reasonably well because they are coming from a position of recognising that for this group of people, it is not a criminal justice issue, it is a human and social support and disability matter. [They] take it out of the realm of criminal justice'.

This is not to deny the importance of other programs which exist that are community-based and at the back-end of the criminal justice system, such as the Community Justice Program in NSW which offers post-release support to people with mental illness and/or cognitive impairment, or support for people in the criminal justice system, particularly during police interviews, such as that offered by the Intellectual Disability Rights Service as noted in an interview with Jim Simpson, NSW Council for Intellectual Disability. However, a place-based community-focused justice reinvestment approach prioritises the importance of front-end holistic support which has the capacity to prevent criminalisation in the first instance.

The social problem of homelessness, and particularly combined with people with mental illness and/or cognitive impairment as a group who need support rather than criminalisation, involves some fundamental changes in both political and social responses to these issues. We know that once police and the criminal justice system begin to manage people with complex needs, these needs are neglected and usually compound into a situation of constant recycling in and out of police custody, courts and prison. In Chapter 2 we provided the JRI example of Travis County, Texas, and Foundation Communities in their response to homelessness in the central business area of Austin. One of the lessons from that initiative was the importance of building a broad-based coalition to tackle the issues at the community level and with community engagement. An important stakeholder in the process was the Downtown Austin Alliance (DAA), which is described as 'a partnership of downtown property owners, individuals, and businesses devoted to preserving and enhancing the value and vitality of downtown Austin' (Downtown Austin, 2015).

Several of the larger shelters for homeless people in Austin are in the downtown part of the city only a few blocks east from the main commercial and entertainment precinct. In an interview, Bill Brice (Downtown Austin) stated:

> We're confronted every day by the fact that we've got three primary social service providers located just three blocks east of where our office is here. If you've passed by there at any time of day or night, it looks completely different from anywhere else in our downtown. It looks like a slum.

While this might be interpreted as a law and order issue by local businesses, who then pressure police and courts for stronger, more punitive intervention, this was not the case.

> Over time we've recognised that our emergency shelters, which by definition are not temporary or permanent housing, have become our de facto housing for people who are chronically homeless and have multiple barriers to housing, people with co-occurring mental health and substance abuse issues, criminal histories and physical health issues...that present barriers to them becoming successfully housed or permanently housed, or successfully employed and so on. So we are involved in the conversations that concern addressing and resolving those issues for Downtown and for the community as a whole. (Bill Brice, Downtown Austin)

The Downtown Austin Alliance went on to support the development of the Travis County JRI housing program, which it saw as successful.

> Number one, we've got people in housing that weren't housed before and were chronically homeless. But secondly, what it's really helped us to do is to shine a spotlight on the fact that we don't have housing for this chronically homeless population with criminal histories and multiple disorders and there is a dire need that we have, and that has really helped to elevate that in the minds of our local elected officials, whether it's city or county, or social service and housing providers. (Bill Brice, Downtown Austin)

In summary then, a place-based and social justice-oriented approach to justice reinvestment offers opportunities for addressing the needs of homeless, criminalised and incarcerated people with a mental illness and/or cognitive impairment. There is the opportunity to develop integrated and more holistic support to people in the community and prior to their becoming caught within the criminal justice system.

The Travis County example shows the importance of building broad-based coalitions that can redefine interventions that are not founded in seeing homeless people as a law and order problem, and instead prioritise community level engagement and support.

Women and place-based approaches

Given the increases in women's imprisonment we have outlined above, the question we pose here is whether the place-based approach underpinning justice reinvestment can meet the needs of women and effectively work to reduce their imprisonment and re-imprisonment experiences. At the outset we note that a specific focus on criminalised women has not featured predominately in the introduction of JRI in the USA. And as far as we are aware, none of the justice reinvestment initiatives in Australia have a specific focus on women and their experience in the criminal justice system. However, the Australian Senate Committee report (LCARC, 2013) on justice reinvestment did consider the needs and interests of women, including criminalised women, those affected by the incarceration of family members, and victims of abuse. The Senate Committee (ibid.: 16) acknowledged that 'poverty, poor education outcomes, unstable housing, domestic violence and/or sexual abuse and trauma' contribute to women's incarceration, and also noted that:

> [t]he social costs of imprisonment are self-evident. With every new generation of criminalised women and children the net widens. Increasing numbers of individuals and families are being drawn into

the cycle of criminalisation, child protection, poverty and despair – at great cost to the state. At the same time, they are being drawn away from social and economic productivity and contribution. (ibid.: 21)

However, the Committee did not specifically address how justice reinvestment might respond to women's social disadvantage, nor to their victimisation and offending.

As Stubbs (forthcoming) has argued, given that proponents of justice reinvestment are insistent that it is evidence-based and a data-driven approach, 'it is surprising that JR literature rarely considers gendered and racialised patterns in incarceration, or in the processes that drive incarceration and their implications'. However, the cost-driven focus of justice reinvestment may militate against consideration of women in the prison.

> At one point Denver wanted to look at women in particular and we said, "they're such a small share of the population". "How does focusing on them really reduce your population and isn't that the goal"? But no, that [women] has not been the nature of the conversation. (Nancy La Vigne, Urban Institute)

Or there may be an implicit assumption that gender neutral interventions across the total population will benefit women. There is little specific literature to assist groups trying to combine justice reinvestment with women's needs. Women-specific programs may be mentioned in passing where they have been introduced as part of a broader justice reinvestment initiative. For example, Wong *et al.*, (2013: 14) in their evaluation of the UK Local Justice Reinvestment Pilot refer to the establishment in Greater Manchester of a women's attendance centre, women's centres and a 'women's only specified activity'. However, there is no discussion of how these interventions fit within the development of a gendered-approach to justice reinvestment. Tentative guidelines have been proposed in the UK to help justice reinvestment programs to focus on women's specific needs (Lanning, Loader and Muir, 2011), and the National Resource Centre for Justice-Involved Women at the CEPP in the USA has been developing gender responsive strategies for women involved in the criminal justice system. However, we note that there is ongoing debate about the use of gender-responsive programming arising from concern that it may have contributed to the use of prisons as if they are therapeutic institutions (Kendall, 2002).

The specific experiences of criminalised women

Before discussing further the implications of a place-based justice reinvestment approach, it is important to acknowledge the differing criminal justice experiences for women and men, including distinctive pathways to offending (Daly, 1998; Simpson, Yahner and Dugan, 2008), and the different characteristics, offence profiles and sentence lengths that are typical of women prisoners. In reviewing the current international research, Stubbs (forthcoming) notes that it has been consistently shown that women prisoners tend to commit mostly nonviolent offences, and are sentenced for less serious offences and for shorter periods than men. Women often have histories of physical and or sexual abuse, high rates of drug and mental health problems, and complex needs (see, e.g., Corston, 2007; UNODC, 2008; Light, Grant and Hopkins, 2013). Women's experiences of re-entry back to the community following incarceration also differ. These differences in experience become apparent in higher rates of relapse and recidivism (Frost and Clear, 2012; La Vigne, Brooks and Shollenberger, 2009).

Stubbs (forthcoming) argues that numerous inquiries and reviews (for example, UNDOC 2008; Corston, 2007) have advocated the greater use of strategies designed to keep women out of prison. These have included for example, decriminalisation, diversion, the repeal of mandatory sentencing provisions and a greater use of community-based sanctions and community-based treatment and services. However, despite what is known about the specific nature of women's offending, incarceration and recidivism, there is little being done in practice to implement on a broad scale, strategies specifically for criminalised women, including those designed to keep more women out of prison, and the planning and programs necessary to assist women transitioning from prison to the community. A number of Australian interviewees drew attention to the fact that services for women have been defunded or received reduced funding in recent years, including women's drug and alcohol services, mental health services, homelessness services, and support for women leaving prison. As Kat Armstrong (WIPAN) told us:

> How many women's services have been cut, and what an enormous effect that has had? So yes, there must always be services specific for women because women have very different issues and needs than men do. Yes, [we] all live in the community together, but...women are women, men are men and both have different needs, wants, abilities, different health issues, different backgrounds and so there

should always be services available to meet whatever those needs are and yes, definitely to have specific women services.

There is also a need to understand the broader changes in economic and social policy brought about through neo-liberalism, and how these specifically impact women, including their offending, their likelihood of incarceration and the specific problems they face on release from prison. Restrictions on access to welfare, the feminisation of poverty, changes in the labour market and a shift to low paid jobs (Mosher, 2010; Kruttschnitt, 2011: 905) are likely to have exacerbated levels of disadvantage that contribute to women's incarceration. In addition the rise of welfare conditionality has imposed a raft of new obligations that involve increased systems of regulation and surveillance as a condition of receiving social services. In some cases, failure to satisfy these obligations can attract criminal penalties. As Wacquant (2009a: 288) has argued, social welfare has come to be informed by the same values and philosophies as criminal justice: deterrence, surveillance, stigma and graduated sanctions. These changes impact on women, and particularly those from racialised groups.

While these macro changes in economic and social policy have specific localised impacts on poor working class and racialised communities, they also pose particular problems for place-based initiatives. As Stubbs (forthcoming) argues there has been little research on how these broader changes have impacted on women's criminalisation and the rising rate of women's imprisonment (see also Kruttschnitt, 2011; LeBaron and Roberts, 2010; Mosher, 2010). The absence of such research 'is likely to hinder the development of JR approaches with the capacity to prevent crime and drive down women's incarceration by focusing on the social determinants of crime' (Stubbs, forthcoming).

The reach of the criminal law will also impact on the criminalisation of women, potential avenues for justice reinvestment reform and the efficacy of place-based initiatives. In particular, we note the higher level of criminalisation of women in the USA for drug offences that do not attract the same level of punitiveness in Australia. And we draw attention to the fact that some activities have been decriminalised in Australia but not in the USA. In particular, prostitution is illegal in all jurisdictions in the USA (except for a few counties in Nevada). Maximum penalties in most US states range from 30 days to 12 months imprisonment for sex workers – which adds significantly to the 'churn' of women through the prison system, women who also may have issues with drugs and alcohol, mental health and homelessness.

One particular issue that emerged from our research which is directly related to the efficacy of justice reinvestment as a place-based approach was the extent to which women exiting prison returned to the communities from where they came. Australian focus group participants from a number of women's ex-prisoner support services noted the following:

> Ms Nash: I think it [a place-based approach] is about where people come from, not where they're going as well. Because the vast majority of women that we work with do not return to their place of origin because they have accrued a history of criminalisation which –
>
> Ms Roach: Or they get housing somewhere else.
>
> Ms Nash: – which will make it very difficult for them to return to that community. So place-based is very problematic from a whole...
>
> Ms Kilroy: I suppose my point is place-based isn't going to work for women coming out of prison. That's the point I'm making, simple and clear, because women go to many different places, they're not going to one place as such. (Women's focus group)

A range of factors is likely to influence whether women exiting prison return to the same communities. Individual decisions are likely to be constrained by, or dependent on, considerations such as protection from violence, access to children, access to housing, on-going legal requirements affecting residency such as parole conditions, and so on. Indigenous women exiting prison may have additional factors influencing their decisions given they have more dependent children and higher rates of mental health disorders, domestic and sexual violence, homelessness and of return to prison, than their non-Indigenous counterparts (Baldry, Ruddock and Taylor, 2008: 9–10). For Indigenous women from remote communities there may be additional factors both pulling them back to the community (such as kinship and relation to land), and preventing their return (the difficulties and costs in travel from regional and urban prisons back to remote communities which can be many hundreds of kilometres from their point of release).

Specific demographic contexts will also impact on the location of disadvantaged and criminalised women. For example, members of women's services in the Australian Capital Territory (ACT) told us in an interview that research had found that:

> [T]he most marginalised populations in the ACT were women, in single parent households usually, but what [the report] really

highlighted was that in the ACT unlike every other state and jurisdiction, disadvantage [is] masked because the concentrations of people are spread through every suburb... So, we have this really different issue around place-based stuff because we can't define them all as being in one area... So Canberra's quite different. (Marcia Williams, Women's Centre for Health Matters)

However, if women do not return to the same community from where they came prior to imprisonment, it is perhaps likely they will return to a community with a similar demography. Baldry's (2014) research on institutional pathways into the NSW criminal justice system for people with mental and/or cognitive disabilities found that 40 per cent of the Indigenous women in the cohort were living in and moving between just three suburbs, while 32 per cent of all women were concentrated in just three inner-city Sydney suburbs. 'Most of the suburbs and towns had chronically low levels of income, poor educational outcomes, high levels of policing, high unemployment, high rates of violence and alcohol and drug use, and lack of culturally appropriate disability services' (ibid.: 383).

Justice reinvestment and women in the USA

There is little evidence that policies or programs have been developed to specifically respond to the identified needs of women, and there have been only a few examples in the USA where concerns about the rising rates of women's imprisonment have informed the development of JRI legislation (e.g., Rhode Island, New Hampshire, Oklahoma, South Dakota and a local JRI initiative in Denver, Colorado). We discuss two differing examples in more detail below: Denver and South Dakota.

Denver, Colorado

At the time of the research, there was a local-level JRI project in Denver, Colorado, that was still in its early stages of development. The project showed some potential to develop programs that were more responsive to women, minorities and other vulnerable groups. However, it also demonstrated challenges that might arise, especially where women were too few to generate adequate savings. An initial assessment suggested the need to focus on a 'population of justice-involved women with families affected by domestic violence' (CEPP, n.d.). However, an analysis of the data yielded a 'target population that was too small to meet JRI objectives' (ibid.). As a consequence, the focus moved to frequent users of the criminal justice system, who commonly had substance abuse and or mental health problems. An application for funding was sought for a front-end approach, that included case management, trauma informed services and 'culturally informed care'. There was explicit acknowledgment of gender, race, ethnicity, religion and other social categories (ibid.). Whether this local-level JRI project develops further is dependent on a range of factors including political support for the proposal and funding.

Stubbs (forthcoming) notes that while the Denver project suggests the possibility of planning JRI programs that are responsive to diverse needs and interests, and to keeping women in focus, that outcome is unlikely without an analytical approach that examines how the drivers of incarceration may work differently for different groups and for those at the intersection of social categories (Bosworth and Kaufman 2013, Bumiller 2013).

Rapid City, South Dakota

We discussed in general terms the development of JRI initiatives in South Dakota in the previous chapter. South Dakota has been unusual because the rise in the women's prison population (and particularly that of Native American women) was one of the drivers for considering and then developing justice reinvestment. As the South Dakota Governor, Dennis Duagaard explained to us, 'The most significant cost that we foresaw was the incarceration pace was leading to us needing to build a new women's prison in a couple of years and a new men's prison a few years after that'. The focus on women's imprisonment was a key factor in building support for change. Jim Seward, general counsel to the South Dakota Governor, observed:

> Our women's population had grown to an all-time high... We looked at our data, and it showed that our incarceration rates were way above the regional average and much above the national average... One of the things we would tell stakeholder groups: in 1976, South Dakota had 13 women locked up, 13 women in prison. We didn't even have a women's prison, it was in Nebraska. We rented beds from Nebraska. When we were doing these meetings we had hit 460 in our [women's] prison and we were about to have to knock a hole in the wall and build another one. That was in less than my life time. And as we were visiting with law enforcement guys, who were maybe 60 years old. They were saying, "Wow, that is in my career, I started in 1976 when we had 13 women, now we have 460". I would say congratulations you have really done a marvellous job. We were locking up

women at four times the rate of Minnesota. Some people would say, "Well we have a lot more drugs here". I would say, well show me the data. I look at Minnesota, and while we don't agree politically, they don't look like they're out of control. They don't look like they have women running around in the streets doing bad things to people and not being held accountable.

A focus on women was also used to get buy-in from conservative groups who might otherwise have perceived justice reinvestment as part of a liberal, soft-on crime initiative. This was achieved by presenting women's incarceration as part of a pro-family narrative.

At the time of the research, South Dakota was applying for funds to establish a pilot program that would involve housing, treatment and support services in Rapid City for women on probation and parole. A number of factors underpinned the decision to develop the project. It was recognised that drug use (particularly crystal meth) was a major contributing factor to women's incarceration and failure while on parole or probation. Further it was an issue that particularly affected Native American women who make-up over 40 per cent of the women's prison population (South Dakota Department of Corrections, 2015). One of the largest Indian reservations in South Dakota, Pine Ridge Indian Reservation, is situated relatively close to Rapid City.

Which place-based justice reinvestment processes are likely to most benefit women?

Lanning, Loader and Muir (2011: 14–6), propose that justice reinvestment for women offenders should involve: pre-court diversion, revised sentencing guidelines and increased investment in community-based alternatives that might increase the confidence of sentencers in noncustodial alternatives. The Women's Justice Taskforce (2011) of the UK Prison Reform Trust recommended justice reinvestment programs for women with savings to be reinvested 'to support women's centres and other effective services for women offenders and vulnerable women in the community' (ibid.: 3). The Corston Report (2007), a major review of women's imprisonment in the UK, endorsed the establishment of women's centres as key sources of support for women offenders. Support has been provided for women's centres as part of the justice reinvestment initiative in Greater Manchester, although, as Stubbs (forthcoming) notes, no other UK schemes appear to focus on women's needs in their programs. As we examine further in the next chapter, analysis of the positive effects of women's centres and the provision of social housing for women offenders can have a substantial cost-saving benefit.

It is apparent that front-end measures designed to keep less serious offenders out of prison are better aligned with the characteristics of many women inmates. As Kat Armstrong (WIPAN) explained:

> Given my experience in prison, which [was] almost 10 years, and given as I say, the women that I walk beside each and every day, the trauma that happens as a result of imprisonment itself is enormous and it continues to have effect on the woman. So if we can actually minimise that and not have that at all and actually look at her as the human being that she is and okay, "Who is she?", "What's her background?", "Why did she commit offences in the first place?" and not even let her go through the trauma of being criminalised and imprisoned, I would definitely say don't even let her go there, don't even go there.

When asked how justice reinvestment might serve the interests of criminalised women, Kathy McFie, an ex-prisoner and now a worker at the Women and Prisons Group in the ACT, replied:

> Access to services [for women] that would give them the support in order to prevent them from going into prison. So by that, they need good access to organisations that can deal with the issues that they have, that would ultimately if they didn't have that support lead them into prison, things like drug and alcohol support, counselling and domestic violence services. All those sorts of things, they need to be readily available... If it comes to a woman being imprisoned, they need to be dealt with right from the word go, not "alright, put them in touch with people after they've left the prison".

The current lack of gender specific policies and programs to assist criminalised women, combined with the increasing rates of female imprisonment, suggests that gender neutral justice reinvestment is unlikely to benefit women. The available research indicates that strategies to reduce women's incarceration rates need to be targeted for women, with a focus on front-end measures (diversion, community-based sanctions, specific programs and social support) rather than on back-end measures such as parole and post-release support which are commonly used in existing justice reinvestment programs in the USA. These front-end measures are also ones that are particularly conducive to development through a place-based approach.

Justice reinvestment and Indigenous nations

There have been many names given to Indigenous collectivities, including clans, tribes, language groups, communities and peoples. However, it is clear that 'nations' is the concept that best conceptualises the importance of Indigenous governance and self-determination (ATSISJC, 2014:130). In both the USA and Australia, Indigenous *nation-building* is an important priority for Indigenous peoples and organisations, and this includes developing and strengthening community and organisational governance structures which reflect Indigenous control, priorities, laws and culture. However, there are significantly different legal and political histories to Australia and the USA which impact on how the Indigenous nation-building is understood at a practical level. Indian nationhood and sovereignty was recognised by the US Supreme Court in a number of judgments in the 1820s and 1830s through the doctrine of 'domestic dependent nations'. Despite subsequent whittling away by US Congress, a number of federally-recognised tribes continue to exercise governmental authority. As far as we are aware, no Indian tribal governments have applied for or received funding under the JRI. In the case of South Dakota, discussed in the previous chapter, three tribal authorities are participating in a JRI project initiated at the state level. The six other tribal governments in South Dakota are not participants. It is important to recognise that Indian tribal participation in a state-based JRI project may be perceived as *negatively affecting tribal authority and sovereignty* if it involves giving up exclusive jurisdiction (e.g., in relation to state-based probation and parole which would normally have no authority on Indian country).

The situation in Australia for Indigenous people is considerably different, where the higher courts have consistently held that Indigenous people had not attained either the numbers or the status of 'civilised nations' that could be recognised as sovereign states governed by their own laws. What is particularly interesting with Indigenous discussions on justice reinvestment in Australia is that they are presented as an *opportunity to exercise authority*. Indigenous approaches to justice reinvestment transform an understanding of the process well beyond simply a technocratic means of crime control and de-incarceration, to one that is centrally concerned with Indigenous-controlled governance. This more radical vision of justice reinvestment has important wider implications: it is conceived within broader social democratic ideals of participatory involvement and localised democratic decision-making, and specifically in the Indigenous context, aligns with the collective right of self-determination.

There is a conceptual, political and policy relationship between a place-based approach to criminal justice through justice reinvestment, and an Indigenous prioritisation of the importance of Indigenous nations and Indigenous governance. There are at least three broad points of coalescence. The first is the emphasis on place. The geographic localism underpinning justice reinvestment strongly aligns with an Indigenous emphasis on Indigenous nations and communities, particularly in regional, rural and remote areas where Indigenous people reside in distinct communities. The second is the value placed on community control, community development and cooperation between local services. According to the ATSISJC (2014: 108) these 'align with what we know about human rights-based practice in [Indigenous] service delivery'. The third point is that a flexible approach to the concept of place-based, and a recognition that community can include both a reference to a 'community of interest' as well as a geographic community, has particular resonance for Indigenous people living in urban locations where they may constitute a small minority in a large non-Indigenous urbanised environment. For example, in Australia in all states and territories the localities yielding the highest number of Indigenous prisoners are in capital cities and regional cities (ATSISJC, 2009: Appendix 2). Recognising the importance of Indigenous nations as extending beyond specific geographic locations means that Indigenous community-controlled organisations can play a fundamental role in developing justice reinvestment initiatives for Indigenous people, irrespective of whether they reside in a remote community or in a large metropolitan city.

Justice reinvestment and Indigenous peoples in Australia

We outlined in Chapter 1 the various justice reinvestment initiatives in Australia. What is particularly distinct about these is that in general the greatest uptake of justice reinvestment has been by Indigenous organisations and other coalitions that are applying justice reinvestment specifically to the context of Indigenous imprisonment.

The former ATSISJC (ibid.: 56), Tom Calma, was among the first to promote justice reinvestment in Australia, which he argued was 'a pragmatic solution to the problem of Indigenous imprisonment. ... based on some sound principles that meld with Indigenous perspectives and approaches'. The current ATSISJC, Mick Gooda (2014:115), has emphasised the importance of the place-based and community-driven focus to justice reinvestment: 'the real underlying power of justice reinvestment has always been in the place-based approach of community involvement and capacity building to create safer communities'.

Three of the four Australian inquiries that made recommendations around justice reinvestment also specifically recommended conducting pilot projects in Indigenous communities (HRSC, 2011; Noetic Solutions, 2010; LCARC, 2013). The National Congress of Australia's First Peoples (2013) and the National Justice Coalition (representing various Indigenous and non-Indigenous legal and other peak bodies) also advocated justice reinvestment in Indigenous communities with high rates of incarceration. The National Justice Coalition has tied the importance of considering justice reinvestment to the failure of successive federal governments to set targets for the reduction of Indigenous over-representation in the criminal justice system, despite other social, economic and health targets being set in the Commonwealth *Closing the Gap* agenda (COAG, 2007; see also ATSISJC, 2009).

As a result of this interest, several coalitions are working to promote the adoption of justice reinvestment in Australia, especially for Indigenous young people, and some groups are now working directly with communities to develop pilot projects. Place-based justice reinvestment initiatives in Indigenous communities are in various stages in Bourke and Cowra (NSW), Palm Island (Qld), Ceduna (SA), Mowanjum (WA) and Katherine (NT). The most developed of these projects is the Just Reinvest Project in Bourke, which we discuss at greater length below. A further distinguishing feature of the development of justice reinvestment in Australia is that in general the focus has been on Indigenous juveniles and young people rather than adults.[2] All of the more developed justice reinvestment projects have this focus, largely because the chronic failures of the justice system are more pronounced and the long-term negative effects more extreme with Indigenous young people as confirmed in our interviews with Priscilla Collins and Jared White (North Australia Aboriginal Justice Association (NAAJA)), Sarah Hopkins (Just Reinvest NSW) and Mick Gooda (ATSISJC).

Thus justice reinvestment in the Australian context, at least as it has been conceptualised by Indigenous organisations and the non-Indigenous community sector, has commonly emphasised the potential it holds for building community capacity using place-based strategies that respond to local needs and conditions, and enhance social inclusion.

> I guess the biggest opportunity I see for something like justice reinvestment is the opportunity for [Indigenous] communities to invest themselves in these issues and to feel as though there is something that could be done by the community to make a change, because so much of the experience is that this happens to us and we have no

control and there are all these forces and powers which we are just washed around in. (Peta MacGillivray, UNSW)

In explaining the development of a pilot justice reinvestment project in Katherine in the NT, Priscilla Collins, the CEO of the NAAJA commented, '[Aboriginal] people just keep getting locked up, and there's so much money poured into the end of it...and it doesn't break the cycle. So that's why we have a huge focus on justice reinvestment, so we look at why people come in contact with the system'. Indigenous victim support groups, including Indigenous family violence legal services in Victoria and the NT, have also supported justice reinvestment (see submissions to the LCARC, 2013).

Justice reinvestment has been conceptualised as a way of strengthening Indigenous culture and existing organisational structures.

> In the Northern Territory you've actually got communities that have these structures in place [such as Aboriginal law and justice groups in the Tiwi Islands and Lajamanu] but would just need the support to actually run those programs properly...The thing about justice reinvestment is Aboriginal people have been doing this early intervention stuff for generations and it's something that's always been there but there's no financial support or resources available, so it [justice reinvestment] can work in a community, it just needs the government to focus on getting it up and running. (Priscilla Collins, NAAJA)

This view was similarly expressed by Tammy Solonec (2014: 6) who, when referring to Indigenous programs in Perth and the Kimberleys, noted that they were 'founded on the concept of culture as a preventative mechanism'. It is important then to recognise that justice reinvestment is evolving to meet the needs of Indigenous peoples. As Mick Gooda has noted, justice reinvestment 'will require thoughtful adaptation to the Australian context' (ATSISJC, 2014: 102).

A core part of this adaptation is respect for Indigenous culture and ways of doing things. For non-Indigenous people and organisations (both government and non-government) this involves a substantial shift and much greater flexibility. As Sarah Hopkins from Just Reinvest NSW recalled in the context of justice reinvestment meetings in Bourke:

> I mean none of it's easy, getting community engagement is not easy. I had to learn myself that you can't set a schedule, you can't tick off an agenda list, that there's that kind of flexibility and organic nature

of the process that you have to respect and, of course, it's culture first you have to respect...We would have a meeting where we got everyone we needed in the community in Bourke and it was like, "Great. Here we are." I'm going, "Great, we're going to get so much done today," and then welcome to country. Phil, this gorgeous man, just says, "Okay. Does anyone want to talk about someone who's passed away, but still has an impact that they're still thinking about a lot?" Well, two hours later, there goes the meeting because everyone just starts talking about how important this person was to them and whatever, and I just think, "Okay. This is what we're doing today."

We turn now to discuss the Just Reinvest NSW project in Bourke in more detail.

Just Reinvest NSW, Bourke

In the case of Indigenous people, many social and economic initiatives that are referred to as 'place-based' are top-down approaches by government, often as a response to social disorder. The problems and the solutions are predefined by government, and consultation and engagement with communities is largely about implementing what has already been decided (see Gilbert, 2012 for some examples of these top-down government approaches). By contrast, we see the Just Reinvest NSW project in Bourke as a good example of a 'bottom-up' approach, where priorities and processes are identified at the local level through community meetings and community-based organisations.

Just Reinvest NSW is an incorporated association established by a small group of people working with Indigenous young people in the criminal justice system. In 2012 it launched the Justice Reinvestment for Aboriginal Young People Campaign with the aim of bringing about a change in government policy through the adoption of justice reinvestment. Latter in the same year the Bourke Aboriginal community[3] approached Just Reinvest NSW with the view to developing a justice reinvestment model in Bourke to reduce the involvement of Aboriginal young people in the criminal justice system. Sarah Hopkins from Just Reinvest NSW explained to us the initial process:

Bourke approached *us*. So the opportunity that arose, we thought that for this to work, because it was such a complex challenge, it had to be a community on the front foot wanting to do it and so because they had sought us out, we thought the data works there, now let's go talk to them.

I think from the outset then...it was about community engagement and making sure there was a consensus in the community. Because again we thought we needed to avoid any sense of a top down approach. We don't want to come and say, "These are our ideas, what do you think?" We really wanted the ideas to come from the community. So the first idea was, "Do you want to prioritise youth offending and incarceration rates and public safety, community safety?"

We had three separate visits really just to get that question answered, and one of those was a community forum where about 60 people in the community came, and the answer has been "yes". I think that it's clearly a priority of the community to address the problems facing the young people, it's the top of the list, and then of course at the top of that list, they want to be a safer community.

On the basis of community support, a proposal was developed by the Bourke community with the assistance of Just Reinvest NSW and the Australian Human Rights Commission to engage government, philanthropic and corporate support for the Bourke project. This led to the development of a consortium of partners providing some funding and in-kind support (ATSISJC, 2014: 111). A number of interviewees noted the importance of developing justice reinvestment in Bourke in a way that was not 'beholden to government'. Support from philanthropists and the corporate sector enabled a much greater flexibility and community control over setting priorities, and the nature of how justice reinvestment could develop in a local setting.

The structure for initiating justice reinvestment in Bourke developed in an organic fashion from the community. Maranguka is a community initiative 'substructure' that comprises an executive officer, a project officer, two consultants, Aboriginal and non-Aboriginal members, the business community, shire council, and key players in the community who support justice reinvestment and can assist in engaging the whole community. As Sarah Hopkins (Just Reinvest NSW) explains:

Maranguka convene meetings of the different service providers, say the drug and alcohol service providers in Bourke, they might include mental health with that, so one big group, early childhood, maybe victims' services – to convene a number of meetings of service providers and with key community members there to identify what is the agenda, what are the priorities, and then what would success look like if things were working in that particular area well, what does the community say success will look like and what's the service provider feedback on that.

Apart from Maranguka there is the Bourke Tribal Council, which is a council of Indigenous families and clans. The Council has developed as a consequence of the justice reinvestment project and has an oversight and approval role for any recommendations arising from Maranguka.

However, community buy-in to the justice reinvestment project in Bourke has also involved the non-Indigenous community. As Mick Gooda (ATSISJC) explained to us in an interview:

> We had fairly good buy-in by the council, particularly at the CEO level... There were a couple of young women on the council who are really important. So they see that's really important that it's seen as a Bourke strategy, not just the Bourke Aboriginal strategy... There's a bit of self-interest in it because they actually think... place-based budgets are something we should be all pursuing. Like what is the Bourke budget, for instance?

An important part of the foundation for developing justice reinvestment was the establishment of a series of youth engagement sessions for young people 16 to 25 years old. A number of issues arose from these sessions including warrants, driver licensing offences and bail. As a result a specific program of warrants clinics was developed. The clinics enable young people with outstanding arrest warrants to meet with a local support team to address their needs (such as drug and alcohol misuse) instead of presenting to police. The aim of the clinics is to show the magistrate that the young person has started to address his or her offending, and therefore persuade the magistrate not to impose a sentence of detention (see Just Reinvest NSW, 2015a).

An important development with the justice reinvestment project in Bourke has been the use of a collective impact methodology. As the ATSISJC (2014: 111) explains, a collective impact methodology involves diverse organisations from a range of sectors committing to jointly solving complex social problems. At a practical level this involves developing a common agenda for change, a joint approach, mutually reinforcing activities, continuous communication and coordination and shared measurement for outcomes and accountability. As the ATSISJC (ibid.: 111) notes, 'collective impact has synergies with community development and may translate the more conceptual elements of justice reinvestment to a practical level'.

The community initiative has been fundamental to developing justice reinvestment in Bourke. Along with its support from the non-governmental philanthropic and corporate sectors, this is seen as one of the innovative outcomes of the Bourke project. Unlike the developments in the UK and the USA, 'we're not talking about state-based, state-wide initiatives, finding funds and then injecting it into a community' (Sarah Hopkins, Just Reinvest NSW). A significant amount of time was spent building relationships and a commonality of approach among stakeholders and the community.

> They spoke for 18 months amongst themselves... From the outside, it doesn't look like they're doing much. But what they did was actually build the community's capacity. My role was really going out there, being an independent chair of community meetings for a while, then using my position to open doors like the council, getting Scullion [the Federal Minister] out there; those sort of things. But they've basically done it themselves, but it's been a long process... That's the main lesson for governments; it takes time. If you went out there, for instance, and said, like governments do; "well what you need is a community plan and just, by the way, we've got someone who'll come and write one for you." I don't know how many plans I've been involved with where nothing happens. (Mick Gooda, ATSISJC)

Indigenous governance and community capacity building has been at the heart of the way justice reinvestment has been conceived within an Indigenous context in Australia. The challenge will be to ensure that governments understand that 'partnering' with communities is not mere rhetoric which too often means that communities do not have genuine involvement in decision-making about identifying, naming and developing solutions to their problems. The requirement of committing to doing things in a way that diverges from past practice has particular resonance given the USA experience of *lack* of involvement of local individuals and community-based organisations in justice reinvestment.

Also at the heart of the Indigenous approach in Australia has been the importance of a place-based focus to justice reinvestment. There is the obvious resonance of this with Indigenous people living in more remote and rural communities where place-based can be seen literally in a distinct geographical community. However, we also acknowledge that place-based approaches can be conceptualised in the context of 'communities of interest'. Indigenous people form distinct communities because of their extended family, clan, cultural and tribal connections, not simply because they live in a particular locality. This point is important if we want to think about justice reinvestment for Indigenous people living in larger urban areas, and the role that Indigenous organisations might play in developing justice reinvestment.

Conclusion

We set out in this chapter to examine some of the issues that arise with place-based approaches and definitions of community that underpin justice reinvestment. As a focus, we specifically examined these issues in the context of people with mental illness and/or cognitive impairment, women and Indigenous peoples. Broadly speaking, we have argued that a place-based approach can have significant benefits for these groups where their specific needs and aspirations are clearly articulated and are developed within justice reinvestment initiatives.

Having said that, we should acknowledge some of the limitations of place-based approaches. One consideration that requires further thought is the extent to which justice reinvestment can make significant inroads into structural conditions of disadvantage. We noted in the USA that justice reinvestment has by and large eschewed confronting directly the racialised aspects of punishment and has mostly ignored Indigenous issues. In the Australian setting, it is important to recognise that the structural disadvantage in Indigenous communities adds a level of complexity that needs special consideration in the justice reinvestment context. The structural disadvantage of Indigenous people is both contemporaneous (all the social, economic and health indicators highlight the depth of this disadvantage) and historical (the position of Indigenous peoples arose directly from historical conditions of colonialism). Or in the case of women, we might ask to what extent can justice reinvestment overcome gender-based inequality that pervades so much of social and economic life? The contemporary absence of gender-based interests in justice reinvestment does little to indicate that these concerns will be addressed unless women's needs are directly considered when developing place-based approaches. To the extent that mental illness and/or cognitive impairment has been a feature of justice reinvestment, thus far it is usually in the framework of addressing homelessness.

The questions identified above become even more complex when placed within an intersectional framework of gender, race and disability. The case of Roseanne Fulton highlights the way place-based approaches working at the community level might offer certain opportunities if they are conceptualised in a way that is cognisant of complex needs and intersectional points of oppression. Roseanne Fulton, a young Aboriginal woman from Alice Springs in the NT, was arrested for traffic offences in WA. She has fetal alcohol spectrum disorder and a history of abuse and displacement. She was assessed by the court as being unfit to plead, but was imprisoned for over 18 months for lack of suitable supported community accommodation. There was a widespread public campaign to have Ms. Fulton released from prison. The Commonwealth government wrote to both WA and NT governments requesting them to take action. Ms. Fulton was returned to Alice Springs in July 2014. However, she was not provided with the intensive disability supports she requires. As a result she was again arrested for behaviour associated with her disability, and again incarcerated, this time in the Alice Springs prison (Baldry, 2014: 370–71). Her story highlights the failure to consider her specific position as an Indigenous woman with complex needs.

Effective place-based approaches to criminal justice reform will require a number of commitments to the way we (and in particularly, governments) do things: political commitments to local decision-making and governance structures, the development and strengthening of local capacity to respond to criminal justice problems, and the actual financial reinvestment to allow these changes to occur. Otherwise we run the risk, as Cadora (2014: 284) laments of the current situation in the USA, that 'if reforms aimed at ending mass incarceration are not formally linked to community reinvestment that addresses the deep collateral consequences of decades of criminalisation, we will have missed the opportunity that today's emerging openness to reform presents'. As we noted with the Bourke example in this chapter, we do not suggest that community engagement and community development is an easy task. And engagement is further complicated in working with marginalised and socially excluded groups. We need to always ask the question: is the focus on community as a 'whole' likely to mask specific needs based on difference?

Throughout this chapter we have discussed the importance of a social justice oriented approach to community and place as a necessary component of justice reinvestment. We have suggested that human rights are a key part of the normative framework of a social justice approach. We note here that there are broad normative principles including non-discrimination and rights to participation, access and social inclusion that are fundamental. Baldry (2014: 380) notes that the principle of least restriction is an important protective principle in the support for and care of people with mental and/or cognitive disability in heath and justice settings. This principle requires that people be treated in the least restrictive environment and with the least restrictive or intrusive treatment needed to protect them and others. In the area of Indigenous rights, there are well-articulated norms such as respect, recognition and specific Indigenous rights, including the right to self-determination. In this regard, the opportunities generated with a place-based approach to justice reinvestment are shown in the Bourke case study above. Indeed, justice reinvestment has directly assisted with developing Indigenous nation-building through the Bourke Tribal Council.

We also acknowledge that what constitutes a social justice approach to crime and punishment is far from settled. One obvious dichotomy is between reform and abolitionism, as Debbie Kilroy from Sisters Inside identified in an interview:

> So it's an issue of language that I have, and it's an issue of what the values [are] that drives this so called justice reinvestment, because it's unclear. So we need to have a starting position. Is the starting position the abolition of prisons and if so, then you can actually move forward and think about what the action actually is to de-incarcerate and decriminalise. Otherwise, if it's just about rearranging the deck chairs well, you know, I'm not interested in being a party to that. Because we're seeing that all the time and that's called reform and, you know, it's just tinkering around the edges of fundamentally failed systems.

However, with the caveats noted throughout this chapter, we see a place-based and social justice-oriented approach to justice reinvestment as offering real opportunities for reducing imprisonment.

4
Justice Reinvestment, Evidence-based Policy and Practice: In Search of Social Justice

Justice reinvestment is avowedly data-driven and evidence-based, features that stand in contrast to common approaches to criminal justice policy-making in many jurisdictions. The added impetus towards evidence-based approaches generated by justice reinvestment largely has been welcomed (Clear, 2010). However, what is measured and what counts as evidence are important considerations with significant implications. These are more than simply technical matters. This chapter examines the way in which evidence-based policy and practice (EBP) has been conceptualised and given effect through the methodologies and measures commonly used in justice reinvestment, and how this, in turn, has influenced the direction of justice reinvestment. The chapter also notes some other possible conceptions of evidence and forms of measurement that may be more congruent with the aspirations towards a justice reinvestment that is social justice-oriented.

As we discussed in previous chapters, early proponents of justice reinvestment saw its progressive possibility, especially to redress the disproportionate effects of mass incarceration on marginalised people and their communities. Tucker and Cadora (2003) stress reinvestment in communities that generate large numbers of inmates and to which inmates return in an effort to ameliorate the conditions associated with crime. Cadora (2014: 279) labels this 'a civic ecology of public safety'. Others describe this as a social justice-oriented justice reinvestment. Within Australia, support for justice reinvestment largely accords with a social justice-oriented approach directed towards (re)building community capacity using place-based strategies that respond to local needs and conditions (Schwartz, 2010), address the social determinants of incarceration and contribute to social inclusion (Guthrie, Levy and Fforde, 2013). Proponents of justice reinvestment have emphasised the potential of such an approach to reduce incarceration rates, especially for Indigenous young people; to benefit victims of crime through reinvestment in community services and to respond to other vulnerable groups such as people with psychosocial, cognitive or another impairment (Gooda, Priday and McDermott, 2013). A social justice-oriented justice reinvestment thus offers both normative and instrumental foundations for reform intended to redress mass incarceration. However, international experience demonstrates that there are significant methodological challenges to realising a social justice-oriented vision of justice reinvestment.

The shift in the focus of JRI from *reinvesting in high incarceration communities* to reinvesting in *'high-performing public safety strategies'* (Urban Institute, 2013: 1, emphasis added) was discussed in earlier chapters. This shift may reflect the pragmatic face of the JRI and the political limits on what is seen as achievable. However, the methodologies employed and the measures used in giving effect to justice reinvestment have also contributed to this shift, and the JRI practitioners have shored up those measures by repeatedly endorsing them. For instance, the premium accorded to some forms of evidence and to 'what works' has encouraged the redesign of criminal justice systems – often focused on programs to reduce recidivism – as a key objective of the JRI (Clear, 2012). This approach undoubtedly has assisted policy-makers and practitioners to choose interventions that have been endorsed within EBP frameworks as (cost) effective. However, this narrower focus on the delivery of programs is in tension with the visions of justice reinvestment that focus on place-based initiatives and community redevelopment (Tucker and Cadora, 2003).

Within the JRI, EBP draws heavily on general theories of crime and much of the analysis has been at the individual level. The risk-needs-responsivity framework developed by psychologists (Andrews, Bonta and Hoge, 1990) to explain individual differences in criminal behaviour and predict recidivism has been enormously influential. However, the origins, focus and purpose of the framework – that is, using theories drawn from individual psychology to predict recidivism and identify principles of effective intervention with universal application – differ markedly from the focus on enhancing public safety by revitalising neighbourhoods within the community ecology perspective associated with Tucker and Cadora (2003). This approach to EBP is also at odds with other criminological perspectives that give greater emphasis to structural factors associated with crime and patterns in incarceration and to the differential effects of social policy and criminal justice interventions upon different groups.

Wacquant's (2009a) analysis of the ways in which the penal state and the retrenchment of the welfare state work together and affect marginalised people has been influential within penology. Commentary suggests that while his analysis may be over-generalised and may gloss over gendered social relations (Bumiller, 2013) and tensions and contradictions within neo-liberalism (Brown, 2013), the themes he identifies are salient in many nations influenced by local cultures, conditions and politics. The differential impact of more punitive laws, harsher criminal justice policies and practices, and tighter welfare eligibility and policing of welfare compliance have been noted in countries such as the USA (Beckett and Western, 2001; Kruttschnitt, 2011), UK (Player, 2014: 281–2, 289), Australia (Cunneen *et al.*, 2013) and Canada (Chunn and Gavigan, 2006). As reviewed in Chapter 3, this suggests the need for significant attention to the social determinants of incarceration and to its effects on different groups.

To date, these concerns have not been front and centre in most justice reinvestment schemes. However, even in narrowly economic terms, 'it makes little sense to speak of the "average" prisoner' (Lengyel and Brown, 2009: 47). The form of EBP common to the JRI has been strongly associated with a focus on programs for offenders and to some extent has displaced other considerations. For instance, less attention has been paid to the social determinants of incarceration, the development of alternatives outside the criminal justice system, reinvestment in communities or how best to measure the social costs and benefits of interventions. There has been limited critical analysis of what counts as evidence, the measures used and to whom they are applied, or the kinds of public safety strategies that are endorsed (notable exceptions include: Austin *et al.*, 2013; Clear, 2010; Fox, Albertson and Wong 2013a, 2013b; Fox and Grimm, 2015).

Economic analysis and justice reinvestment

Justice reinvestment is dependent on economic analysis and quantification. Data measuring correctional expenditures and an analysis of factors driving incarceration are used to generate policy options and identify potential savings. Estimates of the costs of programs – and in some models also the benefits – help identify those likely to be (cost) effective and are used to inform policy choices and reform packages. Conceptions of what constitutes evidence shape the approach taken to evaluation and the outcome measures that are used (Clement, Schwarzfeld and Thompson, 2011: 8). Indeed Wong, Fox and Albertson

(2014: 79) suggest that '[t]he overriding distinguishing feature of JR is its reliance for validity on economic theory'.

Economic theory and assumptions that have their roots in economic theory are used in a range of different ways within justice reinvestment, and some models are more strongly aligned with economic approaches than others. Those that emphasise economic analysis tend to be more instrumental, with a greater focus on the pursuit of efficiencies in the use of criminal justice resources and less attention to normative concerns (Tonry, 2011a). However, an economic approach need not preclude normative considerations. Indeed, as discussed below, UK scholars Fox, Albertson, and Wong (2013a) have presented a new theoretical framework for justice reinvestment that draws on economics in the pursuit of social justice.

Economic analyses of mass incarceration have commonly identified a misalignment of supply side and demand side incentives. There is common agreement that the growth in incarceration evident in many countries in recent decades has been demand driven and largely due to changes in sentencing and other criminal justice practices, rather than crime rates. However, governments typically have responded with a supply side solution, that is, by building more prisons and jails, but this does not address the underlying factors driving the growth in incarceration (on the UK see Fox and Albertson, 2010: 266). However, this misalignment has been understood in different ways and with different implications.

Eric Cadora (2014: 280) has described the era of mass incarceration as 'animated by a mythology of public safety' which relies on 'a zero-sum economy where weak civil institutions (such as failing schools) can be compensated for by strengthening and expanding the institutions and activities of criminal justice (such as juvenile detention facilities)'. He has argued that challenging this mythology requires a focus on the misalignment of supply side and demand side incentives, which he analyses at the level of the neighbourhood and community. The supply side involves substantial and increasing public expenditure on 'discretionary public safety costs (namely, expensive prisons) which were becoming long-term obligations as fixed operating costs; this, despite historic drops in crime' (ibid.). In Cadora's account (ibid.), the demand side involves a 'human services problem – cities and counties were witnessing deepening pockets of concentrated impoverishment in neighborhoods where unprecedented concentrations of criminal justice governance had become the norm...[with] direct cost-for-cost tradeoffs'. He contrasts inefficient state expenditure incurred by incarcerating neighbourhood residents with 'investment policies that could yield returns in strengthened local social services and community-based institutions and networks' (ibid.).

Others have examined the demand side somewhat differently. As the emphasis of the JRI has shifted away from neighbourhoods and community reinvestment, the focus on achieving a better alignment between supply and demand has remained. However, the demand side has been more narrowly construed in criminal justice terms and at the individual level of analysis. In practice, the JRI is now more commonly characterised by reform in the criminal justice sector that is associated with cost-effective programs that have an evidence base. These are the factors that distinguish justice reinvestment from other economic approaches that also aim to cut costs. In some settings where the commitment to evidence-based reform is particularly strong, there has been substantial investment in the development of methodologies and even specialised agencies to conduct cost–benefit analyses or other evidence-based approaches.

Of course justice reinvestment also operates in a broader social, economic and political context and with reference to the specific characteristics of particular criminal justice systems. In any given setting, economic efficiency may not be the only, or even the predominant goal of justice reinvestment. Also in some contexts, forms of justice reinvestment appear to have been pursued at least in part because they are a good fit with broader governmental reforms. For instance, in the UK, distinctive approaches that are aligned with the prevailing ideology of 'marketisation' have been deployed by government.

Cost–benefit analysis

Some approaches to justice reinvestment place heavy emphasis on achieving a cost-effective allocation of criminal justice resources and this in turn has encouraged a greater use of cost–benefit analysis (CBA), which previously had limited application in criminal justice. There is no single approach to CBA within criminal justice. However, a model developed by the Washington State Institute for Public Policy (WSIPP) working with the Pew Center on the States, has been very influential. Drawing on this work, the Vera Institute for Justice has developed the Cost–benefit Knowledge Bank for Criminal Justice (www.vera.org/project/cost–benefit-knowledge-bank-criminal-justice) and associated tools for use by criminal justice practitioners. In Australia, a pilot project to apply a CBA to criminal justice programs based on the WSIPP model is being undertaken by the NSW Treasury (Cowell and Taylor, 2015).

The WSIPP (2014) 'benefit-cost investment model' identifies 'what works' to 'lower crime outcomes' using a meta-analysis of relevant studies with sufficient methodological rigour for inclusion, with a preference for random assignment studies. Next, an economic analysis using complex modelling is used to determine if the benefits of the program, as measured in dollar terms, exceed its costs. The measures used are net present values, benefit-cost ratios, and rates of return on investment. Benefits and costs are measured for program participants, taxpayers and crime victims (for instance, in terms of crime victimisation avoided). Then, the odds that the investment will at least break even are calculated. This allows comparisons to be made between different policy options. A recent WSIPP report on prison, police and programs, was described as 'similar to an investment advisor's "buy-sell" list' (Aos and Drake, 2013: 1). It has 'current information on policy options that can give taxpayers a good return on their crime fighting dollars (the "buys") as well as those well-researched strategies that apparently cannot reduce crime cost-effectively (the "sells")' (ibid.).

The WSIPP modelling methodology is subject to constant revision to refine its underlying assumptions, to improve the reliability of the data and to adjust for the limitations of the available research. For instance, Aos and Drake (2013: 10–11) note that researchers commonly use measures such as 'average daily prison population' for the 'average offender' arising from the 'average policy' but statutes or policies are more likely to target specific offences or affect different categories of offenders differently; the coefficients calculated are adjusted in an attempt to correct for such factors. Findings from the WSIPP (ibid.: 4–6) modelling based on costs in the state of Washington include that:

- community supervision of high and moderate risk offenders using the risk-need-responsivity approach produces $4.91 of crime-reduction benefits per dollar of costs;
- intensive supervision, focused solely on increased surveillance of offenders, does not reduce recidivism and is a poor investment;
- reducing prison stays by three months for lower risk offenders, reducing the prison population by 250 people (equivalent to closing a prison wing) would produce an estimated benefit of $4.34 per dollar of costs. Similar reductions for moderate risk inmates would be neutral but for high risk offenders there was a low probability of producing benefits;
- the Nurse Family Partnership for low-income families program was estimated to produce a benefit of $2.73 per dollar of costs with a 76 per cent probability of producing benefits at least equal to costs.

The cost–benefit analyses of criminal justice interventions do not always rely on meta-analysis and indeed there are relatively few areas where sufficient studies meet the threshold for meta-analysis. Research evidence is especially poor concerning interventions that might be effective for specific groups.

In Australia, as in other settler nations, there is a pressing need to reduce Indigenous incarceration rates. In a recent, rare example of the application of CBA to Indigenous Australian offenders, Deloitte Access Economics (2013) compares prison with residential drug treatment. To produce estimates, the study relies on previous research on the cost-effectiveness of drug courts and other drug treatment programs available to Indigenous people, statistical data from corrections and health agencies, and consultations with stakeholders. They estimate that residential drug treatment could produce net financial savings per offender of AUD$111,458 with a further AUD$92,759 in nonfinancial benefits to the offender based on reductions in the burden of disease of Hepatitis C and in premature mortality, costed for the financial year 2011–2, (ibid.: 60–61).

Also in Australia, a research team (Baldry *et al.*, 2012; Baldry, 2014) recently has undertaken several cost–benefit studies of diversion and early intervention for vulnerable groups. These studies are novel in several ways, most notably because the research team used a dataset linked across 12 criminal justice and social services agencies to track the actual lifetime involvement of their cohort with those agencies. Of a sample of 2,731 people who had been incarcerated in NSW at some time between 2000 and 2008, more than two-thirds had multiple and complex needs related to poor mental health and/or cognitive impairment (Baldry, 2014: 375). The research demonstrates that inadequate support for such vulnerable people resulted in them being left to police and the prison system at enormous cost. The authors illustrate this by presenting the case studies of 11 people who had been repeatedly involved with criminal justice and social service agencies, at costs per person ranging from AUD$900,000 to AUD$5.5million (Baldry *et al.*, 2012: 116). These costs are compared with the costs of supporting those individuals via an existing integrated support program, described as an expensive program, using conservative estimates of effectiveness. The researchers conclude that the support program offered significant savings; 'between [$1.20 and $2.40] savings for criminal justice and tertiary health and human services agencies for every dollar spent on earlier integrated social and disability support such as the ISP program' (Baldry, 2014:383).

However, the use of CBA in criminal justice remains subject to debate. Arguments in favour include: examining both costs and benefits allows an assessment of whether the same outcome can be achieved by an alternative intervention at a lesser cost; the use of standardised, monetised measures allows a single measure of cost-effectiveness to be calculated; valuations make it possible to include factors such as 'fear, pain and suffering' (Fox, Albertson and Wong, 2013a: 108); the effects of outcomes on others beyond those who are directly involved can be measured and included; and, CBA allows policy-makers to select 'the most efficient intervention, that is, the scheme where costs are minimized and benefits are maximised'(ibid.: 109). The arguments against include: the assumption that economic efficiency should be the goal rather than other social benefits and 'that some things, such as safety, cannot or should not be valued' (ibid.); that they are prone to misuse by those who fail to recognise the assumptions on which they are based, or mistakenly take them to be objective and precise measures; and 'the measures may incorporate inequities in society' (ibid.: 109–10). For instance, measuring the income lost among victims of crime will produce a lower valuation of the benefits of the crime prevented if the victims are predominantly low-income earners; and, in measuring the possible benefits from a reduced risk of crime and the public's willingness to pay for crime reduction, public fears about crime risk may be at odds with the actual risk.

Roman (2004: 260) also has noted both benefits of CBA for criminal justice and some concerns about its use. Since a CBA relies on the results of evaluation studies and then applies dollar values to program effects, the threats to validity arising in the evaluation studies are compounded. Also, costs and benefits that were not measured in the evaluation, such as those accruing to people other than direct participants, are also likely to be overlooked in a CBA that relies on the evaluation. While a CBA allows the consideration of trade-offs made between the use of community resources and the benefits of programs, the evaluation studies that form the basis of a CBA typically focus on outcomes at the individual level, not the community level (ibid.: 261).

However, Roman has identified the possibility of using a CBA differently. He argues (ibid.: 271) that '[b]ecause the de facto goal of virtually every criminal justice intervention is to improve public safety, it is critical that welfare effects are measured at the community level.' According to Roman, CBAs could be used to examine different policy questions focused on community level outcomes. He notes that this may offer other advantages, such as quantifying the aggregate effects of changes which might be too small and difficult to measure at the individual level.

These suggestions open up the possibility that CBA could be adapted to pursue forms of justice reinvestment directed towards community-level change.

Financing and incentives

Recently, within justice reinvestment greater emphasis has been given to the use of performance incentives, whereby agencies that successfully meet targets share in some of the savings. In part this reflects an attempt to redress the effects of misaligned fiscal and operational responsibilities in many criminal justice systems (Vera, 2012b) whereby local decision-makers have few incentives to supervise offenders within their communities rather than to send them to prison where the costs are born by a different level of government. In the USA, some states now provide incentives to local agencies such as probation services via mechanisms like up-front grants that must be repaid if performance targets are not met, outcome-based payments or a mix of the two (ibid.). Financial incentives also have been encouraged in order to draw in the private sector. Some commentators take the view that private sector engagement is essential to drive innovation and to try things that governments could not or would not attempt (Clear, 2011).

The incorporation of financial incentives within a scheme has implications for the methodology and metrics used and these may need to be adjusted over time. For instance, a target to reduce probation revocation rates by 20 per cent each year may be unsustainable over time due to diminishing returns; the greatest scope for reductions may be in the early years of a program. Also, outcome measures may need to be refined. As an example, Kansas began with a target of reducing probation revocation rates by 20 per cent but, in order to encourage probation officers not just to avoid failure but to work towards success, subsequently added a performance measure of achieving a 75 per cent success rate (Vera, 2012b: 15).

Models used in the UK have a strong focus on PbR and have been described as not being full justice reinvestment (Fox, Albertson and Wong 2013a: 45). They developed in the context of substantial cuts to public sector budgets and a major shift by the government towards the 'marketisation' and purchasing of criminal justice services. This, in turn, has had a marked influence on the methodology and metrics being developed (e.g., pricing services, measures of demand reduction and 'cashable savings') (Wong, Fox and Albertson, 2014). For instance, the Local Justice Reinvestment pilot scheme at six sites across the UK focused on demand reduction in the criminal justice system. Demand metrics and prices were calculated for different criminal justice outcomes; for example, a reduction of one month in a custodial sentence of less than 12 months was costed at £360 of 'cashable savings'. An interim evaluation found that local agencies had not been given sufficient incentives to change their practices, in part because payment for demand reduction based on 'cashable savings' was low (ibid.: 84–5).

The PbR approach has been described by Fox, Albertson and Wong (2013a: 40 and ch 9) as unproven, possibly not the most effective or innovative way to reduce offending, and unlikely to address community problems associated with offending (ibid.: 199). Cuts to services associated with austerity measures adopted by the UK government also may undermine the community infrastructure necessary to support rehabilitation (Lanning, Loader and Muir, 2011: 22–3). In addition, while such schemes ostensibly encourage partnerships between government, the private sector and non-government agencies, they may limit the services that can be offered because the financial demands of PbR contracts are beyond the capacity of some third sector providers (Fox and Grimm, 2015: 70).

Social impact-based investments

One influential UK development has been financing through the use of social impact-based investments, which shifts risk from government to investors. A pilot program at Peterborough prison, which is funded by a social impact bond with raised start-up capital from philanthropic sources hoping to receive a return on their investment, has attracted international attention. Over half the investors had not previously invested in criminal justice related programs. Payment by the Ministry of Justice is dependent on meeting agreed targets in reducing recidivism. Much of the focus of the trial has been on testing a new funding model (Disley *et al.*, 2011: 44). While the form of financing is novel, the form of offender support is less innovative; the program extends community-based supervision and mentoring to prisoners released after serving sentences of less than 12 months who otherwise do not receive support.

It has been suggested that social impact bonds (SIBs) have a greater capacity to focus attention on evidence-based policy.

> So much social policy is made and so many programs are funded based on little or no evidence. When government decides to invest in something, it may be that there's a range of different reasons for those decisions that drive policy, and evidence is not at the top of the

list. At least with SIBs, evidence is higher up on that list. SIBs prioritize the need for data on program effect. And that's a good thing (Jim Parsons, Vera Institute of Justice in Rudd *et al.*, 2013: 51).

However, the Peterborough pilot scheme seems less focused on delivering an evidence-based program than the JRI models in the USA, although Disley *et al.*, (2011) note that it may contribute to developing an evidence base on the value of mentoring short-term inmates. In this instance, the choice of intervention and the willingness of investors to support the approach was said to be influenced substantially by trust in the financial intermediary and the track record of the service provider, St Giles Trust, which had a history of working with offenders in that area (ibid.: 2011).

The Peterborough pilot scheme was designed to compare reoffending rates over 12 months for three cohorts of 1,000 men, each released after serving sentences of less than one year, with rates for a matched control group drawn from other prisons nationally. Investors would receive a return on investment if recidivism rates, as determined by an independent assessor, met agreed thresholds. These were (1) for each cohort recidivism rates were at least 10 per cent below the control group, or (2) the aggregated recidivism rate for the three cohorts was at least 7.5 per cent below that for the control group. The sample sizes and targets were set in order to achieve sufficient statistical power to test the results. A randomised control design was considered but rejected as undesirable because it would have excluded willing and eligible participants from the program (Disley *et al.*, 2011). Outcome payments are based on the number of 'reduced reconviction events' valued at an undisclosed amount per event agreed between the parties. Commentary indicates that investors expect an annual return of between 7.5 per cent and 13 per cent (ibid.: 40). Interim results show that the target of 10 per cent reduction in recidivism below the control group was not met for the first cohort, but initial results have been described by those involved in the program as promising (Social Finance, 2014). The reconviction rate for that cohort was 8.4 per cent below the control group. Investors remain on track to receive a return on investment if the 7.5 per cent reduction in recidivism target is met in the future (ibid.).

The Peterborough pilot program influenced the development of a trial of SIB at Rikers Island NYC, which funds a moral reconation therapy program – a form of cognitive behavioural therapy (CBT) said to be evidence-based – for juvenile offenders. The program is funded by a loan from Goldman Sachs, guaranteed in part by Bloomberg Philanthropies in the event that the program is not successful. If the program is successful, part of the savings accrued by the City will be used to repay the investment (Rudd *et al.*, 2013).

These initiatives have stimulated government interest in social impact-based investment in criminal justice and other areas of social policy in at least three Australian states. Governments in NSW, WA and SA have encouraged social impact-based investments, in partnership with private sector and non-governmental organisations, that are aimed at reducing governmental costs while delivering 'effective programs' targeted at reducing reoffending (NSW Department of Premier and Cabinet, 2015; WACOSS, 2014; SA Government 2014). The SA approach follows Peterborough in its focus on extending post-release supervision to short-term inmates but is notable because the government has highlighted gender-responsive programming for women offenders and the needs of Aboriginal offenders (ibid.: 17). The NSW government has targeted reductions in reoffending by high risk parolees said to maximise the potential for 'reductions in re-offending and improvements in community safety, as well as returns to investors' (NSW Department of Premier and Cabinet, 2015: 7). The approach is described as evidence-based, with reference to the risk-needs-responsivity framework (Andrews, Bonta and Hoge, 1990; Andrews and Bonta, 2010) and international experience: '[g]overnments around the world have implemented social impact investment mechanisms to help reduce crime and re-offending, and to achieve savings. Key examples are the social impact bonds in Peterborough, United Kingdom and Rikers Island, New York' (NSW Department of Premier and Cabinet, 2015: 7).

It may be premature to model the NSW approach on such developments. For instance, a report on the first year of the Rikers Island scheme was not due until at least six months after the NSW government's announcement. Detailed reports on the financing of the Rikers Island and the Peterborough schemes provide cautions and lessons about the complex requirements for a successful SIB (Rudd *et al.*, 2013; Disley *et al.*, 2011). These include the need to provide funding not just for program delivery, but also for intermediaries to set up the deal and for evaluation; the challenge of reaching agreed reasonable prices for social outcomes; payment schedules that meet investor expectations may not align with the timelines necessary for measuring success; the need for adequate pre-existing data to set baseline measures; the demands of measuring the impact and not just the outcome requires control groups or some other form of comparison – 'a counter-factual'– to establish what would have happened in the absence of the program. Scale is also a significant consideration. The designs of the Peterborough and Rikers Island trials were shaped in part by the necessity to generate large enough cohorts for adequate statistical power in the evaluations. Scale also affects the capacity to generate sufficient savings.

There has been debate about how to characterise SIBs and similar investments. For instance, are they a means of 'increasing competition and outsourcing state services to the private sector'; are they an 'extension of the neo-liberal paradigm'; do they have the capacity to promote social innovation (Fox and Grimm 2015: 70)? It should be noted that the Peterborough pilot was not funded through competitive tender, and most investors were foundations and charities. It has been suggested that the novelty of the SIB means that, at least initially, private sector investors may be wary of investing and likely to 'focus on models that are supported by rigorous evidence' (Rudd *et al.,* 2013: 51). Doubts have been raised as to whether SIBs and market-based approaches are capable of delivering the level of innovation needed to bring about real change, or substantial reductions in costs (WACOSS, 2014).

Technical requirements, and especially scale, are likely to offer significant challenges to adopting similar models in smaller jurisdictions, including Australian states and territories. However, SIBs need not be focused narrowly on government savings. As Rudd *et al.,* (2013: 53) note:

> the goal of most social programs is not primarily to save money but to improve the lives of low-income and at risk individuals and families... [SIBs] could be structured to encompass other socially desirable goals that do not lead to government savings, so long as a government can identify what it is willing to pay to achieve those goals.

Thus, even in small jurisdictions, SIBs may offer one option for financing schemes that are targeted towards social justice objectives rather than cost cutting. However, since both the Peterborough and Rikers Island schemes appear to be more focused on reducing government expenditure through reduced reoffending than on wider social benefits, these might not be ideal models to guide a social justice-oriented approach.

Justice reinvestment as data-driven

The value of reliable data and an evidence base to inform policy, planning, program development, procurement and service delivery in criminal justice is widely recognised. However, many criminal justice systems suffer from the poor quality of data or a lack of data, and from a failure to evaluate programs and practices. Indeed, 'the data landscape often is seriously incomplete' (National Research Council, 2014: 30). Gary Dennis from the Bureau of Justice Administration noted in an interview that 'one of the things that we've found is we seriously misjudged the capacity of States and units of local government to keep accurate data. In most cases they can't even substantially document a baseline recidivism rate'. The absence of data is a significant obstacle to even modest reforms to existing systems let alone to adopting reforms intended to transform systems in significant ways. Such data are essential to justice reinvestment.

The role of technical assistance and independent expertise

Technical assistance funded by government and philanthropy has been crucial in assisting state and local JRI in the USA to introduce or upgrade data systems and to develop capacity in the collection, management and analysis of data to enable its effective use. Technical assistance providers also have developed toolkits, websites, knowledge banks and clearinghouses (e.g., <//whatworks.csgjusticecenter.org/>) and other resources to encourage and support the take up of the JRI. In some instances they have also provided political support through lobbying or policy polling (interview with Marshall Clement, CSG Justice Center).

During our fieldwork in the USA, stakeholders in state and local JRI programs acknowledged the vital contribution by technical assistance agencies and the value of a data-driven approach. Jim Seward describes the process in South Dakota:

> It was a way for us to include more people, to get more buy-in... We began our meetings by showing the data... that was the real key. You have all these people sitting around the room. The very first meeting, I as the chairman, asked each person individually – if there was one thing you can achieve through this process what would that be? Then they would tell us: "I want to fix the drug laws", "I want to fix this or I want to fix that". That started the buy-in of the work group. Then you start to show them the data and it was just amazing to watch. Pretty soon, you would have this very diverse group who were all looking at one problem, with the same dataset. Yes, they have all these external factors, their life experience, that are impacting them or their thoughts. But, they started to see that 81 per cent of South Dakota's prison admissions in 2012 are coming into prison for non-violent felonies. Is that really who the public thinks we should be putting in prison? We would have discussions about that.

Technical assistance providers funded by the JRI offered an independent voice in developing policy options, helped achieve buy-in from stakeholders across the sector and eased the path for reforms that might not otherwise have been well received. They also identified the benefits of working across levels of government and with different sectors of criminal justice because decisions taken in one area could drive change elsewhere. For instance, Marshall Clement of CSG Justice Center described the approach used in Kansas, which identified the potential for incentives to local probation services to reduce state expenditure on prisons:

> At the end of the day we were pretty much just focused on what were the main drivers – as the critique [Austin *et al.*, 2013] says, it's admissions and length of stay, this is not rocket science in terms of prison populations. What is rocket science is having enough of the data to figure out what the drivers are and how you can talk about those drivers in a way that's politically compelling.
>
> When we isolated that, two-thirds of their admissions were revocations from probation and parole systems. That got people's attention. 'Wait a minute, the system we're funding over here in the community is producing most of the volume filling our prisons?'... We talked about, if you can reduce your probation and parole revocations... you can have dramatic impact and savings of millions of dollars, and avoid building half a billion dollars in prisons, and you can give incentives to local probation agencies to do a better job because probation's at the county or community level. That made sense, right?

Without a similar program of technical assistance, UK schemes faced significant obstacles in collecting and analysing relevant data. For instance, a pilot program in Gateshead, England, was hampered by a lack of data to enable adequate justice mapping and other analyses (Wong, Fox and Albertson, 2014). In this and other UK schemes, the capacity and capability 'to analyze data and to use it to inform strategy and delivery through effective performance management' were 'in short supply' which appeared to have been exacerbated by budget cuts to relevant government authorities (ibid.: 95).

Proposals for the adoption of justice reinvestment across Australia are likely to face similar challenges arising from inadequate data systems and the limited capacity and capability to undertake the necessary analyses and funding cuts to research units within state government agencies and within the Australian Bureau of Statistics. However, as noted above, technical assistance providers also bring independence and legitimacy to the JRI process. This suggests that future developments in Australia and other jurisdictions may be well served by including independent technical assistance as an integral part of the design of any justice reinvestment model.

Australian correctional data

Inadequate data presents a significant limitation in most, and perhaps all, Australian jurisdictions. While the Australian Bureau of Statistics analyses and publishes data from departments of corrections in each state and territory, there are significant limitations in the data and not all jurisdictions submit complete datasets. Prison data are derived from an annual census of all prisons. This stock measure is supplemented by quarterly reports, but flow measures that count all receptions into prison are not routinely available. Data on offender characteristics are very limited, and some states and territories do not submit data on the Indigenous status of inmates. In some jurisdictions, inmate health surveys conducted by other agencies on a less regular basis provide data on social characteristics, the physical and mental health of inmates and substance abuse. Data are generally not available on the programs available to inmates or their effectiveness, or the localities where inmates reside prior to their incarceration or where they return to after the completion of their sentence. Recidivism rates are reported and used as performance measures, but there is little detail about the characteristics of recidivists or factors associated with reoffending. Some jurisdictions have begun to develop systems to track offenders across criminal justice sectors but the capacity to do so remains limited. There is a paucity of data on community corrections and parole. Publicly available data often take the form of frequency counts and simple tabulations that do not permit more detailed analysis of associations between variables.

Departments of correction in some states and territories collect other data for their own purposes. For instance, summary information on the risk scores of inmates has been reported in some jurisdictions. However, there is a lack of transparency concerning what is collected, public access to data is restricted and it is difficult to determine whether existing datasets would be sufficient to support the analyses required for justice reinvestment. It is also unclear whether all jurisdictions have the capacity and capability to manage data systems and analyse data effectively.

Evidence from a recent Senate inquiry indicates that a lack of relevant data impeded attempts to assess the feasibility of a justice reinvestment pilot scheme in SA (LCARC, 2013: 117–8). In WA, the need to remedy serious deficiencies in data has been described as the 'number one priority for building a more efficient and effective prison system over the short, medium and long term' (WACOSS, 2014: 6). This was confirmed by Chris Twomey (WACOSS) in an interview:

> The stuff around being data-driven – we've seen as very critical to being able to make the political and economic arguments that we need to make to get a reinvestment approach but it's also our biggest barrier at the moment...we keep tripping up about access to data, sharing of data between different government departments, but then also the ability to actually align that data across areas, portfolios and government departments so that it's actually commensurate. So there's a couple of big problems there. Certainly from our point of view our ability to actually access data, for instance, the data in corrections is very limited here.
>
> It's not even clear to some extent what data they're collecting or what they're actually doing with it. But certainly what we do know and what we do see about it says that both the quality of the data is very poor and the amount of data they're collecting isn't actually sufficiently targeted to allow us to do a lot of that fundamental analysis.

Of course, achieving a fuller understanding of the drivers of imprisonment and the potential for more effective interventions also relies on adequate data across all parts of the criminal justice system, including law enforcement and other areas of government and service sectors. Some studies have demonstrated the substantial value of linked datasets for understanding the drivers of incarceration for those with complex needs (Baldry, 2014), but in Australia such datasets are not routinely available.

Methodology and measurement: Counting and what counts

Justice reinvestment in the USA is coming to be defined through practice and shaped by tender requirements, technical assistance programs, resources and toolkits (e.g., Ho, Neusteter and La Vigne, 2013) which endorse particular methodologies and forms of measurement and provide examples for others to follow. As databases are established or updated to support the JRI, the measures that are included, and just as importantly those that are excluded, shape what counts and what is counted and set limits on the questions that can be examined, the policy options that are considered, and the capacity for evaluation and future research.

Many jurisdictions have inadequate administrative and research data, especially for women, minorities, those with mental illness or cognitive impairment or other vulnerable groups, and those at the intersection of social categories such as racialised women. The paucity of relevant data concerning Aboriginal Australians has been noted repeatedly (Wundersitz, 2010; Willis, 2010). Despite research evidence reviewed in Chapter 3 that people with mental illness or cognitive impairment, and especially those with dual diagnoses and complex needs, are over-represented in jails and prisons and likely to be repeatedly incarcerated, administrative data systems are rarely adequate to allow the identification of such patterns. Data systems or frameworks for analysis that are designed without taking such groups into account may well entrench their invisibility to researchers, policy-makers and program designers into the future. Systems that do not allow data to be disaggregated to the local level are likely to impede the development of localised initiatives.

Administrative data are necessary for justice reinvestment, but may be insufficient without informed analysis and interpretation. In Hawaii, community activists and academic researchers were involved in initial meetings with CSG and had some input into shaping the collection and interpretation of data:

> The [CSG] analysts met with Community Alliance on Prisons...they really liked the fact that they could – that researchers could say "well let me tell you what that actually means. You should actually look over there, because they're not going to tell you to look over there, but you should be looking over there"...So they liked that because it really helped them and it made their data stronger. (Kat Brady, Community Alliance on Prisons)

However, activist concerns did not necessarily prevail, as the decisions taken largely reflected the priorities established by political leaders together with resource considerations. For instance, Kat Brady comments: 'I did ask them specifically about women, data on women and they said they could pull that out but they didn't really have the time or the money to do that. So it's like the state, whoever contracts with them, needs to have certain parameters'.

As we noted previously, racial disparities in incarceration have been given little explicit attention within the JRI. Marshall Clement indicates that CSG Justice Center has never had state policy-makers ask for an analysis by race, possibly because 'people recognise that there's not clear solutions... It's not clear cut in the data'.

Thus, while justice reinvestment may be data-driven, choices are inherent in the priorities established for data collection and analysis. These choices shape how factors that drive incarceration are understood and the policy implications that are, and can be, derived from data. Gaps in datasets and omissions in analysis, such as those noted above, provide significant obstacles towards an adequate understanding of the social determinants of incarceration. They also impede recognition of differences between groups that may signal the need for targeted approaches, and this, in turn, is likely to reinforce universal policies and programs even where they might not be the most effective option for particular offenders or groups.

Measuring the drivers of incarceration

In previous chapters we examined the very different rates and patterns of incarceration for women, minorities and mentally or cognitively impaired people. These patterns may reflect the social determinants of imprisonment (e,g., poverty, homelessness, unemployment, poor levels of education and low levels of literacy), the criminalisation of social and health issues (e.g., when public order offences are used against homeless, intoxicated or mentally ill people), the differential effects on vulnerable groups of usual criminal justice practices or some combination of these factors. This suggests that the drivers of incarceration may differ for those groups. The capacity to measure this will depend on having data, a methodology and an analytical framework adequate for the task and recognising the need to do so. An adequate understanding of the drivers of the growth in incarceration also seems unlikely unless the contribution of policing practices is recognised. While this is especially important in local level schemes and in jurisdictions with unified correctional systems, such as the Australian states and territories, it is also a relevant consideration in state-based schemes. However, law enforcement rarely features in discussions of the drivers of incarceration at the state level.

State and local JRI have to some extent pursued different methodologies. A social justice-oriented justice reinvestment may well necessitate a more holistic approach that draws from both approaches, along with other measures. It appears that the JRI has not yet developed methodologies for the measurement of the social determinants of incarceration. Methodologies emerging in other domains, such as on the social

160 Justice Reinvestment

determinants of health (VicHealth, 2013), may offer some guidance for future work in this area.

Developing policy options

Factors that are identified as drivers of incarceration significantly shape the consideration of policy options. As previously noted, the drivers commonly identified in state-level JRI encourage a focus on back-end measures, such as earned reductions in sentence, parole processing and post-release support or polices for dealing with violations of probation or parole. This focus has been criticised by some commentators as inadequate to reduce prison populations; there have been calls for greater attention to sentencing, policing and prosecutorial policies (Austin, 2011) and to strengthening community infrastructure in accordance with the justice reinvestment envisaged by Tucker and Cadora (2003). Subramanian *et al.* (2015) also have called for more attention to front-end measures such as alternatives to arrest, changes to prosecution practices, pretrial release, diversion and improved case processing to reduce time in custody.

The local JRI schemes are more likely to focus not just on re-entry and back-end measures but also to identify front-end options such as diverting offenders, improved case processing, reducing length of stay, or responding to the characteristics of 'frequent flyers'. The local JRI also appears to engage a wider range of stakeholders including social service providers to contribute to problem-solving that goes beyond the criminal justice system (Lachman and Neusteter, 2012).

Of course the policy options considered are also shaped by other considerations. The messaging used by the JRI – reducing costs while enhancing public safety – is a significant factor. Where public safety is construed in terms of reduced reoffending, the policy focus may become narrowed to reducing recidivism, displacing other possible objectives.

Oklahoma provides an example where the growth in women's incarceration was identified in initial reports as a key concern, but this focus was not maintained in subsequent stages of the policy process. A JRI background report acknowledged that the state had the highest rate of incarceration for women in the USA (132 per 100,000 in 2009) and had experienced a 21 per cent increase in the women's prison population over the period 2000–09 (CSG, 2011: 2). Subsequent documents setting out the analysis and policy options for the JRI in the state appear to make no mention of women (CSG, 2012). The reforms adopted in Oklahoma in 2012 via *House Bill 3052* included enhanced funding for law enforcement to tackle violent crime, risk assessment tools to assist in sentencing, mandatory supervision of all adults released from prison and changes to responses to supervision violations. It is unclear what prompted the shift from the initial gendered analysis to a gender neutral set of policy options; this may have reflected the priorities established by state leaders but also may signal a presumption that gender neutral approaches offer universal benefits and greater potential savings. However, the effects of these proposals for women or others remain untested because the Oklahoma scheme has stalled amid concerns that it has not been given full support or funding by the Governor (Brewer, 2014).

Costs and savings

As noted in Chapter 2, caution is needed about the assumed capacity for justice reinvestment to generate significant savings. There seems to be greater emphasis on savings in some schemes than others, and savings may not necessarily result in reinvestment.

Savings may be in the form of averting future expenditure by limiting growth in prisons. Where costs are averted, such as avoiding the need to issue a bond to fund a prison building program, the savings may be substantial but spread over the life of the bond. The actual savings in a given year may be less than the costs of making the system changes associated with the JRI (Interview, Marshall Clement, CSG Justice Center). Justice reinvestment usually requires initial expenditure before any savings can be realised. However, Marshall Clement also observes that by shifting to more effective, evidence-based approaches, system change may be able to be funded by the reallocation of existing budgets.

State-level JRI schemes often include reforms that shift inmates from prisons or jails into community corrections which cost only a fraction of the cost of incarceration. One study from 2008 estimated the average cost per person per day for parole at US$7.47 and probation at US$3.42 compared with US$79 for an inmate (Pew Centre on the States 2009 as cited by James, Eisem, and Subramanian, 2012: 842). However, due to the fixed costs of incarceration, reducing inmate numbers will not necessarily result in substantial savings unless whole wings of prisons or even whole prisons can be closed. Todd Clear (Rutgers University, interview) observes that the JRI has the best prospects where prison populations are large, otherwise '[t]here's just not much money to be made.' He also notes that the potential savings may differ according to the characteristics and mix of inmates; savings per inmate might be higher for those serving very long sentences, but significant savings might be possible from reforms that affect large numbers of offenders serving shorter sentences.

Tony Fabelo from CSG Justice Center cautions against couching arguments for justice reinvestment in small jurisdictions in terms of potential financial savings and observes that the Australian context is too small to generate significant savings. While Australian developments to date have focused on the possibility for community reinvestment, he warns to not be caught by having to justify this by promising significant savings and suggests that this was 'social reinvestment not justice reinvestment'. The recent review by a Senate committee of the Australian Parliament (LCARC, 2013) indicates that some political leaders were indeed sceptical about the capacity for justice reinvestment to generate significant savings. In a minority report, opposition senators who are now in government following a federal election, stress that they could not endorse the committee's favourable report on justice reinvestment because of '[t]he dearth of evidence that any JR programs to date are sufficiently successful to allow reduced spending on the court and prison systems' (ibid.). It seems that there is some way to go in Australia before justice investment is understood by some key political representatives as more than just a way to significantly reduce government expenditure.

The objective of achieving significant savings does not bode well for the development of approaches targeted towards the specific needs of particular groups and is likely to reinforce a universal approach to justice reinvestment policies and programs. As Gelsthorpe and Hedderman (2012: 386) comment with reference to PbR schemes in the UK, where the objectives of justice reinvestment include generating substantial savings for government, women, minorities and other vulnerable groups who make up relatively small proportions of incarcerated populations may be seen as too few to count. However, the extent to which this represents an obstacle, at least for some groups, may differ. For instance, as discussed in Chapter 3, the over-representation of Aboriginal people incarcerated in Australia is so pronounced in some jurisdictions that they account for substantial proportions of the incarcerated population. Thus, at least in those settings, it may be possible to rebut arguments that programs targeted to their needs and interests are unlikely to generate sufficient savings.

The local JRI schemes discussed in Chapter 2, also suggest the possibility of adopting other benchmarks for savings, not based on the closure of a prison or prison wing, but more aligned with policies that are tailored towards specific groups. For instance, Mecklenburg County identified the high costs of repeat, low level offenders. Almost half of the people jailed returned to jail within a year and 48 people identified as 'frequent users' accounted for 1,704 arrests and 21,445 jail bed days over

2008–11 at a cost of US$2.5 million. Many of these people suffered from mental illness, substance abuse or were homeless and they were also frequent users of health and other services. The county focused on problem-solving and finding a humane response. The county's justice reinvestment policy framework includes: reducing the reliance on arrest for low level offending; diverting the mentally ill and homeless, providing support for them and others in need of drug treatment; and improving bail processes (CEPP, 2012b: 1–2). The cost of providing social housing for these frequent users was US$14–15,000 per person as compared to previous costs to the system of US$38,000 per person. The commitment by Mecklenburg County to the scheme is especially notable since the savings do not necessarily flow to the county.

It may be challenging to develop methodologies with the capacity to recognise and measure benefits and savings across agencies and sectors, disaggregated to a local level, however, enabling and sustaining a social justice-oriented justice reinvestment is likely to require a shift in that direction.

Performance measures and 'success'

Performance measurement is necessary within the JRI. Sites that partner with the CSG are required to meet a minimum standard in capturing relevant data such as admissions, releases, and average daily population. Some states have gone much further developing very detailed tools for tracking performance (CSJ Justice Center 2014). Measuring program outcomes, defining what constitutes success and how this is costed are key, but there is no one approach. Commentary on PbR schemes and the marketised models in the UK have commonly noted the detailed negotiations required and complex metrics sometimes used to measure performance and that these represent challenges to be overcome.

Recidivism measures are commonly used as performance measures within the JRI schemes despite their well-recognised limitations. It also has been noted that recidivism measures are susceptible to manipulation (interview, Todd Clear, Rutgers University). As noted in previous chapters, the absence of a focus within the JRI on specific groups has an impact on the measures used to determine 'success' and may well mean that outcomes are measured only at the general level. In the absence of more adequate measures it may be difficult or impossible to determine if interventions have differential effects.

However, a social justice-oriented justice reinvestment requires a different approach that is more holistic, reaches beyond the criminal justice system, with different measures of success that would include attention to 'pre-habilitation' designed to prevent crime in the first instance, as well as diversion and other front-end measures. The difficulty of measuring crime that is prevented, and the cost savings from reductions in crime, have also been noted by others (Wong, Fox and Albertson, 2014). However, as discussed below, measuring social costs and benefits may offer a different calculation that includes benefits to others outside the criminal justice system and perhaps at the level of the local community.

Local schemes and challenges for measurement

In Chapter 3 we noted that aspirations towards justice reinvestment in Australia have largely had a place-based focus. Interest in justice reinvestment in the UK also has been predicated on localism and the potential to shift budgets and accountability to local level and to provide opportunities for innovation by linking localised costs and benefits (Commission on English Prisons Today, 2009; Fox, Albertson and Wong, 2013b). We also examined the possibilities, and challenges, of effective place-based criminal justice reforms. However, local level schemes may face particular challenges related to measurement.

Where correctional systems and other criminal justice agencies are largely organised at the state or territory level, as in Australia, or the national level, as in the UK, administrative data systems may be poorly equipped to provide analyses of prison, community corrections or other relevant criminal justice data at regional or local levels. Financial systems may also be inadequate to track expenditure or calculate savings across sectors or for specific local initiatives. In addition, the gaps in data for subpopulations of interest within correctional systems that have been noted above may make it difficult or impossible for the kind of targeted approach to local programming that is often considered desirable, and may impede evaluation.

While the pilot projects undertaken in the UK have been PbR schemes described as not full justice reinvestment, and the programs differ in detail, for present purposes it is useful to the review challenges that they face.

Evaluations find that individual offenders in the relevant schemes do not necessarily map on to local communities. For instance in the Diamond initiative in London (Wong, Fox and Albertson, 2014: 2) and the Peterborough prison pilot (Disley *et al.*, 2011) not all offenders released from prison resided in the communities that were the focus of the interventions. In the Gateshead project, poor data generally and a lack of accurate data on where offenders lived prior to incarceration or on release limited the capacity for mapping and the high level statistical modelling commonly used in the USA was not available. Other obstacles to neighourhood resettlement arose because the neighbourhoods were not well matched with where probation staff were deployed (Wong, Fox and Albertson, 2014: 83). Also the scale of the Gateshead project was a significant limitation: '[a]rguably it was unrealistic to expect that such an approach would or could work effectively at the level of a single local authority given that funding decisions about criminal justice were and are made primarily at the national and regional level' (ibid.).

In the six-site Local Justice Reinvestment Pilot, there was a lack of sufficient incentives to encourage local services to change their practices, and a 'perceived inability of agencies to implement interventions that were likely to reduce demand'; payments were low, possibly because of the small scale of the projects, the metrics were too complex and there was no initial investment to support the scheme. In addition, in all but one site there was a lack of 'robust research evidence and cost-benefit analysis to inform local sites' choice of interventions' (ibid.). Scale was also a significant limitation on the Youth Justice Reinvestment Pathfinder Initiative which required participating sites to have no fewer than 50 young people in custody 'in order to deliver significant savings' (ibid.: 86).

Questions of scale also arise with respect to specific groups. Since their numbers may be small in a given local scheme, programs tailored to meet the needs of different groups may be difficult to evaluate to establish effectiveness and may not be seen as cost-effective.

Justice reinvestment as evidence-based

In an influential paper on evidence-based policy, Solesbury (2001: 6) observed that it 'seems to be principally a British commitment'. Less than a decade later this had changed markedly and EBP had been adopted internationally and across policy domains. The appeal to EBP has a long history, but its resurgence in the latter part of the twentieth century has been attributed variously to 'risk society'; the new managerialism in the public sector; or to a 'shift in the nature of politics, [a] retreat from ideology, the dissolution of class-based party politics and the empowerment of consumers' (Solesbury 2001: 9). In the UK, it has been linked to the government of former Prime Minister Tony Blair; during his term in office, numerous reports advocating evidence-based approaches were produced and programs adopted across areas of social policy.

Within criminology, the report *Preventing Crime: What Works, What Doesn't and What is Promising* (Sherman et al., 1998) and the development of the Campbell Collaboration have given added impetus to the growth of EBP (Freiberg and Carson, 2010: 154; Fox, Albertson and Wong 2013a). However, as Freiberg and Carson (2010: 155) observe, despite sophisticated literature on EBP, the notion that '[w]hat matters is what works' offers a 'naïve linear model within which the relationship between evidence and policy is characterized by rationality'. They argue that such a rational and linear model of policy is unattainable due to real world constraints on the operation of rationality and may be 'undesirable'; that it assumes that rationality is value neutral and disinterested rather than relative; and that 'issues of emotion and affect' may be 'even more significant, persuasive or compelling' in public policy debates. They illustrate their argument with an example of particular salience to justice reinvestment: 'evidence about the effectiveness of imprisonment or three-strikes legislation (or more likely ineffectiveness or even its cost) is unlikely to lead to policy changes unless the underlying causes of the public's emotional discomfort are addressed' (ibid.: 158).

However, our research on the ground in the USA and Australia demonstrated the strong practical appeal of EBP. The promise of improved data systems and EBP was welcomed and typically seen as long overdue. Even among some sceptics there was recognition that too often criminal justice policy and practice has had no research foundation. Accounts by key stakeholders confirmed that the emphasis on EBP had been associated with the shift over time from the original vision of reinvestment in communities to investment in the criminal justice system. For instance, as we have previously noted, Marshall Clement (CSG Justice Center) comments that 'there's not much consensus about what an evidence-based methodology would look like to do community redevelopment [but] we actually know what to do with individuals who are high risk of reoffending to give them skills to change their behavior'. Nancy La Vigne (Urban Institute) notes that reinvestment into 'the criminal justice system and not into these communities...provides better and more effective programming and there's more focus on best practice and it funds a lot of things that wouldn't have been funded otherwise'.

The practical appeal of EBP is consistent with the instrumental focus of dominant approaches to justice reinvestment. Normative questions and debates are not prominent within the JRI (Tonry, 2011). This instrumental focus is also a feature of EBP more generally, which it has been suggested 'over-emphasises knowledge and under-emphasises the normative, political, administrative, institutional and organisational context in which decisions are made' (Freiberg and Carson, 2010: 159 citing Majone 1989: 15).

Our interviewees also recognised the rhetorical value of EBP. Some described how EBP had assisted the JRI practitioners in the USA develop political bi-partisanship by offering a more politically neutral, technocratic account of the case for doing justice differently, and of the policy options being considered. It was also said that EBP had provided a focus and a point of common purpose.

Phrases such as 'smart on crime' and 'let the data show us what we should be doing' were described as forms of 'messaging' that had proved to be persuasive in some settings (interview, Jim Seward, South Dakota). In North Carolina, EBP had been adopted by community corrections prior to the introduction of the JRI but there had been some resistance from the judiciary; bi-partisan support and the JRI legislation gave legitimacy to developments that were already underway (interview, Anne Precythe, Community Corrections, North Carolina Department of Public Safety). In the Australian context, bi-partisanship is rare in criminal justice debates and the appeal to evidence is not always sufficient to settle debates.

While the JRI schemes draw on data and EBP to generate policy options, as discussed in other chapters, the political reality is that some options are simply off the table (Austin *et al.*, 2013: 4). Australian proposals are likely to face similar constraints. For instance, US schemes have commonly adopted reforms allowing low-risk inmates to accrue 'good time' and thus reduce time served in custody or reducing the duration of probation or parole through 'earned credits' such as for compliance or participation in programs (James, Eisem and Subramanian, 2012: 835). However, these options seem untenable in some Australian states, at least without a significant political retreat from 'truth in sentencing' regimes introduced in the late 1980s (see Chapter 5).

Within the JRI, EBP is typically strongly endorsed and in some states is required by legislation, although the actual requirements differ. In Washington State, legislation requires criteria to be developed to differentiate between programs that are 'evidence-based', 'research-based' or 'promising'. A review of 65 programs rejected 39 'due to inadequate evidence of effectiveness'; three were designated evidence-based, two were designated research-based and 21 were seen as promising (Pew-MacArthur Results First, 2015: footnote 4). In 2011 alone, five US states passed legislation mandating the use of risk assessment tools and specific programs such as drug treatment, CBT or forms of intensive community supervision (James, Eisem, and Subramanian, 2012: 826). For example, the Kentucky *Public Safety and Offender Accountability Act* mandates the use of EBP for pretrial, inmates, probationers and parolees. The Department of Corrections is required to allocate caseloads based on offender risk, and to use a risk assessment tool pre-trial, before sentencing, at prison intake and at release to parole.

While EBP appears to have strong support, our interviews also revealed some scepticism about the extent to which it had been adopted in practice. For instance, Tony Fabelo of CSG noted:

> Everybody in the country has evidence-based practices. Everybody wants to do justice reinvestment and everybody says they have justice reinvestment. So I encourage you to ask deeper questions...But go to a national conference with 500 people and ask who doesn't have evidenced-based practices? Nobody answers, nobody will raise their hand [laughs]. It's like, do you love your kids?

Thus, while 'let the data show us' might have rhetorical appeal, it can serve to sidestep questions about what counts as evidence and conceal the myriad of factors that shape the policy options that are developed and the political choices that are made (Freiberg and Carson, 2010; see further Chapter 5).

Questions also have been raised about the capacity for EBP to stifle innovation and undermine the development of initiatives responsive to local conditions. For instance, as noted above legislation in some JRI states requires the use of EBP. While some legislated schemes permit local programs, providing that they are designed to follow evidence-based principles (Pew-MacArthur Results First, 2015: 5), this may not overcome the 'risk of missing the very essence of what makes a social intervention "work"' and does little to foster innovation (Fox, Albertson and Wong, 2013a: 142). In our fieldwork, some technical assistance providers described marked differences across schemes and innovative ways in which the JRI was being pursued in different settings. However, in this context innovation was commonly used to refer to various ways in which legislatures put together reform packages at the state level rather than to innovation in the programs per se. As Todd Clear observes (2010: 6), EBP is conservative, and 'a backward-looking standard that requires both a history of action and a systematic pattern of proof of the wisdom of the action' that is not well suited to drive change.

What counts as evidence?

What constitutes EBP and the methodology used differs across disciplines. However, meta-analyses are commonly used in many policy areas and are derived from a synthesis of previous evaluative studies that meet an established threshold for inclusion. Meta-analysis is seen as more rigorous and authoritative than narrative reviews, although there are ongoing debates about the merits of each of these approaches. It is common for a hierarchy of evidence to be adopted with random control trials endorsed as 'the gold standard'. Some disciplines or sub-disciplines, for instance, some schools within psychology, are more likely than others to work with methodologies that readily fit this approach. The risk-needs-responsivity approach (Andrews, Bonta and Hoge, 1990) that is so influential in the JRI, is based on the psychology of individual differences and is founded on meta-analysis. However, despite the privileging of random control trials common within EBP, there remains considerable debate about their strengths and weaknesses, whether they can and do live up to the claims made about them and whether they are the best basis on which to establish evidence (Fox, Albertson and Wong, 2013a: 131–135).

The benefit-cost model developed by the WSIPP (2014: 13) discussed above derives its evidence using meta-analysis:

[W]e carefully analyze all high – quality studies from the United States (and beyond) to identify well-researched programs or policies that achieve desired outcomes (as well as those that do not). We look for research studies with strong, credible evaluation designs, and we ignore studies with weak research methods. Our empirical approach follows a meta-analytic framework to assess systematically all relevant evaluations we can locate on a given topic. (ibid.: 8)

Among the inclusion criteria, the most important is said to be 'that an evaluation must either have a control or comparison group or use advanced statistical methods to control for unobserved variables or reverse causality' (ibid.: 13). Cognitive behavioural therapy has been endorsed by systematic review (Lipsey, Landenberger and Wilson 2007) which is one reason that it has strong support within the JRI. However, few criminal justice programs or practices are evaluated by these standards.

A recent systematic review conducted for the Campbell Collaboration[1] examined studies comparing the effects of custodial versus non-custodial sanctions on reoffending (other possible effects were not examined). The authors (Villettaz, Gillieron and Killias, 2015: 16) describe the number of studies worldwide that met the inclusion criteria (random control trials, natural experiments, or using propensity scores) as 'appallingly weak' even though they included studies of adult and juvenile incarceration without regard to different sentence lengths, type of alternative sanction or other relevant factors. They conducted two separate meta-analyses; the first, based on random control trials, found no difference between custodial and non-custodial outcomes while the second, based on propensity studies, favoured non-custodial alternatives. The authors gave more weight to the finding of no effect, because random control trials were judged to be more rigorous, but they also provided a list of methodological caveats.

Patricia Van Voorhis (2013) argues that the premium placed on EBP has worked to the disadvantage of women and minorities, who have been served poorly by science. Too often research has not used representative samples for these groups but the findings have been inappropriately generalised to them, sometimes with the justification that this is the 'best available evidence' (ibid.: 120–121). The notion that the best available evidence is being used may then serve to 'minimize the urgency to conduct more appropriate research' (ibid.). Van Voorhis also notes that at the time that correctional treatment was coming back into favour, 'there was an appalling lack of research on which to build correctional approaches for women' and 'research fueling the policy transition was conducted largely on boys and men'(ibid.: 112). The weight given to meta-analysis has exacerbated such concerns. While '[e]vidence came to drive policy' (ibid.: 119), for women and minorities it was commonly the case that there was no evidence, or none that counted in the meta-analysis. The body of feminist research on women's pathways to crime (Daly, 1992; Gilfus, 1993), or the needs most relevant to women offenders at that time and subsequently, remains too small to support meta-analysis or when based on qualitative research would be excluded.

According to Van Voorhis (2013) this history of EBP underpins flaws in the conceptual basis of standard risk assessment tools. She traces the influence of two early meta-analyses of correctional programs on the generation of the risk-needs-responsivity approach and the development of 'principles of effective intervention'. Despite caveats about the limitations of meta-analyses based on male only samples, or in which women, girls or minorities were under-represented, the results have been relied on extensively and applied universally. The resultant gender neutral risk assessment tools and principles of intervention have meant that women 'are less likely to be triaged to gender-specific services such as protection from abusive partners, childcare services, access to reliable transport, low-self efficacy, trauma and abuse, parenting programs, healthy relationships, and realistic employment opportunities that allow for self-support' (ibid.: 113).

Some authors of reviews based on meta-analysis recognise the potential difficulties associated with their use. For instance, Lipsey and Wilson (1993: 1200, in Van Voorhis, 2013: 120) caution that '[m]eta-analysis is only possible for treatment approaches that have generated a corpus of research sufficient in quantity and comparability for systematic analysis within a statistical framework'. Thus, meta-analyses only include well-established practices that are in widespread use. New criminal justice practices or programs are often funded for the short term and are rarely funded for the cost of evaluation, providing little opportunity to learn from and build upon the results. Many are not evaluated at all let alone by the standards demanded to be designated evidence-based, and thus knowledge about such innovation may be lost. Programs that are small scale, local and/or targeted to specific groups may be less likely to be funded for evaluation than larger scale and or mainstream initiatives.

One consequence of the reliance on meta-analysis is that few practices or programs are endorsed as evidence-based, and the menu of 'what works' remains restricted. This is likely to have unintended consequences such as stifling innovation and impeding the development of programs that arise from local initiatives or that respond to particular communities and groups. This possibility is greatest where EBP excludes other forms of knowledge and other modes of assessing effectiveness.

What works and for whom?

Evidence-based practice is not only about collecting and analysing particular kinds of data but also involves recommending or prescribing particular practices. Within the JRI, EBP is strongly linked to the 'what works' framework and to risk assessment (discussed in more detail below), and indeed these terms are sometimes used interchangeably. Latessa and Lowencamp (2006: 521–2) define 'what works' as a body of knowledge 'also called evidence-based practice' that in turn reflects 'principles of effective intervention'; these are 'risk, need, treatment and fidelity'.

The 'what works' framework was developed in North America and the UK but has been applied internationally (Worrall, 2000). It is a key element of the JRI (Clement, Schwarzfeld and Thompson, 2011) and is supported by databases designed to assist practitioners and policy-makers to identify 'what works'. Some examples include: CrimeSolutions.gov, developed by the US Office of Justice Programs (www.CrimeSolutions.

gov); the non-profit and non-partisan Coalition for Evidence-Based Policy (evidencebasedprograms.org/); and the National Centre for Justice Planning register of evidence-based policies, programs and practices (<www.ncjp.org/saas/ebps>).

In our fieldwork, technical assistance providers and justice reinvestment practitioners often expressed confidence in the what works framework and some referred to research evidence that underpinned this confidence. Research by Andrews and Bonta (2010; Andrews, Bonta and Hoge, 1990) on risk-needs-responsivity and studies by Latessa and Lowencamp (2006) on halfway houses, residential community corrections facilities and community-based programs in Ohio were commonly mentioned as providing evidence of what works and what does not work in reducing recidivism. These studies together were said to provide support for targeting interventions to offenders with a high risk of reoffending and not low-risk offenders for whom intervention may be counter-productive with programs that respond to criminogenic needs using CBT, an approach that now appears to be standard in many settings.

Another program that has been very influential is the HOPE court – Hawaii's Opportunity Probation with Enforcement program. It is designated as 'near top-tier' by the EBP website 'Social Programs That Work' (<//evidencebasedprograms.org>), where top-tier is defined as 'interventions shown in well-designed and implemented randomized controlled trials, preferably conducted in typical community settings, to produce sizable, sustained benefits to participants and/or society'. An evaluation of the program (Hawken and Kleiman, 2009) showed that as compared with a control group, probationers in the program were 53 per cent less likely to have their probation revoked, 72 per cent less likely to use drugs and 55 per cent less likely to be arrested for a new crime. They served 48 per cent fewer days in prison, on average, than the control group (Hawken & Kleiman, 2009). HOPE has been adopted widely across the USA, and the BJA has used it as a model for a grant program, 'Swift and Certain Sanctions'. It has recently been advocated within Australia (Bartels, 2015).

HOPE has been described by some commentators as based on classical deterrence theory, although Judge Alm, who initiated the program, described its origins in more prosaic terms:

> I thought, "Well this system doesn't work. What would work?" and I thought "How did I raise my kid, my wife and I? How was I raised? Your parents state what the family rules are and then if there's

misbehavior, something happens immediately." You tie together the bad behavior with the consequence and learn from it...

The program is based on close monitoring of probationers, including random drug tests, with swift and certain responses to violations.

> If the behaviour is responsible, [sanctions are] short. If it's irresponsible, it's long. So you'll see the three basic sanctions are if people admit to stuff, it's two or three days, immediately. If they test positive and deny it, we have to send it out to the lab and the lab confirms it, they're going to get 15 days because they're in denial and they're wasting everybody's time; and if they don't show up, it's going to be at least 30. The three, 15 and 30 are the three basic sanctions. But other states have missed that distinction. They can't just give everybody three days because one, the crims have figured this out. They think "If I can go out and party and have a good time and get the same sanction than if I take responsibility, why would I do the former?" (Judge Alm, First Circuit Court, Hawaii)

While our fieldwork demonstrated a good deal of confidence about 'what works', some interviewees raised concerns that the framework and its research base was limited in several respects, including in its failure to acknowledge gender or other differences. Critics have noted that the what works framework 'contends that, with minimal variation, presence of the core risk factors serves to increase the likelihood of offending for both men and women alike' (Martin, Kautt and Gelsthorpe, 2009: 881). They also have challenged the global application of what works, including its use for racialised groups such as Aboriginal people in Australia (Worrall, 2000).

Meda Chesney-Lind from the University of Hawaii offers this appraisal: 'the glass is half full, half empty'. She notes that the what works approach is a welcome shift when contrasted with the punitive approaches that prevailed in the 1980s and 1990s, often based on 'nothing works' – the misuse of Martinson's (1974) influential review:

> It went back to: "no actually there's some things we need to do when we have these people in custody". So from that perspective I think it was a giant step forward because it got us away from that mindless punitiveness and mean spiritedness that characterized that era. Okay, now we get to what are the problems. I think what the problems are – is best summed up by figuring out what does it take to be a program

that has been evaluated using the kind of standards that we typically have...only certain programs are going to have the kind of money to put themselves into that league and those are the ones that are real money makers for the people who develop them.

Like Meda Chesney-Lind, other interviewees raised concerns about the kinds of practices that were endorsed within the what works framework. Australian advocates working on behalf of criminalised women were particularly critical of CBT, which they found to be inappropriate for women and an inadequate response to the circumstances that typically bring women into custody. They were adamant that more attention needed to be given to the social determinants of incarceration. Australian researchers also have cautioned that approaches based on CBT 'de-emphasize contextual or cultural factors' and may be inappropriate for Indigenous offenders, while also acknowledging that '[w]e simply do not know whether existing mainstream rehabilitation programs are effective or ineffective with indigenous offenders'(Day 2003: 11) due to the paucity of relevant and appropriate research or evaluation methodologies.

RaeDeen Keahiolalo-Karasuda of Chaminade University, Hawaii described teaching a class about Hawaiian history and politics to women offenders on a transition program, and how one woman contrasted what she had learnt in that class with the CBT programs she had previously completed:

> I'll never forget one woman who said "Wow, all we learn is cognitive restructuring and I've taken seven classes to restructure my thinking and it's never taken root, and just having this knowledge makes me realise it's not all me and all my fault." She said "Don't get me wrong, I take responsibility for my crimes and stuff, but...now as a Hawaiian I know that there's a whole history and there's external," – what did she say – "external forces that are invested in me being incarcerated. I was like "Whoa, you got it".

Gelsthorpe and Hedderman (2012: 376) observe that '[women] not only believe that they have few legitimate options, but in reality, they have few positive options. Important as enhanced thinking skills are, they can only be, at best, a prerequisite to empowering women to make better choices, if the choices genuinely exist'.

Little is known about 'what works' for women or minorities. However, research has established that there are marked gender differences in pathways to crime and emerging evidence suggests that is also the case for re-entry after prison. For instance, a study by the Urban Institute found that:

> women have different experiences from men, both behind bars and on the outside. They face reentry challenges with a different set of skills and deficits, and those differences are manifested in higher rates of relapse and recidivism. All this suggests that a focus on women as a distinct subpopulation of persons reentering society is critical to the development of effective policies and practices (La Vigne et al., 2009: 3).

Despite such findings, few programs address abuse histories, drug use or poor parenting skills in prison, or in transition to release; and the lack of planning for the re-entry of women offenders has been described as 'striking' (Kruttschnitt, 2010: 38; Bumiller, 2013: 16). The research evidence is especially poor concerning people at the intersection of social categories offering little, for instance, on what might be most effective for racialised women. Kimberle Crenshaw (2012: 1430) has observed in the USA the marked contrast between 'the dramatically visible over-representation of African American women and girls in a wide-ranging net of victimization and incarceration [and] the relative absence of any targeted attention to this overrepresentation'. A search of the CrimeSolutions.gov database generated little that was specifically tailored towards women, racialised offenders or vulnerable groups such as those with impaired intellectual capacity or mental health.

The absence of tailored programs for such groups and the dearth of research on what might be most effective to support them, in part reflects a commitment to universal models underlying the dominant approach to what works. The what works approach, framed in this way, offers little to guide practitioners or policy-makers working with groups that are differentially affected by criminalisation and incarceration. It seems ill-advised at best to continue on the basis that gendered and racialised dimensions of incarceration, or other forms of marginalisation, will be redressed through the general application of what works. As Solesbury (2001: 8) has observed,

> the what works question is too bald. What works for whom in what circumstances is what policy makers and practitioners really need to know. And to answer that there needs to be not just research that is evaluative, but also research that is descriptive, analytical, diagnostic, theoretical and prescriptive.

Risk assessment and the risk-needs-responsivity approach

The heavy reliance on risk assessment within the JRI reflects its programmatic focus. Risk assessment tools are used to predict recidivism, guide expenditure, and inform sentencing, release decisions and re-entry programming. Clement, Schwarzfeld and Thompson (2011: 12) endorse 'validated risk assessment tools [as] remarkably effective at identifying who is at a high risk of recidivating' which ensures that scarce correctional resources are 'correctly' targeted, that is, towards offenders most likely to reoffend so that interventions and supervision are directed to their criminogenic needs (ibid.: 6). Intervening with low-risk offenders is seen as an inefficient use of resources and may increase reoffending (ibid.: 17). For instance, in North Carolina, the *Justice Reinvestment Act* passed in June 2011 requires probation supervision to be concentrated on high risk offenders.

Risk assessment tools commonly draw on the risk-needs-responsivity framework (Andrews, Bonta and Hoge, 1990) which has been described as one of the 'most important findings' for EBP (James, Eisem and Subramanian, 2012). It is based on 'a general personality and cognitive social learning' psychology which the authors state 'has conceptual, empirical and practical value within and across social arrangements, clinical categories and various personal and justice contexts' (Andrews and Bonta, 2010: 7). They contend that this framework applies universally, a claim that is contested as discussed below and that it provides the basis for the identification of principles of effective intervention. CBT is strongly endorsed as an effective intervention (see the overview by Smith, Cullen and Latessa, 2009). Factors such as gender, ethnicity, learning styles and motivation are among those that are considered relevant to the extent that they may pose barriers to successful treatment – this is known as the concept of responsivity.

Andrews and Bonta (2010) describe eight criminogenic needs that predict recidivism. The 'Big Four' are said to be most salient. These are a history of antisocial behaviour, an antisocial personality, antisocial attitudes or thinking and antisocial associates. The remaining factors which are said to have a more moderate influence are family/marital circumstances, low levels of education or poor work history and prospects, a lack of pro-social leisure or recreation and substance abuse (ibid.: 58–59, Table 2.5).

Risk assessment has been institutionalised through the JRI. However, this also has occurred elsewhere through different means; for instance, the Risk Management Authority (RMA <www.rmascotland.gov.uk/>) in Scotland was created in 2005 by the *Criminal Justice (Scotland) Act 2003* to manage the risk of serious violent and sexual offenders. The RMA is one of several agencies that evaluate risk assessment tools. Certain proprietary risk assessment tools predominate in criminal justice and often these are applied universally; the Level of Service Inventory – Revised (LSI-R) is a proprietary tool commonly used by corrections departments across Australia. Some jurisdictions have developed their own tools, in part to avoid the financial burden imposed by adopting proprietary tools but also to ensure that the tools are suited to specific contexts, correctional populations or stages of criminal justice. For instance, Ohio has developed a system of five risk assessment tools used to predict recidivism by adults at different stages of the criminal justice process and a similar suite of five tools specifically for juveniles (Latessa *et al.*, 2009; Lovins and Latessa, 2013).

However, the use of risk assessment tools remains contested. Academic and political debate continues with respect to the conceptualisation and use of risk assessment and the potential for such tools to exacerbate disparities and injustice (Smith, Cullen and Latessa, 2009; Hannah-Moffatt, 2009; Van Voorhis, 2013). For instance, as a recent UK government inquiry noted '[t]he range of services women offenders require is small in volume but complex. Potential providers of rehabilitative services need to recognise that levels of risk posed by women may not precisely reflect the level of support such women require' (HCJC, 2013–14: 50). Meda Chesney-Lind (University of Hawaii) expressed her ambivalence about risk assessment:

> So I'm not a huge fan of risk assessment. It's certainly better than no system at all. It gives a veneer of rationality to what previously was, and it also does make people somewhat accountable, but I think it also blames the people who are at risk of being incarcerated now for poverty and other social attributes that have nothing to do with the crime that's alleged.
>
> The instruments are deceptive, I think they're loaded with all kinds of assumptions about the meaning of certain things and those aren't interrogated thoughtfully. And the other problem is because this is a for profit enterprise

Contrasting views on the use of risk assessment in the USA are illustrated by these 2014 headlines: '*Attorney General Eric Holder to Oppose Data-Driven Sentencing*' and '*To Minimize Injustice, Use Big Data*'. The first headline is from an article in *Time Magazine* in which former US Attorney General Eric Holder, a supporter of justice reinvestment, argued against the use of risk assessment tools in sentencing. His concerns were reported to include that 'they could have a disparate and adverse impact on the poor, on socially disadvantaged offenders, and on minorities' especially where a focus on 'static' risk factors such as educational background and employment history may perpetuate racial disparities in criminal justice while advantaging white collar offenders (Calabresi, 2014). The second headline is from an article by Anne Milgram, former New Jersey Attorney General and now vice president of criminal justice at a philanthropic foundation that has developed a pretrial risk assessment tool. According to Milgram (2014), the pretrial release tool does not focus on factors such as 'education, socioeconomic status, and neighbourhood' that have been identified as potentially discriminatory, and is 'race and gender neutral'. She argues that EBP supported by such tools 'can do more than improve public safety and cut costs'; it 'can help uphold key principles of the American judicial system' (ibid.).

Debates about the underlying assumptions of standard risk assessment tools and their universal use, especially for women and minorities have sometimes been interpreted narrowly. The need for research to validate the tools for women and minorities and to compare whether they have the same predictive capacity for those groups, as for white males, is certainly important. Validation studies have been used belatedly by proponents of the universal approach to dismiss criticism. For instance, Smith *et al.*, (2009: 198) argue on the basis of a meta-analysis that 'the LSI-R performs virtually the same for female offenders as it does for male offenders'. Some critics have worked to develop tools tailored to specific groups; for instance, Van Voorhris (2013) and others have incorporated gender-responsive elements to produce more effective tools for women.

However, it is not just the predictive value of the tools that is an issue. Kelly Hannah-Moffatt (2009: 214) has questioned the 'theoretical and empirical premises of gender-neutral, "empirically based" risk tools'. She has strongly criticised their administration to women and racialised populations. She finds that 'marginalized groups unavoidably score higher on risk assessment instruments because of their increased exposure to risk, racial discrimination and social inequality – not necessarily because of their criminal behavior or the crimes perpetrated' (Hannah-Moffatt, 2012: 281). Gelsthorpe and Hedderman (2012: 375) also note that 'the concepts of "risk" and "need" are themselves "gendered". Others have argued that risk is also a racialised construct (Hudson and Bramhall 2005). According to Blagg (2008: 28), Indigenous people as a group in Australia have always been subjected to forms of risk assessment.

Some Australian judges have expressed scepticism regarding the use of risk assessment tools for Indigenous offenders.[2] For instance, in *Director of Public Prosecutions for Western Australia v Mangolamara* ([2007] WASC 71 (27 March 2007)), Hasluck J observes:

> having regard to the admissions made under cross-examination that the tools were not devised for and do not necessarily take account of the social circumstances of indigenous Australians in remote communities, I harbour grave reservations as to whether a person of the respondent's background can be easily fitted within the categories of appraisal presently allowed for by the assessment tools (ibid.: para166).

He finds that little weight should be given to those parts of the psychiatric reports presented to the court concerning the assessment tools (ibid.: para 165) which he notes had not been validated for Indigenous populations (ibid.: para 172) (see also Cunneen *et al.*, 2013, Chapter 4).

There is a small but growing literature on using risk assessment tools for Indigenous people (Shepherd *et al.*, 2013). For instance, a recent meta-analysis of the commonly used risk assessment tool, the Level of Service Inventory (LSI) in its various forms, found that it was less accurate for Aboriginal offenders (Wilson and Gutierrez, 2014). One of the few Australian studies to assess the application of the risk-needs-responsivity approach to Indigenous prisoners does not dismiss the approach but argues for it to be used differently for Indigenous offenders. The authors (Day, Howells and Casey, 2003:129) conclude:

> First, there appears to be a need to standardize risk measures across different cultural groups. The risk of imprisonment for the Indigenous offender may be determined as much by social factors (e.g. discrimination in the criminal justice system) as well as factors directly related to the individual. Second, given the high level of non-criminogenic needs likely to be experienced by the Indigenous offender, it would seem inappropriate to focus solely on criminogenic needs. On this basis, one could argue that in order for an intervention to be effective, both sets of needs should be addressed concurrently. It is also likely that such an approach would engage the Indigenous offender in the rehabilitative process. Finally, responsivity can also be improved by the consideration of culturally appropriate ways of program delivery.

Despite the debates, Andrews and Bonta (2010) remained committed to a general theory of crime and universal risk assessment, and their stance has continued to influence research and practice. However, subsequent research has resulted in some qualifications to this position in recognition of findings that suggest that there are important differences for young people, women (Van Voorhis 2013: 127), Aboriginal offenders and possibly 'mentally disordered offenders', for whom all eight risk factors are pertinent and not just the 'Big Four' (Bonta, Blais and Wilson, 2014: 280).

Faye Taxman's (2014) influential work has added a different dimension to recent debates about risk assessment. She has exposed unanswered questions and identified myths about the risk-needs-responsivity framework. These myths include:

> All high-risk offenders should be placed in programs; [a]ll low-risk offenders should not be placed in programs; ... [g]eneric programs are suitable for all offenders regardless of criminal behavior or criminogenic needs; [and] [o]ffenders with criminogenic needs related to antisocial behaviors/attitudes/values are the same as high-risk offenders. (ibid.:32)

Her analysis discusses the importance of reshaping the risk-needs-responsivity framework to tailor interventions for individuals by taking account of not just criminogenic needs but also 'stabilizers and destabilizers' such as 'mental health functioning, housing stability, economic stability, and physical location', which may operate at the individual, neighourhood or community levels (ibid.: 38). She also strongly urges that more attention be paid to 'systemic responsivity' that is, factors necessary within a jurisdiction to ensure that a spectrum of adequate and appropriate programs is available and accessible and to complement programming to permit individuals to participate (ibid.: 38–9). This approach seems to mark a shift to a more contextual understanding of the pre-conditions for changing offending behaviour.

Evidence-based practice and social justice

Kimberlé Crenshaw (2012: 1428–9) has observed 'the weakened capacity of social justice discourse to resist the neo-liberal ideologies that underwrite the expansion of social punishment and mass incarceration'. She argues that '[p]roblems that were once debated within political discourse as the product of illegitimate social power are now less controversially seen as individual pathologies and cultural deficits' (ibid.: 1451) with a de-emphasis on structural and historical causes (ibid.: 1452). Some advocates of justice reinvestment have acknowledged this shift but see justice reinvestment as a pragmatic option, using the language of economics to achieve change where appeals to social justice have had little success. Economic analysis and EBP offer potential benefits for criminal justice, including by making the rationale for the policy choices that are made, and the costs and benefits of those choices, more transparent. However, the manner in which the JRI has been given effect, and the commonplace methodologies used, remain in real tension with social justice objectives.

The focus within the JRI on certain forms of EBP, and the reliance on the risks-needs-responsivity framework drawn from the psychology of individual differences, has been embraced by legislators, technical assistance providers and practitioners seeking to reform some aspects of criminal justice. Understood in this way, EBP offers a suite of practices to choose from with a promise that these are likely to be effective in reducing recidivism and generating savings. This must be very compelling. However, the narrow focus on reform of the criminal justice system, with reducing recidivism as a primary goal by using interventions that target the 'Big Four' (Andrew and Bonta, 2010), is very much in tension with the intention of Tucker and Cadora (2003) to bring about change at the neighbourhood level (see Chapter 3). Indeed, Andrews and Bonta (2010) were quite dismissive of social ecology:

> even the best of efforts to link the social ecology of neighborhoods to individual criminal conduct yield minor effects. Social science rhetoric aside, interesting and convincing demonstrations of the impact of broad structural/cultural factors on variations in individual criminal conduct are few. (ibid.: 131–2)

The basis for their dismissal emphasises that their focus is change at the individual, rather than the systemic or community level. Other methodologies and measures are possible and desirable.

Van Voorhis (2013), whose critical review was discussed above, has not dismissed EBP out of hand. Instead, she has given an account of building an evidence base to inform interventions better suited to meet women's needs through a multilayered research program. She draws on an expansive multi-disciplinary review conducted by others with due regard to small scale studies and qualitative research findings, undertaking focus groups, and testing emerging themes sometimes by using experimental designs, none of which would satisfy criteria for meta-analysis. The developing evidence indicates the importance of gender-responsive programming and the need to 'focus on the confluence of mental health, substance abuse and trauma and interventions to improve women's socio-economic conditions.... Incorpor[ating] culturally sensitive and relational approaches that maintain women's connection to community, family, children and other relationships' (Van Voorhis, 2013: 126).

Work by desistance scholars is also instructive. Like Van Voorhis, desistance scholars (Jardine and Whyte, 2013; McNeill *et al.*, 2012) adopt a more contextual approach, moving beyond the individual level to recognise family and community and to take a more strengths-based approach that is not reducible to questions of recidivism. They note that 'the purposes of community corrections vary across both time and place and they are multiple and contested here and now...different purposes suggest different definitions and measures of effectiveness and therefore engagement with different forms of evidence' (McNeill *et al.*, 2012: 38 and 39). Measures of reconviction, which are commonly the focus of evidence-based practice, 'speak to only one of these purposes' but 'research has much more to offer' (ibid.). Like Solesbury (2001), they argue that the evidence that is needed is less about '*evaluating* practices, systems or techniques—it is about *understanding* and *explaining* the processes that practices, systems, and techniques exist to support', that is, bringing about positive change . This includes questions 'about how to motivate change, and how to engage with the family and community contexts in which change is embedded' (McNeill *et al.*, 2012: 50 emphasis in the original). The Good Lives model is one approach that engages with such issues (Ward and Maruna, 2007; Fox, Albertson and Wong 2013a: 146). Qualitative evaluations and methodologies more suited for some programs have a place in such approaches.

Todd Clear (2010: 4) has argued that '[i]f we try to address mass incarceration using the "what works" paradigm, then we automatically are drawn to a programmatic model of change as opposed to, say, a systemic model'. The former model has little influence on the number of offenders who enter prisons and may have 'the perverse effect of forcing the solutions to disregard a great deal of what we know about incarceration' that falls outside the what works framework (ibid.: 11). Thus, the limits of EBP within the JRI are not solely in terms of the type of evidence base used to determine which programs are designated as effective, or the strengths and weaknesses of universal versus tailored programs, although these are very important concerns. Rather as Clear (ibid.: 10) has argued, the what works approach is 'well positioned to inform us about which current practices deserve to be spread more widely' but justice reinvestment requires an 'action-relevant criminological knowledge' to 'enable us to imagine new and potent strategies for improving justice and public safety' (ibid.: 10). Re-thinking evidence, methodologies and measurement is necessarily part of that project.

In this chapter we have flagged both the strengths and weaknesses of commonly used approaches to justice reinvestment. In the section below we highlight some other possibilities that might be more consistent with a social justice-oriented justice reinvestment.

Measuring what matters

As we have discussed above, the emphasis on EBP and what works within the JRI has encouraged measurement and evaluation at the individual level and focused attention on recidivism rates. We have noted that this approach is in tension with aspirations towards social justice and community revitalisation. The limitations of an individual-level analysis and recidivism as an outcome measure have been noted in many quarters. For instance, a recent report by the US National Research Council (2014: 355) argued:

> Much of the research on the effects of incarceration has focused on individual-level outcomes for formerly incarcerated individuals and sometimes their families. Yet because of the extreme social concentration of incarceration, the most important effects may be systemic, for groups and communities.

Other researchers and policy-makers have begun to work towards methodologies and measures beyond the individual level to recognise family, neighbourhood, community and societal factors. Here we describe just a few of these developments.

As discussed above, Roman (2004: 271) has urged the adaptation of CBA to pursue different policy questions, because 'changes in the welfare of the community resulting from a program may be far more substantial than those directly associated with the participants'. He recommends a greater focus on 'economic welfare changes' within the community served by the program.

> Conceptually, this approach links the effects of the program directly to the community served by the program. Therefore, whether the population directly affected by the program is small or large, the

research acknowledges that the program is funded by the larger community and may have effects on the community beyond those that can be observed within an experimental or quasi-experimental framework. (ibid.: 271)

Fox, Albertson and Wong (2013a) have developed a different theoretical framework that seeks to renew the focus on social justice. They reject 'the assumption of instrumental rationality and an extrinsic reward structure' and the influence of rational choice theory that they identify within justice reinvestment models in the UK and the USA. Instead they support a move towards recognition of the 'beneficence and intrinsic rewards of building social capital and tapping into community resources to prevent offending and reoffending' (ibid.: 173). Their model is also normative, and 'considers the offender's rights and responsibilities in relation to their community and wider society' (ibid.: 170). In this approach they draw parallels with the Good Lives model of offender change (McNeill *et al.*, 2012; Ward and Maruna, 2007).

McNeill *et al.* (2012) also point to conceptual and methodological difficulties with recidivism as a measure, recognising that 'some people are more vulnerable to criminalization and penalization than others' (ibid.: 40). They emphasise the need to develop a better understanding of offender change because:

Offender change (as opposed to mere control) is a crucially important means by which community corrections can contribute to a reduction in crime and victimization (and to effective reintegration)—and reduction in fiscal pressures. Supporting long-term change through community supervision holds out the prospect of enabling ex/offenders to progress not just to the point where they are no longer harming others, but to a position where they can become net contributors to their communities—both socially and financially. (ibid.: 41)

This has implications for research and practice, suggesting the need to value ex-offender and practitioner voices.

The need to develop relevant, appropriate and meaningful measures for Indigenous communities and contexts has been recognised internationally and in Australia. For instance, the United Nations Permanent Forum on Indigenous Issues recognises the need to support Indigenous people to participate in developing culturally relevant standards of measurement and indices. Also, the International Centre for the Prevention of Crime has developed a community safety framework for Indigenous communities. These offer models that can be built upon (Willis, 2010: 2). While measures should reflect Indigenous concerns and aspirations, it has been suggested that appropriate measures might include those able to capture incremental change – and not just major system changes that take time to emerge; those that are 'able to be disaggregated in the context of small sample sizes'; and indicators of 'stressors and their impact on well-being, community-level impacts of justice services and the quality of service provided at all levels of the criminal justice system' (ibid.: 5–6).

Joy Wundersitz (2010: 3) has identified the value of an ecological framework in understanding risk and protective factors for offending among Indigenous Australians. Such a framework necessitates moving beyond a singular focus on the individual level to develop relevant measures at family and community levels. It also requires recognition that some factors, like alcohol abuse, have both individual effects and effects on communities. She also highlights substantial differences in offence rates between Aboriginal communities and the imperative for researchers to better understand risk and protective factors across communities. Like other researchers who have seen value in 'strengths-based approaches', she advocates giving greater focus in research and interventions to 'the strengths inherent in Indigenous communities' (ibid.: 97).

Measuring social costs and benefits

The focus of governments on the cost-effectiveness of criminal justice expenditure is unlikely to wane, whatever the state of national economies. However, the need to develop more adequate methodologies and forms of measurement has been clearly identified. For instance, the UK House of Commons Justice Committee (HCJC 2010: para 302) concluded that a better evidence base concerning cost-effective measures was needed, including for groups such as women. The committee urged the development of more sophisticated performance measures beyond reoffending rates, and in recognition that costs and benefits might flow outside the criminal justice system and to a wider range of stakeholders. They saw this as consistent with a Social Return on Investment approach (SROI) (ibid.: paras 368–75). For instance, supporting women in the community may bring financial and social benefits, such as fewer living on welfare and fewer children in care, that do not accrue to the criminal justice system (Gelsthorpe and Hedderman, 2012: 386).

The SROI approach has focused on social costs and benefits. Within justice reinvestment, costs of incarceration, or other criminal justice interventions, are typically measured as the costs borne by the state.

Social cost is conceptualised differently. It has been described as a normative concept:

> the concept of social cost means cost considered from a society-wide perspective. Social costs are incurred when activity is displaced from a normal or expected state of affairs into an alternative, usually less-desired state of affairs. Social cost is in this sense a normative concept. (Lengyel and Brown, 2009: 9 and fn 2)

However, social cost has a second normative dimension of likely concern for justice reinvestment, that is:

> what gets counted as a social cost by some analysts is determined by the moral status of the actor (i.e., whether the activity is condemned by society). Social costs that accrue to the immoral actor are discounted in this perspective. (ibid.: fn 2, citing Mark Cohen, 2000)

However, the authors (ibid.) demonstrate in their work that the choice is open to recognise that the costs to offenders and their families are a social cost and a proper concern. In their study of the social costs of imprisoning parents for drug offences in Hawaii, they recognise that taking the social costs of incarceration into account would properly draw into consideration a raft of other costs such as:

> significant losses to the prisoner and the prisoner's family in terms of reduced quality of life, lost earnings while in prison, lost future earnings of the releasee, lost taxes to the state on lost earnings, up-front criminal justice system costs, the cost of parole, foster care for the children of some prisoners, and a host of other costs, some of which are yet to be estimated. (Lengyel and Brown, 2009: 2)

Despite their comprehensive approach using 24 measures of social cost, they acknowledge that costs to the community of 'reentry cycling' are not included because no one has devised a way to estimate those costs and 'it remains an important topic for future cost–benefit analysis' (ibid.: 47). They estimate that the social costs of incarceration for drug offenders in Hawaii exceed social benefits by a ratio of 7:1 at a significant cost to the state, but with the greatest social costs borne by the offenders and their families (ibid.: 55).

The UK New Economic Foundation (2008: 25) also uses an SROI approach in their report on alternatives to incarceration for women.

They critically examine the measures commonly used in criminal justice and note the disproportionate concern by decision-makers with the financial cost incurred by public spending to the neglect of other costs and benefits –'measuring what matters'. Using SROI they conduct a CBA that includes factors such as the costs of unemployment and family breakdown that would not normally be measured in cost–benefit analyses in order to 'take account of the long–ranging effects and costs that imprisonment has on the children of women offenders' (NEF, 2008: 16). They find that, over ten years, for every £1 spent on support-focused alternatives to prison '£14 worth of social value is generated to women and their children, victims and society generally' (ibid.: 17).

However, SROI should not be accepted uncritically. It may face some of the criticisms of other cost–benefit approaches, such as the concern that not all of what matters can be monetised. For instance, the strengths and weaknesses of SROI are documented in a Scottish study of desistance (Jardine and Whyte 2013). Strengths include the reliance on a theory of change to produce a model, and identify outcomes, allowing key stakeholders to participate in identifying 'outcomes that matter' (ibid.: 22). Weaknesses include that '[a]ssumptions and discretionary or subjective judgements often inform attempts to value social impact and may introduce a lack of transparency and objectivity, or a manipulation of the results' (ibid.: 23). The authors conclude with several cautions. They note that, notwithstanding the appeal of a single measure like the SROI ratio, policy-makers would be unwise to rely solely on that measure. They also note the limits of single outcome measures such as reoffending or 'return to custody' rates, which raise 'questions of power, in terms of whose voice is heard'. They also recognise a 'need to become better at measuring what is often viewed as 'immeasurable'; that is, soft indicators of progress such as individual confidence, personal change and better social relationships on the way to desistence (ibid.).

Conclusion

It is not our intent in this book to design a model of justice reinvestment. Nor do we wish to be prescriptive about how it should be given effect in any context or setting, although we have made clear our view that efforts directed towards challenging the too heavy reliance on incarceration must work to benefit those who are especially disadvantaged by current approaches, consistent with the pursuit of social justice. These efforts should recognise the harmful effects of high levels of imprisonment for individuals, neighbourhoods, particular communities and civil society.

If Eric Cadora (2014: 281) is correct that justice reinvestment is beginning to displace other reform options, then there is a pressing need to ensure that the interests of marginalised groups can be recognised and advanced by justice reinvestment. In part, that means greater attention to the differential drivers of incarceration, and to developing policy options and programs that may be effective for them. Data and evidence matter, and new approaches are needed to measure what matters. However, challenging mass incarceration requires that justice reinvestment is understood as much more than following the data and choosing an evidence-based program:

> In the domain of justice, empirical evidence by itself cannot point the way to policy, yet an explicit and transparent expression of normative principles has been notably missing as US incarceration rates dramatically rose over the last four decades. Normative principles have deep roots in jurisprudence and theories of governance and are needed to supplement empirical evidence to guide future policy and research. (National Research Council, 2014: 333)

We also emphasise that justice reinvestment is not a program to be 'rolled out', as we discuss further in Chapter 5, but rather an orientation or approach which will be given effect differently in different settings; how it is given effect is contingent on a great many economic, political, social and cultural factors. There are choices to be made at each stage of justice reinvestment – some of those are normative and others more instrumental. Those related to evidence, methodologies and measurement are not mere technical details, but as examined above, have had, and will continue to have, a substantial influence on the possibilities of justice reinvestment, and to some extent determine who will share in any benefits, financial or otherwise.

5
How Does Justice Reinvestment Travel? Criminal Justice Policy Transfer and the Importance of Context: Policy, Politics and Populism

The previous two chapters raised a series of challenges to some of the often taken for granted claims made on behalf of justice reinvestment policies. Chapter 3 looked behind the claims of locality and community and in particular interrogated how they may or may not work for over-represented and vulnerable groups, including people with mental illness and/or cognitive disability, women, and Indigenous and other racialised peoples. Chapter 4 examined some of the problematic features behind the methodological and measurement claims of justice reinvestment as 'data-driven' and 'evidence-based', asking what is counted and what counts, and drawing out tensions between 'evidence-based practice' and social justice concerns. This chapter addresses the issue of the portability of justice reinvestment as a form of 'policy transfer', an investigation which places the issue of context centre stage. It looks briefly at the issue of criminal justice policy transfer more generally and through some specific examples in the UK and Australia, before examining some of the key pre-conditions for and barriers to, the successful adoption of justice reinvestment policies in Australia. This is followed by a discussion of various dangers and misconceptions in processes of policy formation, including what we call the 'rationalist fallacy' which is exemplified in the common 'roll out' metaphor and the susceptibility of criminal justice policy to populist backlash.

Instances of what is called 'policy transfer' in the criminal justice realm, emanating from the USA and transplanted elsewhere, have been vigorously opposed by many criminologists, activists, practitioners in the criminal justice sector, social movements and some politicians. Examples include the privatisation of corrections, sentencing policies such as three strikes legislation, 'grid' and mandatory sentencing; and so-called 'zero tolerance' and 'broken windows' policing policies. It would be inadequate to argue that justice reinvestment policies formulated in the USA should be 'imported' or 'transferred' into the Australian and other national contexts, simply because the authors regard it as a broadly progressive development (unlike mandatory sentencing for example). We need to be reflexive here, for one of our aims in this project was precisely to see how justice reinvestment policies might be developed in the Australian context, so that the authors are directly implicated in an attempted diffusion process.

Criminal justice policy transfer

The main context within which policy transfer has been debated in criminal justice research and policy in recent years has been the alleged spread or diffusion of punitive and populist-oriented US policing and sentencing policies to other countries, what Wacquant (2009b:11) calls 'the new punitive doxa', the 'globalization of zero tolerance' (ibid.: 19) and the 'new Leviathon' (ibid.: 172). This debate has often been part of a wider concern about the spread of neo-liberalism and the globalisation or 'Americanisation' of social and economic relations. Wacquant is the leading proponent of the strong version of this 'USA led global spread' of neo-liberalism, replete with its key 'ingredient', an expanding penal system or 'penal surge'. Our discussion starts with a brief analysis of Wacquant's position. This is followed by a discussion of a more sceptical, nuanced and empirically detailed examination of the transfer of criminal justice policy by Jones and Newburn (2007), conducted in the UK. Finally we examine very briefly the limited evidence available in the Australian context.

Wacquant – globalising punitive common sense

According to Wacquant in his two major works, *Punishing the Poor* (2009a) and *Prisons of Poverty* (2009b), the process of policy transfer is not a 'blind and benign drift toward planetary convergence' but rather a 'stratified process of *differential and diffracted Americanization*, fostered by the strategic activities of hierarchical networks of state managers, ideological entrepreneurs, and scholarly marketers in the United States and in the countries of reception.' (2009a: 174, emphasis in original) The 'driving role' is played by 'think tanks and heteronomous scholarly disciplines and academics in the international peregrinations of public policy formulas' (ibid.). In Wacquant's account, it is the Manhattan Institute, a neo-conservative think-tank that was influential in 'applying market principles to social problems' (ibid.: 11) during the Reagan government, that has been the 'crucible of the new penal reason' (ibid.: 10). Wacquant notes the Manhattan Institute promoted Charles Murray's *Losing Ground* (1984), 'the bible for Reagan's crusade against the social-welfare state' (ibid.: 12), together with the 'broken windows' thesis that petty incivilities are a precursor to crime and should be rigorously policed by way of 'zero tolerance' policing which 'propagated itself across the globe with lightening speed' (ibid.: 19).

He summarises the process by which an 'academic pidgin of neo-liberal penality' is developed as follows:

> First there is the gestation and dissemination, national and then international, by U.S. Think tanks and their allies in the bureaucratic and journalistic fields, of terms, theories, and measures that, knit together, concur in penalizing social insecurity and its consequences at the bottom of the class structure. Next comes their borrowing, partial or wholesale, conscious or unconscious, necessitating a more or less intricate work of adaptation to the cultural idiom and state traditions specific to the receiving countries by the officials who then implement them, each in their domain of competence. A third operation intervenes to redouble this work and accelerate the international traffic in the categories of neo-liberal understanding, which now circulate in rush-production mode from New York to London, and then on to Paris, Brussels, Munich, and Madrid: their *academicization*, that is dressing them up in scholarly garb. (Wacquant, 2009b: 47, emphasis in original)

Waquant's general thesis about the globalisation of a USA led 'penal surge' which he argues is an 'integral component of the neo-liberal state' (ibid.: 175) has been widely debated and critiqued (see eg. Brown, 2012; 2011b; 2011c; Cunneen *et al.*, 2013: Pratt, 2011; Bumiller, 2013). Our narrower concern here is whether these somewhat sweeping claims about the globalisation of penal policy through US think-tanks can be justified by actual case studies in specific national contexts. Wacquant's main example is in relation to France, where he launches into what Cohen (2010: 387) describes as a:

> caricature; a savage portrait of these stupid and pompous institutions...which neither hide nor even try to hide their fascination for the supposedly novel and amazingly effective methods of community policing and other such American policies, which they just buy into without any question.

One criticism of Wacquant's account is that his argument 'exaggerates the role of think-tanks and other similar organisations, turning them into the carriers of much too massive a load' (Cohen, 2010: 388). Cohen argues that 'the generation of "meta ideas" are not so much explicitly deployed in changing criminal justice policy as ticking along in the background' (ibid.: 389).

Criminal justice policy transfer in the UK – a 'general steer'

In *Policy Transfer and Criminal Justice: Exploring US Influence over British Crime Control Policy* Trevor Jones and Tim Newburn (2007) set out to test the policy transfer process in the UK context in relation to three specific case studies: privatisation in corrections, forms of mandatory sentencing and 'zero tolerance' policing strategies (see also Newburn, 2002). The analysis is more empirically focused and detailed while still being theoretically attuned. They argue that policy transfer is an important issue for four reasons. Firstly because it is relatively under-researched. Secondly because much of the existing discussion tends to 'underplay or over-emphasise the role of political agency and the influence of particular, political and legal institutions' (2007: 17) and tends to assume 'that the inventions of policy-makers are contiguous with policy outcomes: policy instruments frequently being read as a straightforward representation of policy-makers aims and objectives' (ibid.: 18). This is an important recognition which we will develop later in this chapter. Thirdly a study of policy transfer is important because it raises the more general issue of convergence and divergence, and fourthly, because it opens up the issue of other possibilities and alternatives as an antidote to the overwhelming sense of inevitability and pessimism common to much of the globalisation literature.

Jones and Newburn (2007: 147) summarise their findings as follows:

> the history of UK policy development in these three fields suggests that hard forms of policy transfer – in terms of large-scale importation

of policy goals, content and instruments – are rather rare. In each area, although it is relatively easy to identify US roots for the ideas that were subsequently developed in the UK, in the cases of ZTP [zero tolerance policing] and sentencing at least, it appears that it was primarily policy ideas, symbols and rhetoric that were the objects of transfer. Subsequent developments in terms of policy content and instruments were considerably revised and reshaped in the UK context, with the result that the policies that actually developed were very different from their US forbears. This was less true in the sphere of privatization of corrections, where, as well as the initial idea of contracting out of prisons (and that of electronic monitoring) having clear roots in the USA, there was also a more significant practical input in terms of concrete manifestations of the policy. However even here the specific forms of contracting out of prisons and electronic monitoring that emerged in the UK took on a very different shape from its US precursors.

These more careful and nuanced findings provide a challenge to sweeping stories of policy transfer and the globalisation of US policies. As the authors note:

> Our findings bring into question assumptions that a crude form of 'Americanization' has been developing in UK criminal justice. In fact, our study demonstrates that even in these areas where such a process is widely perceived to have been active, things are much more complicated than they initially seem. If policy transfers even in these particular areas seem to have been rather partial and constrained, then we need to be very careful not to present recent policy changes in terms of a simplified notion of Americanization of British crime control. This supports the findings of other recent work which highlights how the complex changes which are emerging within criminal justice systems cannot be explained by straightforward reference to the global march of neo-liberal reform, nor to simple notions of emulation and transfer. (ibid.: 153–4)

Criminal justice policy transfer in Australia

A brief analysis of some examples of the transfer of criminal justice policy in Australia demonstrates some support for Wacquant's 'differential and diffracted Americanisation', particularly in relation to prison privatisation (although it seems that the UK developments were as much if not more of an influence), zero tolerance policing and risk assessment tools. However overall, and in the absence of Australian research on the transfer of criminal justice policy, we see the pattern as being closer to that outlined by Jones and Newburn.

Turning to correctional privatisation first, as of 2015 there were nine private prisons in Australia, two each in NSW (15.8% of all prisoners); Victoria (31.8%); QLD (18.5%); and WA (20.7%) and one in SA (11.4%) (Productivity Commission, 2015, Table 8A1). Together they held 18.9 per cent of Australia's prisoners (6,044), the highest percentage of any country (Cavadino and Dignam, 2006: 314). There was a period of significant prison privatisation, especially in Victoria under the Kennett government in the 1990s, although the extent to which this was directly driven by US developments is unclear. Certainly particular US companies (e.g., Corrections Corporation of America and Wackenhut Corrections Corporation) were part of consortiums which included Australian companies in the operation of the first private prisons in Australia: Borallon in QLD and Junee in NSW. However these initial prison privatisations drew more upon the general claims of improved efficiency and cost savings involved in privatisation, and a desire to weaken the power of prison officer unions, than in any evidence of specific lobbying by US companies, although there is some evidence of this in relation to the privatisation of the Junee prison in NSW. It is in the area of refugee detention centres, that UK and European based multinational security companies including GSL/G4S and Serco (Grewcock, 2009; Loewenstein, 2013) have had the most reach. With the exception of prison privatisation in Victoria, where the Tasman Institute and Institute of Public Affairs operated to prepare the ground (Woodward, 1999), there is little evidence of any diffusion through Australian think-tanks, or promotion by academics, who in relation to most of these issues have been critical. Wacquant's 'academic pidgin of neo-liberal penality' has not been evident in Australian criminal justice academia (see generally on Australian penal privatisation: Harding, 1997; Moyle, 1994; 2000; McCartney, 2000; O'Neill, 1999; Costar and Economou, 1999; Hancock, 1999; Woodward, 1999; Baldry, 1994; Ernst, 1994; Hogg and Brown, 1998; Roth, 2014).

In terms of sentencing policy there has been periodic interest at the state government level or among the opposition, usually conservative parties, in various forms of mandatory, mandatory minimum or grid sentencing policies based in part on US models such as the Minnesota grid system. However in terms of legislation, the results have been limited. (Brown *et al.*, 2015: 1289–95). Mandatory sentencing provisions, usually mandatory minimums or mandatory minimum non-parole periods, exist in nearly all Australian States and in Commonwealth law. But most are not extensive schemes as in the USA, or indeed the now abolished Imprisonment for Public Protection (IPP) in the UK, but rather relate to specific offences such as the murder of police officers (NSW); repeat burglary (WA); repeat serious child sex offences (QLD); and treachery, terrorism, treason and sedition (Cth). Such provisions have arisen mainly in response to media pressure around specific local cases and against a general backdrop of a long-term struggle between the judiciary on the one hand, and the executive and legislature on the other, over the scope of judicial discretion in sentencing. Legislatures have sought to confine judicial discretion through a range of initiatives including the provision of statistical information, sentencing councils, 'truth in sentencing' formulas, guideline judgments, standard non-parole periods, the preventive detention of serious sex offenders and mandatory sentencing (for a detailed treatment of this history see Brown et al., 2015: 1246–94; Warner, 1999).

'Truth in sentencing' was an influential slogan which came to signify the idea that the public was somehow being defrauded when sentence lengths set by a judge at the time of sentencing were reduced in any way by subsequent legislative or administrative schemes such as remissions, forms of administrative release, or even by parole schemes (Chan, 1992: 192; Cunneen et al., 2013: 52). The high point of 'truth in sentencing' influence in Australia came with the passage of the *Sentencing Act* 1989 (NSW) by the new Greiner, L-NC conservative government. The Act abolished remissions altogether, set a relation of three-quarters between the non-parole and parole period, and abolished the presumption in favour of parole, resulting in an increase in the NSW prison population of 30 per cent over two years (Gorta et al., 1992; Matka, 1991; Cain and Robey, 1992; Roby and Cain, 1992; Johnston and Spiers, 1996; Brown, 1990; 1991). 'Truth in sentencing' rhetoric also lay behind the abolition of remissions in Victoria in 1991 (Freiberg, 1992).

Zero tolerance and 'broken windows' (Wilson and Kelling, 1982) policing attracted significant Australian interest, with numerous Australian police and politicians trooping to New York to listen to Police Commissioner Bratton (1998) and Mayor Giulliani proclaim its success in reducing crime rates (Zimring, 2013). What was transferred was primarily a form of 'get tough' political rhetoric rather than new, on the ground, policing developments (see generally: Dixon, 2005a, 1998; Griffith, 1999; Cunneen, 1999a, 1999b; Ferris, 2001; Darcey, 1999; Grabosky, 1999). However CompStat (the use of local area computer crime statistics for management and accountability purposes:

Henry, 2002; Walsh and Vito, 2004) seems to have been influential in consolidating new forms of performance-driven management (Dixon, 2005a:11; 2005b).

North American risk assessment tools and programs have been influential in various state correctional systems in Australia (Cunneen et al, 2013: 67–90; see also Chapter 4). It is important to note examples which flow the other way (Connell, 2007). New Zealand and Australian restorative justice processes, such as family group conferencing, youth conferencing and circle sentencing, have attracted interest in the UK and the USA (see generally: Braithwaite, 1988, 2002; Morris and Maxwell, 2001; Strang, 2002; Marchetti and Daley, 2004; Chan, 2005; Cunneen and Hoyle, 2010; Marchetti 2014).

The dominant process has been in the transfer of slogans and sound bites, many, but not all, punitive in nature, which politicians have deployed in the Australian context. Slogans such as 'three strikes', 'truth in sentencing', and 'zero tolerance', promoted mainly by politicians, particular journalists and news outlets, and some criminal justice agencies and personnel, have had political purchase, but only as filtered through the complexities and differences of local, mainly state, politics. The long-term 'guerrilla warfare' (Frieberg, 2000: 51) between the executive and legislature on the one hand, and the judiciary on the other, over attempts to restrict judicial discretion, has been a major filter through which the transfer of criminal justice policy proposals must pass.

Jones and Newburn (2007: 163) find in the UK context that the policy transfer process is closer to 'what Page describes as "gaining inspiration" rather than "lesson-drawing". Labels have been borrowed and a general steer in certain areas has occurred, rather than anything that comes close to the ideal-typical model of policy transfer'. They draw the distinction between 'soft' and 'hard' policy transfer, soft being broadly the discourse elements and hard, the actual programs. They note (2007:162) that 'rhetoric, labels, and nomenclature travel much more easily than the nuts and bolts of policy' before going on to echo Melossi (2004: 144) that even here, 'we should be careful of assuming that similar labels *mean* similar things.' Newburn (2010: 344) notes for example that in the UK the Wilson and Kelling 'broken windows' thesis:

> gradually morphed into what became the New Labour government's "anti-social behaviour strategy". Curfews, ASBOS, parenting orders, and changes to tenancy rules and eviction regulations have all been influenced by what is believed to be the core message of the "broken windows" article.

Therefore while there may be little 'nuts and bolts' policy detail behind the 'soft' policy transfer of rhetoric, labels and slogans, that does not mean that they are without effect. Indeed they can play a significant role in condensing a sentiment, shaping a public mood and providing legitimation for shifting positions and new policies. Under the heading of bipartisanship below, we quote the US Right on Crime group characterising the US left's position as 'soft on crime'. While somewhat of a caricature and drawing on familiar '1960s disintegration' tropes, it does pinpoint the expansion of the US prison system in the 1990s under the Clinton presidency. Similar expansions took place under the Blair Labour government (1997–2007) and in the Australian Labor Party's (ALP) state governments in the 1990s and 2000s.

Tony Blair's 'tough on crime, tough on the causes of crime' sound bite, delivered at the 1992 British Labour Party Conference, is a classic example of policy transfer by slogan. It was picked up and recycled widely on both sides of politics in Australia and elsewhere. The slogan appeared to balance punitive 'get tough' sentiments, with a social democratic recognition of the economic and social causes of crime, although in practice there was little recognition of, or action on, the latter. Blair advisers were much influenced by Clinton's 'triangulation' strategy of a 'third way' between left and right, and Clinton's neutralisation of law and order issues for the Democrats with 'tough on crime' rhetoric, and a massive prison building program. Dean (2008: 16) notes that the Blair government passed 53 crime-related Acts creating 3,000 new offences. Jenkins (2012) points out that this was compared with '500 in the equivalent period under the Tories. He ([Blair]...put more people in prison than ever in British history'. Indeed Stephen Farrell and colleagues have revisited the Thatcher law and order policies and shown that behind the belligerent rhetoric and the politicisation of law and order, imprisonment rates, and especially juvenile detention levels, did not increase under the Thatcher government but turned sharply upwards in Blair's term of office (Farrall, 2006; Farrall and Hay, 2010).

Similarly in NSW, Bob Carr's term of office as the Premier in an ALP State government (1995–2005) also coincided with pre-election law and order auctions, 'cement them in' and 'tough on crime' rhetoric, and rapidly rising imprisonment rates. This was a major shift from and repudiation of a reform period during the first two-thirds of the Wran ALP government from 1976–84. In this period Attorney General Frank Walker decriminalised public drunkenness, begging, vagrancy and most prostitution offences, raised the legal threshold for common public order offences such as offensive language and behaviour, abolished imprisonment for fine default, and reformed bail laws (Brown, 2005). The Report of the Nagle Royal Commission into Prisons (1978) ushered in a period of prison reform under Commissioner Tony Vinson (Vinson, 1982; Findlay, 1982; Zdenkowski and Brown, 1982). The NSW imprisonment rates dropped from 126 per 100,000 population in 1970 to 84 in 1984. Carr was a keen student of US politics and like Blair, may well have been influenced by Clinton's crime policies and the triangulation strategy. Catchy slogans provided cover for a shift in NSW ALP criminal justice policy, reflecting a determination never again to be outflanked by the conservative L-NC on law and order, seen as a major factor in the Greiner L-NC election victory in NSW in 1988. They provided what NSW Police Inspector David Darcy (1999: 291) called, 'a golden thread that can be woven through the fabric of the rhetoric of "getting tough on crime"', while gesturing to traditional social democratic concerns.

Newburn's observations (2010: 346) provide an apt summary of the above brief discussion of policy transfer in the UK and Australia:

> [a]pparently similar developments in policy and practice in different jurisdictions may have differing origins, be organised and regulated differently, and be subject to different forms of criticism and resistance. ... [W]hen discussing purportedly globalising trends, we [should] remember that in some respects attention to the "local" becomes *more* rather than less important. It is precisely the focus on the nature of the local that illustrates the limitations of the global.

Having briefly examined some examples of the transfer of criminal justice policy in the UK and Australia, we return to justice reinvestment and the question of its portability, and thus to differences in context between the USA and Australia. As in so many things, context is crucial. Can justice reinvestment policies developed in the USA be transplanted to different social, political, cultural and economic contexts? To answer this question it is necessary to identify some of the pre-conditions which sustained successful (and unsuccessful) justice reinvestment policies and outcomes in the USA and consider whether these pre-conditions are peculiar to the US context.

Context – differences, pre-conditions, barriers

Among the differences in context between the USA and Australia is the relative lack of 'low hanging fruit' (relatively easy changes which will produce quick reductions in imprisonment rates) in the Australian context. This is partly because the War Against Drugs has been more restrained in Australia and has had to compete with a strong 'harm minimisation' approach in the medical and public policy fields. The obvious low hanging fruit would be reintroducing remissions – currently off the table since the rise of notions of 'truth in sentencing' and reducing remand rates and bail revocation rates – not so easy, as we will see. As Sarah Hopkins from Just Reinvest NSW puts it:

> We're hoping we'll be able to knock down some sort of low hanging fruit and say, "Okay. Look, in the first six months, or over the 2013 to 2014 period, this reason was given for breaching bail this number of times but after protocols were developed with police, that reason was given only five times..."

By way of comparison in the USA, simple changes in, for example, three strikes mandatory sentencing regimes and highly punitive and discriminatory sentencing policies for minor drug possession would produce reductions in imprisonment rates, such as those achieved in New York through winding back the Rockefeller drug laws (see Chapter 2).

Another significant structural difference is the role of the Governor in the US system, a position with no equivalent in Australia, the UK or New Zealand. Our interviews revealed that where the state Governor was supportive, their leadership, as in the example of South Dakota, was crucial in the consultation and legislative process. South Dakota General Counsel Jim Seward notes that:

> We had those stakeholder meetings. Those were very easy to organise. Staff members would contact the executive director of the County Commissioner Association, and invite them to bring in 10 or 20 people to sit down with us. I found out then, because I was pretty new to the office, that if you get a phone call from the Governor's office to come in and share your views on something, most people accept and they drive in all the way across the state to do that.

Another difference is that the level of distrust in government is much higher in the USA, especially in the Tea Party and the 'small government-low tax' libertarian wing of the Republican Party. This cuts both ways as it is a factor in some of the conservative support for winding back Federal drugs laws, which are seen as an intrusive manifestation of big government. On the other hand, Todd Clear observes that in the USA, reinvestment has been hampered in part because there is a substantial mistrust of government and the public are unlikely to think that savings in one area should be shifted to another area of government expenditure: 'In the US version, it's – our money is being spent over here. Now you're going to take our money and you're not going to give it back to us, you're going to give it over there to them?' He suggests that this might be less of an obstacle to reinvestment in Australia.

Some pre-conditions are not so different, for example, a key contextual element in the rise of justice reinvestment is the substantial reduction in crimes rates, evident in both the USA (dramatic reductions from the late 1990s) and Australia. These reductions are significant because high crime rates and the fear of crime are key conditions in the development of mass incarceration. Clear and Frost (2014: 11) note that in '2010 violent crime hit its lowest rate in forty years' and that 'as a result of falling crime rates, crime has fallen off the main list of concerns Americans express in public opinion polls'. In Australia most categories of crime, especially property crime, have been declining since the late 1990s, and the NSW homicide rate is half what it was in 1988. Law and order issues did not figure prominently in the 2015 NSW election campaign, and to the extent that they did in the 2015 Queensland and 2014 Victorian campaigns, it was largely by way of critique of the excessively punitive policies of both L-NC governments.

Another similarity is the rise of recidivism as a political issue. In the USA high recidivism rates have been a significant factor in the economic argument that imprisonment is wasteful and inefficient. Since 1995 the Australian Productivity Commission has produced a *Report on Government Services*, such as Justice and Corrections. The reports utilise a framework of performance indicators to evaluate government services, including recidivism rates (Productivity Commission, 2015) . The regular compilation and publication of recidivism rates have provided an edge to arguments that imprisonment is 'inefficient', wasteful and even criminogenic. In this way recidivism rates have become a political issue and state governments are sensitive to them, often setting reduction targets.

The project interviews highlighted some specific differences in context which arguably constitute barriers to the successful adoption and implementation of US-derived justice reinvestment policies in the Australian context. This section of the chapter will examine a selection of these 'barrier' issues, namely:

- the differences in legal and political structures underpinning criminal justice between the USA and Australia which, among other effects,

limit the degree to which economic incentives to reduce imprisonment can be developed and devolved onto front line criminal justice agencies in Australia;
- the widespread acceptance across many diverse constituencies in the USA that mass incarceration has become a major problem, for a range of reasons, and that its consequences need to be addressed and drivers reversed;
- that the level of political bipartisanship over the desirability of justice reinvestment policies evident in many US states is largely absent in the Australian context;
- that the important role played by faith-based constituencies in the USA in promoting justice reinvestment policies and notions of redemption around the *Second Chance Act of 2007* is almost entirely missing in the Australian context;
- that the capacity for coordination among various criminal justice agencies around the promotion of justice reinvestment policies as evident in some US states, is again largely lacking in Australia.

Differences in political and funding structures – limits to incentivisation

Significant differences in the political structures of government and in the operation of the criminal justice system exist between the USA and most other countries, even other federal systems such as Australia. A graphic illustration is found in David Garland's analysis of the retention of the death penalty in around half of US states. Garland's (2010: 310) answer to the question why this is so:

> does not point to Puritanism, or punitiveness, or violent vigilantism, as conventional commentaries would have it. It points instead to one of America's chief values and virtues – a radically local version of democracy –which is the primary cause of capital punishment's persistence into the twenty-first century. If the death penalty is a particle of state power, in America that power has never been so concentrated or so centrally controlled as it has been elsewhere, being instead devolved to the local level and co-possessed by a local electorate.

The allocation of powers in the American Constitution is such that 'jurisdiction over police, criminal, and penal matters has, from the founding to the present day, been a matter for the State and local authorities rather than for the central government' (ibid.: 161). This is markedly different from unitary political systems such as the UK, New Zealand and most European states. It is also different from Australia's federation where most standard criminal justice powers, the police and court systems, are predominantly a state responsibility, and where there is no separate federal prison system. However, Commonwealth criminal laws have expanded considerably in recent years in areas such as anti-terrorism, drug importation and distribution, corporate and welfare fraud, as has the size of the Australian Federal Police force. A key difference is that in Australia criminal justice issues and powers have not devolved to local government, such as the counties and municipalities in the USA or local authorities in the UK. Everyday criminal justice issues are primarily a matter of state jurisdiction.

Perhaps the most significant difference of all is that in Australia and most other Western democracies, criminal justice officials are appointed rather than elected. While the appointments of police commissioners, judicial officers, public prosecutors and public defenders are made by the (state) government of the day, by and large political considerations, and certainly party political membership and allegiances, do not play a prominent, or at least overt, role; the appointments are largely merit-based in a public administration mode. In the USA in contrast:

> Electoral politics affect criminal justice more directly and extensively in America than in any other liberal democracy. Rules and procedures vary from state to state, but in most states...the offices of district attorney, state judge, county sheriff, and police chief are elective. Candidates for those positions run for office. They raise campaign funds from private donors and make electoral commitments to voters on issues that would elsewhere be regarded as judicial matters or questions of impartial public administration. Because they are subject to election, legal officers seek to align themselves with majority sentiment and with popular measures such as tough sentencing laws, harsh prison policies, and, of course, capital punishment. In several states, penal policy has been enacted directly by popular referenda or voter ballot initiative, a process that would be "unthinkable" in most of Europe. (Garland, 2010: 165)

In relation to justice reinvestment, this makes the gaining of bipartisanship in the US context more significant, more local, and more difficult, in that electoral politics are embedded within the operations of criminal justice at a local level. It makes the bipartisanship achieved in various contexts, as discussed in a later section, even more remarkable, although it should be noted that party discipline is much looser than in Westminster-type systems like Australia and the UK.

These structural differences in the division of powers flow through to funding arrangements and to the possibilities for 'incentivisation' attached to criminal justice policies and programs. How do cost savings get calculated and 'reinvested' within existing political and fiscal governmental structures, particularly in a context of weak local government which traditionally has had little or no role in relation to policing and other criminal justice processes? In Chapter 3 we discussed in more detail the problems surrounding the constitution of place-based strategies of locality and community within Australia's largely state-based political structures. We noted that in the UK, local authorities play a much more significant role in the delivery of local services so that the possibilities of devolution of fiscal responsibility and incentivising local authorities to engage in various preventive and mentoring programs with disadvantaged groups are much greater than in Australia (Fox, Albertson and Wong, 2013a).

As discussed in Chapter 4 there are a range of incentives (and reverse incentives) built into the US criminal justice system arising from the division between federal, state and county jurisdictions and administrations. Variations in the justice reinvestment strategies attempt to utilise or reverse these incentives in a way that seeks to reduce prison populations, especially through stemming the heavy flow of probation and parole revocations, particularly because of technical violations. The incentives flow not only along jurisdictional lines, but also within and between departments within the one (usually state) jurisdiction. In a typical example, if a state Community Corrections department reduces the number of people returning to prison for technical parole violations, then the savings are reallocated from the Department of Corrections to the Department of Community Corrections.

In some justice reinvestment reforms, the incentives are offered to prisoners as forms of 'earned discharge', a mechanism to reduce parole officer case loads, as South Dakota General Counsel Jim Seward explains:

> We had to figure out a way to get these case numbers down.
>
> The data shows that if you're going to recidivate or reoffend, you're going to do it in the first two years; 93% of offenders do it in the first couple of years. So we wanted to shorten that parole time. So we did "earned discharge", where if you are perfectly compliant for 30 days, you earn 30 days off the back–end. It doesn't take very long...the

> parolees were well aware of it before the law even came into effect. They would talk to the parole agents: "When do I get this? What do I need to be compliant?" "You have to pay your restitution and your fines and your attorney fees and go to treatment. Go to your work and do all the things you need to do. Stay clean and sober".
>
> In just the first eight or nine months, we have reduced those parole case loads, by holding people more accountable, from about 70 to a little above 50. Our goal is, as we can get those caseloads down to that 40 range, they can hold people more accountable, by spending more time with them and using other evidence-based practices

Not only is the scope for generating incentives much more limited in the Australian context for reasons associated with the structural differences in the political and constitutional framework outlined above, but also prospects of creating internal system incentives of the 'responsibilisation' sort outlined in the 'earned discharge' example above are unfavourable in Australia. This is largely because of the current public and political antipathy to any sort of executive and administrative 'interference' with sentence lengths, widely seen as set by the terms of the original judicial sentence. Attempts to reintroduce a system of remissions, 'earned time' or 'earned discharge', are arguably overdue in the Australian context. However such attempts would need to confront the political and cultural force of the 'truth in sentencing' ethos, noted earlier, and to be argued in normative terms as beneficial, not simply as a convenient way of reducing numbers. For incentives are far from just an economic issue, but are inflected by safety concerns and political risk, as Marc Mauer of The Sentencing Project explains:

> The incentives are skewed here because as a judge in a given county you have a convicted offender so you can send them to prison, or you can place them on probation. If you send them to prison the state pays for it. If you give them probation the county pays for it. Most judges will say : "I don't think about cost issues, I just think about justice and safety and all that", and that's probably true. But it's also the case that they live and work in the county as well, so it's hard to imagine they're not influenced somewhat by these things. It's also not just the cost but the fear too. So you have someone who is on the margins of being sentenced to prison or probation. If you send them to prison nobody's going to come back and say: "you were the judge who let this person out on probation who then went out and committed a terrible crime". So I would think that's more of a driving force.

An appetite for change – mass incarceration is a failure – 'something must be done' – towards a new 'commonsense'

In 2013, then US Federal Attorney General Eric Holder called for a 'frank and constructive dialogue about the need to reform a broken system', arguing that 'sweeping, systemic changes', were needed (Reilly, 2013). He went on to single out mandatory minimum and recidivist enhancement statutes as resulting in 'unduly harsh sentences and perceived or actual disparities'. 'When applied indiscriminately they do not serve public safety ... [and] have had a destabilizing effect on particular communities, largely poor and of colour. And applied inappropriately, they are ultimately counter productive' (ibid.). He went on to describe the US prison population as 'outsized and unnecessarily large', noting that 'we cannot simply prosecute or incarcerate our way to becoming a safer nation'. In April 2015 presidential aspirant Hilary Clinton called for an 'end to the era of mass incarceration', noting that there is 'something profoundly wrong in our criminal justice system' (Terkel, 2015).

Many commentators argue that mass incarceration, 'a kind of grand social experiment', which Clear and Frost (2014: 2–3) call 'The Punishment Imperative', is 'grinding to a halt' (ibid.: 7). '[A] combination of political shifts, accumulating empirical evidence, and fiscal pressures has replaced the commonsense idea that the system must be "tough" with a newly developing consensus that what happened to the penal system can no longer be justified or sustained.' (ibid.: 3)

David Green (2013:140) argues that it is 'striking and undeniable' that 'penal optimism has begun to resonate in recent years, particularly among prominent Christian conservatives'. Green goes on to argue that 'there is growing evidence of a shift – if not in the penal climate, then in the penal-policy "weather" '. He notes that '[a]mong the most vocal and active leaders in this shift are those with deeply held religious-moral convictions with long, historical legacies that criminology has often caricatured or overlooked.' (ibid.: 142) The important role played by faith-based constituencies in the USA will be discussed shortly as another difference in context between the USA and Australia.

In a recent book Jonathon Simon (2014:162) argues that: 'like a biblical flood, the age of mass incarceration is finally ebbing.'

> [T]he last decade and a half have seen the emergence of a set of assumptions about prisons, prisoners, and crime prevention opposite to those lined up behind mass incarceration. This has given us the best opening in fifty years to reinvent our approach to public safety. The *Brown v Plata* three-judge court's recommendation for how to

reduce the prison population without producing more crime is a tool kit for this reinvention; it's already being used in California's realignment policy and can be employed elsewhere.

Simon (2014: 165) cites various sources of this 'new commonsense' as: declining crime rates; much less fear of crime; the emergence of better strategies to deal with mental illness; a rediscovery of rehabilitation and re-entry and investment in re-entry strategies and programs to drive down recidivism rates, programs often involving former prisoners; and 'the ascendance of dignity as a constitutional value within the legal system' (see also Simon, 2012). He stresses the significance of the *Brown v Plata* decision where the US Supreme Court required California to reduce its prison population to 137% of capacity (a potential reduction of 46,000 prisoners) because the gross overcrowding under mass incarceration precluded the delivery of adequate and humane health and mental health care. Simon raises the question whether 'a dignity-animated Eighth Amendment will demand a more proactive and preventive criminal justice regime, one planned to prevent degrading conditions and proactively preserve the dignity of the incarcerated' (ibid.: 167).

Australia has a poor history of litigation over prison conditions, with a highpoint of legal challenges and decisions in the 1960s and 1970s and thereafter a relative quiescence, an acceptance of the expertise of prison administrators and a return to a 'hands off' approach (Brown, 2002a; Edney, 2001; Groves, 2001). It would seem foolhardy to place much store in legal challenges to promote improved prison conditions (but see the critique of remand conditions in *Benbrika*, linked to the right to a fair trial: Carlton and McCulloch, 2008). The *extent* of the prison system is clearly beyond the jurisdiction of the courts in the Australian context.

The acceptance that mass incarceration has failed and that the system is broken and a new 'commonsense' is emerging, is not restricted to progressive criminologists such as Clear and Frost, Green and Simon. It emerged throughout our interviews with a broad range of officials from diverse organisations. Moreover this appetite for change is not restricted to the justice reinvestment sphere as evidenced by significant change in juvenile justice, which has taken place largely outside the justice reinvestment process; the fact that adult prison populations have been reduced in states outside of the JRI; and the ability to get cross-party support and endorsement from leading conservative groups such as Right on Crime and evangelical faith-based organisations. The frequency with which we heard the 'need for change' story from a wide range of diverse interview subjects was surprising to us and unlikely to be replicated in the Australian context.

> It goes to this idea I think that there has been a change – there's a change in the thinking and no matter what political stripe you're on, it's hard to make a case for any more prisons.
>
> The reality is that there is this great convergence at this moment I think in criminal justice in this country and I'm glad other people are looking at it because if we have any humility in the country we will admit that we were wrong and that we need to change things... (Chris Watler, Harlem Community Court).

Speaking of the extensive stakeholder consultations engaged in by the South Dakota Criminal Justice Initiative Working Group, Jim Seward notes the way in which senior justice officials, often staunch defenders of the status quo and past practice, acknowledged the need for change. 'The ladies and gentlemen with a little bit of white hair, the justices usually, the retired attorneys general, they had been in the system long enough to look back and say "you know the things I used to do, don't make sense anymore"'.

This appetite for change, based on a view that the system is broken, is far less widespread in Australia. Prison activist Kat Armstrong from WIPAN argues that politicians admit to the 'broken' characterisation in private, but not in public.

> Julie Stubbs: Well I don't think we've got to that point with politicians... recognising that prison is not working?
>
> Kat Armstrong: When I meet with them, yes, they say that to me.... When they get on the TV and speak, that's another story. So, yes, they directly say to me "I agree with you Kat. Absolutely, it doesn't rehabilitate, it doesn't work, and we've got to do things better", but then it's this whole fear of they're not going to be supported by their voters if they're seen to be soft on crime or that they're giving criminals a better way.

Commentators who have stressed the importance of 'penal hope', and pointed to developments that may indicate that 'penal expansionism may be at a turning point' in Australia (Brown, 2013b: 27) acknowledge that some of the US catalysts of a more hopeful penal climate are either absent or have less purchase in the Australian context.

The GFC has had much less effect than in the USA, although it probably has sharpened cost based and efficiency arguments and boosted "what works" and "evidence-based" policy responses. The crime drop may have lowered the public and political temperature of law and order politics and opened up more space for social responses. There is little evidence of any substantial take up of prisoner re-entry discourse, certainly nothing like the US *Second Chance Act* (2007) and little evidence of apparent shifts in public opinion. The influence of Christian evangelical ideas in criminal justice debate is minimal and there is no evidence of right wing political or lobby groups supporting penal reduction in Australia (ibid.: 33).

Differences in degree of political bipartisanship

Given the structural gridlock in US government at a national level – illustrated by the refusal of the Republicans in Congress to pass budget bills in 2013 that produced the 'fiscal cliff' standoff between Republicans and the US President – it seems extraordinary to outsiders like ourselves that at a state level there was considerable bipartisan consensus on the desirability of justice reinvestment policies in particular states. As Nancy La Vigne (Urban Institute) puts it:

> I'm sure you don't have to live in this country to know how rare it is for [members of both parties] to agree on anything these days and they're sponsoring legislation to reduce the mandatory minimums, to support early release of prisoners under certain contexts – its huge.

Jim Seward describes how the bipartisan approach started early on in the justice reinvestment process.

> As we developed the work group, we tried to find a cross–section. We picked six legislators, and unlike anything that anybody could think of in South Dakota in the past, we said we want three Democrats and three Republicans. Our legislature is...about three quarter Republican, super majority. We said on this project we want to have an equal representation. We want this to truly be bipartisan.

The degree of bipartisanship is even more surprising, as noted earlier, in a system where leading criminal justice officials, such as district attorneys and judges, are elected. Election campaigns often involve various levels of 'vote for me I'm tough on crime' rhetoric which can limit the room for manoeuvre once in office. North Carolina District

Attorney, R. Andrew Murray, describes this process as 'walking a fine line'.

> I try to keep politics out of my office but this is a place where you have to be elected on partisan politics so it's a fine line to walk in that I'm a Republican and Republicans tend to be a lot harder on crime. My constituents on the Republican side want me to come in here and clean up the system and make certain that everyone goes to jail. That's just communication really, that's just me out there trying to get the word out that we are doing that when its needed and when it's not needed, we're collaborating and getting people drug treatment and getting people alternative programs so that they don't recidivate... because ultimately that's better for everybody, it's better for taxpayers and for the dollars.

The way the requirement for bipartisanship affected how justice reinvestment developed into JRI is outlined by Nancy La Vigne of the Urban Institute.

> One of the reasons why justice reinvestment didn't unfold the way [it's proponents] thought it would or could is because it is very much a bipartisan effort. You always have the Democrats on board, they see the value in rehabilitation and they don't think that you need to be locking up more and more people, but it's because crime is a politically charged issue they don't get anything out of being pro de-incarceration so they're unlikely to take it up on their own.
>
> Then of course the Republicans are better placed to take it up because they just look tougher on crime to begin with, but they're not going to make the argument that we should reduce the population because it's the nice or right thing to do. They're going to make the argument that it's the fiscally responsible thing to do.
>
> So take those two together and we're not talking about helping poor communities that are affected by mass incarceration or looking at disproportionate minority confinement, because those people committed crimes didn't they? It's like that. So when you look at those political considerations you end up with a different model if you want to effect change.... I've been working in this field for 20 plus years; to see folks come together and say "We really don't need to be incarcerating all these people" – it's tremendous.
>
> But there's limitations... they're more likely to reinvest in the system, but they're reinvesting in evidence-based practice, they're actually

talking about evidence. There is so much that has happened that's exciting and good but it's just a different model because of the political realities.

Representatives of the Right on Crime group took a longer term view, seeing the leading role of Republicans and 'conservatives' as a response to the loss of credibility of the left on criminal justice and law and order issues in the 1960s and the 1970s. They portrayed the left's approach to crime as:

> it's not your fault if you've committed a crime, it's societies fault and...these people need therapy but they don't need prison and let's let them out. ...That led to the massive increases of crime in the 60s and 70s because they were too soft and then the pendulum, as often is the case, swings the other way, you have this big boom in prison construction in the 90s under President Clinton where a lot of Federal money was given out to the States to build prisons.
>
> So then...from a legitimacy standpoint or a credibility standpoint, the left has no credibility on this issue in America because everyone expects them to be soft on crime and to promote things that are inimical to public safety and so when the conservatives come at it and say, "here's what we want to do", some of the things that they propose the left may not necessarily want, but they accept because they want the larger strategic goal.
>
> The strategic goal is more or less shared by both sides, which is reducing incarceration. For a conservative it's not simply to do it for its own sake but because you can keep families intact, you can reduce crime rates and you can save money.
>
> But some of the things that conservatives would propose that the left may not necessarily agree with, are things like these incremental 'swift and sure' sanctions or monitoring where – you're not just releasing individuals you're keeping track of them using modern technology to do so more efficiently and effectively. Following up with treatment or rehabilitation rather than just letting them out.
>
> I think that because the conservatives are proposing that and the left gets what they want, more or less, or the main thing they want, which is less people in prison, I think they're willing to go along with the right. (Chuck De Vore, Texas Public Policy Foundation, Right on Crime)

This view is built on a familiar neo-conservative trope which views the rise of crime rates in the 1960s and 1970s as an indication of 'a serious breakdown in individual moral responsibility, family values, social discipline (especially in the education and penal systems) and national unity' (Hogg and Brown, 1998: 121). It was part of the rhetorical strategy of Republican presidential contender, Barry Goldwater in the 1964 campaign and was more successfully deployed by Ronald Reagan in the 1980 presidential campaign as part of the 'Southern Strategy' by which the previous Democrat electoral stranglehold on the Southern states was broken and large blocks of white working class voters were won over to the Republicans through the use of race-coded issues such as states rights, crime and welfare (Tonry, 2011b: 106–114). Margaret Thatcher took up similar themes in the UK also during the 1980s. In her rhetoric:

> [T]he rising incidence of crime, disorder, family breakdown and moral permissiveness was the natural concomitant of collectivist social policy and lax penal policy, which together eroded the foundation of individual responsibility in the discipline of the free market and the rule of law. Responsibility and freedom could be restored by removing the crutch of welfare, by properly rewarding individuals for their initiative and holding them to account for their wrongdoing. (Hogg and Brown, 1998: 122)

Other interviewed leading players confirmed the way justice reinvestment provided a common ground for Republicans and Democrats. Todd Nuncio in North Carolina states that 'the Republicans see it as a way to save money, the Democrats see it as a way to have better outcomes for certain populations. So it's a win win'. David Guice is a charismatic former career North Carolina correctional administrator who was elected to the legislature (Republican) and was influential in the unanimous passage of justice reinvestment legislation which is seen as one of the US success stories (see Chapter 2). One adviser described his role as 'really just creating the space for some folks who typically don't talk to each other to come to the table and talk about this'. Guice notes that:

> when I arrived at the legislature it didn't matter to me if you were a Democrat or Republican, what mattered to me was getting things accomplished. So when I arrived, I was in the minority party, but that didn't keep me from passing legislation and building relationships. What I learned, at the end of the day, I just needed a vote to get legislation passed. I didn't care where it came from.

It is important to acknowledge that consensus had its limits, different in different states, placing certain issues 'off the table'. In South Dakota in relation to the initial discussions on the Criminal Justice Initiative Working Group, Jim Seward notes that 'there were things that the work group was not going to look at'.

> We knew that if we studied the death penalty, we would never get anywhere. We weren't going to reach consensus. It wasn't driving the population. Juvenile justice wasn't driving the population. Legalisation of drugs, some could argue that that was driving the population, or we wouldn't have a population if drugs were legal. Politically in South Dakota, that just isn't an option. It was part of the charge [from the Governor] that we tried to narrow our focus.

In states where one party was particularly dominant, some interviewees felt that bipartisan claims were simply a recognition that law and order issues no longer functioned as a political vote winner.

A typical feature in the Australian system is that policies enacted by one political party are reversed or amended when the government is changed after elections. There was fear of this in North Carolina, but the fact that the legislation had been supported by both major parties and passed unanimously made this less likely. Anne Precythe in North Carolina notes that : When we go around and do training with our staff...initially I would hear: "This will change with the next political party". [But when] a new governor came in and he was a Republican...he confirmed justice reinvestment'. Tom Eberly (Mecklenburg County) expresses:

> such welcome relief to be here where the first thing you don't think about somebody in the criminal justice system is whether or not they're Republican or Democrat. There is some of that going on but it's not really in your face which is such a welcome environment to be in.

As noted above, in jurisdictions like Australia which do not have elected judges, prosecutors, police chiefs and other criminal justice officials, political affiliation is not, by and large, in the minds of practitioners in the criminal justice system and particular decisions are not seen as driven by party positions. However at the political level in the legislature and executive, partisan politics is very much to the fore, and positions are often taken on legislative initiatives according to perceived political advantage and the prospect of embarrassing the other party, rather than on the merits of particular proposals or programs and their potential longer term benefits.

In contrast to the generally positive take on bipartisanship by most of our interviewees, some leading justice reinvestment proponents were critical of certain effects of the emphasis on consensus. Todd Clear argues in an interview that the emphasis on consensus tends to constrict the potential range of projects and 'stunt any creativity'. In his view, justice reinvestment 'got too quickly put into a policy framework that a Federal Government liked and it put some grant money to fund justice reinvestment strategies'. Clear sees a key assumption behind the CSG policy framework as:

> we don't want to have a political argument about crime...and the way to do that is we get consensus across the political parties in place and then we move on the consensus. All the areas in which there is opening consensus at step 1 are such low hanging fruit and so inconsequential that it doesn't do anything...on the ground in every one of these locations there were active advocates who were trying to change real things...and all the air gets pulled out of their sails and goes into the CSG agenda.

Marc Mauer from The Sentencing Project has a similar view:

> Essentially you had these reform movements that had been developing over some period of time. Some of them had pretty good traction; connections with legislative leaders and a reasonably broad agenda for reform. Then the powers that be came in and sort of sucked the air out of the room and pushed everybody away. Their agenda was – "let's get a bill passed this year and then we'll check that off and go onto the next state".

Justice reinvestment architect, Susan Tucker notes that:

> Mike Thompson and the Council of State Governments have done an incredible job of really building the consciousness of the need for reform, although they don't use the language anymore of mass incarceration or reinvestment in communities. Partly it's a function of what the CSG is, which is a bipartisan organisation of State policymakers. They operate...from a position of consensus, which means you give away a lot upfront I think. It's arguable that you get more

legislation passed, or you get more done, but then always the questions is, have you compromised away the vision.

The difficulty in assessing the conditions for and attractions of bipartisanship is that people tend to call for bipartisanship in relation to things they support – and not for things they oppose. While justice reinvestment proponents in the Australian context call for a bipartisan approach to promote justice reinvestment programs, they also criticise opposition parties for not opposing what they see as regressive criminal justice legislation, for example for criticizing the recent *Bail Act* 2013 in NSW in the parliamentary debates, but then not voting against the legislation or attempting to refer it to committee (Brown and Quilter, 2014: 88). The federal ALP opposition leader Bill Shorten was recently attacked by the conservative government and commentators for breaching the consensus approach on Aboriginal affairs by criticising the failure to meet 'Closing the Gap' targets and the planned funding cuts to Aboriginal Legal Aid (Gordon and Harrison, 2015).

In Australia calls for bipartisanship tend to be interpreted by governments in power with substantial majorities sufficient to ensure the passage of legislation they propose, as signs of weakness. When shadow conservative NSW L-NC Attorney General Greg Smith proposed a bipartisan, evidence-led truce in the law and order 'arms race' in the lead up to the 2009 NSW State election, the offer was rejected by ALP Attorney General John Hatzistergos, who claimed it illustrated that the opposition were 'soft on crime'. (West, 2009; Merritt, 2010; Steketee, 2010). All too often politics and political advantage takes precedence over the detailed examination of criminal justice issues and the requirement for long-term planning. Then there is the further difficulty of fostering a long-term vision and program within a three-year state electoral cycle. As Marc Mauer from The Sentencing Project put it: 'A lot of the stuff we're talking about is probably long-term impact and political people don't have that kind of vision for the most part'.

Important role played by faith-based constituencies

As David Green (2013:126) notes: '[C]hristian fundamentalism has long been associated with the rise of retributive justice'. Accordingly it surprised many when in his 2004 State address, President George W. Bush declared that: 'America is the land of the second chance, and when the gates of the prison open, the path ahead should lead to a better life'. These words presaged the introduction of the *Second Chance Act of 2007*: Community Safety through Recidivism Prevention, which passed in the House of Representatives easily and the Senate unanimously. The Act launched a program of assistance with 're-entry' projects in nearly all states, which continues to operate through a system of federal grants. At the signing ceremony for the *Second Chance Act of 2007* the President said:

> It's through the acts of mercy that compassionate Americans are making the Nation a more hopeful place...We believe that even those who have struggled with a dark past can find brighter days ahead. One way we act on that belief is by helping former prisoners who've paid for their crimes...The work of redemption reflects our values...The bill I'm signing today...will build on work to help prisoners reclaim their lives...[I]t basically says, we're standing with you, not against you...[T]he Second Chance Act will live up to its name...It will help our armies of compassion use their healing touch so lost souls can rediscover their dignity and sense of purpose...[T]he least shall be first...(Bush, 2008, quoted in Green, 2013: 140)

Green (2013: 126) argues that criminology has focused almost exclusively on the punitive dimension of religious thought at the expense of the redemptive, noting that:

> [G]rowing evidence suggests, however, that religiously rooted rationales and goals have contributed to the success of the Second Chance Act and to a range of other progressive reforms, including the Prison Rape Elimination Act of 2003 and the Fair Sentencing Act of 2010.

He challenges the view that re-entry programs have mainly been justified on reducing cost and recidivism grounds and quotes Bush advisers Michael Gerson and Peter Wehner that promoting re-entry 'depends on more than utilitarian considerations. More fundamentally it has to do with reflecting a view of human persons and their inherent dignity' (ibid.: 128). Thus '[t]he elevation of questions of human dignity is a goal not dissimilar to those of Tonry and others who argue for a fundamental reconsideration of American penal policy on moral grounds' (ibid.).

> The faith-based arguments and the redemptive arguments and wanting to promote programs that allow for the redemption of human soul and spirit is a major driver when you look at the people that are the former ministers and the faith-based groups and the justice fellowships, why they're involved. (Sarah Rumpf, Right on Crime)

> Well that comes from a belief and a creator God that we are all equally human and if we're all created in God's image, then if someone messes up and makes a mistake, you don't throw that person away. (Chuck De Vore, Texas Public Policy Foundation, Right on Crime)

Our interviews revealed the ways in which faith-based redemptive arguments not only provided a moral discourse in support of justice reinvestment but also facilitated alliances by enabling supporters to 'get a foot in the door', an opening into conservative support, especially with Republicans, and provided a 'pro-family' narrative.

> [T]heir personal faith...it's a way of approaching them on a public policy issue...that speaks to a different aspect of what they care about than mere dollars and cents or criminal justice. So it is a big help in that regard. It allows you go form alliances....
>
> My faith was never – you wouldn't bring it up, all right, and yet many of the allies that we have on this issue who are Republican, we can talk to them and get our foot in the door because of the redemptive aspects of justice reinvestment. Something that they personally understand. (Chuck De Vore, Texas Public Policy Foundation, Right on Crime)
>
> We were able, in this very room, to get groups like the South Dakota Family Policy Council, to endorse the legislation, because of the importance. If you have a 30 year old mum, who is addicted to heroin, and you put her in prison for four years, what happens to her four children. Where do they go? We were able to use those arguments to convince those evangelical groups and just about all the conservatives, that this is really pro–family.
>
> The Governor said... "this is as much about humanity as it is anything else, if we save money great, but if we can have mums and dads who were previously addicted to drugs and alcohol, now at home raising their own kids, that really should be one of our goals". (Jim Seward, South Dakota)

As noted in Chapter 1, faith-based groups such as the Prison Fellowship and individuals such as Chuck Colson and Pat Nolan were particularly influential in promoting re-entry programs:

> you have to give the devil his due but in the Bush administration, George W. Bush, there was this real emphasis on the evangelical, the

> faith-based thing, and...you can look back on the time when the church, the religious community, was the social service safety net for the most part. I think we're kind of coming back to that. What's happened is that Second Chance and the justice reinvestment work has begun to change the culture there and to improve the level of professionalism among the NGOs [Non-Government Organisations], particularly the faith-based organisations....we're not...just going in there and somehow helping them save their souls or preaching to them...– you can deal with some of those spiritual elements, but the real situation is food in your belly, a job, treatment for your drug addiction or whatever. (Gary Dennis, BJA)
>
> If you were here yesterday, in this room you would have seen faith-based volunteers here. They hand out toiletries to our guys, they serve coffee and danish, they have what is a called a ministry of presence which came out of 9/11, it's not proselytising, it's just being with people who are in trauma or dealing or working with trauma. (Chris Watler, Harlem Community Justice Centre)

Here then is a significant difference in context between the USA and Australia, which is far more secular politically. As Green (2013: 130) notes: '95% of Americans profess to believe in God' and 'more Americans believe in the existence of Satan as a literal being (62%) than believe in Darwin's theory of evolution'. In relation to the role of religion in penal issues in Australia:

> The established churches have played varying, waxing and waning roles in penal reform movements. The on-the-ground welfare arms of some churches such as the Salvation Army, Anglicare and Mission Australia have been engaged in various forms of practical post-release prisoner assistance. Individual prison chaplains such as Father Brosnan and Father Norden in Victoria have been influential in public debate. Combinations of churches or individual churches have, from time to time, issued joint statements and publications calling for penal reform and greater investment in post-release assistance see, e.g., Inter-Church Steering Committee on Prison Reform 1994; Australian Catholic Bishops Conference 2011–2012). But the US-style evangelical movement is far less significant and they have shown little interest in criminal justice issues either in support of greater punitiveness (at least as organisations, if not as individuals) or in penal moderation and reduction. The role of religion in the history

of Australian penality is significantly under-researched. It is arguably most marked in the role of churches in running Aboriginal missions in the late nineteenth century and first half of the twentieth century. (Brown, 2013b: 32)

Differences in capacity for coordination

In *The Prisoner's Dilemma* Nicola Lacey (2008: 109) argues that the capacity for coordination which is characteristic of social democratic regimes, is one factor in such regimes having lower levels of inequality and lower imprisonment rates than neo-liberal regimes.

In Lacey's (ibid.) and Cavadino and Dignan's (2006) typologies, the USA and Australia both appear in the neo-liberal economy camp. However arguably Australia retains a much greater commitment to social democratic traditions, policies and programs than does the USA, evident in the stronger welfare safety net, higher minimum wages, compulsory superannuation and a national health scheme, Medicare. Nevertheless when it comes to the capacity for coordination *within the criminal justice system*, the authors were struck by examples of coordination within a state between agencies and departments that would be very unlikely to happen in the Australian context.

One of the clearest examples of the capacity for coordination in the USA around justice reinvestment which arises from our interviews was in relation to the process in South Dakota. Republican Governor, Dennis Daugaard, explains the lengthy process of gaining support across a wide range of criminal justice agencies (including the Chief Justice and the judges), other stakeholder groups and legislators from both major parties. Significantly this coordination commenced before a justice reinvestment approach was decided on, continued during the formulation of the policy and the preparation of the legislation, the legislative process, and later in the oversight and implementation process. For this reason it is worth quoting at some length.

> So one of the things we did was to first start out by engaging members of the corrections stakeholders in various areas and what we did was members of my administration, members of my staff, engaged stakeholder groups, one group at a time. So we would visit with court officers in one or more cities, say judges. We would then also engage with prosecutors, get a group of prosecutors together in one city or another city or multiple cities. We'd get together with defence attorneys and the question posed to them was, in your observation of the

efficacy of our criminal justice system, do you have recommendations for improvement? Do you have areas where you see there's a failing from your vantage point? We didn't offer them any thoughts about what we thought was wrong, we just said "what do you think could be improved, if anything?".

So we went through group after group, sheriffs, police, defence attorneys, prosecuting attorneys, judges, victims groups and collected information, just collected information. By those means we identified areas where there might be some opportunity for improvement. We also through those means informed those stakeholder groups that we were looking at it, so they were aware that something was being considered.

Then after doing that for a number of months, we engaged with the Chief Justice and my office and legislative leaders, we announced that we were going to be undertaking a work group study of the criminal justice administration in South Dakota and looking for means of improvement.

Of course prior to that announcement I had to engage the legislative leadership and say, "this is something I want to do, of course we aren't going to do anything legislatively that you don't vote for and don't choose to do. It doesn't oblige you to vote for anything. But it does demonstrate your willingness to look at the subject". By announcing your leadership it demonstrates to the public that you are discharging your responsibility to look at issues of concern to the state.

So we formed a work group and within that work group we had some of the legislative leaders, we had a member of the house, the speaker of the house was a member, the Republican leader in the Senate was a member, we had other legislative members. We had a retired judge, we had a current judge, we had prosecutors, defence attorneys, again a smattering of representation from the stakeholder groups with whom we'd had earlier conversations and the charge to them was threefold. First, maintain or improve public safety. Secondly, hold offenders accountable and thirdly, save money if there is opportunity to save money.

And I would say that the significant reason why we were able to be successful in this area is the engagement of all these stakeholder groups and after the work group progressed to a certain degree down a path towards solutions that they were as a group in support of, then we had to go back to the stakeholder groups. We went to the Police

Chiefs Association and presented to their board why we were doing this, why we thought it made sense and asked for their support, their proactive, affirmative endorsement. We went to the Sheriff's Association, of course we had members of their association on the work group, so we had an advocate who was one of them in each of these cases or in almost all of those cases.

In some cases we had some pushback from some of these groups and we had to amend our package to satisfy them. In some cases we didn't do everything they wanted but we did enough of what they wanted that they agreed to endorse. That was especially in those law enforcement areas, the prosecutors, they don't want to be perceived as soft on crime, so to the extent that they perceive this as softening, that was hard for them to agree to.

So there was definitely a negotiation process involved in discussing with some of these stakeholder groups. But in the end we, in each case, went to the association of each of these groups and asked their board to endorse this plan, so when we came out with the package by the time we got to the beginning of the legislative session and had our package to introduce, we had already secured the endorsement of all these groups. They are the ones that generally will sound the alarm of opposition in which the general population will then resound.

I think we tried through the process to get all the major groups on board and that can be I think a good refutation of the shrill voices in media. We did have, I would say and I don't know how we earned it, but we had generally good support from the media. During the lead up we had some of our work group members produce letters to the editor and my voice opinion page, articles from say a retired Supreme Court Justice or a retired Attorney General, people who are associated with prosecution, endorsing the package. So we had some voices early on even before we introduced the package explaining the problem, explaining the cost and explaining how we're spending a lot of money on low level offenders that don't present a physical threat to us. So we built up with some deliberation and Pew was very good about that, helping us foresee and build up some resistance to opposition before it arose.

So then on the first day of session I made the criminal justice initiative the centrepiece of my state of the state address and literally upon conclusion of the address, I came down from the rostrum and joined with the leadership in the Senate. We handed in that bill together with their sponsorship, it was their bill, not mine. I said, "I can introduce it or you can introduce it". Of course they saw the train coming and they saw that it was apparently well supported and so they liked to have legislation that is publicly known and of their prime sponsorship. So what could have been lukewarm support became – it's their bill, it's not my bill it's their bill.

I would say we did have a little bit of opposition in committee but we were able to argue successfully against it and we had a few no votes but overall it was – we have 105 legislators and we have 70 legislators sponsoring the bill and the number of no votes was just a handful in both houses, it was overwhelmingly adopted. Amended a little bit during the process but almost not at all.

This bill was a very complex bill with many moving parts, many changes and many programs because if you don't incarcerate these offenders you still have to supervise them in some way. You can't just simply add them to a probationer's management list without some tools for that probation officer or that parole officer. So we want to have means to double check that alcohol abusers weren't drinking, that drug abusers weren't using drugs. We wanted to implement some random checking and in some cases routine and regular checking depending upon the nature of the person. So those things cost money and those things take time to implement. We wanted to implement some pilot projects on some of our reservations for our Native American population and that involves government to government negotiation with the tribal government to settle upon jurisdictional issues.

So having an oversight council whose responsibility it was to implement was important because it's a very easy train to get off the track because it had so many elements of change involved. So the oversight group was created as part of the legislation, a statutorily established body with appointments by myself and my legislators and by the Chief Justice of the Supreme Court and they meet regularly to judge progress.

In Australian jurisdictions, the doctrine of judicial independence has historically been interpreted as precluding a Chief Justice from involvement in committees which include police, court officials, prosecutors, government departments, victims groups and other organisations and from overtly discussing and pursuing particular policy goals or objectives, such as the reduction in prison and detention numbers and reductions in parole revocations and so on. There is an exception to this in relation to the President of the Children's Court, who in NSW at least is required by legislation to coordinate policy discussions between various criminal justice and welfare agencies. Similarly in the UK, Lacey (2008: 95) notes that the 'prevailing conception of judicial autonomy and independence would be regarded as inimical...to any overt negotiation or communication between the judiciary and the government or civil service.' This then is a long way from the South Dakota process where as part of the preliminary stakeholder program conducted by the Criminal Justice Initiative Working Group: '[W]e also went out and met with judges in their circuit. We would go to Rapid City and meet with all the judges. We also did an individual interview with every justice on our Supreme Court' (Jim Seward, General Counsel to the South Dakota Governor).

When we put the Australian practice to Jim Seward, he observed:

> If someone was a strict constructionalist with our constitution, they might say, I am not sure the Chief Justice should be working on that. But, he has the obligation to be the administrator of the court system. If your constitution places that burden on someone in the justice system, and they have a duty to administer the justice system, don't administrators have a duty to sit down with others? If the legislature is giving them the money to run that system, they shouldn't be afraid, I don't that it's unconstitutional to sit down and talk about, how is the system working. If the court system thinks they need more money, well why do they need more money? Because the executive branch maybe is bringing them more customers. Then the court system is pushing those customers in the form of inmates, back on the executive branch.
>
> Rather than making it a conversation about a murder case or a drug case, it's really a conversation about administering the system. And then I would think, in any country, you should be able to have that conversation.

Speaking of judges in community courts being involved in policy discussions, Chris Watler of the Harlem Community Court notes that:

> [S]ome judges are more traditional, they want to be aloof, they don't want any matters that could come before them, they don't want to be prejudiced and other judges are like, I want to hear, I want to understand problems in a way so, whatever the judges' take is, either one could be very successful at a community court as long as they want to collaborate. As long as they want to be a team player.

There is no doctrine or convention preventing greater coordination and cooperation between different criminal justice agencies and government departments in Australia, but as a matter of practice it is a relatively rare occurrence, however much the rhetoric of a 'whole government approach' may suggest otherwise. Chris Twomey, from WACOSS expresses the difficulties:

> one of the key things that we see is a big challenge for Government is how do they take a whole of government approach to the justice problems, [such as] justice reinvestment, dealing with some of those social and causative factors. Because a lot of the big problems we have is where is the demarcation between what's justice and corrective services versus what's child protection, what's mental health, what's health services, what's alcohol and other drug services, where does youth services fit into it, child services education?
>
> So far at the moment, that compartmentalisation makes it very hard to do collective approaches, the way money is allocated within budgets makes it very hard for them to actually release funds to do something that's collaborative, it always has to be someone's responsibility.

In the USA by comparison, as examples such as South Dakota show, justice reinvestment policies and strategies were promoted through strong inter-agency and interdepartmental cooperation and coordination.

Policy, politics, populism

The previous section has sketched out some of the main differences in context between the USA and Australia, and similar exercises could be conducted for other countries; although it is important to note that these differences are not only national but also state-based in federal systems like the USA, Canada and Australia, as well as regional and local. These major differences in context illustrate the difficulties and dangers in the simplistic assumption that specific criminal justice policies, whether of the punitive, 'three strikes' sort, or penal moderation and reduction as in justice reinvestment, can be simply uplifted and transplanted. As Jones and Newburn (2007: 162) argue, the process is not one of an 'import-export trade'. For 'policies are not traded like goods... They cannot easily be packaged, put in a container, transported to a new location, and then simply become embedded and established in a new setting'.

Key characteristics of policy are that it is action-oriented rather than simply 'a decision', involves a complex, dynamic and continuing 'web of decisions' (Hobbs and Hamerton, 2014: 8) and typically involves a range of contributors to the process, although that is not always the case. Drawing on a range of sources (Downes and Morgan, 2002; Jones and Newburn, 2002; Muncie, 2005; Pratt, 2007) Hobbs and Hamerton (2014: 3–6) produce a typology of stakeholders in relation to criminal justice policy as follows: political parties, public officials, criminal justice professionals and their representative organisations, penal reform groups, single issue campaign groups, victims and those that lobby on their behalf, the general public, media, traditional and new experts, multinational private firms that provide penal services and international institutions and conventions of governance. This list could be supplemented (e.g., local communities are missing) or broken down (e.g., 'the general public' and 'media' could be further differentiated) but it serves to make the general point that a range of interests, interest groups and constituencies are potentially involved, although this is not of course to suggest that all are involved in specific instances nor that all carry equal weight.

Indeed, a number of scholars have pointed to dramatic shifts in the relative power and influence of specific groups in relation to criminal justice policy since the 1970s. Loader (2006) has argued in the UK context, that in the post second world war period, penal policy was very much an 'in-group' exercise, decided upon by sections of the civil service, politicians and 'insider' lobby groups, who enjoyed privileged access to politicians and the policy-making process. He calls these players, who, in the UK context generally had a 'penal welfare' and rehabilitative orientation, 'the platonic guardians' of the public interest. From the 1970s with the rapid politicisation of criminal justice issues, particularly around sentencing, these 'platonic guardians' were increasingly sidelined by the newer, brasher voices in the tabloid media, individual victims and victims groups, talk back radio hosts and politicians who saw law and order as a potent political force. Ryan (2003, 2005) traces the same process, describing it as the 'rise of the public voice' outside the more referential 'top-down' political structures, utilising talk back radio and the internet to 'operate on politicians through the media' as part of a 'democratic' anti-elites politics. A consequence of the rise of the 'public voice' according to Ryan (2005: 143) is that 'politicians are required to engage with the public in a manner that a generation ago would have been unheard of in most Western democracies...the wider public nowadays refuses to be airbrushed out of the policy-making equation'.

Thus the rise of the 'public voice', frequently but not exclusively punitive in nature, at least as articulated through the tabloids and talk back radio, has taken place alongside what Garland (2001b: 150) calls the 'declining influence of social expertise'. This is part of a wider process in which he argues that welfare professionals have 'experienced a sharp decline in status and political clout' as 'market solutions, individual responsibility and self help have increasingly displaced welfare state collectivism and social policy has come to place more emphasis upon accounting and managerial expertise' (ibid). Criminal justice professionals have experienced the same decline: they have 'lost status and credibility' as policy-making has become 'more politicised, some at least have become more supportive of punitive responses to crime and those who have not increasingly sound like "voices in the wilderness"' (ibid.: 152).

Politicians who indicate reformist views on criminal justice issues are often a target of such populist tabloid campaigns. Greg Smith, a socially conservative NSW Attorney General in the L-NC state government who promoted bail reform, was portrayed on the front page of *The Daily Telegraph* in before and after fashion, turning from Rambo to a marshmallow. Radio shock jock Ray Hadley repeatedly attacked Smith, calling for 'this raving idiot' to be sacked. Smith was later removed as Attorney General (Brown, 2014, Brown and Quilter, 2014: 84). Ken Clarke, Conservative Party Justice Secretary in the Cameron UK government who was on record denouncing the 'bang em up culture' (Travis and Sparrow, 2010) and promoting sentencing reform, was portrayed in the Sun as a Teletubby.

> Ken Clarke is a bit chubby, therefore he's a Teletubby. Haha! Terrific. They've cut out a picture of Ken Clarke's face, and put it into the body of the yellow Teletubby, Laa-Laa.
>
> The readers won't quite understand just how much they're meant to dislike someone unless you literally turn them into a figure of ridicule: a vegetable, a comedy animal, a children's TV character. If you think that something like sentencing tariffs...might be too hard for your readers to understand, don't worry: just wheel out the crudely Photoshopped picture, and they'll get the message. Look at this idiot! He must be sacked.
>
> All we're left with is Ken Clarke in a big yellow suit with an antenna on his head....Punish him. Make him suffer. A bit like how we're invited to see criminals. And that's what passes for a debate about sentencing. (Baxter, 2011)

Clarke was later moved from Justice Secretary to Minister Without Portfolio.

In the Australian context Hogg and Brown (1998) have charted a similar process to that outlined by Garland, Ryan and Loader above, describing the outcome as the emergence of an 'uncivil politics of law and order' (see also Weatherburn, 2004). This has been exemplified in 'law and order auctions' in the lead up to elections as rival parties vie to portray themselves as 'tougher on crime', and by derogatory attacks on the judiciary from politicians, tabloid and TV media, police representatives and victims which portray judges and magistrates as 'out of touch' with public sentiment. In an illustration of this phenomenon, in 2013 then NSW Premier Barry O'Farrell called for the appointment of more police and prosecutors to the judiciary as they were 'more in touch with community feeling'. Individual talk back radio hosts, particularly those enjoying close relationships with police, exercise extraordinary influence. In a prime example Brown and Quilter (2014) outline the lengthy process of law reform of increasingly dysfunctional and oppressive bail laws in NSW, following an extensive consultative law reform process by the NSW Law Reform Commission. The new reform legislation was passed unanimously in the NSW parliament but was 'sabotaged' within one month of its introduction largely through the efforts of one radio talk back host who enjoys strong links with the NSW Police Association and police hierarchy. As will be discussed later, these sorts of examples are in a sense 'the elephant (or Teletubby) in the room' in debates around the 'rationality' in economic, social justice and public safety terms, of adopting justice reinvestment policies. For they show both how tenuous reform processes can be when confronted by powerful populist forces and that 'rational', 'evidence-led' policies are always open to being trumped by emotive media and political campaigns, especially those springing up around individual cases involving horrendous crimes, newsworthy victims or notorious accused.

The lesson of such events in relation to justice reinvestment is that 'rational', cost and 'evidence-based' arguments must confront the emotive appeal of punitive sentiment and its Durkheimian roots in constructing social belonging and a sense of community. This is so, even if, as Alison Young (1996: 10) argues, a community founded on victimisation 'is a simulacrum of a community; a phantasm that speaks of nostalgic desire for oneness and unity, while at the same time structuring itself around its dependence on fear, alienation and separateness for its elements to make sense'. So that justice reinvestment arguments cannot be pitched solely at the level of the 'rational' or the 'evidence-led' but must be situated within a moral and political vision, couched in a 'language that connects with cultural imaginings concerning punishment...for punishment is nothing if not about the imagination, emotion, culture, symbolism, representation and pain' (Brown, 2010: 145).

In short a justice reinvestment policy that relies solely on the recitation of the dismal and worsening statistics of Indigenous incarceration and detention rates, or the cost differentials of imprisonment as against diversion or forms of community corrections, will likely fail to gather the necessary widespread public and diverse constituency support necessary for success. We need to fashion new visions, images, languages, stories and ways of talking, to avoid the 'rationalist fallacy' that 'evidence' will 'win out' over emotion, a fallacy compounded by the way what counts as evidence in 'evidence-based' policy, is constructed, as illustrated and discussed in some detail in Chapter 4. One way of approaching this might be, as Hogg (2012) suggests, by detaching the term populism from its pathologised partner, punitiveness, and taking populism more seriously 'as both a normal and necessary dimension of politics and one with no essential ideological or social belonging' (ibid.: 105). A second feature of the rationalist fallacy involves the formulation and transmission of policy, and it is to that we now turn.

The rationalist fallacy

As Jones and Newburn (2007: 161) note, a policy transfer discussion 'often proceeds with an unrealistically or overly rational model of policy-making' which 'assumes that policy-makers/politicians begin by identifying a problem and then travelling in search of its solution (or alternatively as John Kindon might argue, identifying a solution and then looking for the problem)'.

The assumption here, as Jones and Newburn (2007:18) put it, is that 'the intentions of policy-makers are contiguous with policy outcomes: policy instruments frequently being read as a straightforward representation of policy-makers' aims and objectives'. By way of contrast, outcomes are often the 'messy result of unintended consequences, serendipity and chance' (ibid.). But a critique of the rationalist conception of policy formation and transfer must go further. For even without 'unintended consequences, serendipity and chance', it is important to recognise that the translation of policy formulations into actually operating programs, traverses the complex relationships between theory, government and politics. These domains or 'fields' are semi-autonomous, having their own conditions of existence, rationalities, institutional means, technologies, languages, modes of deportment, mentalities, practices and limits, which are not reducible to a particular theory, principle or practice (Hogg, 1996: 46). In short, there is not some 'pure' set of justice reinvestment principles that can be simply enshrined in a policy document produced by say a think-tank, an Inquiry, a university research project, a government department or political party, and then translated directly into a governmental or political program or process that can be implemented on the ground. Each stage of policy formulation, translation into programs and implementation, involve different modes of calculation, different agents and agencies utilising different strategies and languages, subject to different limitations and different conditions of possibility. This is the case even within one jurisdiction, let alone in situations where policy transfer is being attempted across national boundaries and across jurisdictions.

The carpet model – 'rolling out' policy

The rationalist fallacy that policies are direct manifestations of the intentions of policy-makers and can simply be 'implemented' or 'transplanted', is evident in the common view of policy as some self contained entity that can simply be 'rolled out', like a carpet or role of grass, unravelled to produce a floor covering or an instant lawn. This common formulation constitutes policy as an object, a thing, which can be simply unrolled and is thereafter self-operating and self-generating. But even within this inappropriate conception, a carpet or a lawn cannot just be rolled out anywhere, the building and room, or the ground, must first be prepared, and thereafter further nurturing is necessary. Carpets fade and are stained, scuffed and torn, lawns can die, be dug up by insects or animals, washed away in a deluge or overrun by other plant species. Policy formulations are dynamic amalgams, drawing their potential from the suitability or unsuitability of the context and from the skill and enthusiasm of the various local constituencies and agents who are attempting to implement them in these variable contexts. Thus the common political, media and public discourse of 'rolling out' policies (in any field) profoundly misrepresents the processes of policy formulation and the difficulties of formulating policy and transforming it into on-the-ground processes in widely varying localities, which feature varying landscapes, terrain and conditions of support and opposition.

The 'roll out' metaphor draws some of its force from the desire to seize on a proven successful program which can just be adopted everywhere, a political attraction for those trying to leave their mark within a three- or four-year political cycle. When some of the authors appeared before the Legal and Constitutional Committee of the Australian Senate Inquiry into justice reinvestment (1 May 2013) we were asked by a then opposition coalition senator, whether 'there are programs right now that could be rolled out cross-jurisdictionally that effectively demonstrate and prove the concept at work' (Senator Humphries Hansard 1 May 2013: 59). The response of two of the authors was to emphasise that a community-based focus meant that different problems would be identified in different communities and that the (largely forgotten) 'asset mapping' dimension meant that different communities would have different agencies available as sources of social cohesion and program capacity.

> Mr Cunneen: Part of the strength of justice reinvestment is that in its ideal form it is partly driven by the community. So what are the problems in that particular community that you are looking at? It is not necessarily a program that lends itself to a blanket approach, a one-size-fits all approach. I think it does need to be, to a high degree, community driven... The argument has been that it is not necessarily something you want to introduce into every community and every state. You identify those communities which are providing large numbers of the fodder, if you like, for imprisonment, and target those communities, but at the same time look at the particular issues. They will not be the same. Papunya will not be the same as Blacktown in Sydney. It really is a more precise approach to it.
>
> Mr Brown: There is another side that we have not emphasised as yet, and that is the asset mapping... It is not just identifying the communities to which large numbers of prisoners return; it is also identifying what are the current sources of social cohesion within the community. Again, that rather militates against 'rolling out' some kind of nationally directed program, because they might be very different. In one community it might be a grandmother's group that is operating as mentors and going into prisons, or it might be a local school, church, particular business, youth club or sporting association, whatever. You try to identify which are those organisations within civil society that help keep people together and provide positive role models... and then to what extent might they be either assisted in what they are doing, or drawn into some kind of program which they have a better chance of succeeding with, than some kind of 'nationally rolled out' program. (Hansard: ibid.)

There may well be some forms of policy, for example legislative changes to bail laws, drug laws, to procedures in relation to bail or parole revocations, which are by their nature as legislation applicable across a particular jurisdiction. However, even here the evidence is that there are significant differences in the implementation of legislative provisions on the ground. A clear example is the historical lack of availability of various forms of semi- or non-custodial sentencing options such as periodic detention, probation, drug courts and so on, in rural and remote areas in Australia, precisely those areas where many Indigenous people live (Legislative Council Standing Committee, 2006). One such example emerged in an interview with Sarah Hopkins about the Just Reinvest NSW campaign.

> One of the circuit breakers that we're putting forward right now, ... is there's no mental health nurse that goes to the courthouse in Bourke. If you go to the Downing Centre [a court in central Sydney] and you've identified that someone has got a mental health issue, you can stand the matter down on the list and there's a mental health nurse and you go see her or him, she'll provide a report and then you go back to the magistrate and the magistrate can deal with the matter in terms of bail or sentence or whatever. In Bourke they don't have that, and not only do they not have a community health nurse that can go to court, they don't have a community health nurse in the whole of Bourke.

Similarly wide differences are evident in youth justice diversion across different local authorities and Youth Offender Teams (YOTS) in the UK. Indeed Goldson and Hughes (2010: 217–18) comment in relation to youth justice in the UK that:

> in many important respects the national is an inadequate unit of policy analysis in that it can conceal, or at least obfuscate, local and/ or regional differences within otherwise discrete territorial jurisdictions. For sure, neo-liberal economics, neo-conservative politics and burgeoning practices of policy transfer may well serve to create some standardised and homogenised international/global policy responses, but youth justice is also significantly localised through national, regional and local enclaves of difference... Indeed, in many countries it is difficult to prioritise national developments above widely divergent regional differences, most evident in sentencing disparities (justice by geography). In short, once it is recognised that variations *within* nation state borders may be as great, or even greater, than some differences *between* them, then taking the national (let alone the international and the global) as the basic unit for understanding policy shifts and processes of implementation becomes questionable.

Thus where, as here, the argument is for a local community-oriented approach to justice reinvestment in NSW and its application first and foremost to Indigenous communities, then the 'national roll out' approach is highly inappropriate.

As Gary Dennis of the BJA in the USA put it:

> we like to deal in models – I like to draw little boxes on paper and connect them and think that this is an orderly progression; it isn't. Even though I think we have done a reasonably good job at the state level of adhering to the basic model of how we come in, looking at the data developing, the information about the drivers, and all that sort of stuff, the bottom line is that each individual state and each individual jurisdiction is different. The players are different, the attitudes are different.... In the final analysis it morphs into its own thing. I would say that in trying to adapt this to whatever, wherever you're going to go, you've got to maintain flexibility. You have to understand that it may, in two different areas, look different.
>
> The trick is maintaining the integrity of the process and maintaining some adherence to a model that people can see, but also understanding that it's not a cookie cutter.

On the issue of models, Mick Gooda, ATSI Social Justice Commissioner, had this to say:

> the thing that worries me about justice reinvestment – someone comes out and says there's a Bourke model that's working; that's what you need. Let's pick up Bourke and we'll transplant it to Blackwater in Central Queensland. Or the other mob that's looking at it down in...Ceduna, South Australia. I said 'you guys got to work it out yourself'.

Policy, the 'finer grain' and asset mapping

Laura Kurgan, one of the architects of the 'million dollar block' modelling in New Orleans post-hurricane Katrina, argues, 'policy people don't understand the finer grain'. It is the 'finer grain' that is provided through the asset mapping process, involving the identification and input of local community organisations and figures. Kurgan gives the example of starting 'in the wrong neighbourhood' with a particular justice reinvestment project, but then because of meeting someone already working in the field 'we found the right neighbourhood to work in'. Interestingly, prior to the project interviews, the authors had approached asset mapping as a key part of the original justice reinvestment concept which had tended to 'drop out' of the process with the transition to JRI. However Kurgan stated that it was never really an established part of the justice reinvestment process. She saw the 'spatial language' of the project as vital, pointing to a project in Brownsville, New York, where the mapping revealed that 'there was not one high school in Brownsville. They had all been closed. That is the exact, high school to prison pipeline. There is no place for them to go to school'. As she puts it:

> You had to research the community. You had to know is it black, is this high immigration and also what's good that's going on there? Is there a lot of religion? Are there charter schools? There's so many things. That's why when I say assets I really mean assets. There's always good things in these communities.... If there are people in the community already who are the ones you are partnering with, you don't need to bring someone in from the outside. You go there and you say: "Who are the people doing the most effective work?" That's not hard to find. You work with them.

Sometimes the assets are ground-level forms of informal community solidarity. Peta MacGillivray (UNSW) gave the example of a young Aboriginal man who was granted bail, but was unable to afford transport to return home, five kilometres out of town. He approached an 'Aboriginal woman and he says "Aunty, guess what," and she sort of thought "Oh yeah, I can see what's happening here."' A lift home ensued.

An illustration of the 'finer grain' provided by a combination of 'asset mapping', 'service mapping' and community consultation emerged in the Bourke project. It involved identifying driving without a licence as a major route into the criminal justice system and the issuing of arrest warrants as leading to other offending behaviour, as Sarah Hopkins of the Just Reinvest NSW explains.

> [W]e've got these circuit breaker proposals that we're hoping to start...around warrants, so kind of like a warrant amnesty clinic...and also a driver licensing crime prevention thing. So when police pull someone over and they don't have a licence they don't have to give them a CAN [Court Attendance Notice] they can refer them off to a service.
>
> So the warrant thing was an idea from the community, that basically if you have a warrant out for you, then you go underground and

you create mayhem. It actually I think came from the police. Yes, police and...the community identified warrants as an issue. They are terrible, once you've got a warrant your offending rate just seems to – I don't have the data, that'd be fascinating actually – your offending rate just seems to spiral and I guess there's that 'no care' factor, and the driver licence thing definitely came from the police. So it was at the end of one our sessions – actually, this is a really good example.

We had one of our community engagement sessions where there were some different service providers, and at the end of it, a police officer came up to me and said, "I don't want to be pulling people over who don't have a licence and having to commence proceedings against them. If I could do something there, if there was something I could refer to, I'd do it and I think the police would do it."

The elephant in the room – populist backlash and the trashing of evidence

A prime example of populist backlash which has already been mentioned was the recent sabotage of bail law reform in NSW (Brown and Quilter, 2014). It seems unlikely that justice reinvestment would be a specific target of backlash given its generality, its appeal across the political spectrum at a rhetorical level, and its largely small scale, pilot status. The two objections to justice reinvestment from the then opposition Coalition Senators on the Senate Inquiry evident in their Minority Report, were that 'the criminal justice system (for the most part) and the prison system (in its entirety) are the responsibility of the states and territories, not the Commonwealth' and that there was a 'dearth of evidence that any justice reinvestment programs to date are sufficiently successful to allow reduced spending on the court and prison systems.' (LCARC, 2013: 1.3, 1.13)

The ever present danger is less any specific attacks on justice reinvestment and is more, sudden law and order crises arising around specific events. In the case of the retreat on bail reform in NSW, outlined above, the granting of bail in three particular cases created a media storm which focused on the alleged offences and notoriety of the accused, conflating accusation, guilt and punishment. Such developments will more than offset any gains obtained through justice reinvestment initiatives as imprisonment rates are driven even higher, as is the disproportion of Indigenous people in those rates, making the problem to be redressed even worse. In a three-month period, December 2014 to March 2015 the NSW remand population increased by 800 prisoners as a result of the retreat on bail reform (Brown, 2015).

The other danger is the simple ideologically driven punitive opposition to any penal welfare measures, specialist courts, diversion programs or programs oriented to specific groups such as juveniles or Indigenous people, whatever evidence is available to demonstrate their success. The epitome of this process occurred under the Newman conservative government in Queensland between 2012 and 2015 which abolished the Murri (Aboriginal) courts, the drug court and the youth drug courts; and overturned the proscription on naming juvenile offenders. At the Senate Inquiry into justice reinvestment, Dr. Hughes of the National Drug and Alcohol Research Centre gave evidence in response to a question about 'evidence' of program success. Dr. Hughes noted that:

> [C]ertainly there have been some concerning changes in many parts of Australia – the Northern Territory and also Queensland – with the closure of three drug courts there. This was in spite of a very significant evidence base showing that the programs not only worked but that they were making significant contributions to the offenders and the community. So the steps against the use of the proven strategy are certainly retrograde. (Hansard, 1 May 51)

Punitive backlash irrespective of evidence of counter-productive effects, draws on three major sources of support: highly punitive responses to horrendous crimes; the degree of influence of media 'shock jocks'; and the ease with which politicians invoke 'common sense' notions of 'community protection' and 'public safety' as paramount. One of the considerable successes of justice reinvestment advocacy in the USA is the way it has excavated and 'redefined', to use Tucker and Cadora's (2003: 4) term, the notion of public safety. For 'research proves that public safety is not assured by imprisonment alone'. As they put it: '[T]he question should be "What can be done to strengthen the capacity of high incarceration neighborhoods to keep their residents out of prison?" not "Where should we send this individual?"' (ibid.).

The first and most difficult source of backlash to confront is the deep emotive and cultural attachment in particular societies to punitive sentiments and responses, especially in relation to spectacularly brutal crimes. There are certain crimes that for a range of reasons, often to do with the 'moral standing' of the victim and offender, take on an iconic status in media coverage, popular consciousness and political effects. The image of Willie Horton was used to great effect by George W. Bush in the 1988 US presidential election campaign through the political advertisement of a:

> dark skinned black man, a convicted murderer who escaped while on a work furlough and then raped and murdered a white woman in her home...[which] blamed Bush's opponent, Massachusetts governor Michael Dukakis, for the death of the woman, because he approved the furlough program. (Alexander, 2012: 54)

As Alexander says, the 'ad was stunningly effective, it destroyed Dukakis's chances of ever becoming president' (ibid.: see also Tonry, 2011b: 109–10; Newburn and Jones, 2005).

Emotive responses to horrendous crimes are deeply embedded and visceral in nature, but it is important to note that their force is highly differential and culturally specific to particular societies. This is highlighted by the different responses to the killing of two year old James Bulger in 1993 in the UK by two ten year old boys, and the similar killing in Norway in 1994 of five year old Silje Redergard by three six year old boys. The UK public, media and political response can hardly be over-emphasised. It evoked widespread debate over social and moral issues, parenting, video ratings, single mothers, the state of the society, and legal and sentencing policies in relation to children. It triggered new legislation which 'effectively reversed the decarcerative provisions of youth justice law and policy – in respect to children aged 12–14 years – that dated back to the Children Act 1908' (Goldson and Muncie, 2006: 143, quoted in Green 2008: 3) and appeared to signal a significant shift in penal policy-marking the beginning of a long-term increase in adult prison rates (see Figure 1.3 in Green, ibid.: 5). By way of contrast the Norwegian killing (admittedly carried out by younger boys) was interpreted throughout within a welfare paradigm. As Green (ibid.: 7), who examines the responses to the two cases in considerable detail, puts it: '[T]here was no mass out-pouring of anger or outrage from the family, the community, or the press, no cries for vigilante justice, and no political maneuvering by any party's politicians to politicize the incident'.

While Australia has arguably not seen the equivalent response to an iconic case such as Horton or Bolger, individual cases such as the Anita Cobby and Janine Balding rape/murders and the Thomas Kelly 'one punch' killing, all in NSW, and the Jill Meagher rape/murder by a parolee in Victoria in 2012 have produced widespread public outrage, changes in criminal justice policies such as in eligibility for parole, and a hardening of community and political attitudes towards criminal justice issues, which feed into increasing imprisonment rates.

Peggy McGarry from Vera recounted the following example:

> I think the lessons are that you can't do it that quickly, because then you have one incident, like in one of the States we did implementation with...They had a very big crime committed by a parolee and now a lot of the reforms are either, in practice or otherwise, unravelling. I think you need to educate people about why these reforms make sense, why they are not jeopardising public safety.

In an interview with the Republican Governor of South Dakota, Dennis Daugaard, we asked him whether the justice reinvestment reforms put in place were 'robust enough to withstand a Willie Horton moment?' His reply was:

> On the day of passage, when we were celebrating passage, I predicted just that. I said there will be a crime that is committed by one of these parolees that will cause us to question the wisdom of this reformation.... [we] know that there will be one or two like that. The question today, before it has happened, is should we recognize that that will be the exception and should we let the exception drive our processes? Or should we [recognize that] 95% of parolees are compliant,...and that we have a system that encourages those compliant ones to get off the parolees work list [so that] those non-compliant ones have more and more attention so...there is a smaller and smaller number that the parole office has to supervise. It seems to me that that is a logical means of managing bad behaviours.
>
> You have to acknowledge that those kinds of things will happen and I did that on the very day that we passed it. That question arose and I said 'there is no question it will happen, it will happen, but we can't let the exception drive our behaviours'.

Governor Daugaard's response highlights the importance of engaging the public and building the case for reform proposals. In Australia it has been a common pattern for governments of all persuasions to trumpet 'tough' policies involving increases in penalties, but fail to argue the normative case for, and remain quiet about, programs or initiatives which attempt to reduce imprisonment rates, provide preventive programs or post-release assistance.

> [Such] attitudes have led to the entrenching of a "reform on the sly" approach, whereby more progressive social and welfare approaches to criminal justice issues, however much evidence can be marshaled in their favour and however successful, are not promoted lest they draw adverse attention and claims of being "soft on crime", the automatic assumption being that the public are universally punitive, a "common sense" notion challenged by research (Roberts et al. 2003). One effect of this approach is that little on-going public support is built for reformist measures. So when the spotlight is shone on a sound and carefully constructed reform initiative... and media and political criticisms emerge, there is little well informed and widespread public support to point out that, despite the specific "weakness" that has been identified, the initiative is meritorious and beneficial... Because the discursive ground for this sort of insulating strategy has not been prepared, punitive and exclusionary responses quickly swamp the field (Brown and Quilter, 2014: 90).

Conclusion

This chapter has discussed the general issue of policy transfer in criminal justice and briefly summarised examples in the UK and Australia. It argued that there were some examples of more overt policy transfer through correctional privatisation, CompStat-type policing reviews and the take up of risk instruments in correctional management. However the predominant form of policy transfer was of the 'soft' sort: the adoption of slogans such as 'truth in sentencing', 'three strikes', 'zero tolerance' and 'broken windows' policing, which were then deployed in the local, predominantly state-based context, as part of local histories of political, legal and cultural struggle over criminal justice issues. Drawing on our interviews we discussed some of the key differences in the political, legal, cultural and social frameworks between the USA and Australia, concentrating on some of the potential barriers to the adoption of US-style justice reinvestment policies in Australia. The discussion then moved to an analysis of the nature of policy and its relation to politics and populism as a form of politics. It was argued here that many of the standard approaches to policy fall prey to the rationalist fallacy, assuming that it is the unproblematic echo of its formulators' intentions which can be simply transmitted across the semi-autonomous realms of theory, government and politics. We identified one illustration of an inadequate conception of policy, the common reference to 'rolling it out' in the form of general, national or state-wide programs. This was followed by a discussion of the susceptibility of criminal justice policy to populist backlash and the implications of this for the way justice reinvestment arguments are couched.

Conclusion

In this book we have attempted to simultaneously promote the potentialities of justice reinvestment as an approach to reducing incarceration rates, redressing racial disparities and building community resilience to crime, while also raising a range of questions and challenges. This is a difficult path to tread. But advocacy and aspiration must be tempered by a reflexive impulse which constantly calls into question presuppositions embedded in what is being advocated. As we have outlined, most forcefully in Chapters 1 and 2, the original vision of justice reinvestment in the USA has transformed into a more practical, government-oriented program which attempts to reduce incarceration rates through criminal justice reform. As such it has drawn criticism from some of its original proponents, criticisms we have outlined and to some extent replicated. Nevertheless, we have attempted to understand why this has happened; to show the pressures and processes producing such a shift, together with the benefits and gains obtained; and the way the process has contributed to what we discerned in our fieldwork and interviews to be a growing appetite for change in US criminal justice. Like many of those we interviewed, and many others in Australia and elsewhere, we recognise that such gains are only made within the conditions of possibility operating in particular local, state and national contexts. Political shifts are hard won in the criminal justice field and the original vision must be leavened with a sprinkle of realism in order to both achieve and extend such shifts.

A mapping of the conditions of possibility and their underpinnings must however attempt to identify weak spots: arguments and processes which may constrict the potential for justice reinvestment movements to gather force in specific contexts. Thus we have simultaneously supported a community development approach in pursuit of social justice, while at the same time, especially in Chapter 3, pointing out problems with community and place-based conceptions, especially as they apply to marginalised peoples. Similarly, while it sounds inspiring that criminal justice policy might be 'evidence-led', 'data-driven' and rational rather than emotional, such aspirations and claims contain a myriad of problems, some of which were teased out in Chapter 4. Again, while desiring to use US experience and gains as part of the argument for a justice reinvestment approach in Australia, we felt it necessary to point out in Chapter 5 some of the theoretical and practical problems in simplistic conceptions of policy transfer and to highlight the importance of, and differences in, local context and the need to grapple with populist responses.

We have engaged in our project in this way, not because we are indifferent to the vital issues the project of justice reinvestment responds to or because we are driven by a disposition to critique. Quite the reverse. We wish to contribute to an unfinished, evolving narrative and movement for change in the way crime, criminal justice and penal issues are constructed and managed. Such a contribution is best made, we feel, by a combination of exposition, advocacy and questioning. Thus we have attempted to describe and explain developments, to argue for particular normative conceptions, partially encapsulated in the term social justice, and also at the same time, point out difficulties and inadequacies in the way the policy debate on justice reinvestment is being fashioned and implemented. We hope by this method to strengthen, rather than undermine, the unfolding story of justice reinvestment, a notion only just over a decade old but one ripe with potential to assist in a major re-orientation of criminal justice policy. Such potential can only be realised if advocates manage to hold together three distinct motivations: a vision that what currently is, might be otherwise; an appreciation that reforms must be won within existing political possibilities; and a degree of self-reflection that movements can only progress if they are able to constantly question and refashion their own foundations, values and claims.

In the Introduction we located the point of departure for this book in a previous work where some of the same authors examined penal culture as a means of understanding the increasing use of the prison in recent decades. Our inquiry revealed the highly racially selective nature of imprisonment rates in numerous jurisdictions, but especially in Australia. For this reason the justice reinvestment groundswell in Australia has emerged out of a focus on Indigenous communities and is linked to issues of Indigenous democracy, a term we have used as shorthand for issues of Indigenous governance, empowerment, self-determination and nation building. We noted the way that a 'tipping point' argument which revealed the 'criminogenic' effect of mass incarceration on particular, predominantly racialised, communities has emerged.

The research project identified several key research themes: the key conceptual underpinnings of justice reinvestment; the social-moral aspects of justice reinvestment policy and the way that these are in tension with rational, 'evidence-led' and 'cost effective' approaches; whether place-based approaches can respond effectively to entrenched disadvantage; and how justice reinvestment might translate into the Australian context.

Chapter 1 demonstrated the importance of the historical context of justice reinvestment as a reaction to mass incarceration. It began by telling the story of mass incarceration, as initially defined by Garland (2001a), developed through the notion of hyperincarceration by Wacquant (2010) and revitalized by Alexander (2012). The drivers of mass incarceration in the USA are widely acknowledged as harsh sentencing laws, drug laws which over-criminalise nonviolent offenders, and heavy-handed responses to parole and probation violations. The overview provides some context to the data presented in the chapter, demonstrating similar trends across the USA, the UK and Australia; namely that incarceration rates are at historic highs, particularly for vulnerable groups.

The history of the development of justice reinvestment in the USA identified some of the elements which contributed to reshaping the discourse around criminal justice reform. These elements were the financial imperatives driven by the global downturn, a shift in the political environment with significant bipartisan acceptance that the 'system is broken', legal challenges to corrections systems, a legislative focus on prisoner re-entry, and the untiring efforts of advocacy organisations and researchers.

Some of these components were evidenced in the case studies taken up in Chapter 2 which described the various iterations of JRI as they developed. The primary delineation is between programs that work across the whole of a jurisdiction, and those that are more localised at the county level. The diverse strategies associated with the JRI were explored through brief case studies of state-based and localised JRI which were the subject of the fieldwork undertaken for this project. The selection of sites also incorporated the experience of unified jurisdictions and schemes with a focus on Indigenous prisoners. These sites were Hawaii, South Dakota, Rhode Island, North Carolina (including Mecklenburg County), Texas (including Travis County) and New York.

The progression of the concept of justice reinvestment into the JRI highlighted the complex arrangements of support and interaction between various founding think-tanks and other organisations. The origins, nature and activities of these bodies reveal how this complex coalition arrangement has shaped the continued development of justice reinvestment into the JRI. We identify three influential aspects in this process: the value placed on bipartisanship, the support at an early stage from conservative political organisations and the role played by faith-based organisations.

Mass incarceration in Australia has a different character to that in the USA and the UK. In the UK justice reinvestment has been framed within the marketisation ideology of the government, largely in the form of PbR schemes. It is distinctive that the groundswell of support for justice reinvestment in Australia has been led by the community sector. Justice reinvestment endeavours in Australia now incorporate pilots in three states: specific justice reinvestment focused working groups, academic projects and increasingly, government support. Even a cursory examination of key moments in the history of justice reinvestment demonstrates that to change the conversation about criminal justice reform, a combination of factors and conditions needs to coalesce in order to create the chance to retreat from 'the perfect storm of punishment' that exists today. Chapter 2 is the beginning of a story that highlights the potential of justice reinvestment to open up a new dialogue.

A core argument of this book builds on the analysis of Austin *et al.* (2013), which identifies the differences between the initial principles of justice reinvestment as set out by Tucker and Cadora (2003) and the way that the JRI has unfolded on the ground. We argue that the absence of a commitment to place-based strategies in state-wide JRI, and a failure to prioritise the reinvestment of correctional savings in high-incarceration communities, undermines the prospects of a social justice-oriented program of reform. Rather, the JRI has focused on working with the political leadership to secure the passage of legislation. Some of the ways that the JRI diverges from the original vision of justice reinvestment are the omission of local actors in setting the reform agenda, the dropping of asset mapping (along with other localised evidence) from the collection of data and the shift from the needs of vulnerable communities to system-wide reform.

To track this trajectory away from community engagement and control, and indeed from any location-based focus, the language used to describe the JRI on the CSG website was traced from the time that the initiative began until the present day. The current descriptors entrench the absence of a place-based component and the lack of prioritisation of community-based reinvestment.

However, while noting the losses that arise as a consequence, we argue that the variance in the JRI in practice from justice reinvestment in theory reflects an adaptation to political and practical realities. The conceptual fluidity in justice reinvestment is not necessarily a weakness; the strategy's adaptability to varying contexts and political realities can also be seen as contributing to its robustness.

Chapter 3 critically examined the claims of justice reinvestment to be a 'place-based' strategy and unpacked the assumptions behind such claims. It specifically considered whether a place-based approach can provide adequate recognition of the needs of three social groups who have been particularly affected by the growth in incarceration: people with mental illness and/or cognitive impairment, women and Indigenous peoples.

The chapter argued that there is a distinction that can be made between 'top-down' and 'bottom-up' approaches to public policy development and implementation, and considers how place-based approaches might coalesce with a social justice vision of justice reinvestment. A social justice vision includes a commitment to a process of democratisation and empowerment; the satisfaction of human physical, social and economic needs; and respect for human rights (including principles of fairness, equity and non-discrimination). We also note the danger of reframing basic government obligations to meet human needs around housing, health, education and employment within a discourse of crime prevention, rather than seeing the satisfaction of these needs as fundamental human rights. A key element of a bottom-up approach is that policy priorities, linkages and service delivery models are determined through community decision-making and negotiated with different levels of government. In contrast the state-based JRI approach has been largely top-down and the local democratic participatory focus of justice reinvestment has been lost.

We argue that how we understand and define community has fundamental implications for how we envisage the development and implementation of a place-based approach in justice reinvestment. In particular, it is necessary for some flexibility in considering the concepts of both 'community' and 'place-based', neither of which need to be constrained to particular physical or geographic locations. We draw attention to the fact that the community development approach at the heart of justice reinvestment needs more serious consideration. It is perhaps easier for criminologists and lawyers working in the area of justice reinvestment to concentrate on systemic criminal justice change (through, e.g., reforms to probation and parole), rather than on how local participatory and reinvestment processes can be developed in specific communities, particularly when an understanding of community development is usually outside their professional repertoire. As one interviewee involved in JRI told us, 'we're not community redevelopment experts'.

We note that the racialisation of punishment has largely been disavowed in justice reinvestment in the US context. However, a more open-ended, 'bottom-up' approach to place-based initiatives may also provide opportunities. We determine that this potential is evident in developing justice reinvestment for people with mental illness and/or cognitive disability, women, and Indigenous and other racialised peoples. For all three groups we see justice reinvestment as offering a potential for change to the current criminal justice and penal arrangements that do so poorly in responding to the needs of these groups. In this context, we draw attention to an Australian case study of the Just Reinvest NSW initiative in Bourke, which we see as a particularly instructive example of a bottom-up approach to justice reinvestment that has been developed and sustained through community initiatives.

In Chapter 4 we examined justice reinvestment as data-driven and evidence-based, features with strong practical and rhetorical appeal. Our fieldwork reinforced the important role that technical assistance providers had played in ensuring that datasets were developed and analysed to provide a basis for the JRI, and bringing an independent perspective and providing legitimacy to processes and policy options.

The manner in which evidence has been conceptualised and the methodologies and measures commonly used within the JRI have had important effects. We found little focus on differential patterns in, or drivers of, incarceration for different groups, such as those with mental illness and/or cognitive impairment, women or racialised people, although some local JRI schemes had recognised factors such as mental illness or homelessness among 'frequent users'. Where datasets and analytical frameworks do not address these differences, they may entrench the invisibility of vulnerable groups into the future, and work against assessing the need for more tailored policies and programs. Schemes that emphasise cost-cutting may dismiss minority populations as unlikely to yield substantial savings, although experience with local schemes suggests other ways of approaching savings.

Evidence-based approaches have assisted legislators, policy-makers and correctional administrators to choose cost-effective policy options and programs. However, we found that the premium accorded to some forms of evidence and the 'what works' framework had narrowed the focus of JRI and reinforced the shift from reinvesting in communities to investing in reform of the criminal justice system. The reliance on meta-analysis may enshrine a limited range of programs for which evidence exists in what is deemed to be an acceptable form. The evidence base is poor concerning programs tailored to particular groups. However, the emphasis given to 'what works' may stifle innovation and undermine the development and testing of programs that arise from local initiatives, or respond to minority interests, since these are unlikely to meet the threshold to be considered evidence-based. This possibility is greatest where EBP and the 'what works' framework exclude other forms of knowledge and other modes of assessing effectiveness. A further contributing factor is that the evidence-based framework within JRI, commonly relies on the risk-needs-responsivity approach, with origins in individual psychology and a focus on predicting recidivism. While the universal application of the risk-needs-responsivity framework, which had been staunchly defended by Andrews and Bonta (2010), has been challenged conceptually and empirically, especially from the perspective of its application to women and racialised peoples, it continues to be very influential within the JRI and correctional practice.

As Clear (2010) has argued, the programmatic response of the JRI, often focused on back-end measures to reduce recidivism, is in tension with other approaches to justice reinvestment and penology (such as desistance theory). These include those that have a more expansive agenda for criminal justice system reform that includes front-end measures and decarceration and social ecology approaches that focus on community revitalisation. It also has been largely instrumental in sidestepping important normative questions that cannot be resolved by data alone. In the chapter we also flagged some developments that may have the potential to reshape methodologies and forms of measurement to be more congruent with a social justice vision of justice reinvestment.

Our argument confronts the issue of policy transfer, the question of how 'portable' justice reinvestment might prove to be. Chapter 5 involved a brief examination of Wacquant's (2009a, 2009b) argument of the 'global spread' of US neo-liberal punitive policies, followed by Jones and Newburn's (2007) investigation of criminal justice policy transfer in the UK. A brief overview of the limited Australian evidence suggested that the pattern is closer to that found by Jones and Newburn (ibid.), namely, the dominant forms of transfer are 'soft', that is slogans and labels such as 'three strikes', 'truth in sentencing', 'zero tolerance' and 'broken windows', rather than detailed policy and programs. Nevertheless this does not mean that such forms of policy transfer are without significant effects, but that those effects are contested, not automatic, subject to local political, legal and cultural politics, a politics played out on the terrain of local histories and balance of forces.

The issue of context is thus central to any analysis of policy transfer, and we examined some of the key differences in context between the USA and Australia with an emphasis on a number of differences which might constitute barriers to the take up of justice reinvestment policies in Australia. These were the differences in political and funding structures which present limits to 'incentivisation' strategies; the absence in the Australian context of an 'appetite for change', built on the notion that the system is 'broken' which is widely apparent in the USA; significant differences in the degree of political bipartisanship over criminal justice policy between the USA and Australia; the important role played in the USA by faith-based constituencies and conservatives in the promotion of justice reinvestment, both largely absent in Australia; and the apparent differences in the capacity for coordination over criminal justice policies.

Finally in Chapter 5 we examined some of the difficulties and problems besetting attempts to achieve policy transfer. These included what we called the 'rationalist fallacy' that policy is simply the manifestation of the intentions of policy-makers and can be readily transferred, or in a popular metaphor which exemplifies the problems, 'rolled out', in different contexts. Another problem is the susceptibility of reform movements aiming at penal reduction, to forms of populist backlash, and the implausibility of thinking that such backlash can be adequately rebuffed by a recourse to the self-evident 'rationality' of reform proposals that are advanced under the banner of being 'data-driven', 'evidence-based', or 'smart'.

Our answer to the question of the portability of justice reinvestment is thus a guarded one, hedged about with qualifications. What is clear is that justice reinvestment cannot simply be transplanted from the US context to the Australian (or for that matter elsewhere), for justice reinvestment policy is not a commodity or package and context is everything. The absolute centrality of context in debates on the transfer of criminal justice policy necessitates detailed local mapping to identify the varying conditions which might sustain or present a barrier to the adoption of justice reinvestment ideas, slogans, methodologies, policies and programs in varied national, state and local contexts. The answer we offer is that justice reinvestment can be an *inspiration* for a form of locally-based community development strategy utilising enhanced data and identification of local community assets and current forms of service support, conducted initially in the communities of vulnerability which have the highest contact with the criminal justice system. In the Australian context that is exemplified in Indigenous communities. As outlined earlier in Chapter 3, the Just Reinvest NSW campaign is one such approach and is offered here not as a general prescription but as one fashioned for Australian conditions. Indeed as the discussion of the campaign in Chapter 3 showed, with the development of Maranguka, the bottom up community process, the focus on youth, the role of service mapping, the identification of specific local problems such as driving without a licence and the criminogenic effects of arrest warrants, the focus is not just Australian conditions but specific Indigenous community conditions.

While stressing the local, we suggest a similar argument may well apply in other white settler or post-colonial societies where Indigenous groups constitute such a disproportionate part of the prison population and as subjects of criminal justice institutions more generally (Cunneen et al., 2013). As one of the original proponents of justice reinvestment, Susan Tucker puts it in an interview:

> It's striking...that the places that are considering or doing Justice Reinvestment are New Zealand, Australia, the UK and the USA...All places where minorities are disproportionately incarcerated....I think it's a recognition that the disinvestment in these communities and their lack of political participation or involvement, is part of the problem.

What we wish to avoid is any suggestion that the wide range of developments that have occurred in the USA can be boiled down into some essentialist prescription of a 'pure' form of justice reinvestment that can be emulated in other countries and locations and promoted using the latest 'KPI' or 'best practice' managerial speak. We are sympathetic to the criticism offered by many of the original proponents of justice reinvestment in the USA and outlined in more detail in Chapter 2, that its translation into the JRI has shifted the focus from justice reinvestment as a neighbourhood-based, social justice response to the inequities of racially selective mass incarceration, to a legislative-based mechanism for improved efficiency in back-end penal measures, particularly probation and parole supervision and revocation practices (Austin et al., 2012). However, we are wary of such critiques being used to promote a 'one true road' type approach, structured in dichotomy and dismissive of developments that do not fit a community empowerment model.

In the Australian context, justice reinvestment-oriented initiatives may well travel under different labels in different jurisdictions. In WA there are justice reinvestment-oriented developments currently being promoted under the Social Reinvestment rubric, which utilise the language of 'safe communities, healthy families and also talking about smart justice' (Chris Twomey, WACOSS).

One of the overwhelming impressions gained by the authors during our fieldwork in selected US jurisdictions, was the diversity of developments in different state and local contexts; the widespread recognition across a range of players that significant reforms were required to reduce imprisonment levels; the surprising commitment to bipartisanship; and foremost, the enthusiasm and good will displayed by advocates from legislators, administrators, program managers, criminal justice professionals, think-tank researchers, to non-government and activist organisations. Some of the most impressive developments under way were on the fringes of justice reinvestment policy and practice, indeed in some cases did not draw explicitly on justice reinvestment discourse.

Developments in the New York Probation Department, such as the establishment of NeONs (Neighbourhood Opportunity Network) discussed in Chapter 3, are an inspiring example of how a traditional government criminal justice agency might be transformed from a standard service agency with a 'sign on at reception and wait your turn in a drab office' type approach, to a vibrant local community centre exuding a sense of activity and hope. Susan Tucker had suggested in her interview that a visit to the South Bronx NeON 'will really give you a very different feel for what a local justice investment initiative might look like. It's not perfect but it's a beginning'. Our subsequent visit evoked for one of the authors, recollections of visiting some of the local community mental health treatment centres in northern Italy in the hay day of the democratic psychiatry movement in the late 1970s. There was the similar experience in the colourful and radically redesigned office of it not being immediately apparent exactly who were staff, probationers, parolees, local citizens, community and health workers, friends, family and others. The procession of people reading examples of their poetry included all these and indeed the Commissioner of Probation, reading a poem by her 11-year-old child. Parolees were being assisted with healthcare registrations, employment applications and educational programs. The taxi driver who dropped us off at the NeON office told us it was an excellent place, doing great work. A similar sense of vibrancy and local community campaign activity was evident at the Harlem Community Court. Governors, sheriffs and congressmen launched into trenchant critiques of the futility, waste and injustice evident in mass incarceration and the policies which produced it, and mounted strong and remarkably non-partisan (for elected officials) advocacy of justice reinvestment programs.

To the extent that justice reinvestment was a major source of policy, program or rhetorical support for this diverse range of activities, it served as a source of inspiration to penal reduction, a narrative that avoided the negativity of pure critique and offered something positive in the way of a political strategy and program seeking to fashion a new common sense around criminal justice issues. Such a common sense might be fashioned out of a range of elements, including: appeals to cost savings and 'smarter' justice, data and evidence-based policies; enhanced public safety; reduced recidivism; increased offender accountability to communities; ex-prisoner job creation and other community development programs; redressing racial and other marginalised group disparities and inequalities; promoting Indigenous democracy; unleashing individual and community potential; creating healthier families; providing a better future for young people; enhancing life chances and building social solidarity. In assembling such elements into a narrative for change, it is important to utilise data and appeals to an evidence-based political rationality, but the articulation must ultimately be a normative one, conducted in the name of increased social justice, rather than technical or instrumental rationalities or 'superior' knowledge claims.

Our question, 'how well does justice reinvestment travel?', might more appropriately be recast, to 'how well can elements of the justice reinvestment story and process, inspire and be utilised to generate challenges to our current over-reliance on criminal justice and penal "solutions" to crime?' While we have argued for a local community-based form of justice reinvestment in the Australian context, we are alert to the dangers of prescription, not only because context is everything, but also for the reason that the possible outcomes of justice reinvestment-oriented policy and programs are not given or determined in advance in any particular theory, policy or politics. Outcomes depend on the way that discourses drawing on justice reinvestment are articulated to, and by, a range of constituencies, other discourses, governmental programs, and media and popular imaginings and mentalities, in particular overlapping sites and places (Brown, 2013b).

Appendix: Record of Interviews in the USA and Australia

Washington and New York, USA, 2013

Organisation	Name and title
ACLU	Vanita Gupta, Deputy Legal Director
ACLU	Kara Dansky, Senior Counsel
BJA	Gary Dennis, Senior Policy Advisor
Consultant	Susan Tucker
CSG Justice Center	Marshall Clement, Division Director
Rutgers University	Todd Clear, Professor
Spatial Information Design Lab, Columbia University	Laura Kurgan, Director
The Pew Charitable Trusts	Public Safety Performance Project members
The Sentencing Project	Marc Mauer, Executive Director
The Sentencing Project	Nazgol Ghandnoosh, Research Analyst
Justice Policy Centre, Urban Institute	Nancy La Vigne Director,
Urban Institute	Lindsey Cramer, Research Associate

Local Level, USA, 2013

Organisation	Name and title
Center for Effective Public Policy	Peggy Burke, Principal
Crime and Justice Institute, Community Resources for Justice	Barbara Pierce Parker, Managing Associate

Hawaii, USA, 2014

Organisation	Name and title
Chaminade University	Dr RaeDeen Keahiolalo-Karasuda, Director, Office of Native Hawaiian Partnerships
Crime Victim Compensation Commission	Pamela Ferguson-Brey, Executive Director
Crime Victim Compensation Commission	Amanda Sawa, JRI Restitution Accountability Project Coordinator
Community Alliance On Prisons	Kat Brady, Coordinator
First Circuit Court	Steven Alm, Judge
University of Hawaii	Meda Chesney-Lind, Professor, Chair Women's Studies

New York City, USA, 2014

Organisation	Name and title
Centre on Sentencing and Corrections, VERA Institute of Justice	Peggy McGarry, Director
Harlem Community Justice Centre	Chris Watler, Project Director
Center on Sentencing and Corrections, VERA Institute of Justice	Nancy L Fishman, Project Director
New York City Department of Probation	Clinton Lacey, (formerly) Deputy Commissioner
Neighborhood Opportunity Network, New York City Department of Probation	Catrina Prioleau, Director
Tow Foundation	Emily Tow Jackson, Executive Director
NYC Mayor's Office of Criminal Justice	Vincent Schiraldi, Senior Advisor

North Carolina, USA, 2014

Organisation	Name and title
Mecklenburg County	Kevin Tully, Public Defender
26th Judicial District Charlotte Mecklenburg County	Todd Nuccio, Trial Court Administrator,
Mecklenburg County	Thomas Eberly, Criminal Justice Director
Centre for Effective Public Policy	Richard Stroker, Senior Manager
Mecklenburg County	R Andrew Murray, District Attorney
NC Department of Public Safety	George Pettigrew, Justice Reinvestment Administrator
NC Department of Public Safety	W. David Guice, Commissioner Division of Adult Correction and Juvenile Justice
NC Department of Public Safety	Nicole E Sullivan, Rehabilitative Programs & Services, Director
University of North Carolina	James Markham, Professor, School of Government,
NC Department of Public Safety	Chad Owens, Senior Policy Administrator
NC Department of Public Safety	Timothy Moose, Deputy Commissioner
NC Department of Public Safety	Joseph Prater, Deputy Commissioner
NC Department of Public Safety	Anne L Precythe, Director Community Corrections

Rhode Island, USA, 2014

Organisation	Name and title
Executive Office of Health and Human Services	Steven Costantino, Secretary
Nine Yards Program, Open Doors	Nick Horton, Coordinator
Open Doors	Sol Rodriguez, Director
Office of Health and Human Services	Elena Nicolella, Associate Director, Policy and Innovation Executive
Rhode Island Department of Corrections	Ashbel T Wall II, Director

South Dakota, USA, 2014

Organisation	Name and title
Pennington County	Kevin Thom, Sherriff
South Dakota Legislature	Craig Tieszen, State Senator
Governor's Office	Jim Seward, General Counsel
South Dakota Unified Judicial System	Greg Sattizahn, State Court Administrator
South Dakota Government	Dennis Daugaard, Governor of South Dakota

Texas, USA, 2014

Organisation	Name and title
Center for Effective Justice, Texas Public Policy Foundation	Marc Levin, Director
Center for Effective Justice, Texas Public Policy Foundation	Derek Cohen, Policy Analyst
Texas Public Policy Foundation	Chuck DeVore, Vice President of Policy
Right on Crime, Texas Public Policy Foundation	Sarah E Rumpf, Strategic Communications Manager
CSG Justice Center, Austin	Tony Fabelo, Director of Research
Texas Criminal Justice Coalition	Ana Yanez-Correa, Executive Director
Travis County	Kimberly Pierce, Planning Manager Criminal Justice Planning
Travis County	Cathy McClaugherty, Senior Planner Criminal Justice Planning
Travis County	W Carsten Andresen, Planning Manager, Justice and Public Safety Division

Continued

Organisation	Name and title
Travis County	Efrain Davila, Planner Justice and Public Safety Division
Travis County	Roger Jefferies, County Executive Justice and Public Safety Division
Travis County	Anonymous
Downtown Austin Alliance	William V Brice, Program Director Security & Maintenance
Ending Community Homelessness Coalition	Ann E Howard, Executive Director
Foundation Communities	Sofia Barbato, Supportive Services, Program Manager
Foundation Communities	Edward Crawford, Resident Supportive Services Coordinator
Foundation Communities	Heather Courson, Supportive Services Coordinator
Foundation Communities	Quiana Fisher, Supportive Services Coordinator
Foundation Communities	Timothy D Miles, Director of Supportive Services

Australia, 2013–14

Organisation	Name and title
Australian Human Rights Commission	Mick Gooda, Aboriginal and Torres Strait Islander Social Justice Commissioner
Community Restorative Centre, Sydney	Alison Churchill, CEO
Flat Out, Melbourne	Annie Nash, Executive Director
Independent advocate, Sydney	Vicki Roach, Women In Prison Advocate
Just Reinvest, NSW	Sarah Hopkins, Chairperson
Karralika Programs, Canberra	Sharon Tuffin, Services Director
National Aboriginal and Torres Strait Islander Legal Services	Eddie Cubillo
North Australia Aboriginal Justice Association	Priscilla Collins, CEO
North Australia Aboriginal Justice Association	Jared Sharp, Solicitor
NSW Council for Disability Services	Jim Simpson, Senior Advocate
NSW Department of Corrective Services	Deirdre Hyslop, Principal Advisor, Women Offenders
NSW Department of Justice	Gowan Vyse, Regional Manager, Office of the Public Guardian
UNSW	Eileen Baldry, Professor of Criminology

Continued

Organisation	Name and title
UNSW	Peta MacGillivray, Project manager / researcher
Sisters Inside, Brisbane	Debbie Kilroy, CEO
WACOSS	Chris Twomey, Director Policy
WIPAN	Kat Armstrong, Director
Women's Centre for Health Matters, ACT	Marcia Williams, Executive Director
Women & Prisons Group, ACT	Kathy McFie, Support Worker
Yula-Punaal Centre, NSW	Michelle Knight, Aboriginal Women's Post Release & Case Management Officer
Yula-Punaal Centre, NSW	Tammy Wright, Executive Director

Notes

3 The Politics of Locality and Community

1. Rikers Island – the New York City jail which can house up to 15,000 inmates. See http://www.nyc.gov/html/doc/html/about/facilities-overview.shtml
2. In the USA there was originally no JRI focus on juveniles but this is now changing with South Dakota and West Virginia adopting justice reinvestment approaches to juvenile justice in 2014.
3. Bourke is a small remote town in northwestern NSW with a population of just under 3,000 people. Some 30 per cent of the population is Indigenous (ATSISJC, 2014: 108).

4 Justice Reinvestment, Evidence-Based Policy and Practice: In Search of Social Justice

1. 'Campbell Systematic Reviews follow structured guidelines and standards for summarizing the international research evidence on the effects of interventions in crime and justice, education, international development, and social welfare' http://www.campbellcollaboration.org/.
2. See also: *Director of Public Prosecutions (WA) -v- Moolarvie* [2008] WASC 37, Blaxell J; *Director of Public Prosecutions (WA) v GTR* [2007] WASC 381, McKechnie J. The cases all relate to Aboriginal men being assessed for designation as a serious sexual offender under the *Dangerous Sexual Offenders Act* 2006 (WA).

List of Cases

Australia

Director of Public Prosecutions (WA) v Moolarvie [2008] WASC 37.
Director of Public Prosecutions for Western Australia v Mangolamara [2007] WASC 71; 169 A Crim R 379.
Director of Public Prosecutions (WA) v GTR [2007] WASC 381.
Jurisic (1998) 45 NSWLR 209.
Muldrock [2011] HCA 39; 244 CLR 120.
R v Benbrika & Ors (Ruling No 20) [2008] VSC 80.
Way [2004] NSWCCA 131.

USA

Brown v Plata, 131 S. Ct. 1910 (2011).

List of Legislation

Australia

Bail Act 2013 (NSW).
Dangerous Sexual Offenders Act 2006 (WA).
Sentencing Act 1989 (NSW).

UK

Children Act 1908 (UK).
Criminal Justice (Scotland) Act 2003 (Scot) asp 7.
Criminal Justice and Immigration Act 2008 (UK).

USA

Consolidated Appropriations Act, 2010 Pub L No 111–117,123 stat 111th Congress (2010).
Consolidated Appropriations Act, 2014 Pub L No 113–76, 128 stat 5 113th Congress (2014).
Criminal Justice Reinvestment Act of 2010, S 2772 111th Congress (2010) [bill was not enacted].
Fair Sentencing Act of 2014, Pub L No 111–220, 124 stat 2372 (2014).
Justice Reinvestment Act of 2011, Pub L No 2011–192, NC Sess Law, (2011).
Prison Rape Elimination Act of 2003 Pub L No 108–79, 117 stat 972 108th Congress.
Public Safety and Offender Accountability Act H.R. 463, 2011 Leg., Reg. Sess. (Ky. 2011).
Second Chance Act of 2007, Pub L No 110–199, 122 stat 657 110th Congress (2008).

References

ABS (Australian Bureau of Statistics) (2014a) *Prisoners in Australia, 2014*, catalogue no. 4517.0, Canberra: ABS.
ABS (Australian Bureau of Statistics) (2014b) *Recorded Crime – Victims, Australia, 2013*, catalogue no. 4510.0, Canberra: ABS.
ACLU (American Civil Liberties Union) (2015) *American Civil Liberties Union*, https://www.aclu.org/faqs (FAQS), accessed on 15 April 2015.
ACT Government (2015) *Justice Reinvestment Strategy*, http://justice.act.gov.au/page/view/3829/title/justice-reinvestment-strategy, accessed on 15 April 2015.
AIHW (Australian Institute of Health and Welfare) (2013) *Youth Detention Population in Australia*, Canberra: AIHW.
Alexander, M. (2012) *The New Jim Crow: Mass incarceration in the Age of Colorblindness*, revised edition, New York: The New Press.
Allen, R. (2007) 'From Restorative Prisons to Justice Reinvestment', in R. Allen and V. Stern (eds), *Justice Reinvestment – A New Approach to Crime and Justice*, London: International Centre for Prison Studies.
Allen, R. (2011) 'Justice Reinvestment and the Use of Imprisonment Policy Reflections from England and Wales', *Criminology and Public Policy*, 10(3), pp. 617–27.
Allen, R. and Stern, V. (eds) (2007) *Justice Reinvestment: A New Approach to Crime and Justice*, London: International Centre for Prison Studies.
Allison, F. (2015) *Justice Reinvestment Project: Katherine*, Brochure, March.
Andrews, D. and Bonta, J. (2010) *The Psychology of Criminal Conduct*, 5th edition, Cincinnati: Anderson Publishing.
Andrews, D.A., Bonta, J. and Hoge, R. (1990) 'Classification for Effective Rehabilitation: Rediscovering Psychology', *Criminal Justice and Behavior*, 17(1S), pp. 19–52.
Aos, S. and Drake, E. (2013) *Prison, Police, and Programs: Evidence-Based Options that Reduce Crime and Save Money*, 13-11-1901, November, Olympia: Washington State Institute for Public Policy.
ATSISJC (Aboriginal and Torres Strait Islander Social Justice Commissioner) (2009) *Social Justice Report 2009*, Sydney: Australian Human Rights Commission.
ATSISJC (Aboriginal and Torres Strait Islander Social Justice Commissioner) (2014) *Social Justice Report 2014*, Sydney: Australian Human Rights Commission.
Austin, J. (2011) 'Making Imprisonment Unprofitable', *Criminology and Public Policy*, 10(3), pp. 629–35.
Austin, J., Cadora, E., Clear, T.R., Dansky, K., Greene, J., Gupta, V., Mauer, M., Porter, N., Tucker, S. and Young, M.C. (2013) *Ending Mass Incarceration: Charting a New Justice Reinvestment*, Available at http://sentencingproject.org/doc/Charting%20a%20New%20Justice%20Reinvestment%20FINAL.pdf, accessed on 8 January 2015.
Australian Catholic Bishops Conference (2011) *Building Bridges, Not Walls: Prisons and the Justice System. Social Justice Statement 2011–2012*, Availble at http://

www.socialjustice.catholic.org.au/files/SJSandresources/2011-SJS-Statement. pdf, Australian Catholic Bishops Conference.

Australian Federal Government (2009) *A Stronger, Fairer Australia (Social Inclusion Agenda)*, Canberra: Australian Federal Government.

Australian Greens (2013) *Justice Reinvestment for Australia: The Greens' Plan for a More Effective Approach to Criminal Justice*, August, Canberra: Australian Greens.

Australian Red Cross (2012) *Policy Statement on Justice and the Impacts of Imprisonment*, February, Carlton: Australian Red Cross.

Baldry, E. (1994) 'USA Prison Privateers: Neo-Colonialists in a Southern Land', in P. Moyle (ed.) *Private Prisons and Police: Recent Australian Trends*, Sydney: Pluto Press.

Baldry, E. (2010) 'Women in Transition: From Prison to...', *Current Issues in Criminal Justice*, 22(2), pp. 253–68.

Baldry, E. (2014) 'Disability at the Margins: The Limits of the Law', *Griffith Law Review*, 23(3), pp. 370–88.

Baldry, E., Brown, D., Brown, M., Cunneen, C., Schwartz, M. and Steel, A. (2011) 'Imprisoning Rationalities', *Australian and New Zealand Journal of Criminology*, 44(1), pp. 24–40.

Baldry, E. and Cunneen, C. (2014) 'Imprisoned Indigenous Women and the Shadow of Colonial Patriarchy', *Australian and New Zealand Journal of Criminology*, 47(2), pp. 276 – 98.

Baldry, E., Dowse, L., McCausland, R. and Clarence, M. (2012) *Lifecourse Institutional Costs of Homelessness for Vulnerable Groups*, Canberra: Commonwealth of Australia.

Baldry, E., McDonnell, D., Maplestone, P. and Peeters, M. (2006) 'Ex-Prisoners, Accommodation and the State: Post-Release in Australia', *Australian and New Zealand Journal of Criminology*, 39(1), pp. 20–33.

Baldry, E., Ruddock, J. and Taylor, J. (2008) *Aboriginal Women with Dependent Children Leaving Prison Project*, Needs Analysis Report, Sydney: WSSPAH.

Barlow, M. (2013) 'Sustainable Justice: 2012 Presidential Address to the Academy of Criminal Justice Sciences', *Justice Quarterly*, 30(1), pp. 1–17.

Bartels, L. (2015) 'Swift and Certain Sanctions: Is it Time for Australia to Bring Some HOPE into the Criminal Justice System?', *Criminal Law Journal*, 39(1), pp. 53– 66.

Baxter, S. (2011) 'Why the Sun has turned Ken Clarke into a Teletubby', *New Statesman*, 9 June, http://www.newstatesman.com/blogs/steven-baxter/2011/06/ken-clarke-teletubby-laa-kept,2011.

Beckett, K. and Western, B. (2001) 'Governing Social Marginality: Welfare, Incarceration and the Transformation of State Policy', *Punishment and Society*, 3(1), pp. 43–59.

BJA (Bureau of Justice Assistance) (2012) *Bureau of Justice Assistance Strategic Plan: Fiscal Years 2013–2016*, November, Washington DC: Bureau of Justice Assistance.

BJA (Bureau of Justice Assistance) (2015) *Bureau of Justice Assistance – Justice Reinvestment*, https://www.bja.gov/programs/justicereinvestment/faqs.html (Justice Reinvestment Initiative FAQs, How Do I Participate?), accessed on 15 April 2015.

BJA (Bureau of Justice Assistance) (n.d.) *The Bureau of Justice Assistance*, Factsheet, Washington DC: Bureau of Justice Assistance.

Blagg, H. (2008) *Crime, Aboriginality and the Decolonisation of Justice*, Leichhardt: Hawkins Press.

Bonta, J., Blais, J. and Wilson, H. (2014) 'A Theoretically Informed Meta-Analysis of the Risk for General and Violent Recidivism for Mentally Disordered Offenders', *Aggression and Violent Behavior*, 19(3), pp. 278–87.

Bosworth, M. and Kaufman, E. (2013) 'Gender and Punishment', in J. Simon and R. Sparks (eds), *The Sage Handbook of Punishment and Society*, London: Sage.

Braithwaite, J. (1989) *Crime, Shame and Reintegration*, Cambridge: Cambridge University Press.

Braithwaite, J. (2002) *Restorative Justice and Responsive Regulation*, New York: Oxford University Press.

Bratanova, A. and Robinson, J. (2014) *Cost Effectiveness Analysis of a 'Justice Reinvestment' Approach to Queensland's Youth Justice Services*, School of Economics Discussion Papers, 537, School of Economics, The University of Queensland.

Bratton, W. (1998) *Turnaround: How America's Top Cop Reversed the Crime Epidemic*, New York: Random House.

Brewer, G. (2014) 'Justice Reform Again on State Officials Radar', *Tulsa World*, 24 November, http://www.tulsaworld.com/news/justice-reform-again-on-state-officials-radar/article_78787e22-06be-5e85-a5ba-76e96efcaaa9.html,2014.

Brown, D. (1990) 'Putting the Value Back in Punishment', *Legal Service Bulletin*, 15, pp. 177–85.

Brown, D. (1991) 'The State of the Prisons under the Greiner Government: Definitions of Value', *Journal for Social Justice Studies*, 4, pp. 27–60.

Brown, D. (2002a) 'The Politics of Law and Order', *Law Society Journal*, 40(9), pp. 64–72.

Brown, D. (2002b) 'Prisoners as Citizens', in D. Brown and M. Wilkie (eds), *Prisoners as Citizens: Human Rights in Australian Prisons*, Sydney: Federation Press.

Brown, D. (2005) 'Challenges to Criminal Justice Reform', in B. Opeskin and D. Weisbrot (eds), *The Promise of Law Reform*, Sydney: Federation Press.

Brown, D. (2010) 'The Limited Benefit of Prison in Controlling Crime', *Current Issues in Criminal Justice*, 22(1), pp. 137–48.

Brown, D. (2011a) 'The Limited Benefit of Prison in Controlling Crime: On the Threshold of a Political Shift', in G. Maxwell (ed.) *The Costs of Crime –Towards Fiscal Responsibility*, Wellington: Institute for Governance and Policy Studies, Victoria University.

Brown, D. (2011b) 'The Global Financial Crisis: Neo-liberalism, Social Democracy and Criminology', in M. Bosworth and C. Hoyle (eds), *What is Criminology?* Oxford: Oxford University Press.

Brown, D. (2011c) 'Review Essay: Neoliberalism as a Criminological Subject', *Australian and New Zealand Journal of Criminology*, 44(1), pp. 129–42.

Brown, D. (2013a) 'Prison Rates, Social Democracy, Neoliberalism and Justice Reinvestment', in K. Carrington, M. Ball, E. O'Brien and J. Tauri (eds), *Crime, Justice and Social Democracy: International Perspectives*, Bastingstoke: Palgrave MacMillan.

Brown, D. (2013b) 'Mapping the Conditions of Penal Hope', *International Journal for Crime, Justice and Social Democracy*, 2(3), pp. 27–42.

Brown, D. (2013c) 'Looking Behind the Increase in Custodial Remand Populations', *International Journal for Crime, Justice and Social Democracy*, 2(2), pp. 80–99.

Brown, D. (2014) 'Is Rational Law Reform Possible in a Shock-Jock Tabloid World?', *The Conversation*, 15 August, http://theconversation.com/is-rational-law-reform-still-possible-in-a-shock-jock-tabloid-world-30416,2014.

Brown, D. (2015) 'State of Imprisonment: Prisoners of NSW Politics and Perceptions', *The Conversation*, 21 April, http://theconversation.com/state-of-imprisonment-prisoners-of-nsw-politics-and-perceptions-38985,2015.

Brown, D., Farrier, D., McNamara, L., Steel, A., Grewcock, M., Quilter, J. and Schwartz, M. (2015) *Criminal Laws: Materials and Commentary on Criminal Law and Process in NSW*, 6th edition, Sydney: Federation Press.

Brown, D. and Quilter, J. (2014) 'Speaking Too Soon: The Sabotage of Bail Reform in NSW', *International Journal for Crime, Justice and Social Democracy*, 3(2), pp. 4–28.

Brown, D., Schwartz, M. and Boseley, L. (2012) 'The Promise and Pitfalls of Justice Reinvestment', *Alternative Law Journal*, 37(2), pp. 96–102.

Bumiller, K. (2013) 'Incarceration, Welfare State and Labour Market Nexus: The Increasing Significance of Gender in the Prison System', in B. Carlton and M. Segrave (eds), *Women Exiting Prison: Critical Essays on Gender, Post-Release Support and Survival*, Milton Park and New York: Routledge.

Butler, T. and Allnut, S. (2003) *Mental Health Among NSW Prisoners*, Sydney: Corrections Health Service.

Butler, T., Andrews, G. and Allnutt, S. (2006) 'Mental Disorders in Australian Prisoners: A comparison with a Community Sample', *Australian and New Zealand Journal of Psychiatry*, 40(3), pp. 272–6.

Cadora, E. (2008) 'Open Society', *Criminal Justice Matters* 64(1), pp. 20–3.

Cadora, E. (2014) 'Civic Lessons: How Certain Schemes to End Mass Incarceration can Fail', *The Annals of the Amercian Academy of Political and Social Science*, 651(1), pp. 277–85.

Cain, M. and Robey, V. (1992) 'The Impact of Truth in Sentencing Part 1 – The Higher Courts' *Sentencing Trends and Issue*, no. 2, Sydney: Judicial Commission of New South Wales.

Calabresi, M. (2014) 'Exclusive: Attorney General Eric Holder to Oppose Data-Driven Sentencing', *Time Magazine*, 31 July, http://time.com/3061893/holder-to-oppose-data-driven-sentencing/,2014.

Carlton, B.A. and McCulloch, J. (2008) 'R v Benbrika and ors (Ruling No. 20): The "War on Terror", Human Rights and the Pre-Emptive Punishment of Terror Suspects in High-Security', *Current Issues in Criminal Justice*, 20(2), pp. 287–92.

Carson, E.A. (2014) *Prisoners in 2013*, BJS Bulletin, September Washington, DC: Bureau of Justice Statistics.

Cavadino, M. and Dignan, J. (2006) *Penal Systems : A Comparative Approach*, London: Sage.

CEPP (Center for Effective Public Policy) (2012a) *Justice Reinvestment Initiative at the Local Level, Travis County, Texas*, Silver Spring: Center for Effective Public Policy.

CEPP (Center for Effective Public Policy) (2012b) *Justice Reinvestment Initiative at the Local Level, Getting to Know Mecklenburg County, North Carolina*, Silver Spring: Center for Effective Public Policy.

CEPP (Center for Effective Public Policy) (n.d.) *Justice Reinvestment Initiative at the Local Level, Getting to Know Denver, Colorado*, Silver Spring: Center for Effective Public Policy.

CEPP (Centre for Effective Public Policy) (2015) *Centre for Effective Public Policy*, http://cepp.com (What Makes Us Unique; Justice Reinvestment), accessed on 15 April 2015.

Chan, J. (1992) *Doing Less Time: Penal Reform in Crisis*, Sydney: Institute of Criminology, University of Sydney.

Chan, J. (ed.) (2005) *Reshaping Juvenile Justice: The NSW Young Offenders Act 1997*, Sydney: Sydney Institute of Criminology.

Chunn, D.E. and Gavigan, S.A.M. (2006) 'From Welfare Fraud to Welfare as Fraud: The Criminalization of Poverty', in E. Comack and G. Balfour (eds), *Criminalizing Women: Gender and (In)Justice in Neo-Liberal Times*, Halifax: Fernwood Publishing.

Clear, T. (2002) 'The Problem with "Addition by Subtraction": The Prison-Crime Relationship in Low-Income Communities', in M. Mauer and M. Chesney-Lind (eds), *Invisible Punishment: The Collateral Consequences of Mass Imprisonment*, New York: New Press.

Clear, T. (2007a) *Imprisoning Communities: How Mass Incarceration Makes Disadvantaged Neighborhoods Worse*, New York: Oxford University Press.

Clear, T. (2007b) 'The Impacts of Incarceration on Public Safety', *Social Research*, 74(2), pp. 613–30.

Clear, T. (2010) 'Policy and Evidence: The Challenge to the American Society of Criminology: 2009 Presidential Address to the American Society of Criminology', *Criminology*, 48(1), pp. 1–25.

Clear, T. (2011) 'A Private-Sector, Incentives-Based Model for Justice Reinvestment', *Criminology and Public Policy*, 10(3), pp. 583–608.

Clear, T. (2012) *The Promise and Perils of Justice Reinvestment. Is Justice Reinvestment Needed in Australia?* Justice Reinvestment Forum, Canberra, National Centre for Indigenous Studies, Australian National University.

Clear, T. and Austin, J. (2009) 'Reducing Mass Incarceration: Implications of the Iron Law of Prison Populations', *Harvard Law and Policy Review*, 3(2), pp. 307–24.

Clear, T. and Frost, N.A. (2014) *The Punishment Imperative: The Rise and Failure of Mass Incarceration in America*, New York and London: New York University Press.

Clear, T., Rose, D. and Ryder, J. (2001) 'Incarceration and the Community: The Problem of Removing and Returning Offenders', *Crime and Delinquency*, 47(3), pp. 335–51.

Clear, T., Rose, D., Waring, E. and Scully, K. (2003) 'Coercive Mobility and Crime: A Preliminary Examination of Concentrated Incarceration and Social Disorganisation', *Justice Quarterly*, 20(1), pp. 33–64.

Clement, M., Schwarzfeld, M. and Thompson, M. (2011) *Report of the National Summit on Justice Reinvestment and Public Safety: Addressing Recidivism, Crime, and Corrections Spending*, January, Council of State Governments Justice Center.

COAG (Council of Australian Governments) (2007) *National Indigenous Reform Agreement (Closing the Gap)*, Canberra: Council of Australian Governments.

Cohen, S. (2010) 'Ideology? What Ideology?', *Criminology and Criminal Justice*, 10(4), pp. 387–91.

Cole, D. (2011) 'Turning the Corner on Mass Incarceration', *Ohio State Journal of Criminal Law*, 9(1), pp. 27–51.

Commission on English Prisons Today (2009) *Do Better Do Less: The Report of the Commission on English Prisons Today*, London.

Commonwealth of Australia (2011) *Government Response to the House of Representatives Standing Committee on Aboriginal and Torres Strait Islander Affairs Report: Doing Time – Time for Doing: Indigenous Youth in the Criminal Justice System*, Canberra: Attorney-General's Department.

Connell, R. (2007) *Southern Theory*, Sydney: Allen and Unwin.

Corston, J. (2007) *The Corston Report: A Report by Baroness Jean Corston of a Review of Women with Particular Vulnerabilities in the Criminal Justice System*, London: Home Office.

Costar, B. and Economou, N. (eds) (1999) *The Kennett Revolution. Victorian Politics in the 1990s*, Sydney: UNSW Press.

Cowell, O. and Taylor, R. (2015) 'Piloting the Washington State approach to public policy in NSW', paper presented at *Applied Research in Crime and Justice*, Sydney: NSW Bureau of Crime Statistics and Research.

Cramer, L., Harvell, S., McClure, D., Sankar-Bergmann, A. and Parks, E. (2014) *The Justice Reinvestment Initiative: Experiences from the Local Sites*, November, Washington DC: Urban Institute.

Crenshaw, K.W. (2012) 'From Private Violence to Mass Incarceration: Thinking Intersectionally about Women, Race and Social Control', *UCLA Law Review*, 59(6), pp. 1418–72.

CRJ (Community Resources for Justice) (2014) *Creating Safe, Secure, and More Liveable Communities. 2014 Annual Report*, Boston: Community Resources for Justice.

CRJ (Community Resources for Justice) (2015) *Crime and Justice Institute Justice*, http://www.crj.org/cji (Justice Reinvestment Initiative), accessed on 15 April 2015.

CSG (2007) *Increasing Public Safety and Generating Savings: Options for Rhode Island Policymakers*, New York: Council of State Governments Justice Center.

CSG (2009) *Justice Reinvestment in Texas Assessing the Impact of the 2007 Justice Reinvestment Initiative*, 10 April, New York: Council of State Governments Justice Center.

CSG (2011) *Justice Reinvestment in Oklahoma: Overview*, New York: Council of State Governments Justice Center.

CSG (2012) *Justice Reinvestment in Oklahoma Analysis and Policy Framework* New York: Council of State Governments Justice Center.

CSG (2013) *Lessons from the States: Reducing Recidivism and Curbing Corrections Costs Through Justice Reinvestment*, April, New York: Council of State Governments Justice Center.

CSG (2014a) 'North Carolina Reaping the Benefits of Justice Reinvestment Act of 2011', *CSG Justice Center Justice Reinvestment*, 13 October, http://csgjusticecenter.org/jr/north-carolina/posts/north-carolina-reaping-the-benefits-of-justice-reinvestment-act-of-2011/.

CSG (2014b) *Justice Reinvestment in North Carolina: Three Years Later*, November, New York: Council of State Governments Justice Center.

CSG (2015a) *In Brief: Examining the Changing Racial Composition of Three States' Prison Populations*, March, Council of State Governments Justice Center.

CSG (2015b) *Council of State Governments*, http://www.csg.org (About; Homepage), accessed on 15 April 2015.

CSG Justice Center (2008) *Justice Reinvestment – The Strategy: How Justice Reinvestment Works*, 6 October 2008, http://web.archive.org/web/20081006223018/http://justicereinvestment.org/strategy/quantify, accessed on 6 October 2008.

CSG Justice Center (2010a) *Justice Reinvestment – About the Project*, http://justicereinvestment.org/about, accessed on 1 September 2010.

CSG Justice Center (2011) *Texas Justice Reinvestment: Outcomes, Challenges and Policy Options to Consider*, http://csgjusticecenter.org/jr/texas/publications/texas-justice-reinvestment-outcomes-challenges-and-policy-options-to-consider/, accessed on 30 March 2015.

CSG Justice Center (2011) *Justice Reinvestment – About the Project*, http://justicereinvestment.org/about, accessed on 19 August 2011.

CSG Justice Center (2013) *Justice Reinvestment – About*, http://csgjusticecenter.org/jr/about/, accessed on 11 April 2013.

CSG Justice Center (2015a) *Justice Reinvestment*, http://csgjusticecenter.org/jr/about/ (About Justice Reinvestment; Funding and Partners), accessed on 30 March 2015.

CSG Justice Center (2015b) *Justice Reinvestment State Profiles*, http://csgjusticecenter.org/jr/ (Connecticut, Hawaii, North Carolina, Rhode Island, Texas), accessed on 30 March 2015.

CSG Justice Centre (2015c) 'President's Budget Recommends Continued Funding for Second Chance Act, Justice Reinvestment Initiative, and Justice and Mental Health Collaboration Program', *CSG Justice Center Justice Reinvestment*, 2 February 2015, http://csgjusticecenter.org/jc/presidents-budget-recommends-continued-funding-for-second-chance-act-and-justice-reinvestment-initiative-and-justice-and-mental-health-collaboration-program/.

Cunneen, C. (1999) 'Zero Tolerance Policing and the Experience of New York City', *Current Issues in Criminal Justice*, 10(3), pp. 299–313.

Cunneen, C. (1999) 'Zero Tolerance Policing: How will it Affect Indigenous Communities?', *Indigenous Law Bulletin*, 4(19), pp. 7–10.

Cunneen, C. (2001) *Conflict, Politics and Crime. Aboriginal Communities and the Police*, Sydney Allen and Unwin.

Cunneen, C., Baldry, E., Brown, D., Brown, M., Schwartz, M. and Steel, A. (2013) *Penal Culture and Hyperincarceration*, London: Ashgate.

Cunneen, C. and Hoyle, C. (2010) *Debating Restorative Justice*, Oxford: Hart Publishing.

Daly, E. (2013) *Alternatives to Secure Youth Detention*, C.f.C. Tasmania.

Daly, K. (1992) 'Women's Pathways to Felony Court: Feminist Theories of Lawbreaking and Problems of Representation', *Southern California Review of Law and Women's Studies*, 2(1), pp. 11–52.

Daly, K. (1998) 'Women's Pathways to Felony Court', in K. Daly and L. Maher (eds), *Criminology at the Crossroads: Feminist Readings in Crime and Justice*, New York: Oxford University Press.

Daoust, C. (2008) *The Paradox in Incarceration and Crime Directed Research*, Directed Research Report, Sydney: Justice Action.

Darcy, D. (1999) 'Zero Tolerance – Not Quite the Influence on NSW Policing Some Would Have You Believe', *Current Issues in Criminal Justice*, 10(3), pp. 290–98.

Day, A. (2003) 'Reducing the Risk of Re-Offending in Australian Indigenous Offenders', *Journal of Offender Rehabilitation*, 37(2), pp. 1–15.

Day, A., Howells, K. and Casey, S. (2003) 'The Rehabilitation of Indigenous Prisoners: An Australian Perspective', *Journal of Ethnicity in Criminal Justice*, 1(1), pp. 115–33.

Dean, M. (2008) 'Media Fingers on the Social Policy Pie – and the Seven Sins of the Reptiles', paper presented at *The 15th Guardian Lecture*, Nuffield College, Oxford:

Deloitte Access Economics (2013) *An Economic Analysis for Aboriginal and Torres Strait Islander Offenders: Prison vs Residential Treatment*, Canberra: Australian National Council on Drugs.

Department of Corrections (2015) *Prison Facts and Statistics – September 2014*, Wellington: Department of Corrections (NZ). Available at http://www.corrections.govt.nz/resources/quarterly_prison_statistics/CP_September_2014.html.

Disley, E., Rubin, J., Scraggs, E., Burrowes, N. and Culley, D. (2011) *Lessons Learned from the Planning and Early Implementation of the Social Impact Bond at HMP Peterborough*, Research Series 11(5), Ministry of Justice (UK) and RAND Europe.

Dixon, D. (1998) 'Broken Windows, Zero Tolerance, and the New York Miracle', *Current Issues in Criminal Justice*, 10(1), pp. 96–106.

Dixon, D. (2005a) 'Why Don't the Police Stop Crime?', *Australian and New Zealand Journal of Criminology*, 38(1), pp. 4–24.

Dixon, D. (2005b) 'Beyond Zero Tolerance', in T. Newburn (ed.) *Policing: Key Readings*, Cullompton: Willan.

Downes, D. and Morgan, R. (2002) 'The Skeletons in the Cupboard: The Politics of Law and Order at the Turn of the Millennium', in M. Maguire, R. Morgan and R. Reiner (eds), *The Oxford Handbook of Criminology*, Oxford: Oxford University Press.

Downtown Austin Alliance (2015) *About the DAA*, http://www.downtownaustin.com/daa/about-daa, accessed on 30 April 2015.

Dowse, L., Baldry, E. and Snoyman, P. (2009) 'Disabling Criminology: Conceptualising the Intersections of Critical Disability Studies and Critical Criminology for People with Mental Health and Cognitive Disabilities in the Criminal Justice System', *Australian Journal of Human Rights*, 15(1), pp. 29–46.

Drucker, E. (2011) *A Plague of Prisons: The Epidemiology of Mass Incarceration in America*, New York: New Press.

Durlauf, S.N. and Nagin, D.S. (2011) 'Imprisonment and Crime: Can Both Be Reduced?', *Criminology and Public Policy*, 10(1), pp. 13–54.

Edney, R. (2001) 'Judicial Deference to the Expertise of Correctional Administrators: The Implications for Prisoners' Rights', *Australian Journal of Human Rights*, 7(1), pp. 91–133.

Egan, C. (2013) 'More Crime Remedies Needed: Judge', *The West Australian*, 17 August 2013, https://au.news.yahoo.com/thewest/latest/a/18537944/more-crime-remedies-needed-judge/,2013.

Ernst, J. (1994) 'Privatisation, Competition and Contracts', in J. Alford and D. O'Neill (eds), *The Contract State: Public Management and the Kennett Government*, Geelong: Centre for Applied Social Research, Deakin University.

Farrall, S. (2006) 'Rolling Back the State: Mrs Thatcher's Criminological legacy', *International Journal of Sociology of Law*, 34(4), pp. 256–77.

Farrall, S. and Hay, C. (2010) 'Not so Tough on crime? Why Weren't the Thatcher Governments More Radical in Reforming the Criminal Justice System?', *British Journal of Criminology*, 50(3), pp. 550–69.

Fazel, S., Khosla, V., Doll, H. and Geddes, J. (2008) 'The Prevalence of Mental Disorders among the Homeless in Western Countries: Systematic Review and Meta-Regression Analysis', *PLOS Medicine*, 5(12), pp. 1670–81.

FBI (Federal Bureau of Investigations) (2013) *Crime in the United States 2013*, http://www.fbi.gov/about-us/cjis/ucr/crime-in-the-u.s/2013/crime-in-the-u.s.-2013/violent-crime/violent-crime-topic-page/violentcrimemain_final, accessed on 20 April 2015.

Ferguson, R. (2014) 'America's Punishment Addiction: How to put our Broken Jails Back Together', *The Guardian Online*, 10 March, http://www.theguardian.com/commentisfree/2014/mar/10/how-to-fix-american-prisons,2014.

Ferris, B. (2001) 'Criminology Issues of Zero Tolerance Policing', *Southern Cross University Law Review*, 5, pp. 121–41.

Findlay, M. (1982) *The State of the Prison: A Critique of Reform*, Bathurst: Mitchellsearch.

Fitzgerald, J. (2009) *Why are Indigenous Imprisonment Rates Rising?* Issues Paper, no. 41, Sydney: NSW Bureau of Crime Statistics and Research.

Flatow, N. (2015) 'Supreme Court Justices Blast The Corrections System', *Think Progress*, 24 March 2015, http://thinkprogress.org/justice/2015/03/24/3637885/supreme-court-justices-implore-congress-reform-criminal-justice-system-not-humane/,2015.

Fox, C. and Albertson, K. (2010) 'Could Economics Solve the Prison Crisis?', *Probation Journal*, 57(3), pp. 263–80.

Fox, C. and Albertson, K. (2012) 'Is Payment by Results the Most Efficient Way to Address the Challenges Faced by the Criminal Justice Sector?', *Probation Journal*, 59(4), pp. 355–73.

Fox, C., Albertson, K. and Wong, K. (2013a) *Justice Reinvestment. Can the Criminal Justice System Deliver More for Less?*, London: Routledge.

Fox, C., Albertson, K. and Wong, K. (2013b) 'Justice Reinvestment and its Potential Contribution to Criminal Justice Reform', *Prison Service Journal*, 207, pp. 34–46.

Fox, C. and Grimm, R. (2015) 'The Role of Social Innovation in Criminal Justice Reform and the Risk Posed by Proposed Reforms in England and Wales', *Criminology and Criminal Justice*, 15(1), pp. 63–82.

Freiberg, A. (1992) 'Truth in Sentencing? The Abolition of Remissions in Victoria: Sentencing Act 1991 (Vic)', *Criminal Law Journal*, 16(3), pp. 165–85.

Freiberg, A. (2000) 'Guerrillas in our Midst? Judicial Responses to Governing the Dangerous', in M. Brown and J. Pratt (eds), *Dangerous Offenders: Punishment and Social Order*, London: Routledge.

Freiberg, A. and Carson, W. (2010) 'The Limits of Evidence-Based Policy: Evidence, Emotion and Criminal Justice', *Australian Journal of Public Administration*, 69(2), pp. 152–64.

Frost, N. and Clear, T. (2012) 'New Directions in Correctional Research', *Justice Quarterly*, 29(5), pp. 619–49.

Garland, D. (2001a) 'Introduction: The Meaning of Mass Imprisonment', in D. Garland (ed.) *Mass Imprisonment: Social Causes and Consequences*, Thousand Oaks: Sage.

Garland, D. (2001b) *The Culture of Control: Crime and Social Order in Contemporary Society*, Chicago: University of Chicago Press.

Garland, D. (2010) *Peculiar Institution: America's Death Penalty in an Age of Abolition*, Oxford: Oxford University Press.

Garland, D. and Young, P. (eds) (1983) *The Power to Punish: Contemporary Penality and Social Analysis*, London: Heinemann.

Gelsthorpe, L. and Hedderman, C. (2012) 'Providing for Women Offenders: The Risks of Adopting a Payment By Results Approach', *Probation Journal*, 59(4), pp. 374–90.

Gilbert, R. (2012) *Place-Based Initiatives and Indigenous Justice*, Brief 13, Canberra: Indigenous Justice Clearinghouse.

Gilfus, M. (1993) 'From Victims to Survivors to Offenders: Women's Routes of Entry into Street Crime', *Women and Criminal Justice*, 4(1), pp. 63–89.

Gingrich, N. and Nolan, P. (2011) 'Prison Reform: A Smart Way for States to Save Money and Lives', *Washington Post*, 7 January, http://www.washingtonpost.com/wp-dyn/content/article/2011/01/06/AR2011010604386.html,2011.

Glaser, W. and Deane, K. (1999) 'Normalisation in an Abnormal World: A Study of Prisoners with an Intellectual Disability', *International Journal of Offender Therapy and Comparative Criminology*, 43(3), pp. 338–56.

Glaze, L. and Kaeble, D. (2014) *Correctional Populations in the United States 2013*, BJS Bulletin, December, Washington DC.

Go, J. (ed.) (2013) *Postcolonial Sociology*. Political Power and Social Theory, Bingley: Emerald Group Publishing.

Goldson, B. and Hughes, G. (2010) 'Sociological Criminology and Youth Justice: Comparative Policy Analysis and Academic Intervention', *Criminology and Criminal Justice*, 10(2), pp. 211–30.

Gonnerman, J. (2004) 'Million Dollar Blocks: The Neighbourhood Costs of America's Prison Book', *Village Voice*, 9 November, http://www.villagevoice.com/2004-11-09/news/million-dollar-blocks/,2004.

Gooda, M., Priday, E. and McDermott, L. (2013) 'Looking Beyond Offenders to the Needs of Victims and Communities', *Indigenous Law Bulletin*, 8(5), pp. 13–6.

Gordon, M. and Harrison, D. (2015) 'Coalition MPs Stage Walkout after Bill Shorten Raises Budget in Closing the Gap Speech', *Sydney Morning Herald*, 12 February, http://www.smh.com.au/federal-politics/political-news/coalition-mps-stage-walkout-after-bill-shorten-raises-budget-in-closing-the-gap-speech-20150211-13bla7.html,2015.

Gorta, A. (1992) 'Impact of the Sentencing Act 1989 on the NSW Prison Population', *Current Issues in Criminal Justice*, 3(3), pp. 308–17.

Grabosky, P.N. (1999) 'Zero tolerance Policing' *Trends and Issues in Crime and Criminal Justice*, 102, Australian Institute of Criminology.

Green, D. (2008) *When Children Kill Children*, Oxford: Oxford University Press.

Green, D. (2013) 'Penal Optimism and Second Chances: The Legacies of American Protestantism and the Prospects for Penal Reform', *Punishment and Society* 12(2), pp. 123–46.

Greene, J. and Mauer, M. (2010) *Downscaling Prisons. Lessons From Four States*, Washington DC: The Sentencing Project.

Grewcock, M. (2009) *Border Crimes: Australia's War on Illicit Migrants*, Sydney: Sydney Institute of Criminology.

Griffith, G. (1999) 'Zero Tolerance Policing', 14, NSW Parliamentary Library Research Service.

Groves, M. (2001) 'International Law and Australian Prisoners', *University of New South Wales Law Journal*, 24(1), pp. 17–59.

Guthrie, J. (2015) *Reducing Incarceration Using Justice Reinvestment: An Exploratory Case Study*, http://ncis.anu.edu.au/cowra/, accessed on 15 April 2015.

Guthrie, J., Levy, M. and Fforde, C. (2013) 'Investment in Prisons: An Investment in Social Exclusion? Linking the Theories of Justice Reinvestment and Social Inclusion to Examine Australia's Propensity to Incarcerate', *Griffith Journal of Law and Human Dignity*, 1(2), pp. 254–81.

Hancock, L. (1999) 'The Justice System and Accountability', in B. Costar and N. Economou (eds), *The Kennett Revolution. Victorian Politics in the 1990s*, Sydney: UNSW Press.

Hannah-Moffat, K. (2009) 'Gridlock or Mutability: Reconsidering "Gender" and Risk Assessment', *Criminology and Public Policy*, 8(1), pp. 209–19.

Hannah-Moffat, K. (2012) 'Actuarial Sentencing: An "Unsettled" Proposition', *Justice Quarterly*, 30(2), pp. 270–96.

Harding, R.W. (1997) *Private Prisons and Public Accountability*, Buckingham: Open University Press.

Hawken, A. and Kleiman, M. (2009) *Managing Drug Involved Probationers With Swift and Certain Sanctions: Evaluating Hawaii's HOPE*, Washington, DC: O.o.J.P. National Institute of Justice, US Department of Justice,.

Hayes, S., Shackell, P., Mottram, P. and Lancaster, R. (2007) 'The Prevalence of Intellectual Disability in a Major UK Prison', *British Journal of Learning Disabilities*, 35(3), pp. 162–7.

HCJC (House of Commons Justice Committee) (2013) *Women Offenders: After the Corston Report*, 1, London: The Stationery Office.

HCJC (UK House of Commons Justice Committee) (2010) *Cutting Crime: The Case for Justice Reinvestment*, London: House of Commons.

Heffernan, E.B., Andersen, K.C., Dev, A. and Kinner, S. (2012) 'Prevalence of Mental Illness among Aboriginal and Torres Strait Islander People in Queensland Prisons', *The Medical Journal of Australia*, 197(1), pp. 37–41.

Henry, V. (2002) *The Compstat Paradigm: Managerial Accountability in Policing, Business and the Public Sector*, New York: Looseleaf Law Publications.

Herberman, E. and Bonczar, T.P. (2014) *Probation and Parole in the United States, 2013*, BJS Bulletin, October (revised 21 January 2015), Washington, DC: Bureau of Justice Statistics.

Herbert, N. (2010) *Speech to the Howard League for Penal Reform*. Howard League for Penal Reform Parmoor Lecture 2010.

Herrington, V. (2009) 'Assessing the Prevalence of Intellectual Disability Among Young Male Prisoners', *Journal of Intellectual Disability Research*, 53(5), pp. 397–410.

Ho, H.S., Neusteter, R. and La Vigne, N.G. (2013) *Justice Reinvestment. A Toolkit for Local Leaders*, Washington DC: Urban Institute http://www.urban.org/UploadedPDF/412929-Justice-Reinvestment-A-Toolkit-for-Local-Leaders.pdf.

Hobbs, S. and Hamerton, C. (2014) *The Making of Criminal Justice Policy*, Oxford: Routledge.

Hogg, R. (2012) 'Punishment and "the People": Rescuing Populism from its Critics', in K. Carrington, M. Ball and J. Tauri (eds), *Crime, Justice and Social Democracy: International Perspectives*, Basingstoke: Palgrave Macmillan.

Hogg R (1996) 'Criminological Failure and Governmental Effect', *Current Issues in Criminal Justice*, 8(1), pp. 43–59.

Hogg, R. and Brown, D. (1998) *Rethinking Law and Order* Sydney: Pluto Press.

HRSC (House of Representatives Standing Committee on Aboriginal and Torres Strait Islander Affairs) (2011) *Doing Time – Time for Doing: Indigenous Youth in the Criminal Justice System*, Canberra: Parliament of Australia.

Hudson, B. and Bramhall, G. (2005) 'Assessing the Other: Constructions of Asianness in Risk Assessment by Probation Officers', *British Journal of Criminology*, 45(1), pp. 721–40.

ICPS (International Centre for Prison Studies) (2015) *United Kingdom: England and Wales*, http://www.prisonstudies.org/country/united-kingdom-england-wales (Overview; Further Information), accessed on 4 May 2015.

Ife, J. (2013) *Community Development in an Uncertain World: Vision, Analysis and Practice*, Cambridge: Cambridge University Press.

Indig, D., McEntyre, E., Page, J. and Ross, B. (2010) *2009 NSW Inmate Health Survey: Aboriginal Health Report*, Sydney: Justice Health.

Indig, D., Vecchiato, C., Haysom, L., Beilby, R., Carter, J., Champion, U., Gaskin, C., Heller, E., Kumar, S., Mamone, N., Muir, P., van den Dolder, P. and Whitton, G. (2011) *2009 NSW Young People in Custody Health Survey: Full Report*, Sydney: Justice Health and NSW Department of Juvenile Justice.

Institute for Economics and Peace (2013) *UK Peace Index 2013*, Sydney: Institute for Economics and Peace.

Institute for the Study of Crime and Justice (2009) *Evaluation of the Hartford 'New Day' Building Bridges Pilot Program*, New Britain: Institute for the Study of Crime and Justice, Department of Criminology Central Connecticut State University.

Inter Church Steering Committee on Prison Reform (1994) *Prison – Not Yet the Last Resort*, Sydney: Inter Church Steering Committee on Prison Reform.

James, D., Farnham, F. and Cripps, J. (1999) 'Homelessness and Psychiatric Admission Rates Through the Criminal Justice System', *Lancet*, 353(9159), pp. 1158.

James, J., Eisem, L.-B. and Subramanian, R. (2012) 'A View from the States: Evidence-Based Public Safety Legislation', *Journal of Criminal Law and Criminology*, 102(3), pp. 821–50.

Jardine, C. and Whyte, B. (2013) 'Valuing Desistance: A Social Return on Investment Case Study of a Throughcare Project for Short Term Prisoners', *Social and Environmental Accountability Journal*, 33(1), pp. 20–32.

Jenkins, S. (2012) 'A British FBI has no Chance Against London's Very Own KGB', *The Guardian*, 11 May, http://www.theguardian.com/commentisfree/2012/may/10/police-metropolitan-police.

JFA (2012) *JFA Institute*, http://www.jfa-associates.com/ (home page and publications), accessed on 11 March 2015.

JMC (Justice Mapping Centre) (2010) 'Justice Mapping Center Launches First National Atlas of Criminal Justice Data', *Justice Mapping Center*, 5 October, http://www.justicemapping.org/archive/28/justice-mapping-center-launches-first-national-atlas-of-criminal-justice-data/, accessed on 15 April 2015.

JMC (Justice Mapping Centre) (2015) *Justice Mapping Centre*, http://www.justicemapping.org (About Us), accessed on 15 April 2015.

Johnston, A. and Spears, D. (1996) *The Sentencing Act 1989 and Its Effects on the Prison Population*, Research Monograph Series, 13, Sydney: Judicial Commission of New South Wales.

Jones, T. and Newburn, T. (2002) 'Policy Convergence and Crime Control in the USA and UK: Streams of Influence and Levels of Impact', *Criminology and Criminal Justice*, 2 (2), pp. 173–203.

Jones, T. and Newburn, T. (2007) *Policy Transfer and Criminal Justice: Exploring US Influence Over British Crime Control Policy*, Maidenhead: Open University Press/McGraw Hill.

Just Reinvest NSW (2015a) *Justice Reinvestment in Bourke*, http://www.justreinvest.org.au/jr-in-bourke/, accessed on 19 April 2015.

Just Reinvest NSW (2015b) *Creating a Just NSW Thinking Differently for Safer Communities*, http://justreinvest.org.au/wp-content/uploads/2012/04/2015-Election-Policy-Doc-Final.pdf, accessed on 19 April 2015.

Justice Fellowship (2015) *Justice Fellowship*, http://www.justicefellowship.org/ (What We Do; Michigan Justice in Crisis: Justice Fellowship's Call to Action), accessed on 19 April 2015.

Kautt, P. and Gelsthorpe, L. (2009) 'What Works for Women: A Comparison of Community-Based General Offending Programme Completion', *British Journal of Criminology*, 49(6), pp. 879–99.

Kavanagh, L., Rowe, D., Hersch, J., Barnett, K.J. and Reznik, R. (2010) 'Neurocognitive Deficits and Psychiatric Disorders in a NSW Prison Population', *International Journal of Law and Psychiatry*, 33(1), pp. 20–6.

Kelling, G. and Coles, C.M. (1998) *Fixing Broken Windows*, New York: Free Press.

Kendall, K. (2002) 'Time to Think Again About Cognitive Behavioural Programmes', in P. Carlen (ed.) *Women and Punishment. The Struggle for Justice*, Cullompton: Willan Publishing.

Kim, K., Becker-Cohen, M. and Serakos, M. (2015) *The Processing and Treatment of Mentally Ill Persons in the Criminal Justice System*, March, Washington DC.

Kruttschnitt, C. (2010) 'The Paradox of Women's Imprisonment', *Daedalus*, 139(3), pp. 32–42.

Kruttschnitt, C. (2010) 'Women's Prisons', in M. Tonry (ed.) *The Oxford Handbook of Crime and Criminal Justice*, Oxford: Oxford University Press.

Kruttschnitt, C., Slotboom, A., Dirkzwager, A. and Bijleveld, C. (2013) 'Bringing Women's Carceral Experiences into the "New Punitiveness" Fray', *Justice Quarterly*, 30(1), pp. 18–43.

La Vigne, N.G., Brooks, L.E. and Shollenberger, T.L. (2009) *Women on the Outside: Understanding the Experiences of Female Prisoners Returning to Houston, Texas*, Research Report, 2009, New York.

La Vigne, N.G., Davies, E., Lachman, P. and Neusteter, S. (2013) *Justice Reinvestment at the Local Level Planning and Implementation Guide*, Second Edition, Washington DC: Urban Institute.

La Vigne, N.G., Neusteter, S.R., Lachman, P., Dwyer, A. and Nadeau, C.A. (2010) *Justice Reinvestment at the Local Level Planning and Implementation Guide*, Washington DC: Urban Institute.

La Vigne, N.G., S, B., Cramer, L., Ho, H., Kotonias, C., Mayer, D., McClure, D., Pacifici, L., Parks, E., Peterson, B. and Samuels, J. (2014) *Justice Reinvestment Initiative State Assessment Report*, January, Washington DC: Urban Institute.

Lacey, N. (2008) *The Prisoners' Dilemma*, Cambridge: Cambridge University Press.

Lachman, P. and Neusteter, S.R. (2012) *Tracking Costs and Savings Through Justice Reinvestment*, Justice Reinvestment at the Local Level Brief 1, Washington DC: Urban Institute.

Lamb, H.R. and Weinberger, L. (1998) 'Persons with Severe Mental Illness in Jails and Prisons: A Review', *Psychiatric Services*, 49(4), pp. 483–91.

Lamb, H.R., Weinberger, L.E. and Gross, B.H. (2004) 'Mentally Ill Persons in the Criminal Justice System: Some Perspectives', *Psychiatric Quarterly*, 75(2), pp. 107–26.

Lamb, H.R., Wenberger, L.E. and DeCuir Jr., W.J. (2002) 'The Police and Mental Health', *Psychiatric Services*, 53(10), pp. 1266–71.

Lanning, T., Loader, I. and Muir, R. (2011) *Redesigning Justice Reducing Crime Through Justice Reinvestment*, June, London.

Latessa, E. and Lowencamp, C. (2006) 'What Works in Reducing Recidivism?', *University of St. Thomas Law Journal*, 3(3), pp. 521–35.

Latessa, E., Smith, P., Lemke, R., Makarios, M. and Lowenkamp, C. (2009) *Creation and Validation of the Ohio Risk Assessment System* Final Report, July, Ohio: University of Cincinnati, School of Criminal Justice.

LCARC (Legal and Constitutional Affairs Reference Committee) (2009) *Access to Justice*, Canberra: Department of the Senate.

LCARC (Legal and Constitutional Affairs Reference Committee) (2013) *Value of a Justice Reinvestment Approach to Criminal Justice in Australia*, Canberra: Department of the Senate.

LeBaron, G and Roberts, A. (2010) 'Toward a Feminist Political Economy of Capitalism and Carcerality', *Signs*, 36(1), pp. 19–44.

Legislative Council Standing Committee on Law and Justice (2006) *Community Based Sentencing Options for Rural and Remote Areas and Disadvantaged Populations*, Report, March, Sydney: Legislative Council Standing Committee on Law and Justice.

Lengyel, T. and Brown, M. (2009) *Everyone Pays: A Social Cost Analysis of Incarcerating Parents for Drug Offenses in Hawaii*', Honolulu: Consuelo Foundation.

Levitt, S.D. (2004) 'Understanding Why Crime Fell in the 1990s: Four Factors that Explain the Decline and Six that Do Not', *Journal of Economic Perspectives*, 18(1), pp. 163–90.

Light, M., Grant, E. and Hopkins, K. (2013) *Gender Differences in Substance Misuse and Mental Health Amongst Prisoners. Results from the Surveying Prisoner Crime Reduction (SPCR) Longitudinal Cohort Study of Prisoners*, London: Ministry of Justice Analytical Series (UK).

Lipsey, M.W., Landenberger, N.A. and Wilson, S.J. (2007) *Effects of Cognitive-Behavioral Programs for Criminal Offenders*, Campbell Systematic Reviews, no. 6, Oslo: Campbell Collaboration.

Loader, I. (2006) 'Fall of the "Platonic Guardians": Liberalism, Criminology and Political Responses to Crime in England and Wales', *British Journal of Criminology*, 12(3), pp. 399–410.

Loader, I. and Sparks, R. (2010) *Public Criminology*, London: Routledge.

Loewenstein, A. (2013) *Profits of Doom: How Vulture Capitalism is Swallowing the World*, Melbourne: Melbourne University Press.

Lovins, B. and Latessa, E. (2013) 'Creation and Validation of the Ohio Youth Assessment System(OYAS) and Strategies for Successful Implementation', *Justice Research and Policy*, 15(1), pp. 67–93.

Marchetti, E. (2014) 'Delivering Justice in Indigenous Sentencing Courts: What This Means for Judicial Officers, Elders, Community Representatives, and Indigenous Court Workers', *Law and Policy*, 36(4), pp. 341–69.

Marchetti, E. and Daly, K. (2004) 'Indigenous Sentencing Courts: Towards a Theoretical and Jurisprudential Model', *Sydney Law Review*, 29(3), pp. 416–43.

Martin, J., Kautt, P. and Gelsthorpe, L. (2009) ' What Works for Women: A Comparison of Community-Based General Offending Programme Completion', *British Journal of Criminology*, 49(6), pp. 879–99.

Martinson, R. (1974) 'What Works? – Questions and Answers About Prison Reform', *The Public Interest*, 35, pp. 22–54.

Maruna, S. (2011) 'Lessons for Justice Reinvestment from Restorative Justice and the Justice Model Experience', *Criminology and Public Policy*, 10(3), pp. 661–9.

Matka, E. (1991) *NSW Sentencing Act 1989*, Sydney: NSW Bureau of Crime Statistics and Research.

Mauer, M. (2013) *The Changing Racial Dynamics of Women's Incarceration*, Washington DC: The Sentencing Project.

Mauer, M. and Chesney-Lind, M. (eds) (2002) *Invisible Punishment : The Collateral Consequences of Mass Imprisonment*, New York: New Press.

McCartney, C. (2000) 'Corrections in Australia: Is the Future Private', in D. Chappell and P. Wilson (eds), *Crime and the Criminal Justice System in Australia: 2000 and Beyond*, Sydney: Butterworths Australia.

McNeill, F., Farrall, S., Lightowler, C. and Maruna, S. (2012) 'Re-examining Evidence-Based Practice in Community Corrections: Beyond "A Confined View" of What Works', *Justice Research and Policy*, 14(1), pp. 35–60.

Melossi, D. (2004) 'The Cultural Embeddedness of Social Control: Reflections on the Comparison of Italian and North American Cultures Concerning punishment', *Theoretical Criminology*, 5(4), pp. 651–79.

Meronek, T. (2013) 'Islands in the Sand: Why Thousands of Hawaiian Prisoners are Languishing in the Arizona Desert', *Hyphen Magazine*, http://www.hyphenmagazine.com/magazine/issue-26-south/islands-sand#sthash.1idvL2qZ.24DbgYCL.dpuf,2013.

Merritt, C. (2010) 'State Liberals Walk Away From the Law and Order Auction', *The Australian*, 16 April, http://www.theaustralian.com.au/business/legal-affairs/state-liberals-walk-away-from-the-law-and-order-auction/story-e6frg97x-1225854275877,2010.

Milgram, A. (2014) *To Minimize Injustice, Use Big Data*, Laura and John Arnold Foundation, 20 August, www.arnoldfoundation.org/news/minimize-injustice-use-big-data., accessed on 15 April 2015.

Minton, T.D. and Golinelli, D. (2014) *Jail Inmates at Midyear 2013 – Statistical Tables*, August, Washington DC: Bureau of Justice Statistics.

Mitchell, M. and Leachman, M. (2014) *Changing Priorities : State Criminal Justice Reforms and Investments in Education*, October, Washington, DC: Centre on Budget and Policy Priorities.

MOJ (Ministry of Justice UK) (2010) *Breaking the Cycle: Effective Punishment, Rehabilitation and Sentencing of Offenders*, London: Ministry of Justice.

MOJ (Ministry of Justice UK) (2013a) *Statistics on Race and the Criminal Justice System 2012*, November, Ministry of Justice.

MOJ (Ministry of Justice UK) (2013b) *Justice Reinvestment Pilots: Second Year Results*, London: Ministry of Justice.

MOJ (Ministry of Justice UK) (2014a) 'Offender Management Statistics Bulletin, England and Wales', Quarterly – October to December 2013, Annual – January to December 2013, London: Ministry of Justice.

MOJ (Ministry of Justice UK) (2014b) *Statistics on Women and the Criminal Justice System 2013*, November, Ministry of Justice.

MOJ (Ministry of Justice UK) (2014c) *Costs Per Place and Costs Per Prisoner: National Offender Management Service Annual Report and Accounts 2013–14*, Ministry of Justice Information Release, October, London: Ministry of Justice.

MOJ (Ministry of Justice UK) (2015a) 'Offender Management Statistics Bulletin, England and Wales', July to September 2014, Ministry of Justice.
MOJ (Ministry of Justice UK) (2015b) *Offender Management Statistics Bulletin, England and Wales*, Statistics Bulletin, April, London: Ministry of Justice.
MOJ (Ministry of Justice UK) (2015c) *Population Bulletin: Weekly 17 April 2015*, April, Ministry of Justice.
Morgan, N. (1999) 'Capturing Crims or Capturing Votes? The Aims and Effects of Mandatories', *UNSW Law Journal*, 22(1), pp. 286–94.
Morgan, N. (2000) 'Mandatory Sentences in Australia: Where Have we Been and Where Are We going?', *Criminal Law Journal*, 24(3), pp. 164–83.
Morrison, C.M. (2012) 'Foreword: Criminal Justice Response to the Economic Crisis', *George State University Law Review*, 28(4), pp. 953–66.
Mosher, C.J. and Mahon-Haft, T. (2010) 'Race, Crime and Criminal Justice in Canada', in A. Kalunta-Crumpton (ed.) *Race, Crime and Criminal Justice*, Basingstoke: Palgrave MacMillan.
Mosher, J. (2010) 'Intimate Intrusions: Welfare Regulation and Women's Personal Lives', in S. Gavigan and D. Chunn (eds), *The Legal Tender of Gender: Law, Welfare and the Regulation of Women's Poverty*, Oxford: Hart Publishing.
Moyle, P. (1994) *Profiting from Punishment. Private Prisons in Australia: Reform or Regression*, Sydney: Pluto Press.
Moyle, P. (ed.) (2000) *Private Prisons and Police: Recent Australian Trends*, Sydney: Pluto Press.
Muldrow, D. (2015) 'Bipartisan Summit on Criminal Justice Reform a Triumph of Cooperation, Right on Crime, The Conservative Case for Reform', *Right On Crime,,* 9 April 2015, http://rightoncrime.com/2015/04/watch-bipartisan-summit-on-criminal-justice-reform/.
Muncie, J. (2005) 'Globalisation of Crime Control: The Case of Youth and Juvenile Justice', *Theoretical Criminology*, 9(1), pp. 35–64.
Murray, C. (1984) *Losing Ground: American Social Policy, 1950–1980*, New York: Basic Books.
NACRO (National Association for the Care and Resettlement of Offenders) (1992) *Revolving Doors: Report of the Telethon Inquiry into the Relationship between Mental Health, Homelessness and Criminal Justice*, London: National Association for the Care and Resettlement of Offenders.
Nagle, J. (1978) *Report of the Royal Commission into NSW Prisons*, Sydney: NSW Government Printer.
National Congress of Australia's First Peoples (2013) *National Justice Policy*, Version 1, February, Sydney: National Congress of Australia's First Peoples.
National Research Council (2014) *The Growth of Incarceration in the United States: Exploring Causes and Consequences*, Washington DC: C.o.L.a.J. Committee on Causes and Consequences of High Rates of Incarceration, Division of Behavioral and Social Sciences and Education of the National Academies,.
New Economic Foundation (2008) *Unlocking Value: How we all benefit from Investing in Alternatives to Prison for Women Offenders*, London: New Economic Foundation.
New York City Department of Probation (2015) *Neighborhood Opportunity Network (NeON)*, http://www.nyc.gov/html/prob/html/neon/neon.shtml, accessed on 28 April 2015.

Newburn, T. (2002) 'Atlantic Crossings: "Policy transfer" and Crime Control in the USA and Britain', *Punishment and Society*, 4(2), pp. 165–94.

Newburn, T. (2010) 'Diffusion, Differentiation and Resistance in Comparative Penality', *Criminology and Criminal Justice*, 10(4), pp. 341–52.

Newburn, T. and Jones, T. (2005) 'Symbolic Politics and Penal Populism: The Long Shadow of Willie Horton', *Crime, Media, Culture*, 1(1), pp. 72–87.

Noetic Solutions (2010) *A Strategic Review of the New South Wales Juvenile Justice System, Report for the Minister for Juvenile Justice*, April, Manuka: Noetic Solutions.

NSW Department of Premier and Cabinet (2015) *Statement of Opportunities, NSW Social Impact Investment Policy*, February, Sydney: NSW Department of Premier and Cabinet.

NSW Labor Party (2015) *Labor Proposes New Approach to Tackle Aboriginal Incarceration*, http://www.lukefoley.com.au/labor_proposes_new_approach_to_tackle, accessed on 19 April 2015.

NSW Law Reform Commission (2012) *Bail*, Report 133, Sydney: NSW Law Reform Commission.

NSW Ombudsman (2011) *Addressing Aboriginal Disadvantage: The Need to Do Things Differently*, A Special Report to Parliament under s 31 of the *Ombudsman Act 1974*, Sydney: Office of the NSW Ombudsman.

NSW Sentencing Council (2004) *Abolishing Prison Sentences of Six Months or Less: A Report of the NSW Sentencing Council*, Final Report, August, Sydney: NSW Sentencing Council.

NT Government (2011) *Review of the Northern Territory Youth Justice System: Report*, September, Darwin: Northern Territory Government.

O'Callaghan, K. (2015) 'What Really Matters: Justice Reinvestment', *Western Australia Police*, http://www.police.wa.gov.au/Aboutus/CommissionerofPolice/Whatreallymatters/Justicereinvestment/tabid/2003/Default.aspx, accessed on 19 April 2015.

O'Neil, D. (1999) '"The Quiet Revolution": Public Service reform in the Kennett Era', in B. Costar and N. Economou (eds), *The Kennett Revolution. Victorian Politics in the 1990s*, Sydney: UNSW Press.

Open Society Foundations (2015) *Open Society Foundations*, http://www.opensocietyfoundations.org (About Us: Mission and Values; About Us: Expenditures), accessed on 14 April 2015.

OpenDoors (2015) *9 Yards*, http://www.opendoorsri.org/9yards, accessed on 27 April 2015.

Papalia, P. (2010) *Justice Reinvestment, An Option for Western Australia*, Perth: WA Labor.

Parliament of Victoria Law Reform, D.a.C.P.C. (2014) *Inquiry Into the Supply and Use of Methamphetamines, Particularly 'Ice'*, in Victoria, September, Parliament of Victoria.

Pew-MacArthur Results First Initiative (2015) *Legislating Evidence-Based Policymaking: A Look at State Laws that Support Data-Driven Decision-Making*, Issue Brief, March, Washington DC: The Pew Charitable Trusts.

Pew (2008) *One in 100: Behind Bars in America 2008*, February, Washington DC: The Pew Charitable Trusts.

Pew (2009) *One in 31: The Long Reach of American Corrections*, March, Washington, DC: The Pew Charitable Trusts.

Pew (2014) *The Pew Charitable Trusts*, http://www.pewtrusts.org/en/research-and-analysis/collections/2014/11/justice-reinvestment-national-summit-sustaining-success-maintaining-momentum (Justice Reinvestment National Summit), accessed on 14 April 2015.

Pew (2015a) *Growth in Federal Prison System Exceeds States'*, Fact Sheet, January, Washington DC: The Pew Charitable Trusts.

Pew (2015b) *Pew Research Centre*, www.pewresearch.org (About Pew Research Centre), accessed on 3 May 2015.

Pew (2015c) *Public Safety Performance Project*, http://www.pewtrusts.org/en/projects/public-safety-performance-project, accessed on 4 May 2015.

Player, E. (2014) 'Women in the Criminal Justice System: The Triumph of Inertia', *Criminology and Criminal Justice*, 14(3), pp. 276–97.

Pratt, J. (2007) *Penal Populism*, London: Routledge.

Pratt, J. (2011) 'The International Diffusion of Punitive Penality: Or, Penal Exceptionalism in the United States? Wacquant v Whitman', *Australian and New Zealand Journal of Criminology*, 44(1), pp. 116–28.

Prison Policy Initiative (2015) *Hawaii Profile* http://www.prisonpolicy.org/profiles/HI.html, accessed on 30 March 2015.

Prison Reform Trust (2014) *Bromley Briefings Prison Factfile: Autumn 2014*, London: Prison Reform Trust.

Pritikin, M.H. (2008) 'Is prison increasing crime?', *Wisconsin Law Review*, 2008(6), pp. 1049–108.

Private Prisons Investigation Panel (Vic) (Kirby Inquiry) (2000) *Report of the Investigation into the Management and Operations of Victoria's Private Prisons*, Melbourne: Private Prisons Investigation Panel (Vic).

Productivity Commission (2015) *Report on Government Services 2015*, Canberra: Productivity Commission.

Reddy, V. and Levin, M. (2014) 'Right on Crime: A Return to First Principles for American Conservatives', *Texas Review of Law and Politics*, 18(2), pp. 232–54.

Reilly, R.J. (2013) 'Eric Holder: "Broken" Justice System Needs "Sweeping" Changes, Reforms to Mandatory Minimum', *Huffington Post*, 8 December, http://www.huffingtonpost.com/2013/08/12/eric-holder-mandatory-minimum_n_3744575.html,2013.

Rempe, S. (2014) *Prison Fellowship*, http://www.prisonfellowship.org/2014/01/a-good-investment/ (A Good Investment), accessed on 19 April 2015.

Right on Crime (2015) *Right on Crime*, http://www.rightoncrime.com (Home; The Conservative Case for Reform), accessed on 19 April 2015

Roberts, D. and McVeigh, K. (2013) 'Eric Holder Unveils New Reforms Aimed at Curbing US Prison Population', *The Guardian*, 12 August 2013 http://www.theguardian.com/world/2013/aug/12/eric-holder-smart-crime-reform-us-prisons,2013.

Roberts, J., Stalans, L.J., Indermaur, D. and Hough, M. (2003) *Penal Populism and Public Opinion: Lessons from Five Countries*, New York: Oxford University Press.

Robey, V. and Cain, M. (1992) *The Impact of the Truth in Sentencing Part 2 – The Local Courts*, Sentencing Trends, June.

Roman, J. (2004) 'Can Cost–Benefit Analysis Answer Criminal Justice Policy Questions, and If So, How?', *Journal of Contemporary Criminal Justice*, 20(3), pp. 257–75.

Rose, D. and Clear, T. (1998) 'Incarceration, Social Capital and Crime: Implications for Social Disorganization Theory', *Criminology*, 36(3), pp. 441–80.

Rose, N. (1999) *Powers of Freedom: Reframing Political Thought*, Cambridge: Cambridge University Press.

Roth, L. (2014) *Privatisation of Prisons*, Background Paper, July, Sydney: New South Wales Parliamentary Library.

Rowse, T. (1992) *Remote Possibilities: The Aboriginal Domain and the Administrative Imagination*, Darwin: North Australia Research Institute, Austrlaian National University.

Ryan, M. (2003) *Penal Policy and Political Cultures in England and Wales*, Winchester: Waterside Press.

Ryan, M. (2005) 'Engaging with Punitive Attitudes Towards Crime and Punishment: Some Strategic Lessons From England and Wales', in J. Pratt, D. Brown, M. Brown, S. Hallsworth and W. Morrison (eds), *The New Punitiveness: Trends, Theories, Perspective*, Cullompton: Willan Publishing.

SA Government (2014) *Building a Stronger Society: Social Impact Investment*, Discussion Paper, Adelaide: S.A.G. Economic Analysis Division Department of the Premier and Cabinet.

Sapers, H. (2010) *Backgrounder: Aboriginal Inmates*, Office of the Correctional Investigator, Available at:http://www.oci-bec.gc.ca/cnt/rpt/annrpt/annrpt2009 2010-eng.aspx

Schwartz, M. (2010) 'Building Communities, Not Prisons: Justice Reinvestment and Indigenous Over-Representation', *Australian Indigenous Law Review*, 14(1), pp. 2–17.

Secretariat of National Aboriginal and Islander Child Care (2013) 'Stop the Creation of Another Stolen Generation! Melbourne Forum on Children in Out of Home Care', *Secretariat of National Aboriginal and Islander Child Care*, 25 June, http://www.snaicc.org.au/_uploads/rsfil/02953.pdf, accessed on 19 April 2015.

Sesame Street Workshop (2015) *Little Children Big Challenges: Incarceration*, http://www.sesamestreet.org/parents/topicsandactivities/toolkits/incarceration, accessed on 15 April 2015.

Shepherd, S., Walker, R., McEntyre, E. and Adams, Y. (2014) 'Violence Risk Assessment in Australian Aboriginal Offender Populations: A Review of the Literature', *Psychology Public Policy and Law*, 20(3), pp. 281–93.

Sherman, L., Gottfredson, D., MacKenzie, D., Eck, J., Reuter, P. and Bushway, S. (1998) *Preventing Crime: What Works, What Doesn't and What is Promising*, Washington DC: National Institute of Justice.

SIDL (Spatial Information Design Lab) (2007) *Justice Reinvestment Central City: Rebuilding Community in Post-Katrina New Orleans*, City Council of New Orleans Criminal Justice Committee Meeting Presentation, 12 July, New Orleans: Spatial Information Design Lab.

SIDL (Spatial Information Design Lab) (2009) *Justice Re-Investment New Orleans*, February, New York: Columbia University Graduate School of Architecture. Spatial Information Design Lab, Planning and Preservation.

Simon, J. (2012) 'Mass Incarceration: From Social Policy to Social Problem', in J. Petersilia and K.R. Reitz (eds), *The Oxford Handbook of Sentencing and Corrections*, Oxford: Oxford University Press.

Simon, J. (2014) *Mass Incarceration on Trial*, New York: The New Press.

Simpson, S., Yahner, J. and Dugan, L. (2008) 'Understanding Women's Pathways to Jail: Analysing the Lives of Incarcerated Women', *Australian and New Zealand Journal of Criminology*, 41(1), pp. 84–108.

Smart Justice for Young People (2015) *Starting a Youth Justice Reinvestment Conversation*, http://us4.campaign-archive1.com/?u=79b4f8bbbfce425a5e566499a&id=bf63e19598, accessed on 19 April 2015.

Smith, A. (2015) 'Oscars 2015: John Legend Makes Slavery Comparison in Acceptance Speech', *NBC News*, 23 February, http://www.nbcnews.com/storyline/oscars/oscars-2015-john-legend-makes-slavery-comparison-acceptance-speech-n310816,2015.

Smith, P., Cullen, F. and Latessa, E. (2009) 'Can 14,737 Women be Wrong? A Meta-Analysis of the LSI-R and Recidivism for Female Offenders', *Criminology and Public Policy*, 8(1), pp. 183–208.

Social Finance (2014) *Peterborough Social Impact Bond Reduces Reoffending By 8.4%; Investors On Course for Payment in 2016*, Press Release, 7 August, Social Finance.

Solesbury, W. (2001) *Evidence Based Policy: Whence it Came and Where it's Going*, Working Paper 1, London: ESRC UK Centre for Evidence Based Policy and Practice, Queen Mary University of London.

Solonec, T. (2014) *Justice Reinvestment: What Difference Could it Make in WA?*, The 2014 Sir Ronald Wilson Lecture, 5 August, Perth: The Law Society of Western Australia.

South Dakota Government (2014) *Justice Reinvestment Initiative State Assessment Report*, http://psia.sd.gov/PDFs/2014.01.24%20JRI%20Final%20w-bookmarks129-131.pdf accessed on 15 April 2015.

South Dakota Department of Corrections (2015) Inmates by Race / Ethnicity, May 1, 2015, http://doc.sd.gov/documents/about/stats/adult/InmatesbyRaceMay12015.pdf, accessed on 17 May 2015.

Spelman, W. (2000a) 'What Recent Studies Do (and Don't) Tell Us About Imprisonment and Crime', *Crime and Justice*, 27, pp. 419–94.

Spelman, W. (2000b) 'The Limited Importance of Prison Expansion', in A. Blumstein and J. Wallman (eds), *The Crime Drop in America*, Cambridge: Cambridge University Press.

Standing Committee of Attorneys-General (2010) *National Indigenous Law and Justice Framework 2009–2015*, Australian Government Attorney-General's Department.

Steketee, M. (2010) 'Smith Takes Electoral Sting Out of Crime', *The Australian*, 29 May.

Stemen, D. (2007) *Reconsidering Incarceration: New Directions for Reducing Crime*, January, New York: VERA Institute of Justice.

Stephens, J., Young, C., Steel, A. and Schwartz, M. (n.d.) *Statistics and Charts: Imprisonment Rates*, accessed on 15 April 2015.

Stern, V. (2006) *Creating Criminals: Prisons and People in a Market Society*, London: Zed Books.

Strang, H. (2002) *Repair or Revenge: Victims and Restorative Justice*, Oxford: Oxford University Press.

Stubbs, J. (2013) 'Indigenous Women and Penal Discourse', in K. Carrington, M. Ball, E. O'Brien and J. Tauri (eds), *Crime, Justice and Social Democracy*, Basingstoke: Palgrave McMillan.

Stubbs, J. (forthcoming) 'Downsizing Prisons in an Age of Austerity? Justice Reinvestment and Women's Imprisonment', *Onati Socio-legal Series*.
Subramanian, R., Delaney, R., Roberts, S., Fishman, N. and McGarry, P. (2015) *Incarceration's Front Door: The Misuse of Jails in America*, February, New York: VERA Institute of Justice.
Taxman, F. (2014) 'Second Generation of RNR: The Importance of Systemic Responsivity in Expanding Core Principles of Responsivity', *Federal Probation*, 78(2), pp. 32–40.
Taylor, J., Wilkinson, D. and Cheers, B. (2008) *Working with Communities in Health and Human Services*, Melbourne: Oxford University Press.
Teplin, L.A., Abram, K.M., McClelland, G.M., Duncan, M.K. and Mericle, A.A. (2002) 'Psychiatric Disorders in Youth in Juvenile Detention', *Archives of General Psychiatry*, 59(12), pp. 1133–43.
Terkel, A. (2015) 'Hillary Clinton to Call for an "End to the Era of Mass Incarceration"', *Huffington Post*, 29 April, http://www.huffingtonpost.com/2015/04/29/hillary-clinton-mass-incarceration_n_7166970.html,2015.
The Sentencing Project (2012) *Incarcerated Women*, Factsheet, Washington DC: The Sentencing Project.
The Sentencing Project (2014) *Disproportionate Minority Contact in the Juvenile Justice System*, Washington DC: The Sentencing Project.
The Sentencing Project (2015) *The Sentencing Project*, http://www.sentencingproject.org, (About Us), accessed on 15 April 2015.
Tonry, M. (2011a) 'Making Peace, Not a Desert: Penal Reform Should be about Values not Justice Reinvestment', *Criminology and Public Policy*, 10(3), pp. 637–49.
Tonry, M. (2011b) *Punishing Race: A Continuing American Dilemma*, Oxford: Oxford University Press.
Tonry, M. (2014) 'Remodeling American Sentencing: A Ten-Step Blueprint for Moving Past Mass Incarceration', *Criminology and Public Policy*, 13(4), pp. 503–33.
Tonry, M. and Petersilia, J. (1999) *Prisons Research at the Beginning of the 21st Century*, Washington: National Institute of Justice.
Travis, A. and Hirsch, A. (2010) 'Kenneth Clarke pledges to cut daily prison population', *The Guardian*, 21 October 2010, http://www.theguardian.com/politics/2010/oct/20/kenneth-clarke-pledges-cut-prison-population,2010.
Travis, A. and Sparrow, A. (2010) 'Kenneth Clarke Hints at Prison Sentencing Reform with Attack on "Bang Em" up Culture', *The Guardian Online*, 1 July, http://www.theguardian.com/society/2010/jun/30/kenneth-clarke-prison-sentencing-reform,2010.
Tucker, S. and Cadora, E. (2003) 'Justice Reinvestment', *Ideas for an Open Society*, 3(3), New York: Open Society Institute,.
United States Census Bureau (2014) *QuickFacts Beta*, http://www.census.gov/quickfacts/#table/PST045214/00, accessed on 30 April 2015.
UNODC (United Nations Office on Drugs and Crime) (2008) *Handbook for Prison Managers and Policy Makers on Women and Imprisonment*, Criminal Justice Handbook Series, New York: United Nations Office on Drugs and Crime.
Urban Institute (2013) *The Justice Reinvestment Initiative: Experiences from the States*, Washington DC: Urban Institute.

Urban Institute (2015) *Urban Institute,* http://www.urban.org/about (About Us), accessed on 15 April 2015.

Useem, B., Piehl, A.M. and Liedka, R.V. (2001) *The Crime-Control Effect of Incarceration: Reconsidering the Evidence,* Final Report to the National Institute of Justice, Washington: United States Department of Justice.

Van Voorhis, P. (2012) 'On Behalf of Women Offenders: Women's Place in the Science of Evidence-Based Practice', *Criminology and Public Policy,* 11(2), pp. 111–45.

VERA Institute of Justice (2012a) *Making Justice Systems Fairer and More Effective Through Research and Innovation,* Brochure, New York: VERA Institute of Justice.

VERA Institute of Justice (2012b) *Performance Incentive Funding: Aligning Fiscal and Operational Responsibility to Produce More Safety at Less Cost,* November, New York: VERA Institute of Justice.

VERA Institute of Justice (2015) *VERA Institute of Justice,* http://www.vera.org/ (About Us; Justice Reinvestment Initiative), accessed on 15 April 2015.

VicHealth (2013) *Fair Foundations: The VicHealth Framework for Health Equity,* Melbourne: The Victorian Health Promotion Foundation.

Vieraitis, L.M., Kovandzic, T.V. and Marvell, T.B. (2007) 'The Criminogenic Effects of Imprisonment: Evidence from State Panel Data, 1974–2002', *Criminology and Public Policy,* 6(3), pp. 589–622.

Villettaz, P., Gillieron, G. and Killias, M. (2015) *The Effects on Re-offending of Custodial vs. Non-Custodial Sanctions: An Updated Systematic Review of the State of Knowledge,* Campbell Systematic Reviews 1, Oslo: Campbell Collaboration.

Vinson, T. (1982) *Wilful Obstruction: The Frustration of Prison Reform,* Sydney: Methuen.

Vinson, T. (2009) *Markedly Socially Disadvantaged Localities in Australia: Their Nature and Possible Remediation,* Canberra: Department of Education, Employment and Workplace Relations.

WACOSS (Western Australian Council of Social Service) (2014) 'Submission to the Economic Regulation Authority', *Inquiry into the Effiency and Performance of Western Australian Prisons,* Perth: WACOSS,.

Wacquant, L. (2009a) *Punishing the Poor. The Neoliberal Government of Social Insecurity,* Durham: Duke University Press.

Wacquant, L. (2009b) *Prisons of Poverty,* Minneapolis and London: University of Minnesota Press.

Wacquant, L. (2010) 'Class, Race and Hyperincarceration in Revanchist America', *Daedalus,* 139(3), pp. 74–90.

Walsh, W.F. and Vito, G.F. (2004) 'The Meaning of Compstat: Analysis and Response', *Journal of Contemporary Criminal Justice,* 20(1), pp. 51–69.

Ward, T. and Maruna, S. (2007) *Rehabilitation: Beyond the Risk Paradigm,* London: Routledge.

Warner, K. (1999) 'Sentencing Review 1998', *Criminal Law Review,* 23(6), pp. 364–75.

Weatherburn, D. (2004) *Law and Order in Australia: Rhetoric and Reality,* Sydney: Federation Press.

Weatherburn, D., Hua, J. and Moffatt, S. (2006) 'How Much Crime Does Prison Stop? The Incapacitation Effect of Prison on Burglary', *Crime and Justice Bulletin,* no. 93, Sydney: NSW Bureau of Crime Statistics and Research.

Weatherburn, D., Snowball, L. and Hunter, B. (2006) 'The Economic and Social Factors Underpinning Indigenous Contact with the Criminal Justice System: Results from the 2002 NATSISS Survey', *Crime and Justice Bulletin*, no. 104, Sydney: NSW Bureau of Crime Statistics and Research.

West, A. (2009) 'Truce Called on Hardline Sentencing – Failed Policies on Both Sides: Opposition', *Sydney Morning Herald*, 8 January 2009.

Western, B. (2002) 'The Impact of Incarceration on Wage Mobility and Inequality', *American Sociological Review*, 67(4), pp. 526–46.

Western, B. (2006) *Punishment and Inequality in America*, New York: Russell Sage Foundation.

Western, B., Kling, J.R. and Weiman, D.F. (2001) 'The Labor Market Consequences of Incarceration', *Crime and Delinquency*, 47(3), pp. 410–27.

Western, B., Lopoo, L.M. and McLanahan, S. (2004) 'Incarceration and the Bonds Between Parents in Fragile Families', in M. Patillo, D. Weiman and B. Western (eds), *Imprisoning America: The Social Effects of Mass Imprisonment*, New York: Russell Sage Foundation.

White, P. and Whiteford, H. (2006) 'Prisons: Mental Health Institutions of the 21st Century?', *Medical Journal of Australia*, 185(6), pp. 302–3.

Willis, M. (2010) *Indicators Used Internationally to Measure Indigenous Justice Outcomes*, Indigenous Justice Clearing House Research Brief 8, Canberra: NSW Department of Justice and Attorney General.

Wilson, H. and Gutierrez, L. (2014) 'Does One Size Fit All? A Meta-Analysis Examining the Predictive Ability of the Level of Service Inventory (LSI) with Aboriginal Offenders', *Criminal Justice and Behavior*, 41(2), pp. 196–219.

Wilson, J.Q. and Kelling, G. (1982) 'Broken Windows', *The Atlantic Monthly*, 249(3), pp. 29–38.

Women's Justice Taskforce (2011) *Reforming Women's Justice: Final Report to the UK Prison Reform Trust*, London: Prison Reform Trust.

Wong, K. (2013a) *The Geek Shall Inherit the Earth? Capacity and Capability to Commission and Deliver Payment by Results Services in the United Kingdom*. Australian Institute of Criminology Occasional Seminars, Canberra.

Wong, K. (2013b) 'Integrated Offender Management: Assessing the Impact and Benefits – Holy Grail or Fool's Errand?', *British Journal of Community Justice*, 11(2/3), pp. 59–81.

Wong, K., Ellingworth, D. and Meadows, L. (2015) *Youth Justice Reinvestment Custody Pathfinder: Final Process Evaluation Report*, Ministry of Justice Analytical Series, London: Ministry of Justice.

Wong, K., Fox, C. and Albertson, K. (2014) 'Justice Reinvestment in an "Age of Austerity": Developments in the United Kingdom', *Victims and Offenders*, 9(1), pp. 76–99.

Wong, K., Meadows, L., Warburton, F., Webb, S., Young, H. and Barraclough, N. (2013) *The Development and Year One Implementation of the Local Justice Reinvestment Pilot*, Ministry of Justice Analytical Series, London: Ministry of Justice.

Woodward, D. (1999) 'Privatisation: A Policy or an Ideology?', in B. Costar and N. Economou (eds), *The Kennett Revolution. Victorian Politics in the 1990s*, Sydney: UNSW Press.

Worrall, A. (2000) 'What Works at One Arm Point? A Study of the Transportation of a Penal Concept', *Probation Journal*, 47(3), pp. 243–9.

WSIPP (Washington State Institute for Public Policy) (2014) *Benefit-Cost Technical Documentation*, August, Olympia: Washington State Institute for Public Policy.

Wundersitz, J. (2010) 'Indigenous Perpetrators of Violence: Prevalence and Risk Factors for Offending', *Research and Public Policy Series*, no. 105, Canberra: Australian Institute of Criminology.

Young, A. (1996) *Imagining Crime*, London: Sage.

Zdenkowski, G. and Brown, D. (1982) *The Prison Struggle: Changing Australia's Penal System*, Ringwood and New York: Penguin Books.

Zimring, F. (2013) *The City That Became Safe: New York's Lessons for Urban Crime and Its Control*, New York: Oxford University Press.

Index

Aboriginal and Torres Strait Islander Social Justice Commissioners (ATSISJC), 2–3, 51, 91, 131, 132, 136, 137
Aboriginal communities
see also Indigenous communities; Indigenous people
tipping point effect in, 8–10
academic projects, 52
African Americans
see also minorities; race
incarceration of, 9–10, 23, 25, 26, 89, 113
men, 23, 25, 26
women, 25–7, 114, 175
youth, 113
age, 47
AJR Project, *see* Australian Justice Reinvestment Project
Alberston, K, 44, 45, 96, 143, 144, 150, 184
Alexander, Michelle, 23–24, 234-5, 241
American Civil Liberties Union (ACLU), 35, 81, 92
Arizona, 62
Armstrong, Kat, 110–11, 129, 207
asset mapping, 36, 82, 98–9, 229, 231–3, 242, 246–7
Austin, James, 13, 15, 18, 28, 32, 35, 54, 57, 62–6, 68, 72–4, 77–80, 83, 90, 92, 97, 242
Australia
appetite for change in, 205–8
bipartisanship in, 208–14
context in, 198–223
coordination capacity in, 218–23
correctional data for, 156–7
faith-based organisations in, 214–18
female prisoners in, 114–15
government support in, 51–2
imprisonment rates, 42, 45–9, 113
Indigenous people in, 130–8
justice reinvestment in, 2–5, 12–13, 16, 17, 44–52, 131–8, 242, 248
mass incarceration in, 8, 45–7, 242
penal policy in, 197–8
policy transfer in, 193–8
political structures in, 201–4
prison privatisation in, 194
Australian Capital Territory (ACT), 52, 125–6
Australian Justice Reinvestment Project, 2, 10–14,52, 62

bail law reform, 198, 214, 225, 226, 229, 233
Baldry, Eileen, 100, 111, 112, 114–17, 119, 125, 126, 139, 147, 157
barrier issues, 200–23, 246
benefit-cost model, 169
bipartisanship, 37, 38, 62, 99, 208–14, 242, 248
Blair, Tony, 165, 197, 198
Bourke Indigenous community, 93, 134–8, 140
Brady, Kat, 71, 85
breaching quotas, 57
broken windows policing, 190, 191, 195–6, 237
Brown, David, 2, 5, 8, 9–10, 13, 143, 206, 207, 218, 226–7, 229, 233, 237, 250
Brown v Plata, 30–1, 206
Bulger, James, 235
Bureau of Justice Assistance (BJA), 29–30, 32, 36–7, 54, 88, 154, 231
Burke, Peggy, 58, 85
Bush, George W., 214–17, 234–5

Cadora, Eric, 18, 30–2, 34–6, 79, 83, 87, 94, 139, 141, 144, 188, 242
California, 28, 31, 206
Calma, Tom, 131
Campbell Collaboration, 166, 169
Canada, 113

283

carpet model, 228–31
Carr, Bob, 197
Center for Effective Public Policy (CEPP), 33, 34
change, appetite for, 205–8, 246
Chesney-Lind, Meda, 173–4, 177
children, 97, 235
Christian fundamentalism, 214–15
Clarke, Ken, 225
class, 23
Clear, Todd, 7, 8, 11, 28, 39, 52, 96, 104, 161, 182–3, 199–200, 213, 245
Clement, Marshall, 35–6, 83–4, 87, 88, 90–1, 92–3, 105, 155, 158–9, 161
Clinton, Bill, 197
Closing the Gap agenda, 132
Coalition for Evidence-Based Policy, 172
coercive mobility, 18–19, 96
cognitive behavioural therapy, 169
cognitively impaired persons, 22, 111–12, 115–21, 244
Cohen, Mark, 186
Cohen, S., 192
collective impact methodology, 136
Collins, Priscilla, 133
colonialism, 103
Colorado, 126–7
Colson, Chuck, 216
Commission on English Prisons Today, 96
communities, 182, 242–4, 247
  Aboriginal, 5–6, 10–12, 131
  asset mapping, 36, 82, 98–9, 229, 231–3, 242, 246–7
  capacity building in, 137, 141–2
  concept of, 101–2
  disadvantaged, 94, 96–7, 110–11, 138
  economic welfare challenges in, 183–4
  ex-prisoners return to, 125–6
  high-incarceration, 18, 58, 73, 78–9, 81–3, 88, 90, 96–7, 98, 104, 142, 234, 242
  Indigenous, 5–6, 10–12, 131
  local, 98–9

  minority, 103–7
  in place-based approach, 101–3
  race and, 103–7
  reinvestment in, 98–100, 141–3, 166, 245
community-based justice, 97
community-based organisations, 83, 85
community control, 131
community development programs, 88–91
community ecology, 142
community investment, 74
community supervision, 146
CompStat, 195–6, 237
Connecticut, 62, 89
conservative political organisations, 37–9, 242, 246
Consolidated Appropriations Act, 36
contagion, 8
context, 16, 198–223, 246–7
control
  community, 131
  culture of, 28
coordination, 218–23, 246
correctional data, 156–7
Corston Report, 128
cost-benefit analysis (CBA), 145–9
Cost-benefit Knowledge Bank for Criminal Justice, 145
costs, 161–3, 185–7
Council of State Governments (CSG), 33, 36, 54–5, 58, 74–5, 87–8
Crenshaw, Kimberle, 175, 180
crime, 7, 9–10
  decline in, 31
  emotive responses to, 234–6
  prevention, 103
  'smart on crime', 31, 38, 40, 91, 167
  underlying causes of, 88
Crime and Justice Institute (CJI), 33, 34, 86
crime rates, 28, 31, 97, 200, 206
CrimeSolutions.gov, 171–2, 175
Criminal Justice and Immigration Act, 40
criminal justice policy transfer, 12–13, 16, 189–238

criminal justice professionals, 225
criminal justice reforms, 9, 29–32, 38–9, 54–5, 59, 139, 142, 145, 205–8, 226, 241, 245
Criminal Justice Reinvestment Act, 31
criminogenic argument, 6–10, 52
Cubillo, Eddie, 7
culture of control, 28
Cunneen, Chris 1, 22–5, 101, 103, 106, 111–15, 117–18

Dansky, Karen, 84–5
Darcy, David, 198
data
  administrative, 158
  collection, 158–9
data analysis, 79–82, 141, 157–65
data-driven approach, 141, 153–65, 244
Daugaard, Dennis, 218–221, 236
death penalty, 212
democracy, 5–6
Dennis, Gary, 54, 86, 88–9, 217, 231
Denver, Colorado, 126–7
desistance scholars, 182
desistance theory, 182, 187, 245
De Vore, Chuck, 216
dignity, 206, 215
disadvantaged communities, 94–7, 110–11, 138
Drucker, Ernest, 8, 29
drug laws, 27, 199, 241
drug offences, 124

earned discharge, 203–4
Eberly, Tom, 100, 212
ecological framework, 185
economic analysis, 143–53
economic theory, 144
ethnicity, 42, 103–7
evidence, 168–71, 233–7, 244
evidence-based policy and practice (EBP), 15–16, 79–82, 141–88, 226–7, 244, 245
  data analysis, 153–65
  economic analysis, 143–53
  evidence in, 168–71
  justice reinvestment and, 165–83

  methodologies and measures, 157–65, 168–71, 183–7
  risk assessment, 171, 176–80
  social justice and, 180–3
  'what works' framework, 171–5
expertise, 154–6, 225
ex-prisoners
  re-entry of, 175, 206, 215–17
  support for, 125

Fabelo, Tony, 35–6, 91, 162, 168
Fair Sentencing Act, 31
faith-based organisations, 37, 39–40, 54, 206, 214–18, 242, 246
families, 97, 102, 182
federal funds, 100
female prisoners, 25–7, 42, 48–9, 114–15
Ferguson, R., 28
financing, 149–53
'finer grain', 231–3
fiscal constraints, 29–30
Fishman, Nancy, 106
Foundation Communities, 60–1
Fox, C, 44, 45, 96, 143, 144, 150, 184
France, 192
Fulton, Roseanne, 138–9
funding sources, 36–7, 56–7, 100

Garland, David, 7, 22–3, 201, 224–5, 241
Gelsthorpe, L., 162, 174
gender, 47, 122, 138139,178
  see also women
Gilbert, R., 95
Gingrich, Newt, 38, 39
global financial crisis, 29–30, 88
globalisation, 190–2, 193
Goldwater, Barry, 211
Gooda, Mick, 51, 131, 136, 231
Good Lives model, 182, 184
government, distrust of, 199–200
Governor, role of, 199
Greater Manchester initiative, 108
Green, David, 205, 214, 215, 217, 235
Greens, 3, 51
Guice, David, 211
Gupta, Vanita, 84, 92, 106

286 *Index*

Guthrie, Jill, 52

Hannah-Moffatt, Kelly, 178
Hatzistergos, John, 214
Hawaii, 62, 69–71, 85, 158
Hawaii's Opportunity Probation with Enforcement (HOPE), 70, 172–3
Hazzard, Brad, 51
Hefferman, E.B., 174
Herbert, Nick, 44
high-incarceration communities, 6–10, 18, 58, 73, 78–9, 81–2, 88, 90, 92, 96–7, 98, 103, 142, 234, 242
  reinvestment in, 88–91
Hispanics, incarceration of, 25, 26
Hogg, R., 227
Holder, Eric, 28, 177–8, 205
homelessness, 107, 119–21, 244
HOPE Court *see* Hawaii's Opportunity Probation with Enforcement (HOPE)
Hopkins, Sarah, 6, 51, 82, 133–6
Horton, Willie, 234–5
House of Commons Justice Committee (HCJC), 43
human rights, 103, 243
Human Rights Centre, 52
hyperincarceration, 1,2, 23, 241

Imprisonment for Public Protection (IPP), 195
imprisonment rates
  Australia, 42, 45–9, 113
  crime and, 9–10
  impact of, 6–10
  increases in, 1, 6–7, 19, 144
  Indigenous people, 45, 47, 113, 115, 147
  men, 48
  race and, 9, 24–7, 158–9
  selective nature of, 2
  UK, 20, 40–2
  US, 19, 21–2, 26–7
  women, 26–7, 47, 48–9, 114–15
incarceration
  see also mass incarceration
  as coercive mobility, 18–19, 96
  costs of, 42–3, 56, 161–3
  drivers of, 56, 159–60, 174
  impact of, 96–7
  mapping, 82
  race and, 2, 6, 15, 23–7, 42, 45–49, 56, 90, 103–7, 112–15, 138, 158–9, 178, 211, 234–5, 241, 244
  social determinants of, 143
  of women, 25–7, 42, 48–9, 121–9
incentives, 149–53
incentivisation, 201–4, 246
inclusion criteria, 169–70
independent expertise, 154–6
Indigenous communities, 5–6, 10–12, 131
Indigenous democracy, 5–6, 240–1
Indigenous nation-building, 130
Indigenous people, 62, 103, 247
  imprisonment rates, 45, 47, 113, 115, 147
  justice reinvestment and, 5–6, 130–8, 240–1
  justice renewal for, 3
  measurement issues with, 184–5
  with mental and cognitive impairment, 112
  over-representation of, 112–14
  rights for, 140
  risk assessment and, 178–80
individualism, 28
Integrated Services Program (ISP), 119
intensive supervision, 146
intersectionality, 115, 127, 138–9, 158, 175

jails, 20–1, 22, 26, 58
JFA Institute, 35
Jim Crow era, 24
Jones, Trevor, 192–3, 227, 246
judges, 221–2
judicial independence, 221–2
Justice Fellowship, 39–40
Justice Mapping Center (JMC), 34
justice reinvestment
  assumptions underpinning, 11
  in Australia, 2–5, 12–13, 16, 17, 44–52, 131–8, 242, 248
  capacity for coordination in, 218–23
  context for, 16, 189, 198–223, 246–7
  as data-driven, 141, 153–65, 244

justice reinvestment – *continued*
  economic analysis and, 143–53
  emergence of, 14–15, 17–53, 241
  as evidence-based, 141, 165–83, 244
  evolution of, 50–2
  features of, 15
  goals of, 57–8
  in high-incarceration communities, 88–91
  incentives for, 201–4
  Indigenous people and, 5–6, 130–8, 240–1
  Justice Reinvestment Initiative vs., 73–9
  key players in, 36–7
  at local level, 83–6
  methodologies, 15–16, 157–65, 168–71, 183–7
  as opportunity for change, 118–21
  origins of term, 18–19
  place-based approach to. *see* place-based approaches
  policy transfer and, 12–13, 16, 189–238, 245–6, 249–50
  populist backlash and, 233–7
  portability of, 16
  in practice, 79–92
  principles of, 55–8, 79–82
  as product of think tanks, 31–5
  race and, 103–7, 244
  research project on, 10–14
  social justice-oriented, 141–2, 159–60, 243
  social-moral aspects of, 11–12
  state and local initiatives, 58–61
  strategies, 2, 3
  support for, 38–9
  in UK, 17, 40–5, 96, 122, 149–50, 242
  in US, 13–17, 29–40, 54–93, 126–8, 167–8, 241, 248–9
  women and, 121–9
Justice Reinvestment Act, 67, 89, 176
Justice Reinvestment Initiative (JRI), 32, 37, 241–2
  evaluation of results of, 91–2
  implementation of, 37–40, 54
  vs. justice reinvestment, 73–9
  at local level, 59–61
  in practice, 62–73, 242–3
  risk assessment and, 176–80
  savings from, 161–3
  steps in, 73–9
Justice Reinvestment National Summit, 37
Justice Reinvestment WA, 51
justice system, reforms, 9, 29–32, 38–9, 54–5, 59, 139, 142, 145, 205–8, 226, 241, 245
Just Reinvest NSW initiative, 15, 50–1, 82, 86, 134–8, 199, 244, 247
juvenile detention, 113
juvenile justice system, 3–4, 230

Kansas, 62, 88
Keahiolalo-Karasuda, RaeDeen, 174
Kennedy, Anthony, 28–9
Kurgan, Laura, 82, 98, 231–2

Labour Party, 51–2, 197
Lacey, Nicola, 218, 222
La Vigne, Nancy, 61, 85, 90, 122, 166, 208, 209–10
law and order auctions, 226
least restrictive environment, 139–40
legislative reform, 99
Level of Service Inventory--Revised (LSI-R), 177, 178, 179
Levin, Marc, 30
Loader, I., 10, 12, 224
local communities, 98–9
local initiatives, 58–61, 83–6
localism, 96, 100–1, 107–11, 131, 164–5, 242
Local Justice Reinvestment Pilot, 44, 45, 108, 122, 149–50, 165
Lynch, Paul, 51

MacGillivray, Peta, 132–3, 232
managerialism, 165
mandatory sentencing, 27, 192, 194–5, 199
Manhattan Institute, 191
Maranguka, 56, 135–6, 247
marginalised communities, tipping point effect in, 6–10
marketisation, 145, 149
Martin, Wayne, 52
Maruna, S., 11

mass incarceration
  see also incarceration
  in Australia, 45–7, 242
  crime and, 9–10
  drivers of, 27–9, 144, 159–60, 174, 241
  economic analysis of, 143–53
  as failure, 205–8
  features of, 22–3
  vs. hyperincarceration, 23-4
  impact of, 6–10, 96–7
  Jim Crow and, 24
  over-represented groups, 111–15
  race and, 24–7, 103–7, 112–14, 158–9
  in US, 19–29
Mauer, Marc, 24–5, 73, 93, 204, 213
McFie, Kathy, 129
McGarry, Peggy, 236
McNeill, F., 184
measurement, 157–65, 183–7
  challenges, 164–5
  of drivers of incarceration, 159–60
  performance, 163–4, 185
  of social costs and benefits, 185–7
Mecklenburg County, North Carolina, 68–9, 99, 162–3
men, imprisonment rates, 48
mentally ill, 22, 100, 111–12, 115–21, 206, 244
mentally impaired persons, 111–12, 115–21
meta-analysis, 168–71, 178
methodologies, 15–16, 157–65, 168–71, 183–7
Michigan, 40
Miles, Timothy, 107
Milgram, Anne, 178
minorities, 103–7, 170, 244
  EBP and, 174–5
  research on, 170
minority communities, 103–7
moral reconation therapy, 151–2
Morrison, C.M., 30, 39
Multiple and Complex Needs Initiative (MACNI), 119
Murray, R. Andrew, 209

National Centre for Justice Planning, 172
National Congress of Australia's First Peoples, 132
National Indigenous Law and Justice Framework, 3–4
National Justice Coalition, 132
Native Americans, 72
neo-conservativism, 210–11
neo-liberalism, 28, 102–3, 124, 143, 190–2, 194, 218
NeOn project, 108–10, 248–9
Newburn, Tim, 192–3, 198, 227, 246
New Day, 89
New York, 72–3, 108, 151–2, 249
Nolan, Pat, 38, 216
North Australian Aboriginal Justice Association (NAAJA), 51
North Carolina, 31, 67–9, 89, 98–9, 176, 212
  Mecklenburg County, North Carolina 68–9, 99, 162–3
Northern Territory, 51
Nuncio, Todd, 211
Nurse-Family Partnership program, 89, 146

O'Callaghan, Karl, 52
O'Farrell, Barry, 226
Oklahoma, 160–1
Open Society Foundations, 32, 35
over-represented groups, 111–15

Papalia, Paul, 52
Parker, Barbara Pierce, 86
parole, 20, 21, 28, 161, 195, 248
payment by results (PbR) approach, 17
penal/colonial complex, 1
penal culture, 1, 23, 240–1
penal hope, 13, 207
penal reduction, 249
penal state, 143
Pennsylvania, 90
penology, 143, 245
performance incentives, 149–53
performance measures, 163–4, 185
Peterborough pilot program, 150–1, 152–3
Pew Charitable Trusts, 32–3, 37

pilot projects, 50–1, 150–3, 155, 164–5, 241
  see also specific projects
place-based approaches, 12, 15, 56–7, 87–91, 94–103, 137–9, 242–4
  bottom-up, 95, 110–11, 243, 244
  community in, 101–3
  financial incentives for, 149–50
  Indigenous people and, 130–8
  localised, 107–11, 164–5
  minority communities and, 103–7
  over-represented groups and, 111–15
  for people with mental and cognitive disabilities, 115–21
  top-down, 95, 243
  women and, 121–9, 138
policy options, 160–1
policy transfer, 12–13, 16, 189–238, 245–6, 249–50
  in Australia, 193–8
  context for, 198–223
  globalisation and, 190–2
  neo-liberalism and, 190–2
  politics and, 223–7
  populism and, 223–7
  in UK, 192–3
political structures, 201–4
politicians, 225
politics, 165
  bipartisanship, 37, 38, 62, 99, 208–14
  of localism, 96, 100–1
  policy transfer and, 223–7
  of resentment, 24
  in US, 54
populism, 189, 224–7, 233–7, 246
portability, 16
post-colonial societies, 247
poverty, 56, 94, 124
pre-conditions, 200
Precythe, Anne, 212
Prison Fellowship, 39–40
prison population
  see also mass incarceration
  by ethnicity, 42
  female, 25, 42, 114–15
  growth of, 19
  reduction of, 57–8, 80–1
  UK, 40–2
  US, 58, 206
prison privatisation, 57, 190, 193–4
prisons, 20
  closure of, 91
  conditions in, 206
  politics of closing, 57
  reform of, 198
  as therapeutic institutions, 1
probation, 20, 21, 28, 41, 161, 248
public safety, 17, 30, 33, 38–9, 56–8, 70, 73, 74, 75, 78, 83, 87, 89, 141–4, 148, 160, 205, 210, 234
Public Safety Performance Project (PEW), 33
public voice, 224–5
punitive sentiment, 226–7, 233–7

Queensland, 51

race, 2, 6, 15, 23–7, 42, 45–49, 56, 90, 103–7, 112–15, 138, 158–9, 178, 211, 234–5, 244
racialised communities, tipping point effect in, 6–10
racial justice, 55
racial minorities, 103–7, 112–14, 170, 174–5, 244
random control trials, 170
Rapid City, South Dakota, 127–8
rationalist fallacy, 189, 227–8, 237–8, 246
rationality, 226–7
recidivism, 142, 163, 176, 177, 182, 184, 187, 200, 206, 245, 249
reconviction, 182
Redergard, Silje, 235
re-entry, 31, 175, 206, 215–17
reform agenda, 83–6
refugee detention centres, 194
rehabilitation, 206
remand population, UK, 40–1
Report on Government Services, 200
Republican Party, 39, 199, 208–12, 216, 218, 219
residential drug treatment, 147
restorative justice, 196
retributive justice, 214
Rhode Island, 31, 62, 65–7

Right on Crime, 38–9, 206, 210, 215–16
Rikers Island, 151–3
risk assessment, 171, 176–80, 193–4, 196
Risk Management Authority (RMA), 176–7
risk-needs-responsivity framework, 142, 172, 176–80, 245
risk society, 165
roll out metaphor, 189, 228–31, 246
Roman, J., 148–9, 183–4
Rose, D., 7, 102
Rumpf, Sarah, 215
Ryan, M., 224

savings, 161–3
scale, 152–3, 165
Schwartz, Melanie, 3–4
Second Chance Act (US), 31, 214–15
self-determination, 140
Sentencing Act (NSW), 195
sentencing laws, 27, 28, 144, 190, 192, 194–5, 199, 237, 241
Sentencing Project, 34
service mapping, 232
Seward, Jim, 127–8, 154, 167, 199, 203–4, 207, 208, 212, 216, 222
Shorten, Bill, 214
Simon, Jonathon, 27, 205–6
slogans, 196
Smart Justice for Young People, 51
'smart on crime', 31, 38, 40, 91, 167
Smith, Greg, 225
social benefits, 185–7
social capital, 96–7, 184
social costs, 185–7
social divisions, 103
social impact-based investments, 150–3
social impact bond (SIB), 44, 57, 150–3
social inclusion, 118, 132, 139, 141
Social Inclusion Agenda, 3
social justice, 55, 94, 96, 121, 139–42, 159–60, 180–4, 239–40, 243
social reinvestment, 248
Social Return on Investment (SROI) approach, 185–6

socioeconomic trends, 30–1
Solesbury, W., 165, 175
Soros Foundation, 35
South Australia, 51
South Australia Justice Reinvestment Working Group, 51
South Dakota, 38, 62, 71–2, 127–8, 154, 211–12, 218–21
Sparks, R., 10, 12
stakeholders, 83–4, 85, 224
Standing Committee on Law and Justice, 47
state budgets, 29–30, 57
state initiatives, 58–61
strength-based approaches, 185
Stubbs, Julie, 122, 123, 127, 207
substance abuse, 111, 115
success, 163–4
Swartz, Charles, 34
systemic imprisonment, 23

Tasmania, 51
Taxman, Faye, 180
Tea Party, 199
technical assistance, 154–6, 172
Texas, 29–30, 62, 87, 89, 91
  JRI implementation in, 63–5
  Travis County, 60–1, 64–5, 98–9
Thatcher, Margaret, 211
The After Prison Initiative, 32, 35
therapeutic institution, 1
The Sentencing Project, 35, 57–8, 204, 213
think tanks, 31–6, 191, 192, 194, 242
Thompson, Mike, 35
three strikes legislation, 190, 196, 199, 237
'tipping point' argument, 6–10
Tonry, M., 24, 27–8, 38–9, 57, 215
Travis County, Texas, 60–1, 64–5, 98–9
triangulation strategy, 197–8
truth in sentencing regimes, 167, 195, 196, 237
Tucker, Susan, 18–19, 27, 36, 54–5, 79, 83, 87, 94, 108, 141, 213–14, 242, 247, 248
Twomey, Chris, 110, 157, 223

United Kingdom
  imprisonment rates, 20, 40–2
  judicial independence in, 222
  justice reinvestment in, 17, 40–5, 96, 122, 149–50, 242
  penal policy in, 197
  place-based approaches in, 107
  policy transfer in, 192–3
  politics in, 211
  prison population, 40–2
United States
  appetite for change in, 205–8
  bipartisanship in, 208–14, 248
  context in, 198–223
  coordination capacity in, 218–23
  crime rates, 31
  criminal justice reforms in, 54–5, 59
  diffusion of policies from, 190–238
  EBP in, 167–8
  faith-based organisations in, 39–40, 54, 214–18
  imprisonment rates in, 19, 21–2, 26–7
  Jim Crow era, 24
  justice reinvestment in, 13–17, 29–40, 54–93, 126–8, 167–8, 241, 248–9
  mass incarceration in, 19–29
  political culture of, 28, 31, 54
  political structures in, 201–4
  prison population in, 58, 206
  race in, 24–7
  reform dialogue in, 29–32
  women in, 126–8
Urban Institute, 33, 34, 36, 85, 175

Van Voorhis, Patricia, 170, 178, 181–2
Vera Institute of Justice, 33
Vinson, Tony, 94–5, 198
vulnerable groups, 111–15

Wacquant, L., 23, 143, 190–3, 241, 245
War Against Drugs, 199
Washington State Institute for Public Policy (WSIPP), 145, 146–7, 169

Watler, Chris, 217, 222
welfare programs, 124, 243
welfare state, 23–4, 143
West Australia, 52
Western Australian Council of Social Services (WACOSS), 110
West Virginia, 84–5
what works framework, 15–16, 171–5, 182, 245
whole of government approach, 223
Whole Place Community Budget, 108
Wichita, Kansas, 88
women, 244
  African American, 114, 175
  EBP and, 174–5
  experiences of criminalised, 123–8
  imprisonment rates, 47, 48–9, 114–15
  Indigenous, 115
  justice reinvestment and, 121–9
  place-based approaches and, 121–9, 138
  in prison, 25–7, 42, 121–9
  re-entry of, 175
  research on, 170
  in US, 126–8
Wong, K., 44, 45, 96, 108, 122, 143, 144, 150, 184
working groups, 51
Wright, Penny, 3
Wundersitz, Joy, 185

Yanez-Correa, Ana, 106–7
youth
  engagement of, 136
  with mental and cognitive impairment, 116–17
  minority, 113
Youth Justice Reinvestment Pathfinder Initiative, 44
youth justice system, *see* juvenile justice system

zero tolerance, 190, 192–6, 237